LOUIS XIV

To Georgiana

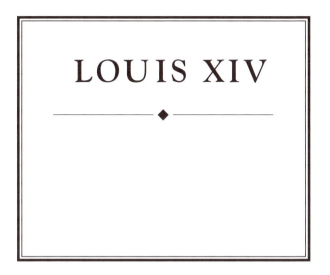

LOUIS XIV

◆

Geoffrey Treasure

Longman

An imprint of **Pearson Education**

Harlow, England · London · New York · Reading, Massachusetts · San Francisco
Toronto · Don Mills, Ontario · Sydney · Tokyo · Singapore · Hong Kong · Seoul
Taipei · Cape Town · Madrid · Mexico City · Amsterdam · Munich · Paris · Milan

Pearson Education Limited

Head Office:
Edinburgh Gate
Harlow CM20 2JE
Tel: +44 (0) 1279 623623
Fax: +44 (0)1279 431059

London Office:
128 Long Acre
London WC2E 9AN
Tel: +44 (0)20 7447 2000
Fax: +44 (0)20 7240 5771
Website: www.history-minds.com

_____

First published in Great Britain in 2001

© Pearson Education Limited 2001

The right of Geoffrey Treasure to be identified as Author
of this Work has been asserted by him in accordance with
the Copyright, Designs and Patents Act 1988.

ISBN 0 582 27958 5

British Library Cataloguing in Publication Data
A CIP catalogue record for this book can be obtained from the British Library

Library of Congress Cataloging in Publication Data
A CIP catalog record for this book can be obtained from the Library of Congress

10 9 8 7 6 5 4 3 2 1

Typeset in 11.5/14pt Garamond MT by Graphicraft Limited, Hong Kong
Printed and bound in Great Britain by Henry Ling Limited, Dorchester, Dorset.

The Publishers' policy is to use paper manufactured from sustainable forests.

CONTENTS

———◆———

Preface   viii
Acknowledgements   xi

1 Preparing for Power   1
The God-given   1
The Fronde   7
Mazarin: minister, guardian and tutor   13
The anointed king   17
The ecclesiastical Fronde   20
A constitutional balance   23
A ruler's duty   30

2 Louis XIV's Subjects   43
The poor have no reserves   43
Peasant farming   48
The feudal régime   51
Nobility   54
Bourgeois France   59

3 Personal Rule   69
The case of Fouquet   69
Absolutism   74
The French royal tradition: inspiration and restraint   78
Parlement and Gallicanism   84
'A delightful business'   88
Councils and ministers   94
The *intendants*   99

4 Wealth and Power: Colbert   109
The perfect royal servant   109
The state's finances   115
Manufactures   118
Trade and sea power   125

5 The Power of the Army   134

A defective instrument   134

Control, discipline and recruitment   137

Weaponry, fortresses and supply   142

6 Power Abroad   150

The world of diplomacy   150

The great treaties   157

Trials of strength   161

'Desire to attack the Dutch'   164

The Dutch war   169

'I fully rejoice in my clever conduct'   173

7 Versailles: The Display of Power   180

'Great buildings, their magnificence'   180

The problem of Paris   182

A new palace   185

Significant rituals   189

An unhealthy dependence   194

8 The Temptation of Power   200

'The grand doge'   200

A defensible frontier   202

Vienna: a decisive moment   208

9 Power and Conformity   212

The Huguenot question   212

Huguenot crisis; Catholic ascendancy   217

The Edict of Fontainebleau   222

Emigrés and rebels   229

10 France against Europe: The Nine Years War   238

Louvois's war   238

Towards total war   245

The *necessity of peace*   249

A new moderation   253

Contents

11 **The Great Prize** 259

Treaty or will 259

12 **The Great War** 270

A war on four fronts 270

'There are murmurs at his very door' 276

'Conditions so contrary to justice' 282

Peace at last 287

Europe's changing face 291

13 **The Price of War** 298

The money famine 298

Desperate measures 301

A crisis of morale: Colbertism challenged 304

An alternative voice: Fénelon 308

Great expectations – and tragic losses 311

14 **Faith, Reason and Authority** 316

Jansenism 316

An uneasy peace 320

Self-inflicted wounds 322

Quietism 324

15 **'A King at Every Moment'** 330

A brave end 330

Post-mortem: another regency 334

Envoi 337

Glossary 343

Bibliography 348

Index 359

PREFACE

◆

Majestic in conception, bold in ambition and splendid in image and ceremony, the monarchy of Louis XIV set standards and posed questions which have challenged us ever since. The reign of Louis XIV, boy and man, was also to be called 'the age of Louis XIV'. During its seventy-two years there could be counted, among his contemporary sovereigns, three kings of Spain, three kings and one queen of Sweden, five kings and one queen of England (latterly Great Britain). Throughout the period, following the turbulence of mid-century, there was an unmistakable trend toward absolutist systems of government. Even in England and Holland, though exceptions to the trend, there was a marked increase in the powers of government and in the size of armies and navies. In these developments, contributing to the emergence of the modern state, France, by far the largest of European states, was the prime mover.

Louis XIV's reign was marred by several critical misjudgements. Whether for victory or for defeat, for glory, or even for the security which is now recognised to be the consistent aim of French policy, his subjects had to pay a high price. Without doubt his reign saw the enhancement of royal power, the extension of its authority in the provinces and, continuing the policy of the Cardinals, significant gains of territory. Stability can be seen to be the key note of the reign as the crown came to terms with its most privileged subjects and connived, where it could not coerce, in ways that might limit the power of royal agents to carry out constructive reforms but ensured a degree of consensus, along with a real enthusiasm for the régime among those who counted most in the stakes of power, patronage and influence. How important that was can be gauged by comparison with the instability of the previous hundred years. Enough of the gains of earlier wars were held at the end to ensure the defensible frontier envisaged by the Cardinals in more dangerous times. This larger France, incorporating Alsace, Artois and much of Flanders, and also poised to take in Lorraine, commanded respect among the powers and enabled the ministers of Louis XV to negotiate from strength. At the same time the cultural hegemony of France is suggested by the general use of French as the language of diplomacy after 1714 and confirmed by the almost slavish imitation of French institutions in Germany, and admiration for French writers generally in the age of Enlightenment, 'Young people', wrote Leibnitz, 'come near to making Germany a tributary of French power.'

In 1715 a tired old man might reflect on opportunities lost and on the family tragedies that meant another five-year old coming to the throne. But he could still hold his head high. He could be sure that there would be no repetition of the Fronde. He could not possibly have envisaged a more serious Revolution to come. Nor, by the longest stretch of the imagination, can we attribute to his style and conduct of government any responsibility for the collapse of what would be called the *ancien régime*. That lies at the door of his successors. To consider the record of Louis XV and Louis XVI is of course to invite invidious comparison. But Louis hardly needs such support. He stands alone, not without faults, in many respects an ordinary man, but uniquely accomplished in the art and craft of kingship at a climactic time in the history of Europe. The main trends, political, intellectual and cultural, combined in one half century, and in one country, to make it possible. Louis XIV sensed the need and braced himself for the task. He was the man for the hour.

The man's stature is beyond doubt. Yet there is still room for a wide range of interpretation of the reign. At one extreme are those, mainly now French historians, who respond with enthusiasm to the rhetoric of the régime, to grandeur and glory. They may hark back, perhaps with nostalgia, to a period when France was plainly predominant, when Germany was more of an idea than a state, before Britain had acquired trading supremacy and an overseas empire, before the appeal of French culture and the Cartesian rule of reason was qualified by the growing influence of English science and empirical philosophy. In that partisan spirit a recent expansive and justly lauded biography by a leading authority on the period can start by quoting with approval Voltaire's salute to Louis XIV: 'Louis always had a sense of exaltation in his soul which drove him to great things.' Bluche writes in a long tradition, his case reinforced by ample scholarship. He also writes scathingly of the 'denigrators', writers, teachers, intellectuals, 'all of them the posthumous, unintentional allies of Marlborough and William of Orange'.

There is indeed a long tradition, whether British Whig in origin, stemming from naturally partisan Huguenot sources and from the hostility engendered by successive wars, or French republican in its influence on their textbooks, in which the king is portrayed as a despot and a bigot. Marxist historians have reinforced such views while at the same time reducing the role of the king by their main concentration on economy and society. Paradoxically, however, the most serious damage to Louis's reputation has been done by the numerous authors of the court, or romantic, school of biography, whether lost in admiration of the king's performance and of the supposed glamour of Versailles, or searching for scandal in the too well documented activities of his court. To this day there seems to be a market for this Versailles version: accepting too uncritically the propaganda of the régime and focusing too narrowly on the court. Reacting strongly against such travesties, and with ever more research filling in the picture, British and American historians have found reason to scale down estimates of what Louis's 'absolutist' government actually achieved, indeed to question the very notion of absolutism. While this has been a healthy corrective to inflated ideas it has left Louis in need of some rehabilitation. For the more we know about the limits and constraints on government, the more we recognise the values of seventeenth-century society and the ways in which the political process actually operated, the more impressive seems to be the achievement of the king and his ministers. I came to write this book after a study of Mazarin and the Fronde. I have ventured to enter a crowded field because I am convinced that there is need to strike a balance and to offer a study of the king and his power which is also – because they should be inseparable – a history of the country. There are several brief but scholarly analyses of the reign, of high value to the students for whom they are intended. There are also, as will be seen in my bibliography, important and revealing biographies of the king. I have sought the middle ground: in scale of treatment, balancing story and analysis, taking account of all that has been written, so profoundly and so well in some recent works, about French mentalities, institutions and values. It has been an exacting task and much has been pruned. I hope that the reader will find interest in the story of the king and some sense in my interpretation of the reign. Louis XIV was, by any standards an impressive human being, his kingship a sustained tour de force, the reign among the most important in the history of Europe. The very idea of kingship is coloured by our idea of this formidable exponent. He was not the state, but the state, in both idea and reality, was affected by the way he conceived and performed his role. A study of France in his time has to allow prime place to Louis XIV.

ACKNOWLEDGEMENTS

———◆———

The bibliography shows how many have explored and surveyed the ground. I have been thankfully content to hack behind them, noting what they have seen and studying the lie of the land. In most of those French travels Melisa has been my companion and aide. My debt to her is beyond words. At Pearson, Andrew MacLennan offered me the chance to write about Louis XIV. Keith Robbins gave generous time to reading my first draft, and invaluable advice. Some years on, and with a longer book than that envisaged, I have tried editorial patience. Pendleton Campbell and Magda Robson have helped see it through. As before I have been especially indebted to the judgement, support and enthusiasm, *rara avis*, of the principal editor, Heather MacCallum. I write this on the eve of our youngest daughter's wedding. She will have more exciting presents than this dedication, but none offered with more love.

Geoffrey Treasure
Kington, Herefordshire, September, 2001

Chapter 1

PREPARING FOR POWER

Kings of France are kings elect and chosen of God,
kings after his own heart.

ANDRÉ DUCHESNE, 1609

THE GOD-GIVEN

When Anne of Austria gave birth to a boy at the palace of Saint-Germain on 5 September 1638, the event was hailed as an answer to prayer, indeed a miracle. He was the 'God-given'. In February Louis XIII had signed letters patent placing the realm under the protection of 'the most holy and glorious' Virgin Mary. Anne had vowed to construct a new church at Val-de-Grâce in honour of the Mother of God. Her pregnancy had been as unexpected as it was welcome. She was thirty-seven years old and she had been married since she was fourteen. Early pregnancies had led to miscarriages. Long neglected by her husband, she had lived a virtually separate life. In 1637, when France had been at war with Spain for two years, she had come under Richelieu's surveillance, suspected of treasonous correspondence with her brother, King Philip IV of Spain. Now the mother of the dauphin became a figure of central importance.

A few days later, in Spain, Anne's brother, Philip IV, had cause to rejoice: his wife, Elizabeth of Bourbon, gave birth to a girl, Maria Teresa. For several years Anne had felt divided loyalties. Now, strong in her own position, she could cherish a hope for the future. Nor was she alone. Chavigny, one of Richelieu's most influential ministers, wrote that 'the coincidence of the two births might bring about, one day a great union and a great blessing to Christendom'.

In France the rejoicing was general and sincere. 'Never', wrote Grotius, 'had a people demonstrated such delight.' It was widely remarked, not least by Englishmen, who tended to be cooler in this respect, that the French loved their sovereigns in an uncritical, possessive, almost religious fashion. The sentiment reflected centuries of struggle against rivals and intruders: enemies of the king and despoilers of the land. It also reflected political reality. In the absence of any visible organic unity, only the person of the king represented the unity of the realm. The words on the medal struck to mark Louis XIV's birth were literally true: he was *Francorum Spes Magna*. Periods when monarchy was weak were associated with disorder and lawlessness. Old men could remember the worst days of the Religious Wars when, before the Edict of Nantes (1598) brought them to a formal end and Henry IV began to rule effectively, religion was invoked to justify extremism: political leaders resorted to assassination, and Spanish armies trampled over French lands. Richelieu's generation was profoundly affected by the experience; he personally, by family misfortunes and his own, near-fatal involvement in the power struggle during the regency of Marie de Médicis that followed the assassination of Henry IV in 1610.[1]

Queen Anne's childless state had given cause for concern since Louis XIII had chronically poor health. Until 1638 the heir to the throne had been his brother Gaston of Orléans (d. 1660), who had conspired against Richelieu and defied the king too often to inspire confidence in his capacity to rule. There would be no place for Richelieu or his policies in the reign of king Gaston. So the cardinal was sincere in his congratulations. In 1640 a younger brother, Philippe, was born. However there remained cause for anxiety. It was likely that the young Louis would come to the throne a minor, that the experience of Marie's Regency would be repeated and his work undone. After Richelieu's drastic measures to assert the authority of the crown over some of the highest in the land it was certain that there would be a reaction and likely that there would be a relapse into anarchy.

For the development of Louis XIV's character it was perhaps fortunate that his father died when he was young. Louis XIII had been brought up abominably. His father was hearty, neglectful and sometimes brutal; his mother openly preferred Gaston; the spoiling attention of court ladies was no substitute for a systematic training. He grew up bruised and bewildered. He was timid with women, preferring the company of men. His best side can be seen in his devout sense of duty to God and to the realm. In an unimaginatively narrow way he was conscientious and just. The stammering, insecure prince grew up into a king who needed to assert his dignity, managed to do so on certain public occasions, yet, towards the end, allowed himself to be compromised in an obsessive relationship with a young favourite, Cinq Mars. At certain critical moments Louis XIII rose to the occasion. He gave a brave lead during the crisis of the Habsburg invasions, the 'Year of Corbie' (1636). He only once wavered seriously in his support of Richelieu. There was little in this remote, unpredictable father to encourage tender feeling in the son. It is hard to imagine a relationship extending into his adolescence being anything but disastrous. There were some features in Louis XIII's rule, as he came to understand it, that Louis XIV would respect. Significantly however he would never hear talk of Richelieu. For a model he would look back to his grandfather, Henry IV.

Anne of Austria was a fond mother; she was also a sensible one.[2] In play and talk she clearly delighted in the child's company. Her hitherto rather empty life, solaced by cards, gossip and chocolate, given purpose mainly by religion, had now become serious and dedicated to the nurture of a king. Graceful and refined in her ways, with a concern for cleanliness unusual for the period, she created a decorous and pious household. Louis's health, conduct, education and spiritual development became her prime concerns. It was her mission to cherish and protect him till he should be old enough to rule. Aware of the effect on Louis XIII and Gaston of their mother's preference for the latter, she pointedly distinguished between Louis and his brother whom at first she would treat, and sometimes dress, as a girl. So was instilled in Louis a sense of superiority, in Philippe acceptance of second place – and a lasting inclination towards effeminacy in dress and taste. Meanwhile, as regent, Anne would be as authoritative as was required to prevent subjects encroaching upon the powers that belonged, as of right, to the king. As a Habsburg, daughter of one king and sister of another, that came naturally to her. Schooled under Richelieu in absolutist principles, her chancellor could assure her that she was in the right. 'There is no minority in kings with respect to powers and authority, no deficiency nor disqualification; the queen is obliged to conserve her authority': thus Séguier,[3] in 1645, after *Parlement* had rejected new taxes.

Louis XIII died on 14 May 1643. He had intended to bind Anne by setting up a regency council. In a *lit de justice*, held a few days after the king's death, she secured from *Parlement* the effective annulment of the will when it accepted her as Regent with full powers, including the vital provision that she could choose her own ministers. Dressed in violet, lifted on to the throne by Mme de Mansac, Louis spoke a few well-rehearsed lines before handing over to his chancellor. Undoubtedly there was less of majesty in the child's words than in the principle he represented. Nonetheless, with Cardinal Mazarin presiding over council and assuming the powers of *premier ministre* and *Parlement*'s satisfactory response to Anne's overtures, Louis XIV's first royal action assumed significance. '*Le roi est mort; vive le Roi*' had been the traditional formula. There would be continuity: as to the crown, of course, and its rights – but to what extent its policies?

'I have come to show my goodwill towards my *Parlement*': the judges interpreted Louis's words as a promise of change, a softening, at least, in the style of government. 'Be the father of your people' and 'Strive to be the prince of peace': such *parlementaire* rhetoric expressed also a longing for peace. The stirring news of Condé's victory of Rocroy (May 1643), removing the threat of invasion, strengthened hopes of peace. It also emboldened those disposed to resist the demands of government. Within weeks the *Cabale des Importants* served warning that some of the highest in the land, notably here the duc de Vendôme and his son, duc de Beaufort,[4] would stop at nothing – including the projected assassination of Mazarin – to further their own ends. The intrigue came to nothing. Its leaders were treated relatively leniently. Beaufort was imprisoned. Would not Richelieu have had him executed? A military triumph and a foiled plot: Louis's reign started well.

Astrologers had vied with each other to offer favourable horoscopes for the dauphin, born under the sign of Virgo when 'this constellation had its greatest force'. His easy temperament and robust health seemed to prove them right. Geneticists might point rather to the hybrid strength coming from a crossing of ancestral strains – by marked contrast with the inbreeding in the Spanish Habsburg line, where the tragically deformed Charles II would demonstrate its dangers. Louis could count among his near ancestors sovereigns of vigour and proven ability. To Ferdinand and Isabella of Spain, Emperors Maximilian I and Charles V, add Burgundian duke Charles the Bold, Lorenzo Medici of Florence and, for good measure, Henry IV; recall that Louis had no share in the French Valois line which had ended so feebly – and we can appreciate the high hopes of all who saw the child, 'handsome as an angel' as he was described in the *Gazette*.

The education of princes is notoriously difficult. Between excessive pressure from the tutor, striving to produce a paragon (as in the case of bishop Bossuet and Louis's own son) and too light a hand from courtiers, timeserving, or simply in deference to rank and prospects (especially when the pupil was already king), it has proved hard to find a satisfactory middle way. Louis XIV's education was to be much interrupted during the Fronde. He did not receive the complete humanist syllabus which might fit a subject for high office. For his unique role he did, however, receive a sound, in some respects excellent training. Anne insisted on a reasonable discipline. She was an adoring mother but she showed that she would not be trifled with. In the absence of a father, the role of his godfather, Cardinal Mazarin, was vital. The duc de Villeroi,[5] to whom Mazarin entrusted guardianship, was a loyal, amiable grandee. Hardouin de Péréfixe – later archbishop of Paris – who directed the staff of tutors, taught him the history of his country through daily summaries of its more instructive parts. From his own history of Henry IV he presented the king with a sanitised and eulogistic view of his grandfather, the restorer of peace and order. He instilled a basic grasp of public laws and rights. He pointed out that a king, with whom lay the ultimate responsibility, placed as he was at the apex of the pyramid of counsel and command, 'must be taught primarily to perform decisive actions'. Louis would never forget such lessons. He was being trained to see the history of French monarchy in terms of successive challenges to its power, only to be overcome by resolute action. Tales from Mézeray's *Histoire de France* about *fainéant* kings aroused a child's ready disgust. He promised 'to follow the example of the most generous of his ancestors, particularly abhorring Louis the Idle'.

Péréfixe also prepared for him a royal commonplace book of moral tags, the *Institutio Principis*, which his pupil had to translate daily from the Latin. In due course many of these maxims would be passed on to his own son who would be assured, for example, that 'the profession of a king is a majestic, noble and delightful one'. Péréfixe had observed that 'a king should delight in his calling'. Louis's path to learning was decked with laurel branches. By his writing master he was required to copy out the sentence: 'homage is due to kings; they may do as they please'. He learned the rudiments of Spanish and Italian. Manuals of geography, rhetoric, logic and ethics were prepared for him. From specially designed playing cards he could consider improving gobbets of history and mythology. Saint-Simon[6] was to say that he could barely read or write. It was an absurdly jaundiced view but it suggests an aspect of Louis's personality that would not change. He was a quick learner and he had a capacious memory. But he did not relish learning for its own sake. His approach was pragmatic. After early difficulties he returned to Latin when he found it essential for studying diplomatic documents. To learn about war and statecraft and their delusory outcomes, both controlled and predictable, he read Caesar's self-justificatory *Commentaries*. Closer to home and dealing instructively with the formative reign of Louis XI were the *Mémoires* of Commines.[7] Horsemanship and fencing were learned from renowned masters. A dancing master found him an apt pupil. Laporte, his self-important valet, took it upon himself to teach practical lessons in deportment. Jealous of Mazarin's influence he became over-bold in his offensive jibes and, in 1652, the cardinal secured his dismissal. His own wiser hand can be seen in Louis's musical studies. Playing the lute or Spanish guitar, he acquired the taste which enabled him to appreciate the Italian opera introduced to the court by Mazarin and later to patronise the great French composers, Jean-Baptiste Lully and François Couperin.[8]

The Spanish mother and Italian minister, entirely devoted but also, up to a point, easy-going, seem to have allowed the king to remain a boy. With a child's gift for assuming that what happens around him is normal and, no doubt, a pleasant sense of his own importance, he enjoyed parades and reviews of the household troops and Swiss guards; later, drilling and staging fights round mock fortifications. He was also to be seen, however, on a Maundy Thursday, washing the feet of a dozen poor people of the parish of Saint-Eustache. Altogether Anne and Mazarin's tutelage leaves an impression of high seriousness, a keen sense of duty towards the most important of pupils, of balance and worldly common sense. Great events could be turned to advantage. The treaty of Westphalia became Mazarin's pretext for a lesson on the history of the Holy Roman Empire. Later he made a practice of bringing Louis into council meetings. When Péréfixe complained that Louis was not giving time to his studies Mazarin reassured him: 'Rely on my judgement and do not be too much concerned. He can know too much; as it is, when he is present in Council he asks me a hundred questions about the subject in hand.'

Mazarin's training and early experience had been as a Papal diplomat.[9] From his first encounters with Richelieu, during the Mantuan crisis and subsequent war, the young Roman had been drawn steadily towards French service. It was his diplomatic skills, knowledge of the European scene and resourceful, self-confident personality that had first appealed to Richelieu. The death, in 1638, of Father Joseph, Richelieu's right-hand man, had left a gap that he seemed well suited to fill. It was a positive advantage to his patron that Mazarin came to France relatively free of the client-ties and obligations that a French minister would bring to his office. Even so, Richelieu is unlikely to have seen Mazarin as his successor as *premier ministre*. That position he owed to the admiration of Louis XIII, who insisted on his being a minister; then, after Louis's death, to Anne. From representing the interest of the Papacy in a general peace it was not too great a move to working for terms advantageous to France. Responsibility overall, as *premier ministre*, for French government, was more testing. In his relationship with the king he had several advantages. He had been chosen by Louis XIII, to be the boy's god-father. (The other, significantly, was the princesse de Condé.) After the king died Mazarin moved closer to the royal household. To Anne he was a trusted confidant and advisor. He was imaginative and sympathetic. Like Anne he spoke French with an accent that invited derision, but he was fluent in her native Castilian. An outsider himself, he could respond intuitively to her sense of being excluded from the élites of French government and society. Bonds were strengthened at times of personal trial, as in November 1647 when Louis was seriously ill of smallpox. Undoubtedly he won her heart and mind. It may be that they were exceptionally discreet. It seems most likely – as it did to those, like Mme de Chevreuse, who knew them best – that their relationship stopped short of the intimacy of lovers.[10] She was schooled to restraint, but aware, with Habsburg pride, of her position, seriously devout and heedful of the church's injunctions. His whole career had shown a diplomat's ability to dissimulate and to adapt his behaviour to the needs of the situation. He was well fitted to be a moderating influence on the regent. Some serious political shortcomings were to be exposed by the Fronde. Meanwhile Louis was fortunate in his paternal interest and far-sighted control.

THE FRONDE

The years before the Fronde saw Louis receive his primary schooling; the Fronde was the tough secondary phase: that by which he would be made or marred. Undoubtedly it came as a shock to the court. 'Until the end of 1647', wrote maréchal d'Estrées, 'it seemed as if the spirit of Cardinal Richelieu, who had governed with such authority, had continued both in the conduct of war, and at court.' In that year the king paid his first visit to troops on campaign. At a critical stage in negotiations for peace, with pay short and mutiny in the air, it was intended to raise their morale. Meanwhile Mazarin had to persuade *Parlement* to make their contribution to peace by registering new taxes. He gambled for high stakes, the frontier gains envisaged by Richelieu and now within his grasp.

The sequence of confrontations, gestures, conspiracies, revolts and civil wars, from 1648 to 1653, which comprised the Fronde, was the culmination, violent, widespread and confused, of many conflicts. It involved all groups in society: princes of the blood, and nobles great and obscure, *parlementaires*, *officiers*, Parisian and provincial clergy, even, though usually as victims, ordinary townsfolk and peasants. To help us understand movements which would never have appeared to contemporaries to be so distinct or separate, several Frondes may be described: that of the *parlements*, led (but not coordinated) by that of Paris, from 1648 to 1649; that of the princes, from 1649 to 1652, and those which occurred in one or other of the provinces until 1653, with a postscript in the radical *Ormée* of Bordeaux. At each level of protest, from *parlementaire* objection to the financial measures presented at a *lit de justice* in January 1648, to open rebellion, particular grievances lent weight to personal ambition. Would-be leaders could count also on a general mood of resentment. Foremost in the mind of most Parisians in January 1648 would be the price of bread. There was a longing for an early peace and lower taxes. The continuing disappointment was correspondingly intense.

The Fronde was the predictable reaction to monarchy's continuing absolutist trend and its wartime financial expedients, its 'fiscal terrorism' (Bercé).[11] In its first paroxysms and spreading effects it empowered those institutions and interests which the crown had struggled to sideline or subdue: notably *parlements*, and Estates, members of other sovereign courts, and financial officers. In one aspect it was but the greatest in the line of the antifiscal revolts which had mounted in intensity and violence (though, like the *Croquants* and *Nu-pieds* of the previous reign, they had been local and essentially popular in character). In another, the constitutional, it was a bundle of claims, never reduced to a single programme but reflecting alternative visions of society. Those of *parlementaire* and noble were different, as had been sharply exposed in the debates and conflicting demands of the Second and Third Estates at the last States General (1614–15). They had in common a desire for some constraints on the royal power, especially as it was exercised – 'usurped' as they would see it – by 'tyrannical' minister–favourites, Richelieu, and now the Italian, Mazarin. He was the necessary villain, representing all that was felt to be alien and out of order.

Within the nobility there were marked differences between what *Les Grands*, the highest in the land, demanded for themselves, and what ordinary nobles called for in anticipation of the States General that Anne promised in 1651 – but managed to avoid summoning. Most dangerous to the crown was the determination of *Les Grands* to recover their traditional place at court, in council and, more realistically, in the province where they had a territorial stake and desired the authority and patronage associated with the still potent office of governor. How great that could be was shown during the Fronde, when Condé, first in Burgundy, then in Languedoc was the effective ruler. Magnates wanted not so much to reduce monarchy's status as to share in its councils, responsibilities – and rewards. Their sense of exclusion had been sharpened during the ministry of Richelieu; their appetite for honours and wealth by the example of his huge fortune.[12] Discredited by reckless and opportunistic leadership during the Fronde their political ideals would come, in some respects, to look anachronistic. Their vision, intrinsically neither base nor entirely materialistic, was of a society bonded by ties of fidelity, where they were seen, by local officials, as well as by *gentilshommes*, as proper leaders, and guardians of the customs, laws and institutions of the province. Associated with this reactionary mentality were the aspirations of that large number of nobles who had the same pride of lineage but were less well placed to come to terms with monarchy. They felt threatened by its growth, directly by what they saw as exploitation, in the shape, for example, of the *arrière-ban*; more insidiously, by the wealth and pretensions of the despised *robins*.

The catalyst for rebellion, after the government's decision to withhold salaries of most *officiers*, was the concerted effort of *Parlement* and the other sovereign courts to protect the material interests of *officiers* and *rentiers*. It led to the radical departure of May 1648, the union of the sovereign courts in a new body, the Chambre de Saint Louis which, in constitutional terms, marks the start of the Fronde. Its members sought to reverse recent trends: in particular, towards dealing in the royal council with cases which properly belonged to the courts, and using *intendants* in the tax-raising role that properly belonged to the *trésoriers*. Magistrates, *noblesse de robe* and members of Europe's most celebrated judicial tribunal, having jurisdiction over a third of France, spoke the lofty language that came naturally to guardians of the 'fundamental laws' who shared, to that extent, in royal sovereignty. It was not hard for them to adopt the cause of the suffering masses, reduced to destitution by the weight of taxation. Could they not see its effects on their own estates? The rhetoric should not be discounted altogether. The best *parlementaires*, whether the conservative *premier président* Molé[13] or more radical Broussel,[14] respected 'tribune of the people', were undoubtedly sincere in their love of the *patrie* and, no less, of monarchy. Judicial and financial offices represented, however, a huge capital investment, inherited and secure, through the device of the *paulette*, for their heirs. To understand the furore that arose from the attempt of government to bring pressure to secure regis-tration of edicts by the threat to suspend the *paulette*; or – always a sensitive issue, since it devalued existing offices – by seeking to raise money by the creation of new ones – it is essential to stress the central importance of venal office.[15] For more than 40,000 Frenchmen it constituted a property and an interest in the state: a source of stability when government was strong but of potential rebellion when, as now, it was driven by financial necessity to withhold salaries or interfere with the terms of renewal. *Parlement*'s aims and priorities can be studied in the concessions made so reluctantly (and viewed by the crown as provisional since made under duress) in the Declaration of Saint-Germain in October 1648. Notable were the recall of the *intendants*, except in the frontier provinces; a promise not to create new offices for five years; the re-establishment of the *trésoriers* with extended powers; a guarantee that no official would be removed from office by *lettre de cachet* or held in prison without trial. Undoubtedly *Parlement* had then won a signal victory. It had already claimed the scalp of the unpopular *surintendant* Particelli d'Hémery (dismissed in July) and a 12 per cent reduction in the *taille*. It could claim the support of the people and point to its power to paralyse government in the capital. Mazarin, whose attempted coup against the leaders (26 August 1648) had been the signal for the raising of barricades, thought that 'the best part of monarchy had been abolished'. He exaggerated, but he spoke the mind of the court.

The course of events during the Fronde lies mainly outside the scope of a study of a long personal reign. Louis's powers were never wholly in abeyance but they were severely limited, at times embarrassingly so. Certain episodes are, however, worth recall since they affected him at an impressionable time. Showing him to be vulnerable they might have taught a boy less secure in the affections of those around him, and less well advised, to be vengeful, tyrannical, duplicitous – to mention a few of the common abuses of power. That he emerged from the Fronde resolutely good-tempered, and buoyant without seeming unduly arrogant, is remarkable. It does not mean that he had come through unscathed; that he either forgot – or, where a political imperative did not require it, forgave. Condé might return to grace; Gondi never. *Parlement* would return to its regular functions; Jansenism remained under a cloud. Paris would cheer, but would soon see a king who intended to keep his distance. The experience of the Fronde helped shape Louis's perceptions and principles, indeed the very style of his rule.

In the *lit de justice* of January 1648 he first experienced open criticism of the policy of the crown. In the following months he learned how strong was *Parlement*'s interest, how far-reaching its capacity to obstruct ministers, indeed to paralyse government – and that, Mazarin would emphasise, at a crucial phase in the war and negotiations for peace. Anne could threaten but *Parlement* learned that it could defy her – and get away with it. In July, at another *lit de justice*, he had to listen, but with an outward composure that won admiration, to heavy lectures. Omer Talon[16] told him that 'kings were indebted for their fortune and their grandeur to the diverse qualities of the men who obey them', and Molé warned him that the throne would be in danger if reforms were not begun in earnest. Did not events across the channel reinforce the warning? There would be much talk at court about the plight of Charles I, defeated, driven to make a humiliating compact with the Presbyterian Scots, defeated again, imprisoned and awaiting trial. In January 1649 he would be executed. Henrietta Maria, his queen, Louis's aunt, was in Paris, a helpless spectator of the tragedy. Mazarin's private note-books show that he took seriously the threat of republicanism. In fact it was abhorrent to Frenchmen in general, in particular to nobles and those who owed their offices to the crown. Moreover it would emerge, from all the proposals about reform, that *Parlement* would not seek the control of taxation that had been the essential weapon for the English Parliament.

One aspect of Louis's experience during the Fronde was that, when in Paris, he was virtually a prisoner in his palace. In one pamphleteer's words it was the two hundred judges who were 'the absolute masters of Paris'. There were, however, carefree moments, with war games in the Louvre gardens. The household was devoted. Ministers like Le Tellier[17] and Séguier served the crown and Mazarin, even if they had doubts about the minister's ability to survive. The élite troops could be relied on. The Swiss Guards were staunch. Louis's wayward uncle Gaston of Orléans contributed at first to the protect-ive shield. Representing an embattled royal authority Louis could win fervent loyalty. The years when his young authority was in jeopardy were also the years when the people's love for the king was to be most effusive. But he learned to associate Paris with a threatening turbulence. The barricades of August 1648 forced Mazarin to release the leaders of *Parlement* whose seizure provoked the people and played into the hands of *coadjuteur* Paul de Gondi. From then to July 1652 and the massacre of the *Hôtel de Ville* when a Condéan mob turned on their deputies, the city was in ferment. In siege and famine, roused by the arguments and slurs of pamphlets, or by the ever-potent gossip and rumour of *Les Halles*, Parisians lived up to their reputation for volatility. In retrospect it may seem that *Parlement* was conservative, even when it appeared to be countenancing revolutionary action. There was no wish among the majority of judges to effect a significant change in the con-stitution or financial system. Restoration of traditional rights, notably that of judicial review, was the essence of their demand. As ever, however, in times of civil conflict, before damage to property brought wiser counsels, extrem-ists made the running on both sides. Steeped in the law and language of ancient Rome, judges could fancy themselves as tribunes of the plebs. The rhetoric might be artificial but the effect in verbatim report and partisan pamphlet was to inflame. Nor need we assume that there was no genuine sympathy for 'the people' whose cause they espoused. *Parlement* was not representative in any constitutional sense. In a wider sense it was. In its central position on the Île de la Cité, having administrative and police functions, it had acquired a sense of responsibility – self-importance in government's view – for the well-being of the city, more generally for good order in the land. Hurrying from the Palais de Justice to their homes in the Marais or Rue Saint-Honoré, from hot debate over issues of law and finance that also affected their own pockets, the judges saw another face of the country's crisis. Famished people, many newly arrived from the country, beggars more numerous than ever, women unable to feed their children – the picture was distressing. There was anger and alarm and an urge to apportion blame. The king was a boy, the mother misguided, so the minister must be responsible. Outside court and ministerial circles, among so many disparate groups and interests, there was near-unanimity. All political issues were subsumed in a chorus of abuse. Mazarin became the public enemy, his very name a coachman's oath.

For one royalist writer the basic question was 'whether king or *Parlement*?' Like its opponents upon Mazarin, court opinion focused upon a convenient scapegoat. *Coadjuteur* Paul de Gondi wanted to be first minister and he had made a study of the science of faction. In January 1649 he brought the Fronde to a more deadly point and provoked Condé to besiege the city when he drew leading nobles into an oath of union with *Parlement* against Mazarin. He actually used the word 'Revolution'. No wonder he was particularly abhorrent to the court. As right-hand man, and designated successor to his uncle, the archbishop of Paris, he had the support of influential *curés*. In the arguments of some of the *Mazarinades*[18] there were alarming reminders of the fanaticism of the Religious Wars. Could it be that if a monarch abuses the powers granted him by God, he ceases to be king and the people are absolved from their obedience? In an unbalanced or vengeful mind that could prompt the murderous dagger.[19]

Louis would be mindful of his grandfather's fate, Mazarin, more fearfully, of Concini's. For the king, as for his minister, liberation from constraint and fear, the free air of true kingship, came with his departure from the city: he could then fight his enemies and appeal to his subjects at large. In January 1649, the royal family left stealthily at night, for Saint-Germain; there ensued the siege of the city. Condé brought it to a successful conclusion. At the peace of Rueil in March the crown undertook to honour many of the demands already ceded in the declaration of Saint-Germain. Mazarin was insincere. But Louis was two years short of his majority and money had to be found for the war. Condé's loyalty was conditional and his terms were ominously high. Already there was much for Louis to digest. Frenchmen were fighting Frenchmen, bringing in foreign troops; two of his finest generals were on opposite sides. The rippling effect as revolts broke out in Normandy, Anjou, Poitou, Bordeaux and Aix made it necessary to temporise, to swallow pride and keep an eye on the main objectives: to prosecute the war against Spain and preserve political independence from the control of an over-mighty subject. Such pre-eminently was Condé, supported by his brother, prince Conti, and brother-in-law duc de Longueville.[20]

The arrest of those princes, in February 1650, was a calculated risk. It narrowed the issues, brought clearer definition to rightful authority and to treason and precipitated a more deadly war. The future of the crown was at stake as Anne, Louis and Mazarin went west to secure the loyalty of Normandy; thereafter south, to fight the rebels supporting the cause of the captive princes in the War of the Princesses. They returned to Paris in November of that year, reluctantly, to reassure the citizenry. In February 1651, to quell rumours that she planned to leave again, Anne allowed suspicious Parisians into Louis's bedchamber to see the supposedly sleeping king. By then the princes had been released and Mazarin had slipped out of the country. For the next few months king and regent were confined to the city. Through his estates, offices and governorships, and those of his associates, Condé controlled a quarter of the country. Anne showed tactical skills, appointed new ministers and maintained contact with Mazarin in Cologne. She promised that a States-General would be called after the king had come of age – the event that could at once be used to defer the meeting.

MAZARIN: MINISTER, GUARDIAN AND TUTOR

Another aspect of Louis's hard apprenticeship needs stressing. Never was he left in any doubt that the target of the *frondeurs* was Mazarin. Louis, they said, was ill-advised but not to blame. His minister was proclaimed the enemy of the people. *Parlement* outlawed him, put a price on his head and (February 1650) declared that no foreigner, even a naturalised subject, should ever be made a minister. That was an infringement of the royal prerogative. Mazarin was driven into exile pursued by the insults of the pamphleteers. Had he not tried to rule France from the queen's bed, this low-born Sicilian, usurer, charlatan, adventurer? Mazarin affected indifference. He was most hurt when he thought that he might not be recalled, that his services were not sufficiently valued. It is unlikely that the king was amused by the scurrilous tone of the

Mazarinades, his mentor being vilified and his mother smeared by association. But he cannot have failed to see that there was little serious argument in the pamphlets; only rare and sketchy proposals for anything like an alternative system of government. 'This was a Fronde of words, not a Fronde of ideas' (Jouhaud). Even in the darkest days it may have been a reassuring sign. The traditional affection for monarchy survived amid the chaos of the Fronde – 'the sad farce' as the *frondeur* La Rochefoucauld[21] would call it in the bitterness of failure. If anything, loyalty to the king was enhanced by antagonism to the minister. With worsening conditions came a widespread longing for the restoration of order. The king was the ultimate source of authority. Much was made therefore of formal occasions when, as at his coming of age, on 7 September 1651, with bells ringing and cannon booming, he could be shown to admiring Parisians. The young English gentleman, John Evelyn, saw the cavalcade and the king:

> Like a young Apollo, in a suit so covered with rich embroidery that one could perceive nothing of the stuff under it; he went almost the whole way, saluting the ladies and acclamators, who had filled the windows with their beauty, and the air with *Vive le Roi*. He seemed a prince of a grave and sweet countenance.

Louis's powers were never in abeyance but they were limited, at times embarrassingly so. From the age of ten from those around him, especially from his mother, he was imbibing ideas that would have a lasting influence. *Frondeurs* were plainly enemies to monarchy; the union of the courts was unconstitutional; those who were responsible for the disorders of the August Days were acting treasonably; promises subsequently made under duress were not binding. It was the duty therefore of royal servants to do everything needful to restore the king's authority. In times of emergency Louis could show politic generosity. In March 1651 he wrote to Turenne, whose earlier defection had so crippled the war effort and was now about to return to allegiance: 'I excuse all you have done and wish to forget it'. In final victory he might show moderation. After 1651 the issues remain complex to the historian who seeks to track the moves of ambitious individuals and their shifting alliances. For the king the fundamental issue was becoming simpler and the way ahead, though strewn with obstacles, was plainer to see. Since certain nobles, taking a lead from his cousin Condé, maintained their defiance and sought the alliance of Spain, there could be no question of peace until they submitted.

Between the proclamation of Louis's majority in *Parlement* in September 1651, and his triumphal return the following October, the court was continually in the provinces. In all, between 1649 and 1653, travelling about the country (and few provinces remained unvisited) Louis learned the extent of his kingdom, its variety and potential wealth. In frontier lands, Picardy, Champagne and Burgundy, in the provinces affected by campaign, he saw the devastation caused by civil war, with little to distinguish between rebel soldier or royal, Frenchman or foreigner. Pillage, terror, the disruption of trade and the collapse of law: Pascal was stating what was obvious to its victims when he declared that there was no evil so great as that of civil war. In effect, from the family's 'flight to Saint-Germain' (January 1649) and subsequent siege of Paris to the surrender of Bordeaux (August 1652), Louis was at war, not only with Spain, but with one group or another of his subjects. No one interest, not that of Orléans or Condé, Conti or Gondi, Longueville or La Rochefoucauld, could be fully satisfied, without upsetting another overmighty subject and, in the process, weakening the authority of the crown. It was Louis's duty to his subjects in general, losers by the destruction of civil war, to reassert that authority.

Through all the political intrigues, through often frustrating campaigns, Louis came to maturity. Meanwhile, the manoeuvres in which Mazarin excelled furthered his political education. He could observe those which made Condé first his ally, then (January 1650) his prisoner; then (January 1651) free again, a self-constituted director of affairs; finally (October 1651) an open rebel. He knew of Mazarin's secret trysts with the arch-intriguers Mme de Chevreuse and the Princesse Palatine to bring about one of those *renversements des alliances* which punctuated the Fronde. He saw Mazarin wield the marriage weapon to extend his *clientèle*, using his strong suit, his attractive nieces: so the dangerous Mercoeur and Conti were eventually drawn into the family fold. Politically sophisticated beyond his years, with a strong sense of priorities, tutored to weigh his words, to watch men closely and to conceal his own feelings, Louis knew to whom he owed success: to his mother, to loyal ministers and generals, above all, to Mazarin. He had learned when to cover his cards – and when to show them; when to bribe – and when to strike.

Perhaps it was inevitable that bribery should be as important as force. It had been so for Henry IV in the last stages of the Religious Wars.[22] In a diffused way it is a feature of most political systems, even the strongest. There is however a significant difference between individual bargains made by a monarch under duress and the discreetly managed system of favours, privileges and pensions that supported the absolutist regime of Versailles. Having experienced the one Louis would not be reluctant to utilise the other. The difference after 1661 would be that he was in control so that his patronage, in general, reflected his free judgement and personal preferences. Meanwhile, the case of the comte de Daugnon is instructive. As *lieutenant-général*, he had authority over vital ports in the south-west. So he was able to strike a hard bargain. In November 1652 he exchanged the office for 530,000 *livres* and a dukedom, with a complete amnesty for him and his followers. Such favour upset the loyalist general Harcourt. He expected large rewards. When he was disappointed he left for Breisach (a gain by the Peace of Westphalia) and treated with the Emperor for the establishment of an independent principality. Before he could be brought to terms Mazarin had to find funds to buy off his mercenaries. Then he received back all his offices and his governorship in Alsace since the king wished to show goodwill in restoring affairs to M. de Harcourt in the state they were in before. With insufficient funds, and a still delicately balanced military situation, the royal fist had usually to be concealed in a glove of soft velvet. There could, however, be exceptions.

Gondi's price had been the highest ecclesiastical office. He had wanted to be first minister, he became the Cardinal de Retz, he aspired to be archbishop of Paris. He received his scarlet hat in September 1652. In December, following Mazarin's advice, Louis oversaw his arrest. To Anne's secret order he added a postscript: 'I have commanded Pradelle . . . to arrest him dead or alive if he offers resistance.' To guard against a rescue attempt the road to Vincennes gaol was lined by soldiers. The arrest was a *coup de maître*. The risk of allowing Retz scope for further agitation was judged to be greater than that of imperilling relations with the Pope and causing unrest among some French clergy. The benefit was plain: here was a king acting as master in his own house. Surprise, boldness and thorough planning, the coup was in Mazarin's style, risky but decisive. It had its intended effect. It impressed those who might question the king's resolve and it boosted the king's self-confidence at a vital time.

Even when Mazarin was in exile (twice, February–December 1651 and August 1652 to February 1653), he was directing by correspondence, through client-ministers and unofficial agents. Realising that most Frenchmen were yearning for their king, like Henry IV before him, to overcome his enemies and to restore order, the minister was content to bide his time, to wait for his opponents to destroy each other. The bloody battle for Paris, fought in the Rue Saint-Antoine, watched by the king and Mazarin from a windmill on nearby Charonne hill (2 July), left Condé in possession of the capital. Within three months he had antagonised its citizens and ridden out to join the Spanish army in Flanders.

Throughout, the king was Mazarin's strongest card. Louis, learning to be a soldier, found little to resent and everything to respect, in his minister's handling of affairs. In camp and council the sole student in a master class in the nature and use of power, he proved remarkably patient and willing to listen. A prime source for our knowledge of the young Louis, until his death in 1654, is his trusted confessor Fr. Paulin.[23] A certain partiality must be allowed for. In his regular reports to Mazarin he depicted Louis as a paragon: 'made to command and to please', 'tough and resolute in everything', 'the most open and sincere soul', 'gallant and genuine', 'knowledgeable and devout'. The tutor was proud and fond and the portrait was varnished – but, in essentials, it was clearly what others saw. There were the normal pleasures of privileged adolescence to be enjoyed. Louis seems, however, to have responded to his position – near enough to full power to be able to envisage it, but still thwarted by faction – by curbing his natural exuberance and self-willed temper and by schooling his behaviour.

In personal encounters Louis learned how to please and impress. At a series of public occasions he experienced the importance of ritual. Simply because he was king he could impress the magistrates who attended his formal coming of age (October 1651) and, two years later, enthuse the Parisians who cheered his entry into the city, the ceremonial reclaiming of his capital. His bearing, on such occasions, appeared both dignified and resolute. He was still a boy playing a part – but he played it in a way that was to become a settled style. The greatest part was enacted at Reims, in June 1654. A coronation was more potent than many pamphlets. Royal ceremonies were especially important in critical times. What was later held to have been the end of the Fronde was less obvious at the time. The lessons of that experience had to be reinforced, and the authority of royal government asserted in the most public and dramatic way. The crowning of *le roi très chrétien*, the heir to Saint Louis, king by Divine Right, was carefully orchestrated by Mazarin to have the maximum impact. Through official accounts and sermons, often through a bishop's instructions to his *curés*, its symbolism reached the furthest parts of the realm.

THE ANOINTED KING

In the heart of Champagne, France's most afflicted province, where many villages in the rolling chalk plains were still deserted, framed by the sublime Gothic of Reims cathedral, and at the climax of an immense ceremony, Louis XIV was crowned king. Tradition had been studied but difficulties had been encountered. It is typical of a church which could show the finest of Christian devotion while living alongside examples of privileged exploitation, that it was realised that the archbishop was not a priest: the bishop of Soissons officiated in his stead. Notable too by their absence were some of the leading peers: inevitably that included Gaston and Condé. Nobles who had not been *frondeurs* or had made their peace in time took their place. With some 2,000 in the tapestry-hung cathedral, it was an impressive parade of the political and social élite. Its focus throughout was the sixteen-year-old king who represented, in each rite, the unity of the realm, its soul and its consciousness of law, right and custom. From an exhilarating entry to the sound of drums, trumpets and oboes, and a procession which marked with every shuffling footstep the grades and values of this hierarchical society, Louis played his part perfectly. For the five hours of ritual that ensued before the cloud of white doves could be released to signify its end, he displayed the studied poise that already seemed to be natural to him and the devout bearing suited to a religious exercise of high secular import. Since 816 and the accession of Louis the Pious consecration and coronation had been carried out in the same ceremony.

In the royal necropolis at Saint-Denis monuments, typically, have two effigies: on top, the king is sculpted, in fine dress and proper accoutrements, holding the sceptre; below, the man, mortal, naked and decaying. After 1422 and the death of Charles VI, it had been customary to place on the coffin a wax effigy of the deceased king to which, until the funeral mass and assumption of powers by the new king, service was due as if he were alive. In 1610, following the assassination of Henry IV, it was essential to assert at once the right of the eight-year-old Louis XIII and the Regent, his mother. His first *lit de justice* had set a precedent for Louis XIV. There remained, however, the potent theory of the two bodies: the physical, defective and mortal, and that of kingship, insubstantial, perfect and immortal. The language was suggestive of divinity, the idea grounded in the dual nature of Christ: at once man and God.

So far however from being blasphemous, the sacerdotal concept of kingship represented the grandest in human aspiration embodied in the highest in the land. It also reflected the political necessity to ensure the unity of the realm under a sole authority, uniquely endowed as lieutenant of God with absolute power – and with corresponding duties. The idea to which Bossuet[24] would lend his towering authority and embed in a convincing frame of history was implicit in the words of the bishop of Soissons. Louis was 'The Lord's Anointed, son of the Most High, shepherd of the flock, protector of the church, the first of all kings on earth, chosen and appointed by Heaven to carry the sceptre of the French, to extend far and wide the honour and renown of the Lily . . . making France a universe and the universe a France.'

Divine Right implied Divine delegation to a privileged and absolute sovereign. It was the highest of mandates, but also the most exacting. It was grounded in a political theory that had evolved over centuries to meet the needs of church and ruler in a partnership of mutual advantage. At an instinctive level it expressed a deep French sense (akin to that in Spain where it was stiffened by the experience of the *reconquista*) that Catholicism was the soul of the state. It made a bond between priest and people. In the expectations of the clergy, reading new meaning into the traditional oath of the sovereign to combat heresy, can be read the ultimate fate of the Huguenots. The bishop's rhetoric expressed a joyful mood – but it was not merely for the day. It drew on a long tradition that had been given substance particularly during the regime of Richelieu. As an element in the mental conditioning of the earnest young man it prefigures the diplomatic and cultural imperialism that would be features of the reign. It prepares us for the essential paradox of the reign: that a king who was so conscientious and honourable in his dealings with individuals, so meticulous in his concern for corporate rights, could be also, at times, so ruthless, even callous, in his pursuit of what he saw to be the interests of the church, his dynasty and his realm.

It was, above all, duty and the sense of responsibility for the good of his subjects that were to be understood from the rites of coronation, each mounted so as to extract the clearest meaning from word and gesture, and accompanied with prayer. From the abbey of Saint-Rémy came the most sacred of all objects, the phial, reputed to have come down from heaven for the consecration of Clovis. With its oil the bishop anointed the king while the clergy recited: 'May the king bring down the proud, be an example for the rich and powerful to follow, be good towards the humble, charitable towards the poor, just to all his subjects and work for peace among nations.' From the abbey of Saint-Germain came the royal vestments and insignia: the Dalmatic, loose-fitting and suggestive of priestly status, the mantle, violet covered with silver *fleurs de lis*, the jewelled royal sword, reputedly Charlemagne's, the sceptre, symbolising absolute authority, and the hand of justice that signified the delegated power of God. With the bestowing of the ring Louis 'married his kingdom'. The crown, undoubtedly Charlemagne's, sealed his place in the unbroken royal succession. Louis then mounted the stairs to the throne in the rood loft to receive the homage of the peers. At last the bishop could present the king, as it were to France: '*Vivat rex in aeternum*' and the doors opened, as the people echoed the answering '*Vive le Roi*'.

Significantly that was not the end. As the shouting, trumpeting and musket and cannon fire subsided the king proceeded to receive absolution and to take communion – as no Catholic layman could – in both kinds. Three days later, touching for 'the king's evil', he would demonstrate one element in his quasi-sacerdotal status.[25] Over each of two thousand sufferers from scrofula he pronounced the traditional words: 'the king touches thee: may the Lord heal thee'. He would repeat this ceremony several times every year of his reign.

It did not lessen the appeal of religion to Louis that there was such emphasis on the high calling of the ruler and the duty of subjects to obey. After such solemn days he may, however, have welcomed the need to return to another kind of active service. Before the coronation could take place Champagne had to be cleared of soldiers, Condéans and other bands fending for themselves: the typically messy aftermath of war. Now Louis went, with Mazarin, to the siege of Stenay, the last Condéan fortress on the Meuse: its capture denied the Spanish army entry to Bar and Champagne. Strategic considerations aside it was vital that the military fraternity should recognise that they had a soldier–king. Unrest in Paris and disorder in the provinces showed that the symbolism of Reims had yet to be translated into the disciplined subjection it implied.

THE ECCLESIASTICAL FRONDE

The central figure in what has been called the 'ecclesiastical Fronde' was the cardinal de Retz. His arrest had made him champion of the rights of the church. His escape from gaol (August 1654), followed by Papal confirmation of his episcopal status, enabled him to be the leader in exile of those who looked to Rome for assurance that those rights would not be subordinated to those of the crown. Among them were groups who had their own agenda. The radicalism of Jean Rousse, *curé* of Saint-Roch, led to his expulsion from the Sorbonne. 'He has always been seditious', wrote Mazarin in 1656, recalling a pamphlet in which he had asserted that 'a king must rule justly or face deposition', and noting his connections with Jansenism.[26] That movement's theology had political implications from its beginnings, as Richelieu had recognised. Mazarin had yet to be provoked into acting against its spiritual homes, the abbey of Port-Royal in Paris and its associated lay community. Besides its Hispanophil ancestry in the person of the Flemish bishop

Cornelius Jansen, its links with *Parlement* and with certain notorious *frondeurs* were sufficient grounds for vigilance: the very names of four duchesses, Longueville, Liancourt, Rohan and Luynes, were enough to raise eyebrows at court. When Blaise Pascal started to write his *Lettres provinciales* in response to the condemnation of Antoine Arnauld by the Sorbonne (in January 1656) and turned his satirical fire upon the Jesuits, Mazarin was deeply concerned. He did not wish to offend the Pope but had to guard against the revival of Gallican spirit in *Parlement*.[27] When *Parlement* demurred at Pope Alexander VII's bull condemning certain Jansenist propositions the king was required to hold a *lit de justice* to secure registration. In his actions during these years Mazarin alternated between apparent detachment and personal intervention: he first closed the Jansenist schools (January 1656), then allowed them to reopen (July), while finding ways of persuading Jansenists to repudiate those doctrines of Jansen that the Pope had declared heretical. He was mainly preoccupied with questions of war and diplomacy. But Jansenism, with its resonances of the Fronde, would trouble him to the end. It would surely not have been near the top of Louis's agenda had Mazarin not ensured that it stay there. The young man may have been less alarmed than irritated by 'that refractory clique' as Mazarin called it. But he needed little prompting by the Jesuits to heed Mazarin's advice 'no longer to endure the Jansenist sect or even its name'. One day, unfortunately, he would act upon it.

The fact that ministers took Retz so seriously and gave priority to dealing with Jansenism points to a vital factor in the incoherence and, in the end, impotence of the Fronde: the lack of a single unifying ideology. There was no equivalent to Puritanism in England, bringing together the worlds of religion and politics, giving a sense of God-given purpose, uniting men and women and stiffening the will to sacrifice all for the cause. In an age of religious war, in a country where religious feeling was strong and differences ran deep, the Fronde was a notably secular conflict. There was no central issue of faith to make men choose sides comparable to the tenets of high Anglicanism which Charles I made his cause. There was nothing comparable to the Irish Catholic or Scottish Presbyterian contributions which sharpened religious debate and deepened divisions in England. The shameless intrigues of Gondi helped ensure that the militant tradition of the Parisian *curés*, monks and friars responsible for much of the propaganda against Mazarin never developed into a coherent force. *Dévôts* were well placed in influential circles yet they never evolved from being occasional pressure groups, challenging the Cardinals' foreign policy, for example, into a party capable of concerted action.

The role of the Jesuits was significant. They were naturally sympathetic to Mazarin, their star pupil. Everywhere in Catholic Europe they worked with the ruler. The confessor's influence may rarely have been so great as in Protestant imagination. That of successive Jesuits who heard and advised Louis in confessional and council can only be guessed at. But the influence of the order as a whole can be measured by their steady favour at court, by the vehemence of Jansenist attacks and the wide audience to which they appealed.

The sympathy of Anne towards the *dévôts* sometimes bothered Mazarin but it was also an asset for it neutralised zealots, some of them members of the *Compagnie du Saint-Sacrement*,[28] who might otherwise have combined to destroy him. Drawing its strength from the respected status of *le roi très chrétien*, with its advocates in *Parlement* and among the bishops, Gallicanism provided a bulwark against the *dévôts*, even if at times its mode of support for the crown disturbed relations with Rome. A key figure in the *conseil de conscience*, Vincent de Paul,[29] was critical of the opportunistic policies of Mazarin, but his prime concerns were pastoral and social. Inspired by him, a number of aristocratic women gave themselves to relief work among the poor and refugees of Paris. The Jansenists, self-confident within their own moral universe, came nearer than any other subversive group to developing a philosophy – if not of resistance, at least, of a kind of independence from accepted authority. Yet their theology and style cut across Gallican and Ultramontane positions and served rather to divide than to unify.

Of course the main threat on the religious front might be expected to come not from within the Catholic fold but from the Huguenots.[30] For nearly a hundred years they had been the prime source of rebellion and civil war. Nor was the spirit of resistance quite dead. In May 1643 a false rumour that a Catholic mob was on the way to burn down the temple of Charenton was enough to cause the congregation to panic while noblemen waited with drawn swords. In 1653 a conflict over the rebuilding of a temple at Vals in the hills above the Rhône led to the setting up of an armed camp of some 6,000. But the psalm singers of Vals and the Huguenot gentry among the *sabotiers* of the western provinces who threatened a general rising in 1658 were not representative of the attitude of Huguenots as a body. So far from exploiting the difficulties of the crown they expressed their own sense of insecurity in repeated assurances of loyalty. The *frondeur* venture of Turenne had more to do with his pretensions as grandee than with his faith. It may not be just a coincidence that the provinces where Condé found most support were those in the south-west, where the Huguenot population was relatively dense. Yet there was no general rising. It could be said that there were not enough Huguenots to make trouble except as individual supporters of a rebellious magnate. A more convincing explanation is the fact that leading Huguenots had become so important in the world of business and had so penetrated the cultural establishment of Paris that they had an overriding interest in supporting the crown. In May 1652, at a critical juncture of the war, when there was anxiety about the south, Huguenots were praised for their loyalty. 'We are highly satisfied' declared the king, the Edict of Nantes was reaffirmed and all judgements made by *parlements* since 1629 conflicting with its letter or spirit were annulled. Mazarin was reacting more by necessity than conviction. As the state grew stronger, the Huguenots would again have reason to feel less secure. Meanwhile their passive attitude had contributed to the apparent failure of the Fronde.

A CONSTITUTIONAL BALANCE

Was it an apparent failure or a real one? Was it partial or complete? Answers to these questions, so crucial to understanding the nature of Louis XIV's regime and its real powers, can only be attempted with reference to the differing aims of radicals and conservatives within *Parlement*, and of the provincial *parlements*. *Parlement*'s aims seem to have changed as the civil wars proceeded. At first there were clear-cut proposals for the reform of government in the areas of finance and justice. It early became apparent that there were some judges who looked to England with a view, not to abolishing monarchy but to limiting its powers through greater control of taxation. For a truly radical programme one has to wait, however, for the *Ormée*[31] in Bordeaux in 1653; and there it was rivalries within the city that fomented the rising. Other judges looked backwards to an idealised Renaissance monarchy as, they claimed, it had been before the cardinals' 'usurpation' of royal authority when the huge growth in the creation of office and arbitrary justice tilted the balance in favour of the executive. As moderates gained the day, taking a lead from Molé, *Parlement*'s stance was concerned mostly with maintaining unity within its ranks and securing its own privileges. It had neither the ability, nor the will, to create a united front. Other sovereign courts and provincial *parlements* were left to fight their own battles. So the separatism which hampered sound royal administration actually favoured the crown. Whole areas of France, the Dauphiné, Brittany and Languedoc, for example, were quiescent. Mazarin notoriously pursued the tactic of divide and conquer. The parochial instincts of his foes played into his hands. Even in Paris,

Parlement and the *Hôtel de Ville*, with overlapping responsibilities for administration, were usually at odds. When there was a semblance of unity it was
because of fear of the mob, of ambitious nobles and demagogues. Then the
bourgeois turned instinctively to the crown as the ultimate authority and source
of justice. Paradoxically, therefore, the kind of crowd action which made the
early Fronde so dangerous to the crown became one of its most potent arguments. As for the nobility, it was so fragmented and marked by frequent
shifts of allegiance that one is reduced to thinking in terms of individual or
family interests and strategies. For different kinds of *frondeur* therefore there
would be different outcomes: some might be satisfied as they saw ministers
respecting their judicial rights; others disappointed as they saw *intendants*
returning to the provinces. Some nobles found restored prestige and promotion. For some, like Rochefoucauld, life would continue to be blighted by the
king's suspicion.

To understand the emerging balance of power within the constitution, it is
revealing to look at relations between *Parlement* and ministers in the years
immediately following the king's return to Paris.[32] 'Henceforth members are
prohibited from taking any cognisance of the general affairs of the state and
the direction of finances.' The *lit de justice* of 22 October 1652 did not prove
to be the absolute defeat of *Parlement* that might be assumed from the king's
crushing words. Neither the civil war nor the constitutional conflict behind it
had a tidy end. With the return of the senior members from Pontoise (those
who had obeyed the king's order in July 1652 to go there) *Parlement* was whole
again and ready to capitalise on its recent moderation. It registered the royal
document defining its powers. Like that of Louis XIII in 1641 and no less
severe in tone, it still allowed *Parlement* scope for the amending of royal
edicts. That would be worth as much or as little as the political situation
would allow. Constitutional history has to take note of the dynamic elements
within a given situation: that of the first years after the Fronde was volatile.
If *Parlement* stopped short of open defiance, the crown was also wary of
provoking it. Its measures were practical, and punitive only in a selective
way that left the majority reassured. No judge was to enter the service, or
join the party, of a nobleman. Leading radicals, notably Broussel and Viole,
were exiled, but there were no executions. Reflecting Mazarin's instinct for
appeasement, but also the fragility of the crown's position, these measures
were moderate by comparison with those following Charles II' s restoration
to the English and Scottish thrones in 1660.

Yet there had been a civil war and several unauthorised rebel administrations. Omer Talon had done much to precipitate the Fronde by his

outspoken criticisms of royal policy. Before he died, in 1652, he wrote what might serve as a text for the personal reign of Louis XIV:

> Factions, parties and undertakings must be avoided so that the king's authority may be defended. . . . It is the duty of a good man to oppose strongly the insolence of ministers, who abuse the name and power of the king in order to do wrong. However this must never come to a schism. Nor should it break the union which should exist between the king and his office-holders.[33]

There would be no dangerous quarrel until 1713, and then over the Gallican issue arising out of Louis's self-wounding assault on Jansenism. The Fronde can indeed be seen to have produced 'the union', a kind of partnership, based on a disturbing experience of the breakdown of order and on recognition of mutual and material interests. Conservative judges might therefore conclude that their early boldness in opposition had been worthwhile. By creating an awareness of limits the Fronde helped ensure that Louis XIV would not rule in an arbitrary fashion. When he did use his absolute power, but with restraint and regard for the susceptibilities of the one body which had the prestige and moral authority to mount a serious challenge, he would not be opposed.[34] Radicals who had been tempted to see themselves as in some way representative of the nation, and claimed the right to control taxation, were, of course, disappointed. Such ideas had never had any basis in history; they no longer had any realistic chance in politics.

The remaining years of Mazarin's ministry can be seen as a testing ground for the constitutional balance. The resulting tensions and conflicts completed the king's political education. There was no formal repudiation by the crown of the specific reforms of 1648–49. Step by tentative step, as if seeing what it could get away with, it clawed back power. *Intendants* reappeared in the provinces. A *lit de justice* in December 1652 re-imposed several of Hémery's ill-fated levies. The king's brother attended the *Chambre des Comptes* to overrule restrictions on the use of *comptants*. There were noisy demonstrations as members of the sovereign courts called for the restoration of suspended colleagues. Behind them were *rentiers* angry at the suspension of interest payments. 'Paris is on the eve of some great sedition', wrote one official. Ministers responded by concessions to the merchant guilds and the abolition of a few levies. The *rentiers* were placated, but not until *Parlement* had authorised a meeting of their representatives. The new *premier président*, Pomponne de Bellièvre, warded off pressure for a plenary session. So both sides drew back from the brink. The sovereign courts continued to be obstructive. *Parlement* exploited to the full the procedure of judicial review.

In March 1655 Louis held another *lit de justice* to enforce registration of four-teen fiscal edicts.

Magistrates continued none the less to deliberate. Was it to be 1648 again? Louis was no longer a child. He decided that the time had come to demon-strate his power. He may have been coached by Mazarin – or prompted by the queen. His action, on 13 April 1655, has the stamp of an impatient young man, acting on impulse. Still in his morning's hunting clothes he strode into the *Palais de Justice* and berated the judges:

> Everyone knows how much your assemblies have incited troubles in my State and how many dangerous effects they have produced. I have learned that you presume to continue them under the pretext of deliberating on the edicts which were recently read and published in my presence. I have come here expressly to forbid you to carry on, and you, *M. premier président*, to allow or to agree with it, whatever [pointing to the row of those judges] the *enquêtes* judges may request.[35]

Bellièvre was left to assuage them. Mazarin reacted nervously and explained that the king was but speaking paternally: he would welcome remonstrances in due course. In the light of what was to come it was not Mazarin's soft words but the king's direct approach that can be seen to have scored. Meanwhile there were further tussles, typically, in 1656, over renewal of the *paulette* which was always an opportunity for bargaining, when judges secured a vital declaration from the crown accepting restrictions on the interference of the council in judicial matters. By and large, moreover, ministers followed Mazarin's line. Dealing with an institution as close-knit as *Parlement* and with individuals whose financial interests were not confined to their legal salaries and fees, it was safer to work on those individuals than to confront the institution. Polite words, a *douceur*, or, where necessary, covert surveillance – such politic approaches were a long way from the high precepts of pulpit absolutists, but appeared to be justified by the overriding need to raise funds for the war. Here the role of the *trésoriers* was crucial.

These financial officials were an easier target, though they had their own syndicates, since they had less prestige and less of a support system than members of the sovereign courts. The trial of strength came in 1653 when they issued an *ordonnance* which, in effect, warned officials against working with *intendants*. Séguier then ordered them to obey the king's orders. The *trésoriers* were deprived of their right of remonstrance except in the form of 'very humble prayers and supplications'. They objected and held meetings; so did the *élus*. It was not until 1661 that such meetings were banned. With their overriding concern for the preservation of their offices in the stricter regime of Colbert, they would be in no position to resist the progressive reduction of their powers.

Their offices were to prove as secure as those of the judicial establishment. It would prove to be as impracticable for Louis XIV to abolish, even significantly reduce, venal office, as it was to overcome the passive, but effective resistance of *Parlement* to the fundamental reforms in the law that were needed if the state were to realise its latent powers. Beyond doubt the crown emerged from the whole Fronde experience, the civil war and its aftermath, stronger both outwardly, in political terms, and in its place in the mind and hearts of its leading subjects. It was well placed therefore to acquire greater strength – especially in the military and diplomatic spheres. Its security and renown came, however, to rest on a consensus, subscribed to by the élites of sword and gown – but much on their own terms. The effect was to limit the crown's freedom of action – and to some extent to distort its priorities – when there was any question of radical reform.

Most Frenchmen did not belong to any kind of élite. In itself, simply to be noble implied little in terms of economic weight or social influence. Of those who could claim noble status, only a few thousand were rich enough to live fashionably or appear regularly at court; fewer still able to play a leading role, to raise troops or bear the costs of royal service. Through royal favour, military service or civil office, the ranks were swelling; others, however, were dropping below the level at which they could even pretend to be living nobly or persuade investigators that they should be exempt from the *taille*. The records of the *ban* summoned in 1639 show that few had been able either to serve themselves or pay much in lieu.[36] Poor nobles were likely to look to the patronage of a local magnate. A large element in the private armies of the Fronde, they can be identified as a significant factor in the problem of disorder in the provinces. Few nobles had been directly involved in the popular risings before the Fronde. It was then, following the rebellious example of great families, that they flexed their muscles. The Fronde spelt opportunities for the aggrieved and ambitious as they gathered to list their grievances and propose remedies. Its ending did not mean that they lost their appetite for political action. In 1651, drawn by Anne's insincere offer of a States General, a number of nobles, mostly mere *écuyers*, assembled in Paris to discuss tactics; others in the provinces drew up *cahiers* which provide insights into what nobles expected from the crown and what drove them to rebel. Louis XIV's conception of the nobility's role in society is generally discussed with reference to the grandest among them. The experience of his early years suggests that policy, insofar as it was deliberate, was influenced by awareness of the plight of the nobles as a whole and the threat it constituted to the good order of the provinces. The expansion of the army and navy, substituting royal service for a grandee's *clientèle*, would have, incidentally, a social purpose.

Nobles wanted a reduction in the number of offices for sale. They condemned financiers, in the words of a *cahier* from Champagne, 'gorging themselves on the blood of the people as a vampire does on that of children'. There we see the familiar resentment of the hereditary privileged towards rich interlopers. Nor was their concern for the well-being of peasants burdened by the *taille* wholly disinterested. Its increase made it harder to secure their feudal dues. The *ban* was high among grievances, as were the *aides* and *gabelles*. Some resented the periodic *recherches de noblesse* that might expose a fraudulent title; others wished for a stricter definition of nobility. In several *pays d'états* they regretted the weakening of the Estates. Loyalty to the crown was beyond question. They wanted a king who would rule – not be ruled by an all-powerful minister; one who would sustain them in their privileges, but not expect too much in return.

After the king's coming of age the meeting of the States General was postponed to an indefinite future. Nobles could not have imagined that neither their children, nor grandchildren would see such a meeting – nor that it would then precede a revolution which would make the Fronde look like a mere hiccup in the development of absolute monarchy.[37] Meanwhile hopes so cynically raised gave way to frustration. In the grim early months of 1652, with the crown at war with its greatest subject, bands of nobles met in informal gatherings. A meeting at La Roche-Guyon, under the protection of the duc de Liancourt, received a *lettre de cachet* ordering its members 'to cease from making unions, addresses and useless assemblies' and to come to the king's aid to fight his enemies. Some then rode to court to offer their service, only to be sent home to await the royal summons. The episode speaks volumes about the nervous political climate of Louis's adolescence. An embattled government is closing ranks, wary of unofficial gatherings, assuming an enemy where loyalty cannot be proven. It did not need Mazarin to instil in Louis the aloof and guarded style that was to become habitual: he had to learn to be gracious without giving anything away; to be regal without giving offence.

'Conspiracies of the forest' were a significant part of the texture of the 'post-Fronde'. The greater the vigilance of government the more secretive were the meetings. It is hard therefore to judge the threat posed by the movement. It centred on western provinces, notably Anjou and Normandy. In 1657 widespread activity was reported, with evidence of careful planning. Each province was divided into cantons: in each, two deputies were charged to call meetings and formulate complaints and demands. Colbert's letters to Mazarin refer often to the '*malintentionés*'.[38] He acted for Mazarin in the special council set up to deal with the problem. When, in June 1657, Louis forbade any such assemblies he received a sobering lesson in the limitations of power. The assemblies continued, typically in the depths of forests where seigneurial hunting rights ensured privacy, in remote châteaux, sometimes, more boldly, at fairs. At one gathering near Argenton 700 horses were counted: it suggests a significant number of nobles. At another, far west in the Vendémois, deputies came from as far as Burgundy. Because some could not be trusted, the government was reluctant to give governors the necessary powers to act; again the experience of the Fronde inhibited action.

Was Colbert unduly alarmist when he wrote (August 1658) that 'a league of lesser nobles might gain all the provinces of the realm'? He was informed that certain *parlementaires* had offered support. Several Huguenots were involved, most prominently the sieur de Bonnesson. In 1659 he was inciting a peasant revolt which threatened to spread, like that of the *croquants* in 1636. The *sabotiers* of 1659 were persuaded to disperse and there was no need for military action. So ministers played down an episode somewhat at variance with the official story of a country at peace. Mazarin's unusually harsh actions tell a different story. Bonnesson was executed, other nobles condemned *in absentia* and their châteaux destroyed. They had to learn that royal government had a long arm. Soon it would reach to the recesses of the Massif Central where lawless nobles had a particularly vile reputation. Unless the king could establish more than a nominal authority over the provinces he would fail in the central aspect of his royal vocation, that which had been emphasised in the rites of coronation: to be the father of his people. Campaigning in the provinces he had seen something of the suffering that is conveyed by contemporary reports and historians' statistics.

War, taxation, its essential agent, and nature's periodic blows were the prime causes of distress. Taxation had increased relentlessly during Richelieu's ministry, particularly since 1635, with the beginning of open war against the Habsburgs;[39] the trend had been sustained under Mazarin and was a major cause of the Fronde. Undoubtedly peasants took advantage of its outbreak, and the withdrawal of *intendants*, to stop paying. Arrears mounted to a level which made some cancellation inevitable. War had a more direct effect in the frontier provinces, notably Picardy, Champagne and Burgundy. The last had already suffered grievously in the ferocious border 'war of the two Burgundies' (the other being that part of the original duchy that remained Spanish), in which local nobles raided and plundered regardless of official strategies. Seriously affected too were the areas around the main campaigning routes of the civil wars, notably the Ile de France, and a mid-western band, between Anjou and Bordeaux. Parish registers show famines and epidemics hurting in provinces untouched by military operations.[40] They were not just a French phenomenon. Three wet summers spoiling crops, creating the high prices of 1647–48 and culminating in the grain crisis of 1652, affected communities across Europe from Exeter to Cracow, from Stockholm to Naples. Prolonged malnutrition weakened resistance to disease. Considering, therefore, the evidence for a dip in the population, between 1640 and 1660, of around two million, the casualties of war have to be treated as part of a wider picture.

It was, for all that, the special effects of the Fronde, forcible requisitioning to feed the soldiers and their horses, mindless destruction and the brutalities typical of military operations during the Thirty Years War, that had the sharpest impact on ministers' thinking, whether they saw the problem mainly in terms of economic well-being, of army discipline, or of civil order. In the countryside around Étampes, besieged in the spring of 1652, Vincent de Paul and his *filles de charité* found utter ruin. Nor did it need fighting. 'We have undertaken at Palaiseau, where the royal army has been encamped for twenty days, as great an operation as at Étampes; there is extreme sickness and poverty.'[41] The incursion of hungry, undisciplined men into a barely self-sufficient community, could only be devastating. They took the grain and livestock – and they left their germs. In camp or on the march armies brought disease. Many of the estates around the capital were owned by prominent Parisians.[42] By bailiffs' reports warning of a fall in rents, by city authorities' concern over the flood of refugees, and soldiers and beggars turning to crime, by fashionable ladies raising funds for relief and tending the sick, opinion was swayed where it counted, at court and among ministers. The wide-ranging reforms of Colbert, the Le Telliers' drive to create a more disciplined army, and the humane initiatives taken further and regularised, by royal edict, in the form of *hôpitaux-généraux*[43] – to take only three examples of state engagement in Louis XIV's personal reign – assume new significance when set against the background of the Fronde.

A RULER'S DUTY

During these years Louis was also seeing what, in his terms, was the acceptable face of war. In 1653, for the first time since 1648, Mazarin was able to deploy the bulk of his troops against the enemy. The financial constraints were severe, the forces relatively small and Spanish resistance was still stubborn. Sieges produced only modest gains. The little walled towns, Monzon, Saint-Ménéhould, Stenay, Quesnoy, Clermont-en-Argonne, captured between 1653 and 1655, were not enough to bring Spain to consider peace. The decisive blow eluded Turenne. Meanwhile his rival Condé was still capable of springing a surprise, as when, in 1656, he broke the French siege to relieve Valenciennes. The issues of loyalty and discipline which underlay French reverses are graphically illustrated by the case of the hitherto steady Mazarinist Maréchal d'Hocquincourt, who threatened to take his army over to the enemy if Mazarin did not pay him 600,000 *livres* and release the imprisoned Condéan (and his beloved) duchesse de Châtillon. He got what he demanded.

The Hocquincourt episode shows Mazarin, typically, making an unavoidable concession, keeping his eye on the greater prize. His next move taught Louis a more significant lesson in *realpolitik*. He was coming to the conclusion that France could not defeat Spain without an ally. England was already at war with Spain. Though his greatest action was to come, the destruction of the treasure fleet at Tenerife, Admiral Blake had already struck blows which affected the ability of the Spanish to supply their troops. However, with Lionne reporting that he could make no headway at Madrid, and the Spanish showing their customary reluctance to match military effort to economic resources, Mazarin decided that it was time to harness the power of England to his campaign in Flanders. The political risk was great. Heretic, usurper and regicide, Cromwell gloried in his Protestant mission. He was anathema to loyal Frenchmen and good Catholics. Alliance with him would be a propaganda gift to Condé and to Retz and his *dévot* friends in Paris and Rome. It would upset Charles I's widow and embarrass Louis's mother. There was a precedent in Richelieu's equally risky alliance with Sweden. As in that case, the military argument was paramount. Louis, in camp with Mazarin and Turenne, took little persuading. By the terms of the treaty signed in Paris in March 1657 the English undertook to wage a joint campaign in Flanders; in return for the anticipated conquests they would receive Dunkirk. On the dunes outside that town, on 14 June 1657, Louis watched the battle which brought complete victory to Turenne and his redcoat allies. It cleared the way for further conquests in Flanders and the subsequent peace with Spain with its significant gains on France's vulnerable northern frontier. Cromwell had served his purpose. It was convenient though that he died in the following September, setting in train the process which would lead to the restoration of Louis's cousin Charles.

Within weeks of the battle of the Dunes the French camp was dismayed by the serious illness of the king. It was probably pneumonia. At the height of the fever Colbert, always on the lookout for signs of trouble, was taking military precautions in Paris. Rarely has so much hung on a young life. So soon after the Fronde the death of the king would be a calamity. But some who might grieve might also see it as a time of opportunity. Fortunately Louis's constitution was robust. Nursed devotedly by Anne, he made a swift recovery. One who had special cause to rejoice was Mazarin's niece, Marie Mancini.

There was always going to be tension between the instinct of a young man, absolute sovereign as he was assumed to be, to follow the prompting of his heart, and the traditional requirement that a king should marry to serve his dynasty. In this case Louis was deeply in love – but the marriage proposed was one that offered the greatest diplomatic prize. Only in retrospect can it be held that there was a degree of inevitability about the marriage of Louis XIV to the Infanta Maria Teresa. Mazarin, had already considered an alliance with the house of Savoy, represented by princess Marguerite. It is typical of his covert style that we cannot know whether Marguerite's visit to the court in the winter of 1658–59 was a sign of serious intent, or a tactical ploy intended to bring pressure on Philip IV to offer his daughter – which he promptly did. Meanwhile Louis kept Mazarin in the fever of uncertainty that is conveyed by the strong pleading of the latter's letters.[44] Mazarin looked to the Spanish match as a splendid climax to his ministerial career. For it he was prepared to sacrifice another, surely tempting kind of triumph, that of the *casa*: an alliance between the house of Mazarin and that of Bourbon. On 21 June 1659, the relationship of Louis and Marie was formally ended when the king, publicly, with royal restraint but evident sadness, said farewell to Marie. Duty overcoming passion; stern resolve; unavailing tears: it was a scene from classical drama. A Racine[45] would not, however, have allowed its sequel. They continued to correspond and Mazarin had to appeal again to Louis's sense of obligation (6 July):

> *La confidante* [code for Anne] has written to me about the state you have been in and I am near to despair, for it is absolutely vital that you find your own remedy unless you are to be unhappy and the death of your good servants. . . . And if you do not find the resolve to change your conduct, your malady will worsen more and more. I urge you for your glory, your honour, for the well-being of the realm.

In case that was not enough to stiffen Louis's resolve he wrote again four days later, applying flattering balm to a painful wound:

You always manage everything better than others when you have a mind to apply yourself and decide that all your passions should yield to that you should have, to be a king, so wise and capable of governing your realm that you are great and already very glorious.

Through Mazarin's clumsy sentences the sense comes out with striking clarity. The direct and familiar tone would have been offensive to Louis had he not had a deep, filial respect for the aging statesman with whom he had shared so many trials. With his feeling for the hazards and toils of power, as well as its rewards, Mazarin had built up a relationship of trust which now served him well. At the crisis of his illness Louis had said to him: 'You are a man of resolution and the best friend I have. That is why I beg you to tell me when I should be facing my end.'

Unaware that Louis had again been seeing Marie, locked into the final stage of negotiations, Mazarin wrote to Louis (13 August) to praise him for the sacrifice he had made. Two weeks later, better informed, he wrote again: 'there is no matter more important than this, or one that demands more urgently that it be finished'. Louis bowed to the inevitable, looked forward to the 'glorious peace' which Mazarin had long promised, and prepared to meet his bride. For Marie there was little consolation: she would give her story in her *Mémoires*. For her uncle there was the relief conveyed in a wry comment to his opposite number, don Luis de Haro: 'how I envy Spain where women do not become involved in politics'. For Louis there were lessons that he would not forget. He would put first the interests of the dynasty. He would not allow his private life to affect his conduct of affairs. The state must come first. It demanded much of the king. The king could demand much of his subjects. Between betrothal and marriage, Louis was involved in an episode which was meant to be read as a warning to trouble-makers that no part of the realm was too distant to be beyond the reach of royal discipline

Mazarin had sought a measure of control in Provence by delegating authority, equivalent to that of an *intendant*, to Oppède, the *premier président* of the *parlement* of Aix. In 1659 a revolt against Oppède's rule in Aix was put down by the governor. The leaders found refuge in Marseille with the party there who had just gained control of the city and now proceeded to defy royal orders to hand over the fugitives. Their timing was bad. The court was in Provence, Mazarin was free from his diplomatic labours on the Isle of Pheasants and Louis was in imperious mood. While Oppède reformed the constitution of Aix to ensure royal control, Marseille was taken over by troops, its walls razed and a new citadel built. The magistrates' proud title of consul was abolished and the nobles, who had long dominated the city were debarred from its government. The merchants gained control but under the crown. So the city lost its virtual independence. It had to accept like any other the authority of the *intendant*. It would prosper – but as an integral part of the realm.

The marriage of Louis XIV and the Infanta Maria Teresa was first celebrated by proxy, under the blue and gold banners of France and the red and black of Spain, on 2 June 1660, in Fuentarabia. That was to accord with two rules evocative of the period – and of two distinctive royal traditions: a Spanish princess could not leave Spain unmarried, and a French king could not marry outside his realm. Carrying on her diminutive frame such a weight of tradition and such varying expectations, Maria Teresa was the same age as Louis – but, by comparison, a child in experience. 'If her body were a little bigger and her teeth better she would deserve a place among the most beautiful women in Europe.' Mme de Motteville was generous – but enough of a Frenchwoman to add that 'her costume was horrible, neither cut nor style pleasing to the eye'.[46] In the second marriage ceremony four days later, at Saint Jean de Luz, when she became also queen of France, she won praise with a dress of red velvet embroidered with the *fleur de lis*. It was clearly a French choice. With her dowry still to pay and the promise of a rich inheritance, she was, in a sense, the possession of her royal spouse and of France. The sombre black of the Spanish courtiers could be held no less to express a sense of loss and national decline that no politeness or presents could quite dispel. The king was courteously attentive to his little bride, and he would continue to be so. It was not expected that he would also remain faithful to her.

Through long months of negotiating before the Peace of the Pyrenees, Mazarin had been sustained by determination to complete his life's work. On 26 August 1660 he was too frail to be more than a spectator at the formal procession of Louis and Maria Teresa through the lavishly adorned streets of Paris. A royal entry was both a ritual civic welcome and a political statement, a presentation of the king to the people in a way that emphasised his majesty and their duty. This one was carefully stage-managed by Mazarin, his advisors and artists. Enthroned on a high dais Louis received the submission of the city and its corporations, including the Sorbonne and *Parlement*. The *prévôt* presented him with a key while leading citizens did homage. The *Premier Président's* minor role in the proceedings was deliberate. Those who had recently defied the crown were being shown where power now lay. Every triumphal arch, statue and inscription proclaimed the glory of the king, but also the careful stewardship of his mother, the fruitful exertions of his minister and the benefits of the peace. Anne appeared as regal Juno, or Minerva, tending wise advice; Mazarin was Mercury, bearing good news or Atlas holding up the world on his shoulders. For Louis therefore it was a shared and relatively modest glorification.

Mazarin was in constant pain but ministers, diplomats and agents, notably his *intendant* Colbert, busy with his own plans for the future, knew him to be in control almost to the end. Concerning himself with the negotiations to end the war between Sweden and Poland which would become 'the peace of the North', he had become, in the words of Père Léon's funeral oration 'the arbiter of great peoples and nations'. In his last days at the château of Vincennes, Louis attended carefully to his worldly maxims and practical advice. He was to record them so faithfully that future readers of his *Testament* would hear the master's voice. Mazarin died in the early hours of 10 March 1661. A few hours later Louis summoned leading nobles and officials to hear what he intended. It was expected that he would name a first minister. Apparently the archbishop of Rouen asked to whom he should go for instructions: '*A moi, M. le archevêque*'. Brienne,[47] Secretary of State, recorded his words. 'He had decided to take charge of the state in person and to rely on no one else.' He discharged them from their duties saying that when he had need of their good advice he would call for it. Brienne was charged to write to all foreign secretaries to explain the decision so that they could advise their princes accordingly. The manner was gracious, the words brisk, unambiguous, almost matter of fact. They may not, at first, have produced the sensation suggested by later accounts – especially Louis's own. No doubt most courtiers were sceptical. Applying their own standards and conceptions of the life proper for a sovereign, they could not suppose that the king would long sustain the necessary discipline of government, the long sessions of councils, the perusal of lengthy documents. He would do so for more than fifty years.

In retrospect it seems that Louis's whole life had been a preparation for this moment. It appeared to be a break in practice, but it was also a fulfilment of the absolutist ideal: given his temperament and capacity, a natural step. His decision followed logically from the idea, expressed typically by Le Bret,[48] that sovereignty was as indivisible as the point in geometry, and from the doctrine of Divine Right, soon to be expressed with matchless eloquence by bishop Bossuet. It was also a pragmatic decision. The king felt that he was ready for the responsibility. He had ruled long enough to acquire the taste for power and to weigh its risks. Looking around him, at home and abroad, he also believed that the time was opportune. His apprenticeship had been thorough and he was ready to show his mastery of the *métier*. In April the *Gazette* which, interestingly, had not reported his initial decision, noted his 'marvellous assiduity' in matters of state.

Even allowing for the luxury of afterthought and Louis's inclination to make the most of his achievement, the opening of his *Mémoires*[49] puts his decision in a wider context: 'I began to look around me at the various organs of the state, not with the eyes of a spectator but with those of a ruler, and I realised that there was not one which required urgently that I take matters in hand. . . . Disorder ruled everywhere.' At the same time action was feasible because there was peace at home and abroad: 'there was neither unrest nor fear . . . which might have interrupted or resisted my proposals'. Abroad too (though easier to identify in retrospect) there were signs of a new political climate. 1660 saw the restoration of Louis's cousin Charles II to his English throne and absolutist pronouncements in the Danish Estates: there the king was declared to be 'supreme head here on earth, elevated above all human laws'. In Brandenburg the Elector Frederick William was subduing his Estates and securing the right to tax which would sustain the growth of his state. In 1661 he crushed the resistance of the burghers of Königsberg. In less spectacular ways, concerning himself less with the Empire than with his hereditary lands, the Emperor Leopold was beginning to acquire the resources that would enable him to combat the Turks and to rule more effectively than his predecessors. The United Provinces prospered – but began to look isolated. Louis had reason to be confident as he considered setting the French house in order. Order here is the key word, representing the ideal that bound, in a common view of what was required, political philosopher, reforming minister and ambitious sovereign.

Louis's words were bold and clear. He acted decisively to assert his authority, as later to dismiss Fouquet. In the main, however, he would prove cautious and notably realistic. The willingness to compromise, to deal sensitively with individual grandees and to recognise the credentials, and power, of corporate interests, that had underpinned Mazarin's strategy of survival during the Fronde, were not cast aside by his royal pupil. Indeed they could not be. Much could be achieved by enforcing justice and tackling abuses but king and ministers had to work within a system which had evolved over centuries, reflecting a society which was closer in forms and spirit to the feudal than to the modern. Inevitably there were entrenched positions and notions of right that limited government's room to manoeuvre and thwarted the reformer. It does not follow that there was some kind of continuing conflict between the crown and vested interests, between 'modern' and 'progressive', and traditional. Louis XIV was a man of his time. He would not have thought in such terms. Even when confronted with a direct challenge or obstruction he would have seen repression or reform as a healthy discipline administered, as was his duty, to erring or inadequate members of the body politic. The state had its own interests but it was not exterior to or separate from society. It was a living organism not a machine. Its rules and principles arose from the nature of its social being; to be respected, therefore by ruler as by subject. To assess Louis XIV's rule we have therefore to start by seeing what he saw at court and in his realm.

Notes

1. In April 1617 Marie de Médici's favourite Concini was murdered at the Louvre. Her young protégé Richelieu lost his ministerial post and was perhaps fortunate not to lose his life. When another Italian, Mazarin, became *premier ministre*, the Concini precedent hung like a sword of Damocles over his head. For an account of this episode, and the role and character of the king, see A. Lloyd Moote, *Louis XIII* (California, 1989), especially pp. 79 ff.

2. See Ruth Kleinman, *Anne of Austria* (Ohio, 1985). Her sympathetic study leaves one in no doubt about the importance of Anne's role, both in the upbringing of Louis and in the political life of the Regency.

3. Pierre Séguier (1588–1672) was Chancellor from 1635 to his death. His role in the selection of members for special judicial courts and commissions, and acquiescence in the transference of business from *Parlement* courts to council, made him unpopular with fellow lawyers. After the Fronde he was more cautious. Louis associated him with the repressive regime of Richelieu and the compromising years of the Fronde and he was edged out of the *conseil d'en haut*. Politically the office of chancellor became less important.

4. César, duc de Vendôme (1594–1665) was Henry IV's illegitimate son by Gabrielle d'Estrées. He had been a persistent malcontent and rebel during the reign of his half brother, Louis XIII. His son, François, duc de Beaufort (1616–69) carried on the family tradition, suffered imprisonment for his part in the *Importants*, but eventually escaped; he then offered his services to the Fronde. In the irresponsible heroics of that period and in his subsequently fervent loyalty to the young Louis he epitomises the problem that Louis and Mazarin confronted and witnesses to their success.

5. Nicolas de Neufville, duc de Villeroi (1598–1685), maréchal de France, Mazarin's client, was to be appointed titular head of the new *conseil royal des finances* set up by Louis XIV after the downfall of Fouquet. One of nature's courtiers he earned his position of trust by his responsible conduct during the minority. Like his son François, the unsuccessful general, he was one of the small inner circle with whom Louis would be able to relax on terms as near to friendship as was possible between king and subject.

6. Louis de Rouvroy, duc de Saint-Simon (1675–1755), son of Louis XIII's favourite, will appear later as a prime source for aspects of Louis's later reign, and particularly life at court, through his incomparable memoirs (see pp. 181 and Bibliography).

7. The reign of Louis XI (1461–83) saw the death of the duke of Burgundy and the acquisition by Louis of a part of his inheritance, the duchy of Burgundy, and Picardy. The realm was further enlarged when he gained Maine, Anjou and Provence.

8. For these composers and the importance of music and the nature of royal patronage see R.M. Isherwood, *Music in the Service of the King* (Ithaca, 1972). Lully, director after 1672 of the Royal Academy of Music and supported by Louis in all vicissitudes, was allowed remarkable freedom and intimacy.

9. For Mazarin's early life see G. Dethan, *The Young Mazarin* (London, 1977) and Geoffrey Treasure, *Mazarin* (Routledge, 1995), pp. 3–40.

10. Marie de Rohan, duchesse de Chevreuse (1600–79) was a much loved, manipulative woman, dangerously adept at the power games of the Fronde. Her political importance was greatest at times of instability. Her role and that of other prominent women in the Fronde is sympathetically analysed by Wendy Gibson, *Women in Seventeenth Century France* (London, 1989), pp. 141–68.

11. Y.-M. Bercé's *History of Peasant Revolts* (Cornell, NY, 1990; orig. French, Paris, 1986) is illuminating on the conditions and *mentalités* of peasant society, the varieties of resistance and insurrection, the grievances and aims of rebels. He identifies altogether 459 risings between 1590 and 1715: the most intense phase, 1635–60, saw 282, after 1660, 130.

12. At 39 million *livres*, the largest of any during the *ancien régime*. Richelieu's, with more in land, had been 24 million. Of Mazarin's fortune about a third was in *argent liquide*, coin, bullion and precious stones stored at strong points around the country. If that suggests the alien adventurer, be it noted that he had used his personal resources to support the crown during the Fronde. For an analysis see Daniel Dessert, 'Pouvoir et finance au dix-septième siècle', *Revue d'histoire moderne et contemporaine*, XXIII, June 1976.

13. Matthieu Molé (1584–1656) was a learned lawyer and reluctant standard-bearer for *parlementaire* resistance. His principled opposition to arbitrary measures and willingness to treat and work for a middle way may support the claim that he was the only statesman of the Fronde. 'No procedural thicket was unknown to him' (Ranum).

14. Pierre Broussel's arrest in August 1648 was a signal for the setting up of the barricades.

15. For the crucial significance of office see also p. 84.

16. As *avocat-général* (see Glossary) Talon was in the uncomfortable middle: interpreter of *Parlement* to the king, and of the king to *Parlement*.

17. Michel Le Tellier (1603–85) was secretary of state for war 1643–75, latterly devolving much to his son Louvois. He owed his early prominence to loyalty to Mazarin and his reputation to his administrative skills and his painstaking construction of a large *clientèle*.

18. Christian Jouhaud, *La Fronde des mots* (Paris, 1985) is the best introduction to the 5,000 *Mazarinades*: faction promotion and public entertainment.

19. Roland Mousnier, *The Assassination of Henry IV* (London, 1973, orig. French, 1964) explores this topic and argues that the assassination of Henry IV strengthened absolutist tendencies in the long run by exposing the shocking alternative.

20. Armand de Bourbon, prince de Conti, was Condé's younger brother: one of the princes arrested in January 1650. After their release it would be a prime object of Mazarin's diplomacy, sealed in 1652 by marriage to his niece, Anne-Marie Martinozzi, to detach him from Condé and secure his allegiance to the crown. Louis de Bourbon, duc de Mercoeur, was married to another of Mazarin's nieces, Laura Mancini.

    Henri d'Orléans, duc de Longueville, the third of the princes arrested, had been titular head of the diplomatic delegation at Westphalia. He was governor of Normandy.

21. François, duc de la Rochefoucauld, was head of one of the oldest families and a great landowner in the west, capable of raising a small army from his tenants and clients. His ardent love for Longueville's wife, was one of several such sub-plots in the many-faceted play of the Fronde. His career and interests reveals much about the 'disorders' which Louis XIV found so intolerable. La Rochefoucauld later distilled some of his life's experience in his *Maxims*.

22. The duc de Lorraine, with 900,000 *écus*, the duc de Mayenne, with 820,000, top the list. Sully reckoned 107 million altogether. Queen Elizabeth thought Henry 'dealt too basely in making composition with his subjects'. He might argue that the alternative would have cost more. See D. Buisseret, *Henry IV* (London, 1984) pp. 44–51.

23. See François Bluche, *Louis XIV* (Oxford, 1990; original, Paris, 1984) pp. 60–3, for the important role of the confessor, constant companion and confidant of the king and, through his letters, an invaluable source for the history of Louis's formative years. Louis felt his death keenly.

24. Jacques-Bénigne Bossuet (1627–1704), bishop of Condom, then of Meaux (from 1681), was a regular court preacher from the mid-sixties, with intervals of disfavour when he was outspoken on moral questions. Appointment as tutor to the Dauphin (1670) indicated Louis's respect for his intellect and probity. Through his influential writings about history and politics he became the leading authority on the rights and duties of monarchy. See pp. 87–8 and pp. 327–8.

25. For this subject and a revealing entry into the world of seventeenth-century monarchy and faith see Marc Bloch, *The Royal Touch* (London, trans. J.E. Anderson, 1972; orig. 1924).

26. For the story and importance of Jansenism see pp. 316–17.

27. The rights of the Gallican church (the Catholic church in France) had been formally defined by the Pragmatic Sanction of Bourges in 1438. For the king's right to censor bulls and the question over his right (the *régale*) to receive the revenue of vacant bishoprics, and the consequent struggle with the papacy see pp. 85–7.

28. Founded about 1630 by Henri de Lévis, duc de Ventadour, it was foremost among societies founded, in the spirit of the Counter-Reformation, to promote mission, the conversion of the Huguenots, spiritual and moral improvement and charitable work. Aristocratic in membership and style, theoretically secret in membership, tending to be conspiratorial in operation, it counted for little after 1660 when Mazarin got *Parlement* to proscribe all assemblies which met without the king's permission.

29. Vincent de Paul (1576–1660) was canonised in 1737 but he was already venerated in his lifetime. Among early experiences his capture and imprisonment by Tunisian pirates and spells as *curé* in a poor district, and chaplain to the royal galleys, prepared him for his life's work: inspiring works of charity, and women to offer their services, through organisations like the much loved *Filles de Charité*.

30. For a useful résumé of the early history of French Calvinism see Robin Briggs, *Early Modern France, 1560–1715* (Oxford, 1977), pp. 11–34.

31. Named after the elm-fringed square used for meetings, the *Ormée* recruited support from artisans and tradesmen, under a leadership mainly of minor lawyers and officials. The prime concern was to protect the privileges of the city, not only against intrusive government and particularly Mazarin, but against the urban élite, the judicial oligarchy in the *parlement*.

32. A.N. Hamscher, *The Conseil Privé and the Parlements after the Fronde, 1653–73*, (Pittsburgh, 1976), offers a detailed guide to this controversial area. His work has led to revised judgements about the relations between the crown and *Parlement*, and so of the nature of 'absolute' monarchy.

33. O. Talon, *Mémoires*. Michaud and Poujoulat Collection, series III, vol. VI (Paris, 1839) offers perhaps the most authoritative of the numerous memoirs of the period (see Bibliography).

34. Two further royal statements have been taken to indicate that Louis would allow *Parlement* no voice in royal policy. In 1667 it was told that acts of remonstrance must be executed swiftly; in 1673 that henceforth it must first register, remonstrate later if it wanted to. It seems that Louis meant, as a matter of wartime emergency, to hasten the passage of fiscal edicts – just what ministers had been unable to do before the Fronde. But there was no suggestion that Louis would not wish on occasion to hear *Parlement*'s views.

35. Quoted by Lloyd Moote, *The Revolt of the Judges* (Princeton, 1971), p. 359. Moote comments: 'It was one of the few occasions when the Sun King could not hide his emotions.'

36. For a revealing picture of the state of nobles later in Louis XIV's reign see P. Goubert, *The Ancien Régime*, translated S. Cox (London, 1973; orig., 1969), p. 195. A typical appeal against the *ban* to the lieutenant-general in 1695 by a nobleman's wife brings a domestic touch: 'If you will trouble to send someone to the house you will see whether I am being honest with you and whether the whole house is not half in ruins and the coverings threadbare.'

37. The States General was summoned by Louis XVI in August 1788; it met in May 1789. The monarchy was abolished in September 1792. Louis XVI was executed in January 1793.

38. As recorded in P. Clément, *Lettres, Instructions et mémoires de Colbert* (7 volumes, Paris 1861–83). Here vol. I. For their value, see Bibliography.

39. The *taille* (amount levied, not the yield) had risen threefold between 1624 and 1648, the steepest rise, as in all forms of tax, being since 1635. For the whole subject of royal finance see R. Bonney, *The King's Debts: Finance and Politics in France, 1589–1648* (Oxford, 1981) and J. Dent, *Crisis in Finance: Crown, Financiers and Society in Seventeenth Century France* (Newton Abbot, 1973). See also pp. 79–80.

40. A priest at Saint-Quentin reported in 1652: 'We see men eat soil, grass, the bark of trees, and what we dare not say if we had not seen it, what is horrifying, they gnaw at their arms and hands before dying in despair.' There are many such reports in Vincent de Paul's *Correspondance*. Here, vol. IV, p. 300. For the general misery see R. Mousnier, *Paris capitale au temps de Richelieu et Mazarin* (Paris, 1978) pp. 285ff.

41. Monsieur Vincent's *Filles* and their supporters, many of them prominent lay men and women, reached 193 villages round Paris.

42. In 1650 70 per cent of the land in the Seine valley. New châteaux were not protected by moats and drawbridges.

43. In April 1656 Mazarin obtained Louis's signature on an edict 'providing for the establishment of an *hôpital-général* for the enclosure of poor beggars in the city'. The resulting building, the Salpêtrière, with Bruant's octagonal chapel, is a splendid memorial to an ideal. Was it less impressive because a work of charity was performed in a way that would also witness to the prestige of the state? The example was widely copied in the provinces where the new *hôpital* was often the enlarged former *hôtel Dieu*. See also pp. 197–8, n. 9.

44. A. Chéruel, *Lettres du Cardinal Mazarin pendant son ministère* (1872–1906), 9 vols. For the Mancini episode, see vol. 9. For the value of the letters, see Bibliography.

45. Jean Racine (1639–99), dramatist, uniquely powerful in his austere, classical vein of high principle and disciplined passion; also royal historiographer (from 1677), in both roles a key figure in the culture of the period. See pp. 187, 188.

46. Her ready pen and shrewd observations of what she was able to observe from privileged proximity to the royal family makes Françoise de Bertaut, Mme de Motteville (1621–89) a valuable as well as entertaining source for the early years of the reign. She was Anne's *dame d'honneur*, and she could speak Spanish. Her *Mémoires*, in Michaud et Poujoulart (eds) *Collection de mémoires relatifs à l'histoire de France* (henceforward referred to as Michaud) vols 38 and 39, 1847) give a court view of affairs – and a woman's view, subjective, but full of common sense.

47. Henri-Auguste de Loménie de Brienne (d. 1666), secretary of state for foreign affairs till succeeded by his son. His memoirs (Michaud , series III, vol. III) seem to be reliable for this period. He was much at the king's side though Louis did not see in him, nor in his son, the qualities required of a minister.

48. Cardin le Bret (1558–1665), author of *De la Souveraineté du Roy* (1632) was 'the greatest political theorist of his generation' (Bonney). His ideas were based on a long career of service to the crown. When commissioner to the Estates of Brittany he enunciated the principle that privileges were held 'purely out of the liberality of our kings'. He believed that the sovereign courts must yield before the supremacy of the council. The virtual consensus between crown and élites after 1661 depended on Louis XIV's acting more in the spirit than in the letter of such pronouncements.

49. Louis seems early to have conceived the idea of leaving for posterity a record of his reign. Cardinal Richelieu's *Testament Politique* was one of several precedents and models for a selective and didactic account intended as much to explain the leading ideas and actions of the writer as to tell his story. The birth of his son and heir, in 1661, provided the spur to his starting notes for the *Mémoires pour l'instruction du Dauphin*. He is addressed directly by his proud father over a hundred times.

Complete, they are singularly incomplete, covering only the years 1661–62 and 1666–68. Louis was rarely free thereafter from the pressures of government. In any case those years provided ample material for the lessons Louis wished to teach and for his commentary on the duties and responsibilities of a French king. Louis collaborated at first with Colbert who produced a first draft, in 1665. In that year Périgny, a tutor to the Dauphin, then after 1670 Paul Pellisson, took over responsibility. Pellisson had a finished version ready by 1672. The memoirs were essentially Louis's work and represent his analysis of the situation of 1661, his notion of kingship and his pride in his achievements. For this important topic see P. Sonnino, 'The dating and authorship of Louis XIV's *Mémoires*', in *French Historical Studies*, iii, no. 3 (1964), pp. 303–37. He is author of an English translation of the *Mémoires* (New York, 1970). The most recent edition is that of J. Goubert, Paris, 1995). For Pellisson, see p. 221.

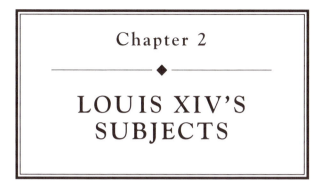

Chapter 2

LOUIS XIV'S SUBJECTS

Another thing rendring this kingdom very considerable is their prolifique
multiplying; for Europe embraceth not a more populous nation.

JOHN EVELYN, 1652

THE POOR HAVE NO RESERVES

When, in 1707, Vauban reported on his meticulous survey of France he estimated the population to be 19 million, of whom more than half a million lived in Paris. Since 1648 approximately a million and a half inhabitants had been gained by war and treaty. Within a range of some 2 million either way Vauban's figure is generally accepted.[1] Allowance has to be made not only for his errors, which seem roughly to cancel one another out, but also for the periodic sharp falls, following the great mortalities which contained an otherwise rising trend within the limits fixed by the rigid framework of a primitive rural economy. Women might expect to have a child every two and a half years after marriage. Late marriages were common as men waited for land to live on, or a craft to pursue and capital to acquire after long apprenticeship. Around a quarter of babies born died within a year. The average life expectancy was barely thirty; in the larger towns, where population was maintained by immigration from the countryside, twenty-five. The poor had no reserves. For many families the birth of a third or fourth child was the last straw. Rural debt was a chronic problem. From borrowing to beggary was a common route. The least accident could put a family on the road. It might be illness or injury to the breadwinner, an extra tax or billeting demand, the death or failure of an employer, the death of a mule or cow, or failure of a crop. Climate was crucial. Wet summers, crop failures and famines increased the numbers of the destitute. The famine of 1693–95 was only the worst of eleven nationwide in the century. La Bruyère put a literary finish on the picture of poverty when he wrote of 'certain wild animals, male and female, scattered about the countryside, black, livid and cracked with sun, bound to the soil that they till with invincible obstinacy . . . in fact they are human. They retire to hovels where they live on black bread, water and roots.'

It is not the stark language that shocks but the likelihood that contemporaries would see little exaggeration in the account. The young king would not have been shielded from such sights as he travelled about war-torn France. *Curés* knew them all too well, the bent backs and rheumatic joints, the women's prolapsed wombs, the prematurely aged, the deformities caused often by unskilled midwifery, the wasted limbs and swollen bellies of malnutrition. John Locke tasted poverty in the form of a Sunday dinner in a Provençal cottage that consisted of 'slices of congealed blood fried in oil'.[2] A peasant woman felt it when she looked at the few beads or scrap of lace that were all she could add to her working clothes on a festival day. The woman who made the lace knew it when she lost her eyesight from working in poor light. Vincent de Paul had sought to palliate it when he founded the *Filles de Charité*. Government recognised it when (in 1662) the existing *hôpitaux-généraux* were incorporated into a national system. Respectable congregations sought to avoid it by commissioning new churches away from the poor parts of town.

To offer impressions of poverty is easy; to account for it harder. Europeans were living in the 'old biological regime'. As Louis would learn, disease took no account of rank, but it took hold most readily where there was malnutrition. A good meal might be an event to remember, associated probably with some festival occasion. Hunger meant weakness and sapped initiative; where only physical energy and sustained toil could improve the land there was apathy. It was widely remarked that the English and Dutch were generally taller and stronger than the French. In a pre-scientific society the fundamental causes of debilitating poverty are to be looked for in the condition of agriculture. For most of Louis XIV's subjects life was hazardous, for many a continuous struggle for the bare necessities of life.

The French rural picture was, of course, patchy: areas around towns, where rich *bourgeois* had lands, where market gardens supplied produce or, as in the vineyards around Dijon, there was specialised production, were usually better off. Famine was most devastating where, as in the Massif Central, communications were most inadequate. There might be found pockets of chronic poverty like that described by the *curé* of Tulle in the Limousin in 1692: 'there are not six families within a radius of ten leagues who have bread to eat . . .'. There was no less poverty to be found in Spain and southern Italy; a more brutalised peasantry in the serf-farmed lands of Northern and Eastern Europe. What struck travellers in France most forcibly was the contrast between the potential fertility of much of France, with the relatively long growing season and generally equable (if not reliable) climate, and the widespread poverty. France had a high proportion of inhabitants to land; only the plains of North Italy, the southern Netherlands and southern England could match its overall 40 to the square kilometre – but they were more prosperous areas. Explanations should be looked for in the striking regional differences, barriers, natural or man-made, to easy communication, agricultural practice, lack of capital investment in the economy as a whole and, affecting all, attitudes in society and the policies of government.

France was several countries united under one crown. When he looks at the outer parts of the mosaic of provinces the British reader, in particular, has to guard against thinking of the province as a larger shire. Rather one is looking, as it were, at Ireland, Wales or Scotland. Mediterranean France was quite different, in ecology, laws and customs from the rest. The Alps, Pyrenees and Juras fostered a distinctive mountain life. Hills, high plateaux, dense forests and remote valleys created in the lands stretching out from the Auvergne another world apart. Here travellers needed guides, and officials, armed escorts. In the eastern provinces laws which favoured the *seigneur* reflected the lax rule of former dukes of Burgundy. Normandy was too near the capital to be able to resist high levels of taxation but exhibited a separatist tendency that reflected centuries of English rule. Celtic Brittany had not been finally secured until 1532.[3] Like Languedoc it would preserve until the Revolution its Estates, favoured tax status and pride in being different. In 1675, reacting against a new tax, it produced the most serious revolt of the reign.

Language defined the chasm that separated the articulate, propertied minority, a few hundred thousand, from the mass of the population. French, as it was used by Racine, Boileau[4] or Bossuet, as it was guarded by the *Académie française*,[5] was the language of the educated: courtiers and churchmen, lawyers and officials, men and women of the *beau monde*. Away from the capital the traveller soon found himself in regions where country dwellers, even the inhabitants of small towns, spoke a *patois* that was efficient for their simple needs and that varied even from one *pays* to another: he needed an interpreter. Three-quarters of the people were illiterate. The ordinary countryman was at a disadvantage in dealing with the professional agents of king or *seigneur*. Strong in family memory but weak in law affecting rights that might be crucial to his well-being, he had to put a cross, or symbol of his work, a pitchfork or hammer, to a document which he could not read.[6] Literacy and capital could be formidable allies in a society in which the *bourgeois* valued above all the possession of land and the rights that might go with it. The peasant did not, however, stand alone. Everything in his faith, work and recreation fostered the instinct to join with fellow villagers to hold his ground. He had a keen sense of belonging. Had he not lived his life within sound of the bell of the church in which he was baptised and married? He knew little of the outside world. He could easily be swayed by rumour; within hours it could bring out a mob to harry an old 'witch', the tax collector or, in communities divided between Catholic and Huguenot, against the rival camp. When rage and fear were sharpened by hunger, it could send men out to a more general muster. Then the violence which was never far from the surface but was normally expressed in charivari,[7] feast-day brawls or fights with another village, was directed against the greater enemy, the town with its presumed grain hoards, or the Parisian tax official and his minions. Then the governor and *intendant* had a rising on their hands. In 1636–37, the revolt of the *Croquants*, affecting, at one time or another, over a quarter of the country before the main band was defeated by a royal army, had only been the expression on an alarming scale, in protest against new taxes, of the determination of inbred communities to defend themselves. Occasionally they found a *seigneur*, more commonly the *curé*, to lead them.

The landscape showed little change over the years. Only in parts affected by war, as in Champagne and Burgundy, were villages permanently abandoned. There were forest clearances, draining of swamps and some enclosures, as in the Gâtine Poitevine, but the overall picture was one of equilibrium. Within the village that could be deceptive. At best the community had the coherence and discipline which was needed to keep the balance between individuals and the community in such matters as the upkeep of roads and bridges, the election of village hayward or shepherd and – most dreaded – responsibility for assessing and collecting the *taille*. As important to the government as to the community was the church, not only a shrine but the place for meetings and elections. Government ordinances would be read out from the pulpit; also adjudications and notice of royal and seigneurial *corvées*. Within communities there were also intense competitive forces, a relentless struggle to survive. The village hierarchy was likely to be more various in status and esteem than differences of income or acreage might suggest. Conditions varied between provinces, even *pays* within a province. There were, however, general tendencies. There was an increasing polarisation between the few relatively well-off peasants and the many living off minute holdings. Here was scope for interference by government, using the *coqs de paroisse* who, with most to lose, would be the most willing to collaborate. The erosion of the rights of small communities, vulnerable through communal debts, price falls and tax pressures, is one feature of the rise in the power of the state.

Certain differences stem from variations of soil and climate; less obvious factors include proximity to a large town or seaport, availability of transport by road, river or, more rarely, canal. The grain lands of the Beauce or the Beauvaisis and the tumbling slopes and narrow valleys of Quercy or Périgord; the stony soil and Atlantic climate of Brittany and the terraced slopes and stone enclosures, the olives and vines of Languedoc; the chalky plains of Champagne and the enclosed farmsteads of the Norman *bocage*: such comparisons can be multiplied and still convey only half the picture. Even within one northern region there could be distinct economies: the pastureless plateau of Picardy, yielding little but grain, was the setting for a society of starkly simple social distinctions, between the handful of *laboureurs* and the mass of *manoeuvriers*.[8] As elsewhere, industry was generally rural and domestic. Many families depended on the woman at the loom. The gentler southerly parts beyond Amiens allowed more scope to the smallholder. Accessible urban markets and demand for craftsmanship everywhere ensured a better balanced economy. Paris had more immigrants from the further regions, like the Limousin, than from its neighbouring provinces. Throughout the south there was such diversity of cultivation as to defy generalisation. Provence had its Alps, its *garrigue* and its fertile plains. Around Bordeaux vine growing was stimulated by the export trade. From the Landes cattle were exported to Spain. In the Cévennes, chestnuts were a staple food. In most regions bread made from wheat was luxury, rye or buckwheat being more common. Everywhere the ox was most precious, the mule more common and in general use for the transport of goods. Analysis of the rural economy as a whole is further hampered by differences in external conditions. Goubert, writing about the Beauvaisis, and Baehrel, about Provence, divide the years of their study, 1600–1720, into four identical periods; there coincidence ends. When prosperity reigned in Beauvais, Provence was depressed; when in the latter years Provence began to expand, Beauvais was severely afflicted. Such examples only suggest the extent of the historian's problem. It would have been understood by the minister who received the *intendants*' letters: they were reporting from different countries – but they reflected also certain common experiences.

In any account of the period diplomacy, war and government loom large. They determine France's place in the world; they are the preserve of an élite of birth, wealth and education, expressing its main interests and values. Consciously separated from the mass of their fellow-countrymen, its members could order their own lives and direct others in ways that could affect the well-being of the community. But their scope and condition too was limited by the condition of the rural economy which underlay the whole: the world of 85 per cent of Frenchmen, it was the primary mode of production and source of wealth and therefore of the taxes that determined what government could achieve. Attempts to build a superstructure grander than the base, to embark on ventures more demanding, in resources and cash, than the economy could support, were bound to be impoverishing and destructive of social order. That had been the lesson of the régime of the Cardinals. It was a lesson well learned by Colbert, imperfectly, we shall see, by the king.

PEASANT FARMING

It is necessary therefore to look more closely at agriculture. The typical lowland farming landscape can be depicted with some confidence. It was to be seen in districts north of the Loire and east of the Seine, and in many other patches elsewhere. Only about a third of the kingdom in extent, it comprised its most densely populated land. It was of a European as well as specifically French type. As it was to be seen in lowland England (though there enclosures were becoming more common) and in much of the Netherlands and Germany, it was what the traveller might think of as normal. Journeying on stony tracks, dusty in summer, deep-rutted and muddy in winter, he might go from Calais to Tours, or to Reims, and see little else, probably no more than twenty miles a day. Even if he were on one of the main routes, maintained or improved by the *corvée* which gave France some of the best roads in Europe, when he passed through remote or forested areas he would be in danger from brigands. Around château and church was a huddle of buildings: some housed the landless *journaliers*, but most – the majority – of those villagers owned or rented a few strips. Even they could hardly sustain their families without some ancillary employment, typically spinning and weaving. Except where stone was available, the one-storeyed cottages were of wood, a cob of clay and straw, or rubble and plaster. Essentially shelters against cold and damp, they might appear like an extension of the farm shed.

For warmth, Louis XIV's peasant subjects lived close to their animals, under the same roof, separated by a partition which did not always reach to the thatched roof. A wide open hearth, crude benches and table, a chest containing a few cherished fineries, a gown, some trinkets bought in the first years of marriage when there were *sous* to spend at the tinker's cart; a couch or two – such are the objects, along with bowls, platters, jugs and cooking utensils that appear in peasant inventories and in the paintings of Louis le Nain. That master of realism did not, however choose the poorest of subjects or scenes of squalor. He painted to please. His peasants might be barefooted, their clothes plain and food simple but he does not show dirt or deformity. One does not see the bed on which several children would sleep, perhaps with parents or grandparents. His farmhouse is likely to be that of one of the few more substantial peasants, a *laboureur*. He would have a plough team, own land and livestock worth thousands of *livres*, employ other peasants. He might have the capital, crucially, to lend to others at rates that ensured that he could one day foreclose and take the land. His family ate off pewter, his cupboards were full of fine linen; his second son might train to be a priest or aspire to some modest office. Indeed he might be specially privileged as a *fermier-receveur*, tenant and farmer of church or seigneurial lands and dues, with ample stocks of grain, a pigeon loft and ducks and geese for his table. Such a man might have half a village in his debt. The tentacles of his power stretched through the region.

Around such a village stretched arable land in great fields farmed in three-year rotation: typically winter corn, spring corn and fallow. The fields were subdivided, often minutely. Even where there was consolidation of holdings the fields were usually unenclosed. Beyond the cultivated land were meadows, rough pasture, scrub, marsh, heath or woodland. These fringe lands provided grazing, wood for building, toolmaking and fuel, litter, rushes for floors and candles, and the berries, nuts and fungi to supplement the peasant's diet. They were subject to communal rules over pasturing, and gleaning. Peasants resisted the introduction of the long-handled scythe in place of the sickle which left the straw longer and more suitable for thatch; also the enclosures which experts declared were needed for the improvement of land and stock. They were not alone in their attachment to old ways. *Parlement* consistently opposed the enclosure of ploughland in Brie. Such conservatism only increased the pressures on the fast-disappearing marginal land. All came down to the need to grow enough grain to make the bread to keep the peasant alive. The father who made a cross on a new loaf with the point of his knife before cutting it or told his son that 'wasted bread meant a broken head' was saying the same thing as the farmers who brought 'waste' land under the plough.

The case of Poitou illustrates other aspects of the agrarian malaise. The soil was good and climate benign; water was plentiful, communications generally adequate. Here the Picts had once fertilised their fields with marl and lime; the peasants neglected to do so. In 1660 France was an importer of wool, though Poitou, for instance, was suited to sheep. Few were to be seen. Dominating the landscape were Renaissance châteaux like Chambord and Chenonceaux, particularly grand emblems of the values of court and counting house; the concentration and, for the interests of the rural economy, misapplication, of the country's wealth. Even in the valleys of the Auvergne farmers cultivated cereals, though climate and soil favoured the rearing of livestock. Generally therefore there was a shortage of meat and milk. More serious, shortage of dung meant the impoverishment of the soil. 'He who has hay has bread' – but peasants would or could not follow the old adage. It seems that grain yields declined in the seventeenth century by as much as 20 per cent. Hence the pressure to cultivate the marginal land, so reducing the grazing and perpetuating the deadly cycle within which peasants were trapped, short of capital and the means of improvement.

Debt played a significant part in communities where crops represented wealth and peasants made up for shortages by barter and extra labour. Peasants tended to patronise local artisans, making purchases by exchange or with copper coins worth less than face value. Only at market might they receive silver coins of small denomination with which to pay tax or the *seigneur*'s dues. Cash was a supplement to barter and the surplus of income tended to be too small to amass capital. It was not unusual for a whole community to fall into debt and to sell their commons, sometimes to pay the costs incurred in a court action to protect their interests. Louis XIV's *intendants* and their *subdélégués* might then move to assume control of the village's finance and oversee assemblies, using its leading men, who had most to lose and were most amenable to pressure. What made possible this intrusion of central government was the steady reduction in the number of independent proprietors. With all the charges on a crop – from implements to seed reserved for next year – seigneurial dues and tithe, and royal taxes, a peasant needed twenty-five acres, about twice what might otherwise have supported his family. Most had five to fifteen acres, worked for others and relied on the earnings of their womenfolk and children. In bad years a few would sell their land and fall to the lowest level, that of the *journalier*. To survive on irregular wages he had to hunt for vacant leases, send his wife and children to scavenge or beg. At best, if he left his village, he might become one of the immigrants who provided the bigger cities with crafts and labour; at worst he joined the growing army of beggars. He was one of the *lie du peuple*, as the numerous indigent were described in official documents.

It is in this setting that the widespread practice of share-cropping, *métayage*, can be seen to have offered stability, while doing nothing to encourage enterprise. With services and payments precisely defined, *métayage* gave the tenant a chance to work and survive without capital, protected the landowner against price changes, strengthened his hold over the peasant – and ensured him a gratifying supply of food. The *fermier-général*, typically a businessman or lawyer, leasing *métairies* (including often seigneurial rights) en bloc from one proprietor to another in order to sublet, appears to represent the concentration of capital which, on the analogy of Holland, might be conducive to improvements. He could trade profitably in farm produce. He also, however, had a vested interest in the old system which secured his position: the small units survived.

Métayage affected some, tithe and feudal dues many, royal taxes most. The weight of dues and taxes that might have been bearable, if exacted in a buoyant economy, was crippling at a time of falling prices. Tithe, the way in which a community supported its priest, varied so much, between 3 and 15 per cent, that it is hard to establish what was normal. At the mean, around 8 per cent, though levied only on the main cereal crops and on vines, it was burdensome. It was unavoidable because it was taken in kind from the sheaves or grapes. It was often objectionable because the proceeds were diverted from the *curé* to agents acting for a cathedral chapter, abbey, even, sometimes, a lay proprietor. The beneficiary was supposed to maintain the fabric of the church and the *curé*'s salary and the relief of the poor. When that was evidently not happening, tithe was regarded as just another feudal due.

THE FEUDAL RÉGIME

When Louis XIV's France is described as being 'still feudal', when, in 1789, the National Assembly is said to have 'abolished feudalism', we need to understand what is meant. Feudal attitudes permeated the political life of the seventeenth century in the sense that the client relationship that bound a man to serve his patron, be he nobleman, minister – or the king – was still conceived of in personal terms. Little distinction was made between public and private interest. It was assumed that faithful service entailed rights and expected reward. The very language is revealing. In June 1658 a Captain

Deslandes thus addressed himself to Fouquet: 'I promise and give my fealty to my lord the procurator-general . . . never to belong to any but him, to whom I give myself and attach myself with the greatest attachment of which I am capable.' Here, with a man 'belonging' to another, we might be in the mediaeval world of vassalage. It is also the world in which most Frenchmen still lived, with little chance to rise in status by service but owing dues and labour which had their origin in the idea that the lord had his duty too – to fight, protect and do justice. The idea had not lost all vitality. The widespread *Croquant* risings of 1636–37 had few noble leaders but they were not directed against the *seigneur*. The peasants' enemy was the outsider, the urban office holder, the *traitant* and *élu*, each feathering his own nest, the instrument of a minister who abused the trust of the king in whose name he claimed to act. In the few serious disturbances of Louis XIV's reign the only *gentilshommes* involved were untypical renegades or impoverished soldiers, like Bernard Postel, sieur du Clivet, 'a drunkard and libertine' according to the *intendant* who reported on the revolt in the Boulonnais in 1661.[9] By 1675, the year of the Breton rising, again essentially about royal taxes, a change of tone may be noted. Peasants were not looking for the support of the *seigneurs*. Some châteaux were attacked and manorial records destroyed. The Breton *Code païsant* called for the abolition of tithes (to be replaced by a fixed stipend for priests) and limitations on hunting rights and seigneurial monopolies. As landowners reacted to low prices and falling rents by trying to exact more, using new map-making and surveying techniques to support claims, or farming out dues to businessmen solely interested in making a profit, the feudal regime was starting to look not only oppressive but anachronistic – as much in Mme de Sévigné's beloved Brittany as in the Dijonnais of the wine merchants or the Île de France of wealthy officialdom.

Vast or tiny, a whole district or part of a village, the *seigneurie* could be bought. It did not confer nobility but it was a step towards that coveted status. Its institutional nucleus, with château, park, chapel, mill and farm, was the *domaine*. Around it, the land was composed of *censives*. The peasant-farmer paid a variety of dues of which the *cens* was most significant because its annual payment meant recognition of the authority of the *seigneur* and corresponding limits on his own freedom. The land might be his to work, sell or bequeath it but he possessed only what jurists called *domaine utile*, as opposed to the *seigneur*'s *propriété eminente*. Peasants owned about 50 per cent of the land by 1700 but much of that 'ownership' was limited. Around this core of tradition and law ranged rights, monopolies, restrictions and dues as diverse as the mosaic of provinces that composed the realm: *banalités*, conferring rights over mill, oven or winepress; *saisine*, a death duty on the assets of a *censitaire*; *champart*, a levy in kind on crops; the *corvées*, obligatory labour services. There was scope for evasion as for exploitation – and endless friction. Evidence from *terriers*, charters of rights and dues drawn up when *seigneuries* changed hands, suggests that *bourgeois* purchasers, aided by new surveying and mapping techniques and conniving lawyers, were usually keen to secure the maximum return. The *seigneur* might renounce his right of criminal jurisdiction because it was too costly, but he retained the crucial right to judge quarrels over boundaries, inheritances and dues.

Over much of the centre and south of France there survived allodial, or absolute tenures free of feudal obligations, upon the Roman principle which was to become the basis of Napoleonic law. The allodial position was starting to crumble before the assaults of lawyers acting for great *seigneurs* and the crown. The Midi remained, however, relatively immune from *seigneurial* claims and exactions. Less fortunate were the peasants in the country's flanks, Brittany and Burgundy, long remote from the control of government. Breton *seigneurs*, more often resident than those in other parts, in many respects closer to their peasants, contrived to live largely off their labour and extensive dues. In Burgundy the ethos and practice resembled the German, more starkly feudal than elsewhere: the *seigneurie* was a fief, the tenant a vassal. Here, as in Franche-Comté (French after 1678) and other eastern provinces, were to be found the last serfs, nearly two million altogether: *mainmortables*, they were tied to the soil, unable to marry without the lord's consent, owing him special *tailles* and *corvées*.

The advance of some *bourgeois*, with fortunes made from finance or trade, only sharpened the sense of resentment of the many nobles, dependent on rent from agriculture, seeking to hold on to mortgaged estates. They were trapped by the very attitudes and rules in which they took most pride. *Dérogeance* was a technical term with serious meaning: loss of noble status for engaging in commerce or manufacturing. To the extent that feudal dues provided a substitute for active farm management, while they reduced the surplus needed by the peasant if he was to improve his land, they impoverished the rural economy. Its condition was of critical importance in determining what government could achieve in the economic sphere.

Related more closely to that condition than many nobles were willing to accept, and no less important in its influence on the political regime, were the fortunes of those at the receiving end of the peasants' dues. Impoverished often by the effort 'to live nobly', with retainers, horses, hounds, all hungry mouths; or by the costs of soldiering, gambling or fashion; and – in the case of a grand or ambitious noble, the expense of attending court, landowners seem generally to have been interested more in dues than improvements. Some simply abdicated their responsibilities; others adopted businesslike methods. A financier who acquired a *seigneurie* for title, and seized the chance to build a fine château, was still used to seeing a return on his capital. A world apart from that of finance or fashion was that of the petty *écuyer*. There might be little to differentiate him from his peasants but the sword he could wear and the *taille* he did not pay. He might be less well off than a *laboureur*; he might have gone to the same school as the villagers; he went to the same church. If he went soldiering it might not be with a commission. The state of such *hobereaux* was revealed when, in 1675, undeterred apparently by the lamentable turnout of 1636, the crown summoned nobles to military service – the *ban* – and found most of them bereft of military skills or equipment. Because they were poor, they were not the less tenacious of privilege. The government's periodic *recherches de noblesse* showed them as keen to show their pedigree as ministers were to tax them.

There were other less bleak aspects of the rural regime. Some landowners undoubtedly followed the precepts of the duc de Luynes in his *Devoirs des Seigneurs* (1668): he advised them to live frugally so as to have money to spare for charity, to visit the poor, to keep in touch with peasants' needs. Louis XIV's *dévot* minister Pontchartrain spent large sums on hospitals, churches and schools, beside food and clothing for the destitute on the large estates from which he took his title. Contemporary accounts enable us to picture communities where the village bell was rung to announce that the *seigneur* was going hunting and peasants flocked to the château to enjoy the sport. As typical a scene was the *seigneur* enjoying the *droit de chasse*; the peasant reckoning the damage as the hounds plunged in to flush out the game; or watching pigeons from the manorial dovecote settling on his corn. An edict of 1669 forbade hunting over land when corn was in stalk, but, also renewed the ban on hunting by commoners, even on their own land. The issue reveals a set of values, a code of conduct which did not allow for lesser men's rights or needs, and which, in the cruel or psychotic, could lead to serious crime. There were unfortunate places, such as those revealed by *Jours d'Auvergne* (1665),[10] where the *seigneur,* long unchecked, could terrorise a whole community.

NOBILITY

Faced by such diversity in the origins, types and circumstances of nobility, it is tempting to view the matter in simple economic terms, making no distinction between one degree and another, measuring only by size of property and other interests. That is not how Louis XIV would have seen nobility, its appeal, its social symbolism and its nuances. French jurists' categories are also, therefore, of limited use in defining its status and role because they are concerned with methods of obtaining nobility; government pronouncements too are unhelpful because they are aimed at preventing evasion of tax through false titles. One approach, that of Loyseau and influential through the writing of Mousnier,[11] is to see France as a society of orders, in which everyone knew where he belonged. Loyseau produced an account of this society, every section of the community in rank according to its dignity and occupation. The same approach, turned to fiscal use, is to be seen in the lists compiled for the *capitation* of 1695.[12] Loyseau's scheme can only be useful as a framework, having the same connection to the subtleties in relationships and the aspirations that fired social action that a written creed has to religious feeling. Or it can be seen as one of those creative fictions which theorists might adopt to construct the neat model that appeals to academic minds. Here it was lawyers used to Roman law with its codifying tendency. In their own lives and dealings they would perfectly understand the distinctive social groupings and the ties that bound men together: those of *lignage*, blood and marriage; of *ordres*, based on *dignité*; of *fidélités* reflecting affection and sentiment; and of *corps*, through formal association. They would know the currency of social life and its values: competitiveness, men's ambition, women's urging, the allure of noble title.

At first it seems that Loyseau's view is confirmed by what is known of marriage patterns. The country nobility tended to marry one of their own kind. But here one comes to the first of the important distinctions within the 'order'. The Norman nobles studied by Wood[13] were mostly quite small fry, typical of the majority. The highest ambition of such a man – a mere *hobereau* to the scornful courtier – was to keep his land and his honour. He did not aspire to go to court; if he did it would be in the train of some grandee. He might prefer to stay at home and have his supper with his dogs in the kitchen. He still claimed the right to wear a sword and cherished his coat of arms.

At any time there might be some ten thousand nobles who were sufficiently wealthy, well connected, well educated, able or bold – to aspire to a place at court, or career in diplomacy, church or army. There were some notable models, the Poitevin nobleman, Cardinal Richelieu, among them, to inspire them to strive to be 'considerable'. Some learned the hard way, during the Fronde, that the way would lie in service to the king, not to a rebellious magnate. At the summit of the noble order was a small group whom men called, simply, *les grands*: either *enfants de France*, children, legitimate or otherwise, and grandchildren of the king, or *pairs*, those among the *ducs* who were entitled to play a part in the coronation. Twenty-five in all had been Richelieu's estimate. He had understood – and sought to deny – what they expected as of right: to counsel and be consulted at court, to have controlling powers, as governors, in the province. In the minority of Louis XIII and the Regency of Marie de Médicis he had seen their claim to be uniquely fitted to serve the king tarnished by faction and greed. Between 1611 and 1617, fourteen million *livres* was paid out to nine nobles. The Fronde, we have seen, presented another opportunity. The failure then of *les grands* to present a viable alternative to absolutist government was to prove decisive. Louis successfully excluded them from policy-making, and attracted them to the substitute role of courtier. Towards the end of the reign, with an excess of sentiment verging on the absurd, Saint-Simon would chronicle the decline of 'the immemorial race of noblemen' and dream of the resurgence that would not occur. What did occur, ironically, through a process already under way in Louis XIV's reign, was the transformation of a warrior caste into an open plutocracy and the consolidation of an élite less conscious of differences of rank as measured by the origins of noble title than of its material resources, though no less determined to maintain noble privileges.

The distinction within the *noblesse*, between *épée* and *robe*, had been sharp enough in the minds of some of the 'old nobility' when they were confronted, as during the States General of 1614 by the pretensions of 'mere lawyers'. On the criterion of age it was, however, weak and weakening. In *parlements* offices were transmitted from father to son or nephew, within well-established dynasties. In Brittany, of 216 *robe* families in 1670, 136 had nobility dated from pre-1500. The entire 2,000 noble Breton families had only 560 of such early date – and even that figure is above that for France as a whole. In a regulation of 1760 the year 1400 would be made a deadline: in all France under a thousand families passed that test – and few among the wealthiest. In Brittany, as in Languedoc, the prestige of the *robe* was high. Generally, however, there persisted a prejudice which became evident when, as during the Fronde, there was a need for cooperation between *épée* and *robe*. It was one thing for a Condé to view a *parlementaire* as an important client and ally; quite another to treat him as an equal. Civil war accentuated the traditional difference between sword and gown, the man of action and the man of words. In calmer days after the Fronde, when the emphasis in noble tactics was on improving the material base for a life at court, traditional taboos were forgotten. Indeed, the higher the level of the noble pyramid, it seems, the less prejudice there was against intermarriage between the nobilities. Not only is there a perceptible merging of the greatest families in a single élite but a further tendency to seek profitable alliances with high functionaries and financiers. Ministers could now look very high. Three of Colbert's daughters married dukes. Louis encouraged such ambition creating, as he wanted, the tightly knit groups of advisers, a new aristocracy of service prepared to work, under the firm direction he knew he could give, for the good of the state.

When it was held sensible thus 'to manure the estate' traditional noble values were indeed in question. Yet they clearly counted as a vital aspect of court and army, and a constant concern of the king himself. Birth and race could not be held to be the sole criterion, yet there persisted a sense of separateness: of having acquired a transmitted excellence. Those who became noble were expected to leave behind the values of the counting-house, the mill, the quayside. By and large it seems that they did. Louis XIV's court both exploited and reinforced the great divide. Two exclusive systems of values would persist into the age of Enlightenment. The social and political consequences of this development were indeed profound. Further explanation is called for.

The word 'privilege' has to be rescued from modern usage with its overtone of disapproval, as conveying some unearned advantage. In the seventeenth century it was closer to its derivation: private law applying to certain rights and distinctions, whether useful or honorific, enjoyed, exclusively, by certain members of society, either as individuals or as members of corporate bodies, or of particular communities. None, in that sense, were more privileged than the nobility. Outstanding was exemption from direct tax for which military service had originally been deemed substitute. So even this material benefit connoted honour nor would that have seemed an empty notion to anyone at court during Louis XIV's wars. No one made money out of service in army, navy or embassy. As a proportion of overall numbers, noble casualties between 1689 and 1714 bear comparison with those of twentieth-century wars. Even harder to define but plainly powerful were the outward marks of privilege that others would see: title, with always the lure of a step upward, from *sieur* (only denoting lordship), to *comte, marquis, duc*; the coat of arms; the special pew in church or prior place in ceremonies. At home the genealogical tree recorded past glories or more recent prowess in the marriage market. Certain values were held dear, implicit in rules and standards by which a noble life should be lived. One reason why the crown found it so hard to stop duelling[14] was that it rose from a keen sense of obligation: honour was to be guarded like a sacred flame. A nobleman was expected to be heroic, magnanimous and generous. Unmilitary, frugal, litigious commoners, who might have amassed fortunes or accumulated offices by eschewing such virtues, strove through ennoblement to leave their base concerns behind them. At least they could draw upon the idea, no less potent than transmitted excellence, that there was something superior in royal service.

Commoners could acquire nobility by letter, representing the will of the king; by virtue of office, ranging from high crown offices to such sinecures as were to be found in provincial courts; in some favoured towns, like Toulouse, by virtue of municipal office. There were some 2,000 ennobling offices by 1715. Increasingly, however, the best offices, as in *parlements*, were purchased or inherited by those already enjoying noble status. New men came in, however, in sufficient numbers, to ensure that the nobility was a growing body, with the dual character that offended the traditionalist but did not diminish its prestige or appeal. It was still a hierarchical caste in which income was not the sole or even chief criterion; yet also open-ended, increasingly affected by the power of money, altogether more adaptable than its image would suggest. Such growth and adaptability could only favour the crown. It contributed significantly to the stability of Louis XIV's régime.

The court was the great arena for the exercise of noble manners and satisfaction of noble aspirations. In its highly developed form, the Versailles of the second half of Louis XIV's reign was also the centrepiece of a style and system of government: it is in that context that the role of the court nobles will be examined. Patronising remarks were made by courtiers about the *noblesse de campagne*. Some would indeed cut a ridiculous figure, with ill-cut clothes, strange accents and lapses into *patois*. It does not follow, however, that all who could afford to, or bear themselves well, wished to go to court. Nobility had its middle ranks, sedentary, quietly influential in their own area. Neither political nor financial considerations tempted the *noblesse parlementaire* to leave their provincial capitals. Among the *noblesse d'épée* were many who remained impervious to the charms of the palace. The uneasy combination of being near to the heart of government, yet outside it, of being important yet dependent, of hovering at the edge of an exclusive set, the endless waiting and standing, the smart gossip, made no appeal to a man who liked to spend time with his family. He might be content to divide his time between his château and his *hôtel* in the nearest big town, supervising his *métayers*, consulting the *curé* or the *procureur-fiscal* of the *seigneurial* court. It might be enough for him if he could find dowries for his daughters, for marriage or a place at the convent, and for his son fees for college or seminary, more probably a commission in the fast-expanding army. He would expect, however, to enjoy influence locally. His loyalty to the crown might be assumed by government, but it would only be translated into positive cooperation through close attention to his particular concerns and those of his clients. It was in that largely hidden area of provincial deals and favours that Louis XIV's *intendants* and governors exercised a degree of control, less imposing than absolutism's outward face but more effective than anything that had gone before.[15]

BOURGEOIS FRANCE

Inevitably it was those nobles least well-placed to take advantage of new wealth who were most resentful of new entries, *arrivistes*. Typical of many was the Norman noble who wrote (*c.* 1656): 'Another kind of person has risen among us. . . . The *rentiers*, ignorant and unlettered, who amass wealth without labour and risk; great do-nothings. . . . They have chased the two pillars of the state, gentry and peasantry from their ancient holdings.' Whether such an advance is measured by accumulations of office, by profitable contracts, or – convincing evidence – by the handsome Mansard-roofed houses to be seen in so many French towns, it is clearly not an illusion born of the envy of the dispossessed. Yet the solid and all-pervasive presence of the *haute bourgeoisie* (most of whom did not attain noble status) tends still to be seen in negative terms, even approaching caricature, and it is easy to see why. Court values dominated the cultural world, nourished by feudal tradition and humanist education, sustained by the patronage of the great. Ministers might plan for economic developments but most of the crucial decisions reflected ways of thinking alien to those of business: religious conformity, the expansion of frontiers, dynastic rights, the sovereign's *amour propre*, were normal criteria.

A man with capital to invest had to choose between the toils and risks of business and the security of office and land. He had to take into account the trading and fiscal conditions engendered by the wars which were the normal state of the country (in 56 out of 80 years, 1635–1715). Nor was this a novel state of affairs. The disruptive experience of the Religious Wars (1561–98) had discouraged investment and instilled habits of caution in French traders and manufacturers. By contrast with contemporaries in England and Holland they seem to have been lacking in enterprise – and even in a proper sense of identity. Molière's *bourgeois gentilhomme*, Monsieur Jourdain, yearning to figure as a man of quality, absurdly fleeced by the seedy nobleman Dorante, stands for the pretentious shams that were a favourite target of moralists and playwrights.[16] (Is it significant that his counterpart in English Restoration comedies is typically the boorish country gentleman?) There was in England the same appeal of land. But the Englishman buying an estate, reaching perhaps towards a title, did not then enter a new world of values. Nobility was not a caste apart. There was no *dérogeance* for the English nobleman who invested in trade. Nor was there a resplendent court to attract the wealthy and ambitious. Court favour was – as by John Churchill – a well-trodden route to high place. But nobleman or commoner could pursue a political career in a chamber where the voice of the merchants and financiers would be almost as loud and influential as that of the landed interests.

Alongside the English experience and the evidence for its growth, through war and peace, in power and prosperity, the French record is, at first sight, unimpressive. Obsession with office, reluctance to invest in productive enterprise: indisputably such *bourgeois* attitudes persisted, to the dismay of reformers. It would be misleading, however, to describe characteristics of an important segment of Louis XIV's France in the light, exclusively, of Colbert's notion of usefulness and of his efforts to stimulate trade and manufactures.

Not only was the *bourgeois* élite, around 10 per cent of the three million inhabitants of towns, a rising class. It was also responsible for some of the most important achievements of the reign. In commerce, particularly towards the end of the century in overseas trade, enough was achieved to show the potential for further expansion. As patrons of builders and artists they were building another, durable France that owed little to court or château. They were the willing task force in the extension of royal government in the provinces. Even as landowners, where the record generally is ultra-conservative, they were responsible for the restoration of estates in war-torn provinces. They were also responsible for the significant growth of office, an area where the fiscal needs of the crown were matched by desire for status. Crucially the sale of offices diverted capital from business investment. Concentrations of urban wealth did, however, create employment for large numbers of domestic servants, demand for a wide variety of goods and a market for fine arts and crafts. The furniture, ever more ornate, gold and silver objects, jewels, clocks, tapestries, pictures, prints, maps and books, that filled the houses of rich *bourgeois* all represented skilled employment. Colbert had this to build on when he devised plans to promote French manufactures. There was another less tangible effect of the office phenomenon. Affording more leisure it contributed to the development of a distinctive *bourgeois* culture, a new intellectual and moral order based on wider reading. It was open to new ideas, especially scientific ones, and it wore a new kind of respectability that depended less on the teaching of the church. Relatively emancipated from traditional constraints, placing a special value on honesty, moderation and the common sense that would soon be lifted to the level of philosophic discourse in the name of 'reason', this bourgeois culture would be the matrix of the next century's enlightenment.

Stability was a feature; the sense of belonging was of the essence. To become *bourgeois* it was necessary spend a qualifying period of at least five years' residence. In Paris a *bourgeois* forfeited his rank if he spent more then five months a year outside the city. The new *bourgeois* usually had to take an oath of allegiance to the city. The *bourg* was the sum of the separate *corps*, representing the interests of professional men, merchants, tradesmen and master-craftsmen. But it was more than that and the *bourgeois* enjoyed peculiar rights. In Lille, for example, where the *bourgeois* amounted to only a twentieth of the population (the rest, *manants* having no special rights), they were eligible for the magistracy and enjoyed the right to trial by town magistrates alone, in both civil and criminal cases. In certain cases, where history had left its mark, particular groups might enjoy valuable privileges. In Rouen, as the *premier président* of its *parlement* informed Colbert in 1675, the city's arquebusiers, its police force, had enjoyed since 1222 exemption from billeting and from the *taille*, with the precious privilege too of the *franc-salé*.

Among the privileges of the town the most important was that of appointing its own government. Every town had a council under various names, typically *échevinage* in the north, *consulat* in the Midi. In theory at least officials were elected; in effect they represented interests rather than individuals, with a natural bias towards the stronger bodies. In Lyon (the only town beside Paris with a population approaching 100,000) and seaports such as Marseille and Nantes the merchants dominated. Nearly everywhere else the diversion of business wealth into land and office had created civic oligarchies, consolidated by intermarriage, self-perpetuating and, to an increasing extent, adorned with titles which 'pure' nobles might scorn but which had resonance in the streets of Toulouse or Dijon. They had sufficient power to make control of town government a prime aim for Louis XIV's *intendants*. In many cases they were sufficiently indebted to justify an *intendant* intervening. Sometimes political motives prompted government action. Absolutist principles were incompatible with civic independence. Bordeaux, the city which witnessed the most radical of popular movements during the Fronde, provides a special case of civic independence and local power. The councillors were allowed to retain civil and criminal jurisdiction; fifty officers dealt with finance, justice and administration. When Colbert wanted to have a mercantile tribunal to deal with cases rising out of the manufacture of textiles he revived the city's old communal court. It was a compromise typical of the period between new authority and old privilege.

All towns had the right to raise taxes for the repair of walls, roads, pavements and lights, to maintain the poor house and other civic amenities. Many towns, like Angers and Beauvais, were exempt from the *taille*, though not from all taxes: *aides* had been a prime cause of the *émeutes* which affected several towns during Richelieu's ministry. There were other levies and the periodic exercise of the detested right to billet soldiers. Special lower rates for *aides* and exemptions from the full *gabelle* featured among a miscellany of privileges. As in the wider case of the province the range reflected the time and manner of a town's incorporation in the kingdom, and special concessions, usually granted when the crown had been in no position to dictate terms. Now it was. Town walls reduced to rubble, La Rochelle besieged and stripped of its privileges by Richelieu, Marseille brought to book by Mazarin: such dramatic episodes served notice that the crown would not tolerate resistance to its laws.

Much of a country's history is likely to be the history of the great, those who have left some record of their activities. So it is with the history of villages and towns: it is the *coq de paroisse*, the *noblesse de clocher* who can be traced. To give a complete picture the brush needs to be more generous. Most towns in Louis XIV's France had but a few thousand inhabitants. Each, however, had a crucial role, as market and provider of services, in the self-sufficient economy of its *pays*. When more affluent citizens were buying land around it a peasant might see his local town as a parasitic growth, a nest of lawyers and tithe-eating upper clergy, monopolist merchants whose capital enabled them to control work and wage rates, and the *fermiers* who exploited his land and labour. There would be many, of course, whom he would recognise as one of his known. In the poorer *quartiers* he might find friends and relations who had come in search of work. They could tell him that town life was less cosy than he might imagine as the town gate closed behind him and he trudged home to his village. Behind him lay the animation of the market, the clangour of bells, enticing goods in shuttered workshops, the wares of cutlers, pewterers and locksmiths, saddle-makers, haberdashers, hatters. On the fringe of town he has left the premises of brewers and vintners, coopers, ropemakers and wagon-makers, the butchers' shambles and the tanners' malodorous racks. Before him was the unremitting toil on which that world depended.

Strained though it was in times of scarcity, when violence might ensue from rumours of profiteering and hoarding, the relation of the town to its orbital villages was essentially one of mutual dependence. The specialist craftsman provided services for which the single village might have insufficient need. Towns provided a market: indeed for most it was the prime *raison d'être*. They needed fresh food, hay and straw, wood, rushes, tallow and hides. They would not willingly pay extra for carriage from further parts, for the fodder for ox and mule, for the tolls on road and river. Such extra costs ensured that markets remained local, communities isolated, the country's economy sluggish. In textile districts like Normandy and Picardy there lived bleachers, dyers and finishers of the cloth that was woven in village homes. Needing merchants' funds and knowledge such specialists were tied in to the early capitalist world but they were also an integral part of the 'natural economy', working within sight of the fields in which they too might have a small stake.

Yet the town also represented to peasants a separate, in some respects alien culture. Urban rules and standards were set by a literate group of professional men and master tradesmen. Towns were places where men read books, even if, for the most part they belonged to the genre of the *bibliothèque bleue*, the cheap tales and compilations of traditional magic and astrology that poured from the presses of Troyes.[17] Here educated French might be heard beside the local *patois*. It was an outward sign of an even more significant cultural divide. Villages had their own peasant hierarchies, place being determined by what a man owned, produced and earned: there were no precise categories. In the towns each *bourgeois* belonged to a *corps* which enjoyed a distinct legal status and had a religious character expressed by dedication to its own saint and by special rites in its own church. The *corps* had a fixed place in the hierarchy, with professional groups to the fore, followed by merchants, then by master craftsmen. In Paris, by 1673, there were sixty artisan *corps*, each with its own elected officials. Such compact urban structures reveal a corporate, ceremonious society in which men would find it hard to think of life in terms of the individualism that is characteristic of 'modern' society. They lived within a framework provided by bodies which provided a degree of security against the vagaries of markets and by the rituals, religious in form and spirit, which enhanced the sense of community and enriched narrow lives. In a century of slow and patchy economic growth, there were inequalities as ever, but also a general lack of opportunity for betterment: the hierarchical urban régime seems to have done much to contain the resulting stresses. Where there were still walls they no longer meant much to the soldier but they could be said to represent the determination of city fathers to defend the status quo. To envisage the scene within the walls is to take a further step towards understanding the world within which ministers had to operate: the ground rules which limited what even the most ambitious minister could achieve in the economic sphere; limited, therefore, the power of the state.

The seven larger towns, and the numerous small ones of a few thousand, exhibited such features; but if any town can be called 'typical' it would be one of the sixty with populations between ten and fifty thousand. Around the city centre and main square is a tracery of narrow streets and alleys interspersed with smaller squares. On or near the main square stands the cathedral or collegiate church. The ecclesiastical presence can be overwhelming – though few to the extent of Angers where, by 1700, there were 69 religious houses, churches and chapels, in a town of 35,000. The centre is separated by gates or rampart from the market, round which live tradesmen and shopkeepers, with their parish churches, guild chapels and halls. Another focal point may be the citadel which, if there is a garrison of any importance, will have its own services, its domestics and victuallers. Here, though not only here, are the town's prostitutes who find constant recruits among domestic servants, perhaps desperate enough to take this route to a sort of independence; sometimes cast out by employer or family after being found pregnant. A girl who left her village at 13 to earn enough for a dowry and a husband, whose life for the next ten years was largely confined to a kitchen or attic or cellar workshop for twelve to fourteen hours a day was naturally vulnerable to the rare excitements of festival evenings of dancing and drinking.

Former concentrations of special occupations can still be read in street names. Convenience has brought together certain trades and crafts. Fine craftsmen, producing goods of value, tend, for security, to congregate together; tanners and dyers need running water; butchers, anti-social neighbours, need access for beasts to slaughter. In the centre, tall houses, with a narrow frontage, reflect the high price of land and the usual rule that *bourgeois* should have a street frontage. In the deep, ill-lit interior, the workshop is on the ground floor, the family above it, with servants and apprentices in an upper storey or garret. Richer *bourgeois* tend to move out from the oldest districts, sometimes breaching the walls to gain space. The main features of the town centre, not only in the decayed tenements where immigrants have joined compatriots and perpetuate slum conditions, are the crush of people, dark ill-ventilated houses and filthy streets, swarms of flies on refuse and manure, lice and fleas on bodies and clothes, water supplies that are too often contaminated – all constituting a chronic fire risk. Attracting the landless and workless from the countryside major towns like Marseille and Lyon receive a steady flow – yet their population remain stable. In that dire context the most generous arrangements to relieve the needy are insufficient. The middle years of Louis XIV's reign will see a spate of bequests and foundations, a corporate but also specifically Christian commitment to charity. The *hôtel-dieu* for the sick, the *hôpital-général* or *bureau de charité* for the rest, exhibit the *grand siècle* at its most admirable.[18] Yet ironically, such is the crowding, so crude are standards of care and treatment, that they are often the worst breeding grounds for disease. Further out from the dense streets are the tiny hovels where live many of the town's workers, clustered round the communal well. Around the main roads beyond the walls are numerous gardens, orchards and grazing plots. Few of the more substantial citizens are without pigs and hens; towns often have communal herds on town fields which are themselves an obstacle to further building.

Only in the big seaports and textile districts, Bordeaux, Marseille, Nantes, Lyon, Amiens, Rouen, for example, was there a substantial merchant class. The typical merchant was still a small operator. But as in all backward communities merchants prospered more than producers. They had benefited as a whole from the long price rise and secured advantages which they now held on to in more depressed conditions. The constraints that characterised such a conservative, in places ossified urban society, as well as the typical urge to form associations, could be seen in the *compagnonnages* in which artisans achieved a semblance of solidarity. Especially militant were printers and workers in skilled, exacting trades, such as leather. But nothing like class struggle could grow out of the polarisation of capital and labour until such men lived en masse. In the pre-industrial society, businesses were usually family units, extended, if at all, by artisans and apprentices. In the dominant textile industry spinning and weaving was done mostly in the villages. Plutocracy operated on the fringe of the economy, where concentrations of capital provided scope for tax-farming, loan-mongering, contracting, and other business secured by personal dealings with government. At the centre, working in ways that determined the vitality of the economy, were the *médiocres*, small masters, with their odd parcels of property, house, shop or workshop, garden, vineyard, field strips farmed *en métayage,* hoard of silver and bundle of IOUs. A few of this class were always accumulating property, but more likely by carefully planned marriages than by risk-taking business ventures. The general diffusion of capital obstructed growth while it gave stability to an economy, in which the supply of labour always exceeded demand, and to a political régime which did not make excessive demands.

Notes

1. The most recent estimate is at the top: 22.4 million in 1705 (but, note, midway between periods of acute distress) in J. Dupaquier (ed.), *Histoire de la Population française* (4 vols, Paris, 1988): ii, *De la Renaissance à 1789*. For general considerations see W. Roosen, 'The demographic history of the reign', in P. Sonnino (ed.), *The Reign of Louis XIV* (New York, 1990), 9–26.

2. John Lough (ed.), *Locke's Travels in France, 1675–9* (Cambridge, 1953), p. 88. Locke's Journal is a rich source for information about French life from a keenly observant, meticulous and statistically minded observer.

3. The process had begun with the marriage of Charles VIII, then of Louis XII, to Anne of Brittany. The process of acquisition did not mean assimilation. The Breton Estates remained vigorous, the *noblesse* who dominated meetings vociferous in defence of their rights. Brittany was the last province to receive an *intendant* – in 1689.

4. Nicholas Boileau-Despréaux (1636–1711) was the most influential critic of his time. He brought to literature the reverence of the theologian and the combativeness of the lawyer. This *legislateur de Parnasse*, standard bearer for classical values and Cartesian method, can be seen with Bossuet as a twin pillar of the literary establishment. The message of *L'Art Poétique* (1675) was think well if you wish to write well. Racine exemplified his principle that the hallmarks of good art were lucidity and elegance.

5. The *Académie française* (1635) was a state-directed body from the start. On to Valentine Conrart's *salon*, meant to be a refuge from official business for cultivated minds, Richelieu, whose image remains on its seal to this day, grafted his conception of a body committed to promoting the image and interests of France.

6. A sample of marriage certificates investigated by Maggiolo (*c.* 1877) from the years 1686–90 reveals (with wide regional variations) 71 per cent illiterate among men and 86 per cent among women. Comparable figures for a hundred years later were 53 and 73 per cent. Quoted by P. Goubert, *L'Ancien Régime* (1969, trans. S. Cox, London, p. 278).

7. For feasts and other episodes of misrule see Natalie Zemon Davis, *Society and Culture in Early Modern France* (Stanford, CA, 1965), pp. 97–123. She writes mainly about the sixteenth century, but custom changed slowly in the countryside and small towns, despite increasingly censorious church attitudes.

8. J. Goubert, *Beauvais et le Beauvaisis* is the prime source for conditions in a cereal-growing region. More accessible is his *Ancien régime*, op. cit. pp. 101–47. For the south see R. Baerhel, *Une croissance; la basse Provence rurale* (Paris, 1961) and E. Le Roy Ladurie, *Les Paysans de Languedoc* (Paris, 1966). Everywhere the skills and labour of women, in house, yard, field and workshop were as important as those of men. Children too had to work for their bread from an early age. See Olwen Hufton, 'Women, work and family', in Natalie Zemon Davis and Arlette Farge (eds), *A History of Women*, vol. III (Boston, 1993), pp. 15–43.

9. For this episode see *Government and Society in Louis XIV's France* (ed. R. Mettam) (London, 1977), and the reports (pp. 255–70) from *intendant* Machault to Colbert,

and the fearful punishment he has ordered (arms and legs cut off while still alive) for Clivet.

10. See p. 102.

11. R. Mousnier, *Les Institutions de la France sous Louis XIV* (2 vols, Paris, 1974, 1980), is available in English translation, as *The Institutions of France under the Absolute Monarchy, 1589–1789* (2 vols, London, 1679, 1684). Charles Loyseau (1564–1627), more jurist than political philosopher, conveys a static view of the categories of French society. He throws valuable light, however, on the degrees, corresponding value and status, and psychology of office-holding.

12. See p. 303.

13. James B. Wood, *The Nobility of the Election of Bayeux, 1463–1666* (Princeton, 1980). Wood does not see the nobles, in his sample (by 1666 he reckons that there were around 2,700 individuals), as declining. His conclusion (p. 170) is that 'developing governmental institutions may have been forced to accommodate themselves to the prevailing aristocratic social regime as much as the nobility was forced to conform to the new political regime ... This class was strong and prosperous enough to ensure that the emerging political regime served its social interests as well as it served the political interests of *raison d'état*.' This view is borne out by several other provincial studies; see also pp. 117 and 132, n. 9.

14. By persuading Louis XIII to stand by his prohibition and insist on the execution of the notorious dueller, Montmorency-Bouteville, Richelieu (whose brother had been killed in a duel) had put down a marker. There was more duelling during the Fronde. Louis's known disapproval was enough to ensure that it was, thereafter, exceptional. Louis's wars offered plenty of opportunity for men to defend their honour in battle. Between 1651 and 1715 there were only seven decrees against duelling, half the number of the previous sixty-four years. G.N. Clark, 'The analogy of the duel', pp. 29–51, in *War and Society in the Seventeenth Century* (Oxford, 1958).

15. The process is well documented, for example, in W. Beik, *Absolutism and Society in Seventeenth Century France: State Power and Provincial Aristocracy in Languedoc* (Cambridge, 1994).

16. Molière, real name J.B. Pocquelin (1622–73), was author of social comedies such as *Le Misanthrope* (1666), *Le Bourgeois Gentilhomme* (1670) and *Les Femmes savants* (1672). The approval of the king gave him an assured position but it could not save *Tartuffe* (1664), a play about a religious confidence man, censored at the instigation of the *dévôts*. He was more interested in the weaknesses of human beings than in the misdirection of institutions though, in *Le Malade imaginaire*, he could make a damaging indictment of a class he disliked. He stressed the virtues of moderation and naturalness at a time when those qualities were being over-looked. Did the courtiers who laughed at the titled boobies on stage think of the artifices of their own lives? It is a tribute to Louis's confidence, as to his taste, that he countenanced, and enjoyed, the comic genius whose sallies went so near to the bone. He was safe from the pensioned playwright – and in Molière's time he was still successful. In later days, when court manners were more staid, would he have been so confident?

17. The danger posed by the proliferation of small presses had been exposed by the *Mazarinades* during the Fronde. Under the direction of Colbert, later of Pontchartrain, royal government introduced systematic regulation of the printing industry and made possible a degree of censorship, and an instrument of propaganda, by driving the smaller houses out of business and reducing others to dependency through preferential privileges. See J. Klaits, *Printed Propaganda under Louis XIV* (Princeton, 1976), pp. 35–7.

18. For these institutions see pp. 197–8, n. 9.

Chapter 3

◆

PERSONAL RULE

No people have a better opinion of their king than the French,
which is owing in a great measure to the clergy.

JOHN NORTHLEIGH, 1702

In all the kingdom the king is perhaps the man who thinks most
succinctly and expresses himself most agreeably.

ABBÉ DE CHOISY

THE CASE OF FOUQUET

'I have decided to take charge of the state in person.' Eyebrows were raised and there were sceptical reactions to Louis's announcement. Mazarin's dominance and Richelieu's before him, the king's warm-blooded pursuit of pleasure, his studied discretion in public dealings, weighed more with courtiers than the precedents of Henry IV or of the Valois sovereigns before the Religious Wars. Is it likely that courtiers would expect a king to endure what they would find so uncongenial, the stern disciplines of administration, its regular routines, the heavy paperwork? How could they imagine the profession of kingship to be 'delightful'[1] – unless it be the gathering of laurels earned by other men? What if they had been told that Louis would rule in such conscientious fashion, maintaining his energy and command to the end, for fifty-four years? Yet a personal rule may have been in Mazarin's mind when, on his deathbed, he advised Louis to choose his ministers according to their talent – and made no particular commendation. Certainly no one knew Louis better than Mazarin, his tutor in business, his mentor in personal conduct. Was not this earnest, reserved, principled young man his masterpiece, his legacy to his adopted country? He did not advise Louis to be his own first minister.[2] But it is not surprising that Louis should have concluded that it was the right step: that for which his training had prepared him, for which the times were propitious, which in the situation, as he saw it, was essential.

When Mazarin died there was a general peace and a widespread yearning for good order. With the end of wars foreign and civil (not a distinction that would mean much to people near the passage of armies) logic and sentiment pointed to the exercise of a strong authority from the centre. Louis's own words convey his sense of what was needed. He wrote later of 'calm and peace', but also of 'disorders' which required that he should act. He was in fact in that rare situation: free to carry out reforms without fear of interference from outside or serious revolt within. That drastic reform was needed he did not doubt. 'Disorder ruled everywhere.'

Everywhere indeed royal authority had been tested by those 'disorders': in *Parlement*, church and provinces; by officials clinging to the advantages gained during the Fronde; by the supporters of Retz; by restless nobles. In 1661 a revolt in the Boulonnais[3] revealed the desperation that could drive peasants to take up arms when the tax collectors failed to make allowance for the effect of a bad harvest. Across the land, however, from Boulogne to Marseille the lesson was taught: the king would brook no defiance of his authority. That is the message of his *Mémoires*. Louis was in a happy mood when he composed them, following the birth of the dauphin (November 1661) which added extra security to the king's position. Allowance may be made too for a retrospective ordering of earlier more random thoughts and plans; but the *Mémoires* reveal much of the king's mind. When allowance is made for the deceptive clarity of afterthought the early decisions he records still appear to amount to a programme of government as coherent as any that can be attributed to Richelieu. Some were ad hoc, to teach a particular lesson. Such were the exile of judges in the *Cour des Aides* to teach them not to question financial decisions, the closure of the Church Assembly to show that the Church should not try to capitalise on his piety, restrictions on the powers of governors, and the exile of the comte de Soissons, convicted of duelling. Several show Louis's concern with issues that were to acquire further significance: the suppression of the office of *colonel-général de l'infanterie* was a vital step towards creating a truly royal army; measures against Jansenism reflect his conviction that the sect was politically dangerous; cautious words concerning the Huguenots implied no immediate threat but offered them no long-term security; the choice of 65 *chevaliers du Saint-Esprit* (the first since 1633) showed that he meant to use his patronage to enhance the appeal of a court committed to his service. Drawing together several of these themes was the disgrace of Fouquet. Bold in conception, sensational in the process, it informed the privileged official world that no one, however rich, distinguished or influential, could be secure if his position offended the king or appeared to threaten the well-being of the kingdom.

When Mazarin was dying and men discussing who would be the new *premier ministre* the name of Nicolas Fouquet was foremost. Fouquet had been promoted to high office unusually early. In 1650, at 33, he became *procureur-général*. In 1653 Mazarin appointed him *surintendant*. So he had a crucial double role, fostering the interests of the crown in *Parlement* and raising money for the war. It was his connections in the closely related worlds of magistracy and finance that enabled him to serve Mazarin so well. In the hand to mouth conditions of war finance no one could secure loans on better terms. His achievement was to make the most of the system – if the individual bargaining process to which royal finance had been reduced can be so called. He had been the intermediary who brought Turenne back to his allegiance to the crown. In 1657, with armies on the point of mutiny, he saved the day, raising nearly a million *livres* in four days from his family and friends. Mazarin died, the richest of royal subjects: his fortune was not beyond reproach or audit but he was safe with his fame. By contrast his *surintendant* was vulnerable. The king did not need the lavish festivities of August 1661 at Fouquet's palatial Vaux-le-Vicomte[4] to convince him that his *surintendant* had enriched himself at the expense of the state. Colbert was there to supply chapter and verse.

Fatally, Fouquet underestimated Colbert, seeing him as a superior clerk. For all his brilliance he was imprisoned, in his thinking, by the presumptions of his world of high office and finance. In this sphere, the state hardly existed. It was not France that taxed and borrowed but the king, as an individual; and the king depended on intermediaries. They, *trésoriers* or *traitants*, holders of royal office or private contractors, worked for the *surintendant*, hoping for high reward but – *traitants* particularly – accepting high risk to purse and person. Colbert knew this world, no one better after years of working for the cardinal, and he would work within it, building his own *clientèle*, with the energy and command of detail that had first commended him to Mazarin. But he envisaged a new financial order, with the crown directly in control, acting not through a *surintendant* but through a *contrôleur-général* who would be empowered by the crown to act in the interests of the economy as a whole. With this in mind he had tried, in a memorandum of 1657, to convince Mazarin that Fouquet was responsible for the confusion in royal finances. Naturally Mazarin rebuffed him. Now *intendant des finances*, he found Louis ready to listen. He needed to play a clever game for the stakes were high. Louis XIV had set aside Mazarin's wishes and ordered an inventory: the contrast between his vast fortune and the penury of the state was disturbing. For Colbert, who would be compromised as the cardinal's chief agent, attack was the best form of defence. He contended that Fouquet, whose own wealth was so blatant, was responsible for the misappropriation of funds and – falsely – that Mazarin himself had thought of dismissing him. So he presented a formidable double case, political and personal: it would be the ground for Fouquet's arrest and trial.

Essentially the case was that the disorder of the finances crippled the state and that the enrichment of financiers challenged the king's authority. Fouquet's evident position as leader in Parisian society, his generous but calculating patronage of writers and artists, and his air of *grand seigneur*, touched the young king at sensitive points at a crucial time. For Louis was schooling himself to project the image of supremacy, control and omniscience that was to be a hallmark of his reign. Up to a point it seems that Fouquet invited disaster. Dominating the financial world, with strong support in *Parlement* and an admiring coterie in the *salons*, he knew that he had enemies and rivals but may simply have underestimated the capacity of the king to act against him. The host of Vaux-le-Vicomte was like a skater on thin ice doing ever more extravagant pirouettes. Whom was he trying to impress? The king, or the financiers whose loans underpinned the financial régime? Did he think that Louis, signally gracious and giving nothing away, accepted that he had been acting under Mazarin's orders? Was it for this reason that he accepted Louis's request that he sell his key post in *Parlement* which carried with it the right to be tried by his fellow judges? Did this strong-nerved veteran of crisis-management now decide that to dare was to win? Or was it because he was still so insecure that he thought it wise to buttress his position in the traditional manner by establishing his own stronghold? It was his extensive fortification of his island marquisate of Belle-Isle that provided Colbert with the most convincing evidence of treasonous intent.

Fouquet was arrested in September 1661. His office of *surintendant* was abolished. He was tried by a special court. Papers were produced, some forged, to show that he planned treason. Much was made of the fact that the fortifications at Belle-Isle were constructed at break-neck speed. It was thought sinister that he had found the money to enable Créqui to secure generalship of the royal galleys. It was alleged that he looked for support abroad. Fresh memories of the Fronde helped the crown case. Colbert's uncle Pussort helped prepare it. Yet his trial dragged on for three years. Fouquet defended himself with skill and courage. Some of his friends stood by him. *Premier président* Lamoignon[5] was judged too lenient and replaced mid-trial by chancellor Séguier. La Fontaine[6] composed an ode urging clemency. Fouquet's written defence was smuggled out of prison, secretly printed and distributed. The hand-picked court failed to come to a clear-cut verdict and sentenced him to banishment for careless administration. The king was vexed by the publicity and delays. He had expected a death sentence. With untypical disregard for the law, he now ordered imprisonment for life. From the Bastille Fouquet went to distant Pinerolo to expiate his faults.[7] Chief among them had been that he had been too great a subject.

Looking back on the case, Louis accused Fouquet of 'fortifying his properties, adorning his palaces, forming cabals and securing key places for his friends, bought at my expense in the hope of making himself the sovereign arbiter of the state'. Indeed Fouquet's private empire covered the main areas where Louis saw disorder: aristocratic insolence, the entrenched privilege of the sovereign courts and financial malpractice. He was piqued at seeing his minister living more grandly than he was yet able to do. He was realist enough, however, to know that he must deal cautiously with the élites of sword and gown, seeking consensus through perception of mutual advantage. Only in the third area was it feasible to take radical initiatives. The fall of Fouquet opened the way to an assault on leading financiers, through the *chambre de justice*, which offered dividends both financial and political, the prospect of a sound financial base for the military power that Louis craved. The opportunity was there and the man ready to take full advantage of it. Colbert took Fouquet's place, with Le Tellier and Lionne, in the *conseil d'en haut*. In the same month a regulation drafted by Colbert created a new branch of government, the *conseil royal des finances*. From the outset it was plain that Colbert, modestly termed *intendant*, was its driving force. By 1665, when he became *contrôleur-général* he had already carried out important reforms and transformed the financial position.

The case of Fouquet complements Louis's decision to be his own first minister. His aggressive action over the 'Affair of the Ambassadors'[8] (October 1661) made an issue out of precedence; the destruction of Fouquet was ostensibly about financial management: in both cases Louis was making a statement about power: where it lay and what it meant. The Fouquet affair did not, however, show him to be an autocrat who could act above the law. If the destruction of a powerful subject was significant so was the protracted legal process that preceded it. It suggests the need to look beyond the principles of absolute monarchy to the true nature of royal power. The theory is also, however, important and should first be considered since it represents the trend of the time and the core assumptions of responsible people. Absolutist philosophy does not belong only to France: it is of its troubled time, its intellectual ferment, its political upheavals and a war-torn Europe.

ABSOLUTISM

It is not surprising that the term 'absolutism' is open to differing interpretation since it was first used in the 1790s by revolutionaries with reference to the *ancien régime* and all that it implied: 'despotism' was assumed.[9] Taking their cue from nineteenth-century writers, warmed by the afterglow of European liberalism, then appalled by the abuse of authority in the age of the dictators, historians have used this term until recently to denote the efforts of seventeenth- and eighteenth- century rulers to create more efficient states. They have rightly seen in such states more extensive civil powers reinforced by an ever-growing bureaucracy and large armies. They have looked at the way in which sovereigns sought to subdue the law courts, political assemblies and local administrations that guarded the rights of subjects, and have tended to take the absolutist intention for the deed. In the face of now-plentiful evidence of the way in which 'absolutist' régimes actually operated the term has come to look less convincing. It is particularly misleading when applied without reference to the differences between European states and to changes over time. To apply the same label, for example, to Richelieu as to Frederick the Great, is simply absurd.

Men of the seventeenth century ranged widely in theories about the nature of *imperium* while accepting that it should be *absolutum* . Through all the commotions of mid-century they still held on to the old principle of Aristotle that, in the best states, laws rule. For Spinoza,[10] absolute sovereignty, if it exists, is the sovereignty held by the whole people. Beside the question of definition, there is a another reason for treating 'absolutism' with caution. The term suggests that sovereigns and ministers would be guided by theory; yet all political experience suggests that they would be mainly concerned with mundane questions of solvency and security. Even for that educated minority of subjects, 'the political nation', capable of thinking in abstract terms about rights, law and rule, indeed about the interests of any community larger than their own, the form of government mattered mainly to the extent that it affected them in purse or place. Meaning release from all constraints, and therefore the ultimate in authority, the notion of absolutism is seductive when it implies the static and definite character that fits theoretical models. To read Loyseau,[11] for example, author of the influential *Traité des Ordres*, is to envisage a ruler bound by no human ordinances, whose absolute power is 'perfect and entire in all particulars.' He can make laws, confer and remove office and privilege, do justice, coin money and raise taxes without consent; moreover he can command goods and services 'for the proper necessity of his people'. Yet Loyseau, writing in 1613 to make a case for monarchy during Louis XIII's minority, knew perfectly well how strongly supported was *Parlement*'s traditional view: that the king was not free to dispose of the kingdom as he wished; he was not owner but administrator of the body politic.

Quite different in reality from the model offered in the course of such special pleading was the dynamic relationship between rulers and ruled, the former striving to keep freedom of manoeuvre in the pursuit of control, the latter defending their rights and properties against royal trespass. Equally misleading is the picture of a ruler who could deliver more than was possible in the conditions of the time: such is the Louis XIV portrayed by most biographers.[12] The nearer historians have come to the world in which Frenchmen lived and the state operated, the more guarded they have become, until the point has been reached when absolutism is seen as much in terms of resistance and limitations as of effective authority. Or it may be seen, with some plausibility in the case of Louis XIV's régime, as cover for a marriage of convenience between the sovereign and his most privileged subjects. The reader may judge differently after further study of this portrait of royal power – but may also accept that politics, in absolutist as in other régimes, is ever the art of the possible.

Meanwhile the term need not be jettisoned. As the animating principle of royal government it remains valid. Absolutism may belong to the realm of historical myths when it is used as a label for an entire political system. Properly used, with reference to monarchs like Louis XIV, who certainly saw himself as absolute, it points to a general tendency in the theory and exercise of power. It leads us into a long-vanished political world which had grown around a hierarchy of orders; also to an aristocratic culture whose common ideas were more important than any differences of country, language or even religion. It relates to a time when monarchy was neither popular nor national; to states in the transitional stage between the feudal and bureaucratic. It belongs to the new intellectual order emerging from the ferment of ideas from which came the 'scientific revolution'. It benefited from the great advance in printing technology and from a growing appetite for books about history, politics, theology and philosophy; from the opinion-forming influence of the *salons*; from a better educated and more assiduous clergy and the increasing prestige of the sermon. Richelieu's propaganda machine had been at its service. Working for him, talented writers like Le Bret had contrived to make an intellectually satisfying system out of the mixture of coercion and compromise that was the reality of his government. Whether they liked it or not subjects were becoming familiar with the concept of an impersonal state which could make a prior claim on their allegiance.

Absolutism belongs to a phase of political thought which, emerging from prolonged debate over origins, hypothetical contracts, and resulting sanctions, is marked by a broad measure of agreement over the need for stronger rule, and obedience in subjects. Most important in the French tradition was Jean Bodin (1530–96). His dates show that most of his adult life coincided with the Religious Wars. If absolutism is the child of war – explicitly so in the case of Hobbes[13] for whom it gave rise to 'slaughter, solitude and the want of all things', when 'force and fraud are the two cardinal virtues' – Bodin's absolutism is the child of civil war. If one man were to be selected for prophet, it should be him; if one source, his *Six livres de la République* (1576: ten editions by his death in 1596); if one founding principle, his postulate of a supreme sovereign authority in the state in which are united the legislative, executive and judicial powers. Bodin is discursive, repetitive and prone to take the reader into the byways of astrology and myth, but he had many readers in France and abroad. He is the point of departure for the most significant French seventeenth-century political philosophers: he can be seen in Loyseau, Le Bret and Bossuet. It is therefore important to grasp his approach to the question of sovereignty and to see where it led him. He is Aristotelian in the way he starts with the family as the model for sovereignty in the larger community; French of his troubled time in his concern for order. In a well-ordered state, as in a family, there must be a sovereign authority and 'the principal mark of a sovereign, and also the power, is the right to impose laws generally on all subjects regardless of their consent'. While sovereignty can be vested in a few, comprising an aristocracy, or in the people, the preferable form is the single monarch, for aristocracy breeds faction and democracy leads to anarchy. The monarchy should, moreover, be hereditary since election implies sharing, contracting – therefore limits. Experiencing the Fronde, looking to England – or to Poland – Frenchmen would readily accept these propositions. In its political climate the seventeenth century, with the apogee of monarchy which he did not live to see, belongs to Bodin as much as the eighteenth century was to belong to Montesquieu.[14]

After allowance is made for the extreme ideas of intellectuals who do not have to implement their ideas, there remains a significant degree of harmony between the philosophers and practitioners of government, even when it did not, as in Bossuet's case, arise from shared experience in court or council. Here, however, a warning note should be sounded. Philosophies, fashions in thinking and styles of living, change more rapidly than forms of government. Absolutism is embedded in the humanist culture of the Renaissance, in the exploration of classical literature and philosophy; in respect for rule and proportion in architecture, the search for restraint and purity in language; indeed in the yearning for classical order. Richelieu's *Académie française* is essentially absolutist in spirit. Absolutist values achieved their most striking expression in the grandeur of the baroque. In its French version it was restrained. Exuberance was for southern Europeans. As can be seen in Versailles, the greatest showpiece of the cult, it was heavily dependent on symbolism. Intellectually absolutism owed much to trends in religion, especially the authoritarian tenor of post-Tridentine Catholicism; nearly as much, the visitor to Versailles might think, to classical themes. It was consistent with Cartesian concern with logic and clarity. It would prove vulnerable to the advance of empirical science with its stress on observation and experiment.

Absolutism would eventually be undermined by the contradiction within divine right monarchy which is exposed when it is translated from theory to practice. If it was God's purpose to endow absolute rulers with powers to establish a harmonious and hierarchical political universe, they must recognise the rights and status of their Christian subjects, deriving from their own place in the hierarchy. Even that respectful concern for rights which is to be seen in Louis XIV's mainly conservative government would not be enough to bring the king closer to the society he was committed to protect. Legislative sovereignty supplies him with the power to act creatively. Given the power implicit in the king's commission, and the ultimate weapon of his signature, his agents will try to extend their power and that of the state they serve. When obstructed they will seek to bypass constitutional checkpoints. When necessary they will create new agencies for direct action. Even when the purposes of government are lofty and its conduct responsible, at least in terms of the higher interest they assume, that of the state, they will be exposed and opposed as 'ambitious', their policies 'unnatural', their régime oppressive. Richelieu's ministry and the reaction to it provided precedents both in what could be achieved and what must be avoided. When Louis is his own managing director the most deadly charge against the cardinals, that of 'usurpation' of royal authority, can be avoided. If, however, he should authorise any reform that goes further than mere tinkering with existing systems, he is liable to be seen – and personally – as 'despotic'. That is the familiar cry of those privileged groups manning the checkpoints. They will do everything possible to deflect or block innovating policies. That they do not hold the commanding heights of political thought makes no difference to the tenacity with which they will resist on the ground. There they are entrenched within the gains of history and heartened by their own ideas about community and property. And there they will be until 1789, representing 'the monstrous and contradictory mass of inequalities' denounced by a liberal nobleman in the States General of that first year of revolution which will sweep them away.

THE FRENCH ROYAL TRADITION:
INSPIRATION AND RESTRAINT

The French royal tradition drew upon the country's past, ancestral memories evoking great names and shading into legend, reaching back from Renaissance monarchy, epitomised by Francis I, to Louis XI, conqueror of Burgundy, and to Joan of Arc, saviour of the realm; to another saint, Louis IX, crusader-model for the devout; to Philip Augustus, who recovered Normandy; back through the Capetians to Hugh, first of that name; to Charlemagne and the imperial tradition, and through misty times to Clovis, Christian convert after victory over the Alemanns in 496, and first to make his capital in Paris. The tradition contained everything needed for inspiration and example; also salutary warnings against complacency which had been reinforced by recent experience. It engendered the patriotism expressed by Jacques Auguste de Thou, humanist, diplomat, historian and a central figure during the years when Henry IV was struggling to establish himself. He recalled 'this opinion of the ancients, that one's country is a second divinity, that laws come from God and that those who violate them are sacrilegious parricides'. How are we to envisage royal government in a country which evoked such fervent concern?

There was a variety in the laws, institutions and customs of France comparable to that within the German Empire, that loose confederation of sovereignties still nowhere near to being a political nation. France was such a nation – and had been for centuries – but its nationhood did not consist in the expression of the abstract principles that would be asserted in 1789: uniformity of rights and a sovereignty derived from the will of citizens enjoying such rights. It was grounded in the single fact of the acceptance by subjects of the sovereignty of the king. 'Nation' might convey to educated men and women a culture which was specifically French, together with certain institutions with which they were familiar. When, however, those are examined, it appears that they have no common base beyond allegiance to the king. The sovereign courts of the *Parlement* of Paris, guardian of the 'fundamental law', cherishing the right of registration without which a royal edict had no validity, only had jurisdiction over a third of the realm; there were nine other *parlements* whose status tells the story of the successive stages in the kingdom's growth.

Whether achieved by marriage, escheat or conquest, it had been a slow growth. Involved in each case was some kind of transfer or enhancement of sovereignty but carrying with it throughout the idea of personal allegiance which had belonged to the feudal apanage. The result was a mass of rights as various as the events which had led to the province's absorption into the realm. In Provence, for example, Louis was count, not king. In Brittany, where the duchy had been attached to France by marriage of its duchess Anne successively to Charles VIII and Louis XII (the latter in 1499), he was king; but the province remained stubbornly independent. It was the last province to receive an *intendant* (in 1689) and its Estates were, with those of Languedoc, the other important *pays d'états*, the proudest and most zealous in defence of privilege. In Provence and Burgundy, the representative body was less prestigious but the province retained its valuable rights. In his drive to impose *élections*, with the *taille* levied on income, Richelieu had only managed to secure the change in the Dauphiné. In the other four provinces the officials of the Estates continued to negotiate with the crown the total sum, and to assess and collect the *taille*, otherwise personal, on the basis of property.

So, over an area approximately a third of France, the crown's main tax was levied on a different basis and produced about an eighth of its total yield. At least there some nobles, if they held *terre roturière* (land not classified as noble), paid the *taille*. Elsewhere they were exempt, as were most *bourgeois*, either as office-holders or as citizens in an exempt town. The indirect taxes should have been more equitable since, in theory, they fell on all. In fact there were numerous exceptions and anomalies. The nobility and clergy had gained exemption in the fifteenth century for the products of their domaine lands. The *pays d'états* raised their own indirect taxes and paid a contribution to the crown. As with the *taille* the amount due was arrived at by an annual round of bargaining with the government. Customs duties, *traites*, were levied not only at the frontiers but also between certain provinces, towns and private estates. Covering much of northern and eastern France was an internal customs union, the *Cinq Grosses Fermes*. The diversity of such duties was a serious obstacle to trade. The *aides* were levied mainly on drink but also on selected commodities such as cloth, fish and wood. The most important *aide*, a wine tax, affected both production and distribution from vineyard to tavern: an army of officials struggled to prevent evasion.

It is the *gabelle* which offers us, in one tax, a cameo of the *ancien régime*, its chequered history and present assets and problems. It was the advantage of this salt tax that demand was ubiquitous and steady. The way in which it had grown, yielding by 1661 around a quarter of the yield of the *taille*, having therefore a central place in the royal finances, reflects the piecemeal way, here by conquest, there by concession, in which the kingdom had grown. The *pays de grands gabelles* in the north and centre of France corresponded to the provinces occupied by the English when the tax originated in the fourteenth century: there the salt was stored in royal warehouses and sold at a price set to give producer, merchant and crown a reasonable profit. Every household had to buy a minimum amount a year. That was not the case in the *pays de petites gabelles* where collection was so difficult that government had also to be satisfied with a smaller duty. Certain areas, like Brittany, were exempt altogether, *franc-salé*. Like the *aides* the *gabelle* was farmed out to a consortium or to individuals. Coping with smuggling, armed with stringent royal decrees, their agents crossed the usually vague lines between the interests of the state and the subject, and between the powers, executive, legislative and judicial in a way typical of France, indeed of continental Europe at this time. In two main areas of government, law and finance, Louis XIV's France can be seen to fall short of the uniformity which, since the Revolution which destroyed the *ancien régime*, would be regarded as a criterion of national sovereignty.

The detailed picture of the realm reveals a patchwork of infinite variety. It is not even contained within clearly marked bounds. Neither Alps nor Pyrenees could provide a secure 'natural' frontier when Savoy straddled the Alps and Spain, more dangerously, the Pyrenees. Indeed, apart from sea coasts and some stretches of rivers there was no frontier in the modern sense of a line within which all was French. One should envisage rather a patchwork of estates. The confusion of lands and lordships explains the cardinals' concern, inherited by Louis XIV, for secure bases and the later drive behind the *réunions*.

Within the two main areas, the north covered by customary law, the south showing the influence of Roman codes, there were around 360 local varieties of law. Innumerable private tolls benefited local interests at the expense of the country's economy. Though the fate of Marseille showed that even the grandest city could not defy the crown with impunity, there remained many local exemptions and privileges, usually, like those of Rouen, dating from the terms of first acquisition. Nor, for all its outward parade of the principles of uniformity and conformity, would Louis XIV's government break with traditionally prudent practice. When, for example, Besançon was captured in 1674, its inhabitants were allowed to keep their corporate privileges and promised exemption from the *gabelle*. The story of Colmar, a largely Lutheran town in Alsace, is one of patient work by royal officials to unravel its ties to Imperial jurisdiction and steady pressure on Protestants to conform. So from its conquest in 1673 and the destruction of its walls Colmar gradually became French in institutions, language and character. In Strasbourg, annexed in 1681, Lutherans were allowed free exercise of their religion; they even kept it after that overtly principled act, the Revocation of the Edict of Nantes. Meanwhile, within the frontiers there survived independent, even foreign enclaves. In the Clermontais and the vicomté of Turenne,[15] inhabitants paid their taxes to their suzerain. Avignon was papal territory; Orange belonged to the eponymous prince. Some of the greatest families, Guise, Bouillon, Soissons, had lands outside France for which they owed allegiance. They enjoyed a special status at court as *princes étrangères*. When minded to rebel, as in Richelieu's ministry, again during the Fronde, they had pretext, support and refuge.

So the administrative, judicial map of France records the country's history – but only part of it. As the young king was made painfully aware, the building of the realm had been a protracted operation, marked by crises and reverses, sealed, *faute de mieux*, by concessions which ran counter to recognised principles of government. During the course of the Religious Wars the scattered forces of the crown proved incapable of quelling the Huguenot minority which created a formidable political and military structure. In reaction to the crown's apparent vacillation in the face of heresy Catholic zealots created another organisation, the Holy League, with alternative local systems of control. In the name of higher loyalties, but evoking feudal tradition, magnates pursued their own ambitions, attracting followers who saw better prospects in faction than in royal service. External powers, notably England and Spain, intervened on behalf, respectively, of Huguenots and League. In both camps there were radical theologians who questioned the right of the sovereign to allegiance if he were 'unjust' – in the context a subjective term. Successive sovereigns, Henry III and Henry IV, were assassinated by fanatics, convinced that tyrannicide was their sacred duty. As monarchy suffered so did the people. What might be called 'popular absolut-ism' represented the widespread desire of subjects for a strong arm. *Politiques* demanded that Frenchmen fight not each other but the Spaniard. 'If the king is a devout Catholic and sent by God, it is a matter of indifference to us to which nation he belongs. We are not concerned with the nation but with religion.' Opposed to this typical Leaguer sentiment (1593) was the *politique* author of the *Satire Ménippée*.[16] In the next generation he would be called *bon français*. 'We want a natural, not an artificial king, already made and not still to be made . . . the king we ask for has already been made by nature. He was born in the real garden of the flowers of France, a straight green shoot from the stem of St Louis.' When in 1593 Henry IV renounced his Calvinist faith and espoused Catholicism this 'natural' king became an acceptable king for most Frenchmen. When, however, in 1610, planning war against Spain he fell to Ravaillac's dagger, it was because, to one zealot acting, he thought, for many, he was an apostate. It was a precedent of which Richelieu would have been acutely aware as, enlisting Lutheran Sweden as an ally against Spain, he fell foul of the *dévôts*. The danger on that one flank made all the more import-ant his successful action against the other, the Huguenot. The Edict of Nantes (1598) had granted, perforce, political rights, notably that of fortify-ing towns, which no seventeenth-century ruler would regard as acceptable. Richelieu's suppression of revolt, with the showpiece siege and capture of La Rochelle (1627–28), demonstrated the authority of the state in the face of religious schism and political separatism. It has a place, midway between Henry IV's conversion and Louis XIV's assumption of personal rule, as one of the great landmarks on the way towards absolute monarchy.

The experience of two minorities and regencies, those of Louis XIII and Louis XIV, further reinforced the lessons of history, as Marie de Médicis, then Anne of Austria, struggled to uphold the authority of the crown and to contain the forces of disorder. In the aftermath of civil war both Richelieu and Mazarin were able to exploit the revulsion of sentiment and row with the royalist tide. Richelieu had to employ all the devices of propaganda. Mazarin, eventually, we have seen, had an easier row, though not before wreck and rescue. His young master provided the perfect focus for royalist enthusiasm. In all this period, even when war-finance and rising taxes bore down on the people, even among rebels, peasant or noble, though his minister might be reviled and his officials defied, allegiance to the person of the king was constant. Republicanism was virtually unknown. The most radical *parlement-aires* condemned the English regicides. In part this was simple sentiment. 'The French love their sovereign personally', wrote archbishop Embrun,[17] contrasting them with the Spanish 'who love their state more than their rulers'. The positive aspect of the surviving notion of fealty cannot be dismissed. Louis XIV would promote the development of government more by appealing with new force and attractiveness to personal, feudal aspects of loyalty than by advocating progressive attitudes and procedures. Also traditional and very influential was lawyers' training in the principles of Roman law, with its stress on authority. 'The king of France is Emperor in his realm.' Having been used first to ward off the Holy Roman Emperor, this legal formula was older than the seventeenth century. By then it fairly defines the king's authority. He enjoyed *pleine puissance*. He was sole proprietary of the land of France – though it was left to Louis XIV to amplify this to full ownership of goods as well as of land. He was almost free of obligation to Estates and he was the supreme financial authority. He was the highest judicial authority, the only source of the law which was always administered in his name. He was the living law. As lawyers' old French had it: '*si veult la roi, si veult la loi*'.

Well grounded though it was in sentiment and theory, mainly royalism was just realistic. There was no viable alternative. The States General of 1614–15 had demonstrated its futility as disputes between the orders and incompatible demands nullified any chance of a serious programme of reform and disqualified it for a role in government. Demand for a meeting during the Fronde came, significantly, in the main, from lesser nobles: neither magnates nor *parlementaires* were interested.[18] Once its authority had been restored, the crown could safely ignore the initial fuss. More significantly the movement for a union of *parlements* came to nothing. The legal élite of Paris would rather work with the crown to preserve their privileged position than attempt even an ad hoc working arrangement with their provincial allies. In this judges and royal ministers thought alike, the one group in terms of rights, the other of control. It was out of the question for Louis XIV to carry out wholesale rationalisation. He would accept as natural, if at times exasperating, the discrepancies between provinces and authorities, judicial, fiscal and ecclesiastical, the overlapping lines within which his taxmen, judges and bishops had to work. He would have no option but to accept the individual and family power networks, the *clientèles*[19] which promoted favouritism but also gave government cohesion. There was no realistic alternative but to deal with provincial institutions and their dominant members through working within the networks of family and officialdom. The face and voice of monarchy, and the essential idea behind it, was absolutist. The rhetoric was compelling, the sanctions formidable. But the crown had to operate through the numerous bodies which stood, at all levels, between it and the people. Its main activities were still, as during the régime of the cardinals, those of diplomacy: estimating the other side's strength and resources – what it could actually deliver – and using persuasion, bribery or coercion as the situation appeared to require. There was no 'civil service' in the modern sense. Instead, at the heart of public life, representing government, affecting all its activities, was the greatest of vested interests: its own creation through regular sales, the army of office-holders, some 46,000 strong in Colbert's reckoning in 1661.[20]

Venal office regarded as property might be detrimental to sound finance and administration. This will become apparent when the work of Colbert is considered. In political terms it was actually a support to the crown. Richelieu, the man most responsible for its rapid expansion, had seen the paradox when he described it as 'a disorder that was part of the order of the state'. Its existence insured the state against radical constitutional change. The independence that came from effective ownership of valuable offices, noble title, family traditions stretching back usually through several generations, produced a proud and independent spirit that brought periodic stress to dealings with the crown, occasionally, as during the Fronde, to serious conflict. In self-esteem *parlementaires* were the weightiest political class in Europe. But the fact that they, with other members of sovereign courts, and *trésoriers*, were the greatest of office-holders, having therefore the greatest stake in the régime and interest in its being law-abiding and peaceful, meant that there could be no serious revolutionary intent.

PARLEMENT AND GALLICANISM

It is not surprising therefore that the symbiotic relationship between crown and *Parlement*, was also a prime source of absolutist theory. Apologists for the crown, Loyseau, Priézac, Balzac,[21] most notably Le Bret, were not academics but jurists, insiders who understood the system, making a case but working within the bounds of the possible, in touch with political reality. 'The greatest political theorist of his generation' (Bonney), Le Bret, who maintained that sovereignty, though 'anchored to the common good' was a supreme power which gave the ruler 'the right to command absolutely', was an *intendant* before he became *avocat-général*. It was when he was Richelieu's hard pressed commissioner to the Estates of Brittany that he enunciated the fundamental principle that privileges were held 'purely out of the liberality of our kings'. In the period between 1610 and 1661 which saw the cardinals pressing forward with the absolutist agenda, but also two minorities which encouraged *Parlement* to recover ground, there were two main but related areas of dispute, the political and the judicial. The judges fought to preserve the element in the crown's sovereignty represented by their guardianship of the 'fundamental laws' and right to register royal edicts after prior scrutiny. Liable to be disputed here was the right claimed by the more radical to refuse registration or to insist on modification. They fought more consistently to preserve their prestige (and fees) as judges, and the value of their offices, against royal encroachment. This occurred on four fronts. They were the wholesale creations of new offices, the commissioning of special courts, the extensive use of *intendants* and the evoking of certain cases direct to the royal council. Along with the crown's increasing use of *lettres de cachet*, the wrongs of other groups of officers and a number of specific grievances, those concerns could be said broadly to represent *Parlement*'s case in 1648. In such periods of conflict both sides would make general statements about their powers. The king's standard claim was not about absolute sovereignty but his standing as the fount of all justice. *Parlement*'s, naturally, was to be the guardian of that justice as, they asserted, previous kings had required them to be. It is of the nature of debate that some claims are pushed to extremes. It is also usual among lawyers for cases to be pursued with logic and tenacity. It was characteristic of the culture that produced – and was influenced by – Descartes and Pascal[22] that history and custom should be subsumed in systematic theoretical constructions. Absolutism, as practice, had evolved within the bounds of traditional sovereignty. Absolutism, as theory, gave the appearance of a coherent system to what, in effect, it would always be, an untidy set of compromises worked out between individual royal servants, struggling to overcome inertia, raise money and carry out reforms, and the vested interests which clung to the status quo.

The way in which constitutional questions, practical politics and theories of government could interact to the advantage of the crown is illustrated by the history of Gallicanism. For this prolonged saga of conflict between Papal decrees and 'Gallican liberties' there are two points of departure: the Concordat of Bologna (1516) and the start of what was to turn out to be the Lutheran reformation in 1517. The Concordat, following Francis I's military triumph in Italy, gave the crown almost complete control over the disposal of the higher positions in the French church. It was a major reason why neither he nor his successor Henry II was tempted to follow the English king Henry VIII's example and break decisively with Rome. Meanwhile, however, Lutheranism, by replacing the sovereignty of Rome with that of the ruler, the hopefully designated 'godly prince', added significant rights and sanctions to the idea of Divine Right. Control of the church meant the opportunity to acquire lands and increase revenues. In Catholic France too there were economic aspects to its sometimes tense, always ambiguous relations with the papacy. Supreme authority over the church was divided between Pope, the bishop-dominated Assembly of the Clergy and the King. The Pope's authority in France was compromised by the Italian-Spanish predominance in the College of Cardinals and by his own ambivalent position, involving him in Italian politics and wars, as both spiritual head claiming *plena potestas*, and a territorial power. Meanwhile the substantial fact was that French bishops usually owed their promotion to the crown. If they needed a reason for according a uniquely independent status to their king they could find it in the well-worn formula: 'the kings of France are so pleasing to God that He chose them to become His lieutenants on earth'. The standing of the 120 French bishops was weakened by lay patronage, by the local concerns of cathedral chapters and the independence of the regular orders. In the ordering of rituals, choice of catechisms and even interpretation of doctrine they did, however, enjoy considerable freedom, even after the belated acceptance of the decrees of the Council of Trent, because *Parlement* steadily blocked the directives of Rome. Bishops usually sought a middle path, keeping a convenient distance from Rome but standing on their dignity as regards *Parlement*. Some judges there reflected the experience of the Religious Wars in their *politique* attitude; some were sternly anti-Jesuit. After the elder Arnauld had led the opposition to the restoration of the Jesuits in Henry IV's reign, the prejudice became a family tradition, affecting crucially the nature of Jansenism. Few judges dissented, however, on the main tenet of *parlementaire* Gallicanism: Papal bulls should be re-formulated as royal edicts, then submitted to scrutiny. On occasion the lawyers provided the crown with a valuable weapon, as over the *régale*[23] issue which brought Louis XIV close to schism. The precedents thus established could be embarrassing, as when Louis needed Papal support for his campaign against the Jansenists – then found himself opposed, and the Papal bull blocked, by *Parlement*. Matters were sometimes complicated by the attitude of the Sorbonne which claimed the special right to pronounce on theology; that led to disputes with both Papacy and *Parlement*.

The support Louis received from most French bishops for his anti-Papal policy culminated in the Gallican Articles of 1682, with their uncompromising declaration: 'kings and sovereigns are not subject in any temporal matter to any ecclesiastical power by the order of God'. Later in the reign Louis would squander the advantage he had derived, in domestic authority, if not international standing, from his stand against the Pope. Meanwhile, habituating Frenchmen to think of Louis as effective head of the church in France, adding a further dimension to the doctrines of Divine Right, Gallicanism made a vital contribution to royal absolutism.

All seems to come together in the remarkable career of Jacques-Bénigne Bossuet,[24] the co-author of the Gallican Articles. Most high-minded of courtiers, most firmly moderate of Catholic theologians, Bossuet was not, as would first appear, the most orthodox of political philosophers. Born into a Burgundian *parlementaire* family, educated by the Jesuits, he was appointed tutor to the Dauphin in 1670. In 1680 his tutorship ended and he was made bishop of Meaux. As a preacher his majestic prose, with its exuberant descriptive flights, carried conviction because it embellished arguments that were logical and disciplined in structure. He exulted in the potential for kingship under God: 'The royal throne is the very throne of God', and again: 'Majesty is the image of the greatness of God in a prince.' Yet he had the moral authority, and nerve, with the king sitting before him, to condemn adultery. He was a staunch controversialist, defender of Catholic orthodoxy against all comers: Luther and Calvin in his *Histoire des Variations*; within the Catholic camp Malebranche's[25] neo-Cartesian attack on Divine providence; later Fénelon's 'quietism'. Though he acknowledged the power of Hobbes's *Leviathan* (1651), he rejected absolutely the rational case for absolutism grounded, by Hobbes, on the depressing premise that man was impelled in all his actions by the instinct for self-preservation.

Few were better placed than Bossuet to study court and government, in particular to observe and assess the king. He made good use of his point of vantage. Formally for the benefit of the Dauphin, but really, of course, for a wider readership, he offered, in his *Discours sur l'histoire universelle* and *Politique tirée des propres paroles de l'écriture sainte*,[26] a vision of Louis XIV's monarchy as the apogee of human history and a model anticipated and sanctioned by the Old Testament. In his way of proceeding 'geometrically' through a logical series of propositions buttressed with fragments of scripture, he shows himself to be a disciple of Descartes. He approved his method though critical of the use to which it was put by the neo-Cartesians, putting reason before revelation in their analysis of the Bible. It is in his reliance in the *Politique* on the Bible, and in particular the books of Kings and Chronicles in the Old Testament, that Bossuet is original, indeed Judaic rather than conventionally Christian in his argument. The Bible was little read by French Catholics, but for Bossuet it was *un livre parfait*. Scripture showed him 'the original principles which have formed empires'. There he saw 'the government of a people whose legislator was God himself'. He opened the *Politique* with the claim that Moses, 'instructed by Divine Wisdom' was 'moved to form the wisest of all empires and to bring it to the last degree of certainty and perfection'. That is – his readers would surely assume – until the arrival of Louis XIV, called to rule 'the most Christian house of France . . . after 700 years, an established monarchy . . . the most illustrious realm there ever was on earth in the sight of God or man'. When he promotes the idea of a 'special providence' from which France, like the Jews under the Covenant, has specially benefited, Bossuet reveals himself the good Frenchman. He is so confident, under God, about the essential rightness of the absolutist régime – and his place in it – that he can use the language of Divine grace to express the special favour shown to Louis, for example, in his marriage. 'It is God who gives great births, great marriages, children and posterity.' He is so far from objective in his reading of the Old Testament that he seems to idolise king David, seeing him as the spiritual ancestor of Louis XIV. As David was guardian of 'the order of the ministry and of all the functions of the priests . . . according to the law of Moses', so Louis XIV was of Christianity, in his actions against heretic Huguenots.

Bossuet is rightly the man most closely associated with the idea of Divine Right. There was nothing new about the mystique of consecrated monarchy. Shakespeare appreciated it when he made Richard II maintain that 'not all the waters from the rough rude sea can wash the balm from an anointed king'. God's blessing on the *fleur de lis* was a favourite theme of Valois publicists as the English gave up their hold on France. It was at the heart of the coronation service in both countries. It now had real political meaning and force. Its central tenet, that the king was God's lieutenant on earth, answered several needs. It provided continuity from the anointing and the solemn vows of the Coronation to the occasions in the reign when Louis, never shrinking from this role, spoke and acted as one responsible for the church in his domains. Divine Right lifted loyal sentiment to a higher plane. It offered an answer to the central question of sovereignty so bitterly fought over in Stuart England and eased the way for great nobles to accept the paramount claims of the state. The king, divinely ordained, in any process of government where there might be a question of rights, corporate or individual, could invoke a higher authority, above man-made laws and conventions. Hard to judge, but worth pondering, is the effect it had on the king himself.

'A DELIGHTFUL BUSINESS'

No one could fail to see the unwavering application to the business of ruling, which he professed to enjoy but which must often have been onerous. Did he not see government, under God, in terms of duty and responsibility? In the principles of Divine Right there was a source of strength for government and an inspiration to the ruler. There were also, as would become clear, dangerous implications. The king was being offered a book of blank cheques when he could interpret his own convictions – and prejudices – as the will of God. The more closely he was identified with the church as favourite son and self-constituted guardian, and the more he gained through its commanding position, the more he would lose when that was challenged. When policies failed, battles were lost, or, most seriously, when influential opinion, following intellectual trends, turned towards rationalism and relativism, his ideological stance, combined with his personal direction of government, left him vulnerable to criticism. We will see that isolating, disillusioning process exemplified in Bossuet's later career. The preacher laureate of Versailles, the most eloquent voice, not only for the rationale of absolutism but for its pervading sentiment, the man who saluted the Revocation of the Edict of Nantes as 'the miracle of our times', would end his days embattled in defence of orthodox faith against double attack: from the mystically inclined who claimed not to need the orthodox services of the church, and from sceptics who challenged a version of history in which all came together in glorious fulfilment in the reign of Louis XIV.

Such troubles could hardly be imagined at the personal reign's bright dawn. The sun shone and would be a fitting, though far from original motif for anticipated years of glory. To royalist tradition, the country's history, recent turbulence and present consensus and the cumulatively persuasive effect of royalist propaganda, add peace after twenty-five years of war, with substantial gains of territory. To the significant political precedents from the régime of the cardinals add the experienced ministerial team bequeathed by Mazarin – and, all in all, it will seem to have been a hopeful time.

The real nature of Louis's power and the ways in which he would exercise it are the central themes of this study. During a long reign it might be expected that structures would evolve and practices change. There were important extensions of royal government in certain areas, economy, war, police, poor relief, for example, and with them , in the powers of the *intendants*. The setting changed. Only from 1682 was Versailles the permanent base of both court and government, and that date conveniently marks a point of transition to the settled routine and style associated with the name of the palace. The year before, Mme de Maintenon,[27] governess to his illegitimate children, became Louis XIV's mistress; in 1683, though secretly, she became his wife. In that year Colbert died. Heroism in war featured largely among the values promoted by the palace, but these events seem in retrospect to indicate the passing of the heroic phase in Louis's personal reign. In the first decades everything seemed possible: the accomplishment of all military aims, genuine economic reforms, comprehensive legal codes, patronage of the arts and sciences on an unprecedented scale.

Matching the heroic, expansive mood was the behaviour of the young king, enjoying without inhibition the rites of spring, but also sincerely admired for the professional and steady way in which he rose to the challenges of government. Handsome, gracious, courteous, spirited, hard-working, above all competent: these adjectives fairly represent contemporary opinion. Unprecedented political authority had an attractive human face. We might see faults, especially his tendency to measure all state activities by the extent to which they enhanced his glory, and his readiness to 'unleash the hounds of war'. Even if recognised, they would be more easily forgiven by those who subscribed to his notion of glory, rushed to join in the hunt and, after easy first kills, bayed for more.

The change of the 1680s in the outward face of the régime and in its manners, personified in Louis by a middle-aged respectability and a more rigorous piety, but also by a growing insensitivity to the opinion of others, is in one respect delusive. At the heart of the régime, in government's forms and functions, *la mécanique* of Saint-Simon's phrase, there was a striking degree of continuity. From the first day Louis worked at perfecting his *métier*, both in council and before the court. It is as if he resolved never to forget that he was king and never to allow his subjects to forget it. Regular habits, self-discipline and a rigid separation of the intimate and personal aspects of life from the public and professional, are impressive aspects of his performance. We may wonder at what human cost the performance was perfected, not obviously to him, but surely to the young women who had to learn that the price of the king's love was that it could not be for ever, had to be concealed and should in no way affect the routines of his day or his formal relationship with the queen. He would consider that a woman's feelings mattered little in relation to the interests of the state, and to the personal needs of the man on whom the state depended. The court would, of course, concur. They regarded Louise de la Vallière,[28] his mistress of the first decade, 'the shrinking violet', who seemed innocently loving and undemanding in a situation she had not sought, and her successor, Mme de Montespan,[29] beautiful, intelligent, competitive and better fitted to enjoy her privileged position, as the most fortunate of women.

From contemporary accounts, however much they may differ, it is possible to recapture some aspects of Louis's daily performance, at the Tuileries, more usually at Saint-Germain, at the vast building site of Versailles where Le Vau's first palace was largely built by 1668, or during wartime summers. In camp he would still be accompanied by wife, mistress and leading courtiers. The word 'performance' is apt because he was aware of the need to act a part and project an image. He was around five feet, four inches, strong-featured, with full mouth and the long Bourbon nose – but less prominent or curved than Henry IV's. He wore high-heeled shoes to give extra height – but not yet the full wig adopted when he lost his hair. Undoubtedly he cut an imposing figure. He rode well, fenced skilfully and – most important in one who was constantly 'on parade' – he moved easily and gracefully. Like his father he was particularly fond of dancing, and one of his first acts was to establish a school of dancing in Paris. For some years he took a part in the masques and ballets at court and saw to it that he had opportunities to lead and shine. The birth of the Dauphin in 1662 was celebrated at the Tuileries with a sumptuous frolic, part ballet, part circus, in which Louis appeared as a Roman Emperor, followed by squadrons of 'Persians' under Monsieur, 'Turks' under Condé, 'Indians' under Enghien and 'American Indians' under Guise. In May 1664 the court was bidden to Versailles, still essentially his father's hunting box, to enjoy the *plaisirs de l'île enchantée*, a three-day festival on the theme of Roland Furieux. There were cavalcades, declamations, pageants, tilting, ballets, plays, notably Molière's *Princesse d'Elide* and *Tartuffe*, music composed and arranged by Lully, fireworks and banquets. Art, display and revel, and, for once, royal patronage with no overt political message – nothing quite like it had happened before and nothing could better express the exuberance of the time.

Trained to give nothing away, Louis already cultivated the detachment that would become second nature. Mme de Motteville,[30] a seasoned observer, saw him to be 'polite and readily approachable but with a lofty and serious air which impressed all with respect and awe and prevented even his most confidential advisers from forgetting his position'. He spoke slowly and picked his words with care. He adapted his comment to the person. He smiled pleasantly, but rarely laughed. He would not have scorned the idea that he was '*un roi de théâtre*' because he knew that he was putting on a necessary show: that he managed so well suggests that it gave him much satisfaction. The show was not yet continuous but he was already showing an actor's poise and timing. The man who would require that his mistresses conceal their pregnancies and make arduous journeys whatever their state would doff his hat to a maid as to a duchess. All were equally his subjects. But no one's discomfort should disoblige the king. There was a message in the manners.

Even more deliberate was his habitual response to petitioners: 'we will see'. It conveys the prudence of a man who must always be in control, who has to be on his guard against impulse, who knows that patronage is his most powerful weapon and must not be cheapened. He was neither particularly clever nor imaginative; he read little outside official documents. He ensured, however, that he was well informed about the personal circumstances of those around him, the women as well as the men, but especially the ranks and prospects of officers in the army of which he was so proud. He would know more generally about bishops and diplomats than he would of lawyers, financiers or other officials. In short his vision was an aristocratic one: nobles, at least if they attended court, saw most of his benevolent side.

Whatever the restraints, Louis's sovereignty, was shared with no body or individual. Yet it was limited, we have seen, by practical obstacles; by his own sense of what was due to tradition in the form of fundamental law, and by his innate caution and conservatism. If society was not ready for truly radical initiatives, nor was the king. In this aspect a representative Frenchman of his time, he was imbued with the idea that his place at the summit of the hierarchy required respect for the occupants of each inferior niche. So he accepted broadly what he had inherited, requiring only order where there had been disorder and clear lines of authority stretching, without question or interference, from the king. It was what lay behind the gracious manners, the firm face he presented to the world, and his self-esteem. A case can indeed be made for the proposition that his idea of government came down to such exertion of authority, and such use of the apparatus, as was needed to provide the resources for the war, diplomacy and civil projects that would win glory for himself and the dynasty. In this reductionist view control of the state was but a means to an end. Thus stated the proposition takes us but a short way to understanding Louis's own appreciation of kingship, his instinctive need to exercise control and mastery and the distinctive style resulting that made it so influential. Nor does it convey adequately the ideals and expectations of those around him.

Louis's deepest concerns and the spirit of his régime are revealed in his use of patronage and propaganda. The image, which we will see perfected in Versailles, is certainly not all. There were to be substantial achievements. Nor, however, will the image turn out to be superficial, mere decoration or camouflage. The king's serious idea of himself as leading actor in a continuing play informed his whole rule. He believed in grandeur and splendour as prime constituents of power. If he had genius – at least in the sense of an infinite capacity for taking pains – it lay in the formal performance of kingly duties, those of theatre and those of administration. They may appear to belong to separate compartments but they were really, to his mind, parts of a whole: an absolutely single-minded career of service. It was this that so impressed his ministers and courtiers, and influenced foreign contemporaries. The man had weight, presence and a constant sense of purpose; the royal state was thereby empowered.

It can still surprise us, as it did Louis's courtiers, that this king, with so much to please him, not only took seriously the business of government but actually enjoyed the long hours spent in council and reading reports. 'Grand, noble and delicious' is how he described the *métier de roi*. It was to this labour of love that he was born: 'it is by hard work that one rules, for hard work that one rules'. But he claimed no remarkable gift beyond his sense of vocation: 'the function of kings consists primarily of using good sense, which always comes naturally and easily'. Rules meant much to him: 'I made it a rule to work regularly twice a day for two to three hours at a time with various persons beside the hours that I worked alone or might give to extraordinary affairs if such arose.' Ministers had to understand that no important matter would escape his eye: 'I commanded the four secretaries of state to sign nothing in future without discussing it with me, and the same for the *surintendant*.' Significantly, in view of Fouquet's downfall, he proposed special vigilance in finance, where nothing was to be transacted 'without its being noted in a special book that was to remain with me'. He recognised the way in which patronage could work for the crown – but also against its interests when powerful patrons built up their own *clientèles*. 'All requests for graces of any type had to be made directly to me, and I granted to all my subjects the privilege of appealing to me at any time.' Intending to be, in reality, his own first minister, he would keep his ministers on their toes. 'As to the persons who were to help me in my work . . . in order to concentrate the whole authority of a master more fully in myself . . . I resolved to enter into [details] with each of the ministers when he would least expect it.' It is perhaps the most revealing of all his statements of intent. He had grasped at the outset a vital aspect of team leadership. Ministers acted in the name of the king; it was to be no empty phrase. The king would know what was going on. It was to be the basis of an extraordinary phase in the history of government. After Fouquet no minister was disgraced. Pomponne,[31] who was dismissed was later re-appointed. Several, like Colbert and the two Le Telliers served until their deaths. Between 1661 and 1715 ministerial position was occupied by only sixteen men.

COUNCILS AND MINISTERS

The word 'team' is appropriate for the inner circle of ministers and secretaries of state. Each of the four secretaries of state, besides any special ministerial brief – Lionne's, for example, for foreign affairs – had responsibility for certain provinces. An early action was to reduce the size of the more unwieldy royal council of his predecessors to a council of three which came to be known, from its meeting in an upper floor of the palace, as the *conseil d'en haut*. At the outset, providing continuity, there were Mazarin's men, Le Tellier, Lionne and Fouquet. In September Colbert replaced Fouquet. Here, meeting most mornings, more often when there was urgent business, the greater policy decisions were taken. Finance was dealt with in the *conseil des finances*. Set up in September 1661 it met twice a week. As understanding grew between Colbert and the king it tended to take important decisions informally before presenting them to the council. In this way, without burdening himself too much with the detail, the king remained abreast of all questions affecting the revenue and the wider economy.

The largest council, dealing with domestic affairs, was the *conseil des dépêches*. It dealt with the reports that flowed in from royal officials in the provinces. At first the king, then usually the chancellor presided, attended by secretaries of state, and also, if they wished, by the princes of the blood. The latter might appear therefore to be participating in royal government. Face was saved. In reality they were excluded from the process that counted. They had no formal share in what they, like the king, would regard as the major concerns of government. That is not, however, to say that individual grandees had no influence. The king was a good listener, specially, it might be added, when the opinion offered matched his own. A Turenne,[32] a Villeroi, latterly, specially, Beauvillier – who did sit in council – and Chevreuse[33] – might be consulted privately. But on the essential principle, that his ministers, the engine of government, sat, not by virtue of the office of secretary of state that they had bought, but by his mandate and under his direction, there was to be no compromise. To that extent this was a new style of government.

The veteran Séguier, who had been Richelieu's iron chancellor and a significant figure during Mazarin's time, was now less important as the king became more directly involved and ministers assumed greater powers. For all his prestige as former war minister it was the same for his successor, Le

Tellier (1677–85). It seems, however, that the *conseil des dépêches* did not decline with the chancellor's office. Its work actually increased with the advance of government. It acted as mediator in provincial struggles, monitor in church affairs, coordinator of patronage and was an essential part of the machinery that kept the state intact during the last years of the reign.

Between 1664 and 1676 and from 1701 there was a *conseil de commerce*. Throughout the reign an informal group, Anne's *conseil de conscience* re-born, dealt mainly with ecclesiastical appointments and came to consist generally of the king, his confessor and the archbishop of Paris. In these respects Louis was acting traditionally, setting up ad hoc bodies, improvising to meet need. Moreover, even in council, decisions were essentially judgements; only through the subsequent dispatch of letters by the appropriate secretary of state were they translated into the administrative orders that we view as the hallmark of modern government .

Louis had been an apt pupil of Mazarin in political affairs; he had a good understanding of diplomatic principles and knowledge of the current scene; he had an excellent memory. Yet he does not seem to have been imaginative. Subtle in petty matters he could be insensitive to the point of blindness in the judgement of major issues. Is it therefore probable that he was influenced more than he realised by advisers who had their own agendas to pursue? It was his custom to hear all his ministers' arguments, state his opinion, then decide in line with the majority. When they had heard what he thought, would ministers be likely to oppose him? Was it not a condition of their long tenure of office that they should strive to please the king? No minister was more outspoken – or in a stronger position to be so – than Colbert. Yet he came round to the king's view about war with Holland in 1672, having originally opposed it. Louis knew that he could not be master of all departments of government. There was always that persisting streak of realism. He was attentive therefore to experts. His sympathy lay, however, with those who shared his values, and any minister who had private reservations had, at some point, to choose between suppressing them and risking office, career and family. Before the death of Lionne, in 1671, Louis was starting to make his own bellicose foreign policy. Since war had an immediate and direct effect on the finances and so, eventually, on the economy as a whole, Louis was therefore, in effect, subjecting his realm to its outcome. Territorial gains were sought at the expense of higher taxes in as arbitrary a way as if he had been the autocrat that he was determined not to be. Revoking the Edict of Nantes in 1685, he proceeded from conviction, fortified by the evidence that his action was approved at court – in 1685 undoubtedly by the Catholic population at large – and not opposed by his ministers. He would indeed have been a prescient and prudent sovereign if he had resisted in either case the urge to improve upon what he saw as the legacy of the cardinals.

Louis was encouraged to believe that his procedures were justified by the undoubted expertise of his ministerial team. Each had been tested in dark days. Hugues de Lionne (1611–71) was responsible for foreign policy. Nephew of Abel Servien who had been a principal negotiator for the cardinals, he had been an invaluable client to Mazarin during the Fronde and had enjoyed a leading role thereafter. He was now a veteran of the treaty-making, with its tedious, nerve-testing preliminaries, which, under Mazarin's direction, had brought such valuable gains. No one had a better understanding of the interests of states and rulers. His intelligence shines out of his dispatches, instructions to envoys abroad, and letters, written often in his own hand, to foreign rulers. He had the courage to remain loyal to the fallen Fouquet. We cannot know if he would have proved a restraining influence in 1672. His successor, Pomponne, for all his diplomatic skills, carried less weight in council.

Michel le Tellier (1603–85) had been war minister since 1643. He had been responsible for the raising and deployment of troops under the most testing circumstances. Mazarin had secured his promotion because he was impressed by his robust performance as *intendant de l'armée* in Piedmont. He had flourished under Mazarin's patronage and helped sustain his cause during the minister's exile. Louis's diligent reforming minister was by now head of a bureaucratic dynasty, fortified by acquisitions of *seigneuries* and by several noble marriages (including his own), a widening circle of family appointments in church and state, and a large *clientéle*. In 1656 he purchased the marquisate of Louvois from which his son, François-Michel le Tellier (1641–91) took his title. From 1664 he shared the office of secretary of state with his son, then only 23. Louvois's head start, his father's careful training, his own ambition and capacity, ensured continuity in the reform and enlargement of the royal army, and the continuing favour of the king. His father became chancellor in 1675. By then Louvois was already, in effect, war minister and, till his death in 1691, arguably the most influential in council. Certainly that was the case after Colbert's death in 1683.

Jean-Baptiste Colbert (1619–83) was one of the greatest of Frenchmen, perhaps, after Richelieu, the greatest of ministers. Like Richelieu – for him always 'the great cardinal' – he displayed, during his single-minded pursuit of high office, a ruthless willingness to destroy the man who stood in his way. Like Richelieu too he came to power with a clear idea of what he intended to do with it. The trend of modern scholarship is to stress the obstacles to reform and innovation, political, economic or judicial, and the limited nature of Colbert's achievement.[34] The régime that was destroyed in 1789 was indeed, in many respects, that of 1661. Colbert was sustained by the appreciative support of the king over two decades; at the same time he was thwarted by the nature of the régime to whose values he so enthusiastically subscribed. All that may be granted, and his failures allowed for; yet his vision was comprehensive, his commitment total, his application heroic, his talent for administration prodigious. It is only when compared to what he planned and envisaged that his achievement overall can be called disappointing or 'limited'.

Like that of Le Tellier, the family venture that led to Colbert's ascendancy offers a glimpse of a competitive high bourgeois culture in which the capital amassed in trade and converted into office, and the appetite it roused, were now directed towards the opportunities of royal service. The family, originally from Reims, had grown rich through international trade, financial dealings and accumulations of office. Ever extending their contacts through business deals and marriages, the several branches seem to have acted almost like a single firm. What was good for one must be good for the family; the most promising member of the firm must be promoted so that he could bring the rest up with him. Colbert was one of nine surviving out of eighteen. Each had to play his or her part – if it was only to save money from the expected dowry: while one daughter married a *trésorier*; four others entered convents. Though he had, since 1631, a financial office in Paris which brought useful entrée into the world of *traitants* and *partisans*, those whom Richelieu called 'a separate class, prejudicial to the state, but necessary', Nicolas Colbert was not remarkable. His son was. He pushed – and was pushed. Through the influence of his cousin Saint-Pouange he became an aide to Le Tellier. During the Fronde he acted first as a go-between between Le Tellier and Mazarin. Its emergencies suited his mole-like ways: he tunnelled extensively; casts did not always reveal his whereabouts. Transferred to Mazarin's service he toiled to enlarge his master's fortune. In the process, becoming expert himself in exploitation and chicanery, he learned about the weaknesses in the system that made it possible.

Entrenched in council after Fouquet's fall, master of financial policy, Colbert only acquired the title of *contrôleur-général* in 1665. In the same year he became *surintendant des maisons* and *surintendant du commerce*. When in 1669 he became secretary of state for the *Marine*, and for the *Maison du Roi*, he acquired a range of authority – embracing many of the departments of modern government – that appeared to make him master in the entire economic sphere. In a limited sense he had been that already, since that was how he envisaged his role, and his undisputed authority in finance led inevitably to incursions into most areas of expenditure: only the army and foreign policy – crucial exceptions – were completely outside his control. Meanwhile his own family advanced in his wake. His younger brother, Colbert de Croissy (1625–96), became an *intendant*, was given important diplomatic tasks, then succeeded Pomponne as foreign minister in 1679, ensuring the future strength of the clan in council. An uncle, Henri de Pussort, was given a leading role in the drawing up of the legal codes. One son, taking his name from the family marquisate of Seignelay, was trained to take on the marine portfolio: he became a minister in 1689. When Seignelay's cousin, Colbert de Torcy (1665–1746), became foreign minister the family interest was assured till the end of the reign. For another son there was a distinguished ecclesiastical career. Three daughters married into the high sword nobility. Some *bourgeois* attributes the Colberts and Le Telliers might evince: not least their spirit of self-improvement. To see them as '*bourgeois* ministers' is, however, absurd. Though jealous voices might murmur they had, by any standard, attained aristocratic status. No less than three of Colbert's sons died in war; few families had a finer record. The king smiled on their great marriages – as if he wished to draw together his principal subjects in a single élite.

Though no individual of the family achieved the distinction of the great ministers, the record of the Phélypeaux[35] dynasty, older in state service than the Le Telliers or Colberts, serves to broaden our picture of the kind of service that the oligarchs of high office, supported by their networks of financiers and *parlementaires*, could give to a necessitous crown. At best it can be seen as a collaboration, mutually advantageous but limiting, with a deadening tendency from its being so heavily biased towards maintenance of the bureaucratic and financial status quo: this would become increasingly clear in the eighteenth century. There was a Phélypeaux in government in 1610. One or other of the two branches, La Vrillière and Pontchartrain, supplied a secretary of state without a break from then till the Revolution. Under Louis XIV there were five. No signature on royal edicts occurs more often under that of the king – or in place of the king's. One after another trod the corridors of power, but discreetly and in a way that makes it hard to weigh their importance. Though Jérôme de Pontchartrain was an efficient secretary for the navy in stringent times, only one of the family, his brother Louis, became a minister: ten years *contrôleur-général* (1689–99), then chancellor till 1714.

THE INTENDANTS

It was Louis XIV's decision to govern himself, without first minister, that gave confidence, cohesion and energy to his ministers. The decision would, however, have been a risky one, if government had not already been relatively well-organised, more so than in 1610 or 1624, or even in 1642, when Richelieu died. It is possible to see the advance of royal government to this point in negative terms. Consider the defeat of the great nobles as a political force prepared to challenge the crown to the point of rebellion, the corresponding reduction in the powers of governors (though they could still play an important part), for some towns the loss of independence, and the apparent retreat of the sovereign courts from any claim to participate in affairs of state – and repression will seem to be the unifying theme. But these salient achievements together amount to an opportunity for the state to play a more positive part. Involved crucially in each part of the absolutist process, and having the potential for creative government, were the *intendants*, with the invaluable weapon of the crown commission.[36] Their recall had been a prime demand of the *frondeurs*; their restoration, tentative at first, an indication that the Fronde was finished.

In the *Code Michaud*[37] (1629) the role of *intendants* had been formally defined: they were then seen primarily as fact-finders on mission. Richelieu's view was enlarged first by the sequence of conspiracy and revolt, then by the demands of war, until he saw them as essential instruments of government. The *intendant* found himself at the rough end of the evolving body of public law. Regularly urged by ministers to act the *intendant* found that he was relatively free to act decisively because he was bound by few considerations beyond that of *raison d'état*, as spelt out in the terms of his commission. In legal terms his powers derived from that part of the king's justice, *justice retenue*, which could be granted – and withdrawn. A further advantage to the crown was that the *intendant* operated outside the well-protected world of venal office-holders. He would have bought his office as *maître des réquêtes*, but his commission as *intendant* was an appointment for a limited period (typically three years) and for specific purposes. This was a manageable instrument of government without the risks that went otherwise with delegation of local powers.

During the 1630s and 1640s *intendants* became a normal part of provincial government. By 1635 it had become the rule that there should be one in every *généralité*. With expenditure, mainly on war, running at around 25 million *livres* above disposable income, and growing dependence on borrowing, office sales and other short-term expedients, ministers concluded that the existing system must be reformed to ensure fair and efficient collection. In 1642 Richelieu defied the financial establishment by a measure both desperate and radical: the power to assess the *taille* was transferred to *intendants*. Even backed by special armed brigades they could claim only limited success. Clearly in the front line, agents of 'fiscal terrorism', they were more exposed than ever to attack. With the Fronde the *trésoriers* and *élus* went back to their former role. Nor did they lose it afterwards, though under closer supervision. Meanwhile the *intendants* were given ever wider powers.

Intendants were drawn mainly from the Parisian magistracy, the class most affected by the *dévôt* spirit of the time and aware of the paramount need for observance of the law and the protection of the poor. The Fronde had already shown contrasting aspects of society: the savagery of war, the spiritual ardour of Port Royal and the humanity of Vincent de Paul and his relief workers. After the Fronde there was a yearning for the rule of law that looked beyond its fiscal benefits. It is improbable, anyway, that Louis and his ministers would have made that kind of distinction: were not social disorder and plummeting tax returns two sides of the same coin? Most disturbances originated in efforts to raise taxes. More generally they showed determination to uphold local institutions, customs and officials against the outsider. Experience showed that when government was weak violence paid. In some areas, like the Limousin plateau, during the fifties, peasants paid virtually no taxes. Tax farmers and their agents lived dangerously. Innkeepers were chary of giving them lodging. An attempt to distrain goods or imprison a defaulter could quickly rouse a mob of neighbours who would then be sympathetic, perhaps imaginative witnesses in a subsequent trial. A pregnant woman knocked out as she clutched her cooking pot; a priest abused by soldiers, becoming a Christ-like figure in the description of loyal parishioners – such accounts fill the archives of law courts. More serious than the lead often given by *curés* and *seigneurs* was the evident complicity of lawyers. In the running war in the south-west over the *gabelle*, for example, courts might refuse to prosecute or actually encourage resistance by the way they treated its agents. It was this kind of local solidarity which represented the most dangerous threat to government. It lies behind the decision to make an example of the Boulonnais, both in the imposition of tax in 1661 and the suppression of the subsequent revolt.[38]

The Boulonnais had adopted measures of self-help over years of war. They raised their own militia. In return they claimed immunity from a range of taxes. Louis's decision to impose a token tax was more to do with principle than with financial necessity. It was a small area round an important seaport and it was relatively close to Paris and northern garrisons. A military response could be swift and effective. Ministers may have been surprised by the strength of resistance and the armed gathering of some 6,000. Most, however, dispersed before royal troops reached them. Louis, who recounted the affair in his *Mémoires*, was clear about the importance of exemplary punishment: 'I thought it my duty to follow my reason rather than my imagination'. A few were executed, 400 sent to the galleys (the exact number required by the navy). Those insurgents over 70 and under 21 were pardoned. Stern justice was to be tempered by royal mercy.

Another view of the problems created by the defiance of royal authority by the privileged and the endemic violence to which it gave rise is afforded by the show trials known as the Grand Jours d'Auvergne (1665–66). This province, central, yet remote, was a byword with officials, inhospitable to the tax collector, a place of dread to the outsider. A situation in which great nobles had instituted régimes of terror reminiscent of the Thirty Years War with Germany had been exacerbated by the collapse of government during the Fronde. The decision to send a team of judges to the province under the *avocat-général* was an indication of the crown's new-found authority and confidence. His brief was 'to deliver the people from this oppression by the powerful'. Of 692 sentences delivered, 87 concerned nobles. 23 of them were executed. Of Gaspard, comte de Espinchal the justices' clerk wrote: 'A book could be written of the crimes of this man'. The baron de Sénégés had imposed his own taxes, collected them with a private army, established his own table of weights and measures, used his peasantry as slave labour and, the indictment ends: 'has already committed two or three murders . . .'. Twelve towers on the estates of the marquis de Canillac housed his 'twelve apostles', at whose head the marquis would roam, 'catechising' with cudgel and sword, burning down peasants' hovels or persuading some luckless traveller to pay him ransom. *Salus provinciarum repressa potentiorem audacia*: the words were inscribed on the medal that commemorated these grim proceedings. Important families had learned that no one was out of reach of the king's justice. To be noble meant more than enjoying privilege. The local *intendant* expressed the theme of service: 'When men of quality are somewhat surer of themselves I do not doubt but that I shall enrol many of their sons in the musketeers.' Ordinary Frenchmen could learn that the king was their protector, not their oppressor.

Complementing the work of the assize courts, Colbert's responsibility, pursued from 1665 with typical zeal, was the thorough investigation of noble privileges.[39] It was bitterly resented. Poor nobles could not finance defence lawyers. It was humiliating even for those with strong title to sit before the new *robe* nobles. Some surely sensed in Colbert's approach a more serious threat in the idea it implied, of nobility being earned by service, validated by royal grant. They would prefer the idea of a nobility of blood, superior because it was racial heir to the Franks: poor history of course but balm to the poor *gentilhomme*. What may have sufficed for local respect, acceptance as *gentilhomme* – as ever, in matters of class, instinct counting for more than formal status – was not enough for government. The *taille* rolls showed that exemption cost the state dear. The king sincerely respected the noble ideal; his ministers paid it lip service; *intendants* looked at where power lay – and it was not with the poorer nobles. They were required to show legal title going back at least a hundred years. *Intendants* were required to establish whether a suspect noble 'lived the life of a gentleman', had engaged in 'manual crafts' or 'retail trades'. The crown's need to maximise revenue against profitable social climbing or unjustifiable clinging to privilege: it was a stern and recurring struggle unlikely to have a more than marginal effect.

'The *intendant* gives constant intelligence of all things to the court.'[40] As Locke saw he provided the information on which the government decided its policy. This, to a greater extent than any before it, was a government seeking to base its policies on accurate information. Colbertism rested on a flow of facts and figures. Amid so much that was traditional it is the most modern characteristic. If not, in all respects, 'the king in the province', the *intendant* was his eyes, ears and voice. He had to watch notables in his province and arbitrate in disputes over justice, taxation, communal or individual rights. In a circular of 1670 Colbert told *intendants* that to see to the sound operation of the *taille* was the most important work entrusted to their hands.[41] In 1672 he wrote: 'It is vital that you should have a particular and detailed knowledge of all the *élections* entrusted to your hands'. 'May a collector seize a cow?' asked the *intendant* of Orléans in 1680. The law of the land allowed it, replied the minister, but 'it is up to you to see that matters do not come to this extremity'. *Intendants* were drawn into the affairs of towns by the general policy of extending control and the opportunities offered by disputes among civic leaders and the tendency to fall into debt. Even where they were not interfering in town politics they were likely to be regulating markets, police or the operation of the poor law. In frontier provinces they had some of the functions of the quartermaster, some of the political agent alongside the general. Billeting, discipline, supply and pay were all likely to impinge on civilian lives and need the *intendant*'s attention.

Conquered towns and lands might require special treatment. The *intendant* of Lille, after 1668, was much taken up with trade and tariffs between newly French and still Spanish areas. *Intendants* had to tread warily around the preserves of local officialdom. The rights of *élus* and of the *cours des aides* must be respected. He was expected to accomplish the multifarious demands of government, yet restrict delegation. Inevitably it grew and with it, through the local recruitment of *subdélégués*, just that meshing of crown and local interests that the use of the *intendant*, the outsider, Parisian, minister's client, was expected to prevent. That was to be a problem for the next century. Already, however, compromises were made which are so typical of this régime, so bold in theory and pronouncements, so needy in resources and therefore, in practice, so cautious and opportunistic. An edict of 1692 enacted that towns had to accept mayors approved by the crown. Two months later Dijon was allowed to pay 100,000 *livres* for the right to nominate its own.

The drive against the Huguenots, after 1679, provided further duties and opportunities for the devout, ambitious, or merely efficient. Men like Marillac and Foucault helped, by their initiatives, to shape policy, pioneering the use of troops, providing optimistic reports of the numbers of converts. The record of Bâville, the long-serving 'king of Languedoc', illustrates the power that an *intendant* could wield under such special circumstances. He could judge, with two counsellors, cases arising out of Huguenot legislation and there was no appeal against his sentences, ranging from confiscation of goods to service in the galleys, even execution. Where there were Huguenots, or famines, revolts, or other emergencies, as in the 'great winter' of 1709, the *intendant* was in the front line. He bore the brunt; he could relish the challenge or be reduced to a nervous spectator of events. He was kept up to the mark by the threat of recall or transfer to a less desirable province.

The *intendant* could cut a great figure in the province. Potentially he had a power to affect peoples' lives that could breed arrogance or sustain a sincere idealism. A few excelled, making roads with forced labour, the *corvée*, improving postal systems, directing new ventures in town planning. De Muin, much admired by Locke,[42] supervised the re-building of the new town and port of Rochefort. Foucault founded a school of hydrography at Caen. Such men built fine houses and enjoyed some of the influence that was slipping from the hands of the governor, bishop and mayor. Others slipped into survival mode, exaggerating success and disguising failure. *Intendants* knew at first hand the limitations of seventeenth-century government, the obstructive pedantry of *officiers*, the tricks of the *coq de paroisse*, the insolence of the *hobereau*, the complacency of cathedral canons, the tenacious conservatism of the peasant. Their reports reveal how little, by modern standards of administration, they could achieve. Being more of the magistrate and policeman than today's civil servant, with aspects of a colonial situation in their attitude towards the people they strove to control, they may recall to the British historian the efforts of the Resident Magistrate of Ascendancy Ireland – even the District Commissioner of Imperial India. Yet they represent the most ambitious and effective effort of any European power to govern from the centre.

Notes

1. For the source of this and following quotations from the *Mémoires* (ed. Goubert) and for comment on their provenance see pp. 41–2, n. 49.
2. For the last days and intentions of Mazarin see Treasure, op. cit., pp. 304–10.
3. For this revolt see also p. 52 and pp. 67–8, n. 9.
4. The masterpiece of Louis le Vau (1612–70), commissioned in 1657, roofed by 1658 and decorated by 1661; what could be achieved by wealth and influence.
5. Guillaume de Lamoignon, a distinguished member of the great legal family, he was much respected by Louis, as an architect of consensus, despite his independence. He had already showed courage in his stand against Mazarin over the *évocation* of cases to council. He was a leading opponent of judicial torture. An important source for this trial (and earlier the Fronde) is the *Journal* of Olivier Lefèvre d'Ormesson (2 vols, ed. Chéruel, Paris, 1860–61). Appointed *rapporteur* in Fouquet's trial, which entailed the duty of summing up before judgment, he was led by dislike for arbitrary proceedings to declare that the evidence was insufficient for a capital sentence. Colbert was disappointed. D'Ormesson's legal career did not prosper thereafter. But the episode shows more about the constraints than about the power of the state.
6. Jean de la Fontaine (1621–95) is best known for his poetic *Fables* (the first came out in 1668). His neat verses, having, as Mme de Sévigné said, the quality of painting, could be enjoyed by the highest in the land without fear for any covert political or social message.
7. Fouquet was not the legendary 'man in the iron mask'. Although it cannot be established with a certainty, it is convincingly argued by John Noone, *The Man Behind the Iron Mask* (Sutton, 1988) pp. 275–6, that the much debated person (in a velvet mask) was a valet, Eustache Danger, treated as special by his gaoler Saint-Mars, not for what he might have been but for what he knew. What that is Noone does not claim to know. J.C. Petitfils, *L'Homme au masque de fer* (Paris, 1970) suggests that Danger had been a valet of Colbert and that Louvois's undoubted concern about the matter arose either from his having been bribed by Louvois to poison Colbert, or (surely more likely) having invented that story and passed it on to a fellow prisoner, Lauzun, to blackmail Louvois. Danger had to wear the mask up till his death (one of few certainties in this sequence of hypotheses) in the Bastille in 1703. He had been transferred there after Louvois's death. Was the rather melodramatic concealment due to the fact that it had been put about earlier that Danger had been

released (thereby countering rumour hostile to Louvois) or was it simply an effort of Saint-Mars to boost his self-importance as gaoler of a political prisoner? The mystery persists and will no doubt inspire further speculation.

8. See also p. 84.

9. A good introduction to this still contentious subject is to be found in the essays in *Louis XIV and Absolutism*, ed. R. Hatton (London, 1976).

10. Baruch Spinoza (1632–77), lens grinder and philosopher, rationalist and Deist, expelled from his Dutch synagogue by fellow Jews; an isolated figure, not influential till the next century.

11. For Loyseau see p. 67, n. 11.

12. Even, recently, by F. Bluche, *Louis XIV* (Paris, 1984, tr. Greengrass, Blackwell, 1990): rich, magisterial and emphatically sympathetic.

13. Thomas Hobbes (1588–1679) was in Paris from 1640 to 1652. He was the friend of Gassendi and respectful critic of Descartes – though he accepted the latter's basic notion of the mechanistic character of nature. His *Leviathan* (1652) was influenced by his view of the English Civil War (from across the Channel) and of the Fronde. The political society projected in *Leviathan* was controlled by expediency. The sanctions of religion and morality were cast aside. Hobbes returned home after *Leviathan* made him obnoxious to the authorities in Paris.

14. Charles-Louis de Secondat, baron de Montesquieu (1689–1755), senior lawyer and political philosopher: he would argue that the corporate and individual rights of subject were the first line of defence against arbitrary rule.

15. Straddling the borders of Haut-Quercy, Bas-Limousin and Haut-Auvergne the vicomté of Turenne comprised 96 parishes. The ruling family claimed that it was not a fief, bestowed on them by the crown and at its disposal, but a free domain: their obligation went no further than homage and respect for the verdict of the courts.

16. Pierre Pithou was among several authors of the *Satire*, patriotic, *politique* – that is to say in religious terms moderate, but anti-Roman, and powerfully royalist. Marie-Madeleine Martin (trans. B. & R. North, 1951; original, Paris, 1948) uses the *Satire* to good effect (pp. 139–45) to show how patriotic feeling was strengthened by the religious wars, so smoothing the way for absolutist theories. In 1594, in *The Liberties of the Gallican Church*, Pithou comes close to declaring that, as responsible to God alone, the king should be judge of his own morality.

17. Quoted by Martin, op. cit., p. 18.

18. See pp. 27–8.

19. The seminal and authoritative study in this field is S. Kettering, *Patrons and Brokers in Seventeenth Century France* (Oxford & New York, 1986). See bibliography for case studies. There was always potential conflict beneath the surface of equilibrium, as factions struggled for control. In larger towns and in *parlements*, there was usually a faction for the governor or *intendant*, always threatening the independence of local institutions, another seeking to uphold that independence. Rivalries which could embarrass the crown when it was weak, as during the Fronde, could be an instrument of power when it was strong. The brokers of crown patronage could outbid local faction chiefs.

20. See pp. 115–16.

21. J.L. Guez de Balzac (1597–1654) wrote memorably about the restoration of France after the civil wars: 'No longer are the French the enemies of their country, idle in the service of their king and scorned by other nations. Behind their faces I see other men; in the same realm another state.' The aspiration of *le bon français* in Richelieu's day was the orthodoxy of 1661.

22. René Descartes (1596–1650), author of *Discours sur la Méthode* (1637) was the most influential thinker of his day – influential indeed in French thinking to this day. The method expounded was one of doubt: all was uncertain until established by reasoning from self-evident propositions, on principles analogous to those of geometry. There was a mechanistic model for all things. It was significant for the developing sense, important to Richelieu, assumed by Colbert, of a distinctive and superior French culture, that he wrote in French. Blaise Pascal (1623–62), Auvergnat, the son of a *président* of the *cour des aides*, was a mathematician and scientist of genius, whose work on atmospheric pressure, the equilibrium of fluids and the infinitesimal calculus was each of the highest importance. His theological and moral concerns, expressed typically in the *Pensées*, were no less profound. His involvement with Port Royal ensured that the author of *Lettres provinciales* would lend distinction to the Jansenist cause and heighten controversy.

23. The right, with feudal origins, possessed by the crown to receive the revenues of the see so long as bishoprics remained vacant, had long been recognised in Northern France. Only when it was extended by fiscal edicts in 1673 and 1675 to the whole of France, did it bring about a conflict with Rome.

24. See also pp. 327–8.

25. P. Nicolas de Malebranche (1638–1715), priest of the Oratory, Cartesian, was author of *La Recherche de la Vérité*, 'last essay in Christian philosophy'. For his role (subversive in terms of orthodox theology) in the changing intellectual climate of Louis XIV's later years see p. 327.

26. The latter may now be studied in an excellent new edition and translation, ed. Patrick Riley (Cambridge, 1990) From it the following quotations are drawn.

27. Françoise d'Aubigné, Mme de Maintenon (1635–1719), 'the widow Scarron' as she was first known (or the 'Indian princess', with reference to Indian childhood years), had found a niche at court, as governess, in 1669, of Louis XIV's illegitimate children by Louise de la Vallière. From unpromising childhood, and marriage to the crippled poet Pierre Scarron, to a title derived from the important estate of Maintenon (Louis's gift in 1675), then to such an exalted position, is about the most extraordinary personal story of the reign. For her character, interests and influence see pp. 325–6.

28. It is improbable that Louise de la Vallière, later duchesse de Vaujours, eventually Sister Louise de la Miséricorde (1675), mistress *c*. 1661–67, actively sought the king's attentions. It is certain that she was uncomfortable in her position, making several attempts to retreat to monastic life before she was eventually granted leave to become a professed nun. The difficulties, indeed distress, in reconciling her natural feeling for an ardent young man to an unnatural situation – the limited private life allowed a royal mistress, the regular pregnancies, the semi-detachment of her children and the final humiliation of being supplanted by a rival – may be imagined.

An unassuming and decent figure in a court milieu so decidedly chauvinist and mercenary, she kept her good name.

29. Athénaïs de Rochechouart (1641–1707), mistress *c.* 1667–81, had been married, in 1663, to the penurious Marquis de Montespan who was inconveniently reluctant to disappear, but willing enough to accept royal favours. The king was not, evidently, much disturbed by his theatrical appearances at court; Athénaïs more so by censorious churchmen and her own uneasy conscience. As Saint-Simon records, she prayed much. When she left court she spent time directing the Saint-Joseph mission to the poor. By all accounts a lovely and gifted woman, she held the king's affections for nearly fifteen years. She allowed him joyous hours away from the formalities of court and she gave him eight children, four of whom attained adulthood. Louis had built for her the beautiful château of Clagny.

30. For Motteville see also p. 41, n. 46.

31. Arnaud de Pomponne (1618–99). For his early career see Herbert. H. Rowan, 'Arnauld de Pomponne. Louis's Moderate Minister', *American Historical Review*, LXI (1956) pp. 531–49.

32. Henri de la Tour d'Auvergne, vicomte, maréchal de Turenne: for his unique prestige and influence see p. 172.

33. Paul, duc de Beauvillier and Charles-Honoré, duc de Chevreuse were both married to daughters of Colbert and active, after his death, in support of his family and connections. As R. Mettam points out, in *Power and Faction in Louis XIV's France* (Oxford, Blackwell, 1988), p. 88, the willingness of the king to countenance such *mésalliances* between high noble and ministerial families (against his principles and usual inclination) suggests 'a deliberate attempt to create tightly-knit groups of advisers bound together both socially and politically'. In the last years of the reign the two dukes, Beauvillier in council, Chevreuse much in Mme de Maintenon's confidence, worked together for *dévôt* causes and, with Burgundy and Fénelon, for peace. Saint-Simon admired them and they figure largely in his *Mémoires*.

34. As notably, and with much supporting evidence, Mettam, op. cit., contrasts the wide scope and freedom enjoyed by the king in making foreign, and even religious policy with the constraints he faced in domestic administration. He stresses the conservative nature of the king's rule and the care taken to distribute patronage evenly and to respect local rights.

35. For this remarkable family, and an illustration, through its record, of the way France was governed, see C. Frostin, 'La famille ministérielle des Phélipeaux: esqisse d'un profil Pontchartrain', *Annales de Bretagne*, 86, 1979: 117–40. The material is usefully summarised in P.R. Campbell, *Louis XIV*, pp. 27–8.

36. For a comprehensive study of the evolving role of the *intendants* see R. Bonney, *Political Change in France under Richelieu and Mazarin, 1624–61* (Oxford, 1978) and Mettam, op. cit. Also, for relevant documents, Mettam's *Government and Society in Louis XIV's France* (London, 1977).

37. So named after its author, *garde des sceaux* Michel de Marillac, Richelieu's most formidable rival. Since he was arrested, lost the seals in 1630, and subsequently died, his 'alternative programme', absolutist but not anti-Habsburg, was never put to the test. The *code* was a miscellaneous collection of rules for legal, commercial and

administrative practice, much of it obsolete or unenforceable, some of it replaced by Colbert's *codes*.

38. For the subject of popular revolts, with much about their motivation and *mentalités* (in particular the *Croquants* of 1636–37), see V.-M. Bercé, *History of Popular Revolts* (trans. A. Whitmore, New York, 1990; orig., Paris 1986). For the 1661 revolt see Mettam, *Government and Society*, op. cit., pp. 255–60.

39. The whole text of the instruction is in P. Clément (ed.), *Lettres, Mémoires et Instructions de Colbert*, vii, pp. 233–56.

40. Locke, op. cit., p. 156. 'The king's man is guard and spy on them both [Governor and Lieutenant-general]'.

41. Clément, op. cit., vol II, i, p. 77. See also Locke (usually well-informed) pp. 110, 140.

42. Locke, op. cit., pp. 234–5.

Chapter 4

♦

WEALTH AND POWER: COLBERT

Without a theory the Facts are silent.

F.A. HAYEK

In all ages history has been used to treat national power and national wealth as sisters; perhaps they were never so closely associated as then.

G. SCHMOLLER

THE PERFECT ROYAL SERVANT

If Colbert had done nothing more than bring order into the finances so that Louis could embark on his early wars with sufficient resources, he would still have a prominent place in history, especially when the achievement is set against the recession and monetary famine of the period. Since he aimed to do so much more – and the record there is patchy – he has become a controversial figure. From his being visualised in a way that came naturally to historians of the nineteenth century as the great instrument of centralising reforms and economic development, to subsequent scornful treatment of his mercantilism; then to scrutiny of his early career which has shown him to be, not so much innovator as successful manipulator of the old financial system to his own advantage; so to a reductionist position which allows him to be little beyond the supremely efficient bureaucrat, Colbert's reputation has been at the mercy of changing fashions in history.[1] Certainly his record should be looked at in the context of what was possible at the time. As in the case of the master he served so zealously, and as in that of Richelieu – the absolutist rhetoric should be read with caution. It is still possible to make a case for his being among the greatest of royal servants – indeed, of Frenchmen.

That greatness does not consist mainly in his thinking about economics, which was very much of its time, nor even in his planning which was immensely thorough, but rigid. It lies rather in the sheer scope of his operations, the energy and intelligence to make the most of his unique concentration of authority, combined with a kind of boldness in his initiatives which should command admiration. There was, no doubt, an ambiguity in his approach, as he pursued the interests of his family and of the state. One can point to a central contradiction in his policies. He subscribed whole-heartedly to the great royal idea: *la gloire*. As Louis fulfilled personal ambitions in war, revenue was diverted from commercial and industrial projects and the benefits of financial reforms were lost. Colbert's vision was grander, however, than his master's. It was grounded in a more comprehensive idea of the state and its potential. It expressed the essential rationality to be found, for example, in his efforts to reform and codify law that had in it the germs of a later generation's 'enlightenment'. It encompassed science and the arts, reflecting a sense of their value even beyond what they might offer to the glory of the king.[2]

Colbert was driven off course after 1672 by the demands of war. His most promising schemes were starved of resources. If he had sustained his opposition to the king's aggressive plans he would have been disgraced. Everything we know about the king's frame of mind in the years before the Dutch war points to that conclusion.[3] Colbert was only allowed independence of judgement and action in his own economic sphere. It was his prime role, as Louis saw it, to ensure sufficient revenue. Colbert knew well what he was about. He was, indeed, as much concerned with the state's authority as with its wealth but realised that the one depended on the other: 'Only the abundance of money in a state affects its grandeur and power.' It is unrealistic to suggest that Colbert could have been a moderating influence on the young king. He could demur. If he went too far he could expect to be reminded of that position, as famously, in 1671, after he had persisted in opposing the king in council. The next day he received a letter from Louis, courteous, but stern: 'do not take the risk of angering me again because when I have listened to the advice of you and your colleagues, and made my decision on what course should be followed, I do not wish the subject to be mentioned again. . . .' Of course Colbert would not so err again. He was the king's servant. Under God, the king represented the entire authority under which he served. There was no other constituency. To look for one was to rebel and to incur disgrace. In retrospect Colbert may have looked secure but it was a security that had to be earned by constantly dutiful conduct. He had good reason to remember the fate of Fouquet. The head, as it were, of a now-great family firm, he had an overriding responsibility: to maintain the presence and influence of the family and to keep that of the Le Telliers within bounds. That did not mean that he did not know his own value or that of his policies. In office he might not achieve all that he wished. Out of office he could achieve nothing. Common sense as well as an instinct for self-preservation dictated that he travel with the headstrong king and do some good along the way. When to all the social and institutional obstacles to change is added the limiting conditions under which he enjoyed the king's support, it appears remarkable that he achieved as much as he did. The man himself was remarkable.

Courtiers noted his invariable black, his stern brow, his unusual preference for water over wine. To Mme de Sévigné he was simply 'the North'. Indeed he had little time for courtly manners. As a young man he wrote of himself: 'I take no holiday. I have no pleasure or amusements. My whole time is spent on the cardinal's business for what I love is work.' A sixteen-hour day took its toll. He grew morose and dyspeptic, beset with the cares and frustrations of office, aware that he was unpopular – but strong enough to bear it. It meant much that the king valued his services. He also believed in himself, in the efficacy of his methods and the validity of his personal mission.

He was the true Cartesian, incarnation of rational method. His rules for work were simple and optimistic. For all matters, evidence and data must be collected and collated. Thus armed, the minister must think 'continually', with 'application' and with 'penetration'. In 1663 he launched a great inquest, which provided government with a new social and economic geography of the realm. His official map-maker, Sieur Nicolas Sarson, was instructed to ensure that the divisions between the four administrations, ecclesiastical, military, judicial and financial were clearly drawn. He too well understood the scope for confusion when lines were blurred. He had an appetite for statistics but they were gathered for a purpose. Indeed he is interestingly modern in his reluctance to base legislation on guesswork. Repeatedly he is to be found beside the king, showing estimates and projections, a sometimes unwelcome but respected voice of caution. Through his letters, memoirs and directives his distinctive badgering voice can be heard reiterating the themes of classification and regulation.[4] They amount to a significant expression of the analytical spirit of the time. They are also a monument to ambitious government, vigilant and peremptory.

For a French minister concerned with finance and trade the international scene offered two clear examples: Spain's decline, now borne out by military weakness, illustrated the danger of a state's living continually beyond its means. The strength of the United Provinces was derived from the prosperity of its commerce. That in turn reflected its social and political structure, engendering values favourable to investment. Colbert had to work within a system that offered every kind of obstacle to such investment. That for him was the challenge. He would only succeed if he could create opportunities for investment in productive enterprises sufficiently attractive to overcome deep-rooted preferences for investment in land and office. His main weapon was the power of the state. His main hope, at the outset, was to achieve a foundation of sound finance, with lower interest rates. His prime aim therefore was to balance the budget. When that was achieved he could expect to find the cash to subsidise new ventures in commerce and industry.

It was a personal mission, expressing his ideas about work, wealth and the community. He liked to think of a country rid of *rentiers* and monks, in which men strove, in disciplined lives, to increase the wealth of the kingdom and the prestige of the king. He was of his time – how could he not be? – in assuming that the state must act to foster its trade and manufactures. That implied regulation and protection. It was the guild-mentality writ large. As with the smaller urban unit, so with the state, individual craftsmen and merchants must accept a system of mutual aid, with detailed rules to fasten wages and prices, conditions of manufacture and sale, even the movement of goods. Individuals are thus protected from the uncertainties of free trade; in return they accept restraints. Where, as in France, the state secures control of the towns, it assumes, in some degree, responsibility for trade: the citizen's right to work for a fair return and protection against the foreigner. Working for social order in alliance with the trading community the state also finds one answer to its constant need – ready money. That necessarily simplified introduction to the age of 'mercantilism' only takes us so far. To go further is to understand why the term (not used by contemporaries) was found so useful by Adam Smith and his school of free traders.

Colbert worked upon principles that were generally accepted in his time. Where writers like Laffemas or Montchrétien,[5] with the same concerns about France's meagre production and consequent reliance on imports, had been able to do little more than prod government, and Richelieu found himself diverted by the more pressing concerns of diplomacy and war, Colbert was empowered to act. From principles to programmes, comprehensively on paper though patchily in reality, 'mercantilism' became a recognisable system.

It was conventional in ideas, yet bore so distinctively the stamp of the *contrôleur-général* that it may more properly be called Colbertism. To see that it was based on realistic assessment of the contemporary economic situation is only to do Colbert justice. To criticise him for not seeing the world as it was to be after a century of colonialism, fast developing trade and early industrialism is to enter blindly into the mental world of the Enlightenment, allowing too little, in judgements about the past, for the conditions of the time.

Credit was inadequate, bills of exchange uncommon, so that capital, in the form of bullion, was an urgent necessity. 'Mercantilism' evolved from the economic needs and political aims of the time. The state depended on the money that it could find to finance armies, navies and diplomats. 'Only the abundance of money in a state effects its grandeur and power.' Colbert was expressing the received wisdom. He was also influenced by what he had observed in his years under Mazarin. The country was suffocating, the treasury starved, through shortage of good coin. Much of that in circulation was of debased silver or copper and foreign, notably Spanish. He could see no end to the depression in agriculture: declining grain prices meant chronically low consumer demand with an adverse effect on manufacturing. The only sure remedy lay in state action to stimulate commerce. He envisaged the world economy as near-static as to both quantity of money in circulation and the overall volume of trade. It was the prime goal of the state to increase its share of those amounts. To that end a favourable balance of trade should be sought. The most desirable form of trade, that which government should promote, was the export of goods, especially manufactured goods of high quality, for which, in return, the purchasing country shipped gold and silver.

France was not alone in seeking to increase exports and reserves of bullion. There must be some degree of free trade. Hence arose the central tension within economic policy: between one concern, the protection of native industries from foreign competition, and the other, the expansion of trade. France was well placed to supply its essential needs but was never able to dispense with Dutch-supplied goods. There was also a strong demand for luxury goods from abroad, strengthened by the usual preference of the fashionable for the foreign. The puritan Colbert might deplore it. He could only tackle it by promoting native manufactures of high quality. He put trust in the tariff weapon but applied it at first with sensible caution. He had a double aim: to simplify the muddle of internal and external dues which were the legacy of past hand to mouth policies, and to use them to protect French, and obstruct Dutch and English trade. He was never primarily interested in the revenue that might come from tariffs. That of 1664 actually lightened burdens, freeing raw materials and abolishing some internal tolls: a desirable measure of simplification. In 1667, however, protection was tinged with aggression in the doubling, for example, of duty on imported cloth. In 1669 he sought a trade agreement with England in the hope of increasing French exports of wines and silks, both carrying a heavy English duty. It is revealing of Colbert's priorities that negotiations broke down over his insistence on English imports conforming precisely to his regulations for French manufactures. In the context, moreover, of the crown's aggressive stance towards the United Provinces it was inevitable that his policy would invite a chain reaction. The preferential sugar duties of 1670–71, the tariff of 1672, went beyond what was required to protect France's young industries; they served notice of economic war upon Holland. For English ministers, they strengthened the case for alliance with France. The temptation that came from such tariff policies, as strong in England as in France was to take a short cut to trade supremacy. From seeking to debar a trade rival from your ports it is a short step to destroying his trade by armed force.

Colbert's tariff policy was increasingly unpopular with French merchants who saw benefits in the free interchange of goods that the minister seemed to ignore. At a general council held in 1701, only the advocate for Rouen would defend the policy which had been Colbert's; the rest declared for the reciprocal benefits of free trade. By then, of course, there had been two prolonged wars. Meanwhile new areas and types of trade had been opening up, undermining the central 'mercantilist' argument based on the assumption of fixed volumes. In any case Colbert's tariffs should not be judged on economic grounds alone. They represented an aspect of 'mercantilism' that was more than economic theory: it was a political approach to economic problems. The incarnation himself of the work ethic, confessed admirer of the Dutch whom he wished to emulate as well as to destroy, Colbert undoubtedly saw value in the growth of a manufacturing and trading economy beyond immediate fiscal advantage. It was not merely jealousy of the ascendancy of Louvois that made him uneasy about the prolongation of the Dutch war. He knew its cost, not only to the king's revenues but to his commercial schemes. But to go from there to arguing that he was a man of peace, fairy godmother to the economy, thwarted in civil purposes by the militarists in court and council, is a step too far. Colbert was a fervent statist who saw himself as the instrument of the king's glory. In England it was from the pressure of private interests that government came to adopt the policy that culminated in the Navigation laws. In France, by contrast, the impulse towards regulation came from the top. He might canvass the view of merchants but they were allowed little influence over policy. 'They nearly always understand merely their own little commerce, and not the great forces which make commerce go.' Colbert's words reveal the office-holder, the desk-visionary, the chauvinist, and the courtier. At heart this 'Little Frenchman' was convinced that manufactures were a potential source of contentment in society. He certainly detested the effete and wasteful luxury of the court. He fought to defend the main parts of his plan against the corrosion of war budgets. The fact remains that he subscribed fully to the notion of power that had so firm a hold over the king. Colbertism bears out the view, now generally accepted, that 'mercantilism' was primarily concerned with the pursuit of power.[6] For Colbert the creation of wealth was a sort of power politics, state-making and national economy-making at the same time. It had to begin with the reform of the royal finances.

THE STATE'S FINANCES

Through the operations of the *chambre de justice*,[7] from 1661 to 1665, Colbert showed the financial world what a minister could do with the king behind him. He also gained a crucial personal advantage, and secured a short-term gain for the treasury. The *chambre* brief was to fine financiers found to have profited excessively during the Fouquet years and, in the words of the edict, to have 'given the public a scandalous example by their gross pride and opulence and by a vulgar display capable of corrupting behaviour'. Nearly 500 were fined 156 million *livres*. Most was paid by a relatively small group of Fouquet's clients. Colbert's, the growing connection on whose fortunes would rise with his, escaped lightly. He needed goodwill to have a chance of succeeding in his financial strategy, with its twin-pronged assault on offices and interest rates.

In 1659 Colbert had presented Mazarin with a memorandum concerning the financial ills of the state. Its key proposal was the abolition of 20,000 purchasable offices. It would reduce exemptions from tax and encourage the dispossessed to put their capital to better use in industry, working for 'the welfare of the kingdom instead of for its destruction'. Richelieu, too, had begun with hopes of abolishing the evil, 'prejudicial' he wrote, 'to royal authority and to the purity of justice',[8] but had soon come to authorise further sales. Defending his retreat in the *Testament* he had written what many surely felt, but few dared to say: 'prudence does not admit of this kind of action in an old monarchy, whose imperfections have passed into custom, and whose disorder forms part of the order of the state'. Order purchased at the cost of disorder; quick capital realised at the expense of future income: such short-term measures were anathema to Colbert. Could he do better? Could he afford not to?

In the *généralité* of Rouen, where taxes had an above-average yield, Colbert found at the start of his ministry that 41.6 per cent of the revenue was absorbed in payment to the office-holders who were only receiving a third of their dues: to pay them in full would have entailed finding a million *livres* in extra tax. This situation, widely reproduced, was critical. Exemptions had grown to a point at which few wealthy *bourgeois* paid any direct tax. Colbert's memorandum of 1664 showed that 46,000 office-holders enjoyed exemption in the departments of Justice and Finance by virtue of their office. Of these, 40,000 were unnecessary having been created only to be sold, and bought for exemption and prestige. They represented the haemorrhage of capital accruing from the profits of trade that Colbert rightly identified as a prime weakness in the economy. When the rich could put half their money into *charges* and the other half into *rentes* they could not easily be persuaded to take risks in manufacturing or foreign trade.

Reflecting the weakness of the crown, especially in the past twenty years, the *rentes* had become an exorbitant levy on the revenue for the benefit of a few rich financiers. Colbert undertook a 'conversion', in effect an enforced reduction in interest rates. To examine the titles of certain *rentiers*, he used the same special tribunal that had tried Fouquet; many claims were repudiated. That he was able to force through these reforms in the face of opposition in city and court witnesses to his courage and to the new political climate. Here was absolutism as influential people were made to understand it. Undeterred by riots and threatening deputations he acted for the crown without scruple or favour. The results speak for themselves. In 1661 interest on debts amounted to about 27 million *livres*; in 1683 the figure was 8 million. To Colbert there was something anti-social, even repugnant in living off usury but he was driven to accept the need for state borrowing through a regular channel. In 1674 he established a loan fund and compelled *fermiers-généraux* to invest in it at 5 per cent. It was a tentative step towards the concept of a national bank. It was abolished after his death. Not until after the revolution would France have a bank like those in the United Provinces and England which played such an important part in ensuring a flow of investment at low rates of interest. Meanwhile war-finance continued to present golden opportunities to the financiers and those aristocratic syndicate members who stood behind them, whose credit was so invaluable, and influence so great, that they were protected by the state.

That glimpse into a darkening future serves to show how notable were Colbert's early reforms of detail. Though far short of his target, thousands of offices were abolished. Benefiting from his experience of managing Mazarin's estates he increased the revenue from crown lands. He fulfilled his undertaking to bring order into treasury accounts. His new registers of receipts and expenditures were combined and submitted to audit before the annual compilation of the *état au vrai* for the *chambres des comptes*. They offered a degree of transparency and some aspects of a modern budget. There would be less excuse than before for framing policy on the basis of guesswork. Meanwhile the state tightened its grip on its financial agents. The leases of tax farmers were checked, many of them cancelled, while commissions were docked. Aware of the furore created by Richelieu's attempt to introduce *élections* into the *pays d'états*, Colbert accepted the existence of the two tax systems but did secure larger contributions from the *pays d'états*. It is in those annual rounds, when his agents, usually *intendant* and governor, presented their demands, that one can see 'the complex mixture of ritual, social interaction and hard bargaining'[9] which, with the informal client contacts and subtly persuasive hints about the value of royal favour, shows what government meant in the further reaches of Louis XIV's kingdom. Compared to Richelieu's day the style was less authoritarian and confrontational because the message came directly from the king. The royal image was that much more appealing and the patronage more valuable and secure.

Colbert was still concerned about the disproportionate burden borne by the *pays d'élection* and its adverse effect on the economy. Fouquet had lowered the rate and cancelled some arrears. Colbert carried the process forward. Paternalist edicts decreeing smaller payments for young peasants with large families, letters urging *intendants* to use discretion and allow for local problems, to be vigilant, for example, in preventing the seizing of livestock from defaulting peasants, show as much common sense as humanity. Peasants were more likely to pay if the demand was reasonable and assessment relatively honest. And Colbert could point to remarkable results. In 1662, little over half of the gross revenue, 87.6 million *livres*, reached the treasury; in 1667 the proportion had reached two-thirds and the net yield was 63 million. For 1671 the respective figures offered by Malet[10] are 104.5 gross and 77.6 net. The net yields would stay around that figure for the next ten years: providing the 'sinews of war' – but never enough for its voracious appetite.

Even preparing for the Dutch war put a brake on the process of reform. As it proceeded, the *contrôleur-général* had to fall back on the very 'extraordinary revenues' he had condemned: further sales of office and new taxes. The money was found, without recourse to high levels of borrowing. But the cost was high: in reduced subsidies for commercial projects (though not for the royal palaces), in pressure on the peasant taxpayer, and consequent resistance. Only brutal repression brought Bordeaux and Brittany to heel after the big uprisings of 1675.[11]

In Brittany the *papier-timbré* revolt, which lasted from April to September, exposed the potentially dangerous interaction of fiscal and social concerns, especially when local officials were prepared to exploit them for their own ends. The rising started as a protest against the government's imposition of stamp duty on legal contracts and a tax on tobacco (which Bretons chewed). It appealed to special interests and gained force from other grievances. Peasants resented seigneurial justice and other feudal obligations; members of the estates conceived that royal officials were encroaching on their authority (though Brittany would have no *intendant* till 1689). It was rumoured that the province was to lose its exemption from the *gabelle*. The governor's harsh repression served as a warning to others, particularly to southerners tempted, like the Bordelais, to imitate the Bretons. It may have enhanced the political authority of the crown. Yet it also revealed the fiscal limits within which Colbert had to operate.

On one occasion Colbert wrote to the intendant at Limoges: 'You can publicise the fact that the king keeps ready, twenty leagues from Paris, an army of 20,000, ready to march into any province where there is a suspicion of a rising, in order to inflict exemplary punishment and to show the whole people the obedience they owed to His Majesty.' Writing these words did Colbert think of opportunities lost? Or did he accept such measures, the harsh, unadvertised face of absolutism, as a reasonable precaution to ensure that the people paid for the sovereign's glory. Colbert's financial legacy was an efficient revenue-raising system. Louis was the envy, in this respect, of fellow sovereigns. Yet, with the threat of force hanging over the taxpayer we are not so far from the fiscal regime of the Cardinals. With many defaulting collectors languishing in gaol we see how impoverished was the base for Colbert's plans to revive the economy.

MANUFACTURES

In his compendious planning Colbert was inspired by the potent myth of a more prosperous past. Nostalgia coloured the short reign of Henry IV when the restoration of peace and a last burst in a century's inflation had made for busy markets and fortunes for trader–banker families like the Colberts.

Whatever the source of Colbert's vision of a golden age when French crafts were booming, when Spanish merchants sent their wool to France to be turned into cloth, and French money did not pour out of the kingdom – it was very different from what Henry's contemporary, Laffemas, described: indeed his diagnoses bore marked similarities to Colbert's own, fifty years on. However, Colbert's mission to restore France to former prosperity was, in one respect, well founded. The land of France was generously endowed by nature; the climate mostly favourable; there were sound established industries; the long coastline had good harbours on the Mediterranean, Atlantic and Channel. The thriving United Provinces, with meagre natural resources (little timber for example), showed what a trading community could achieve. There Colbert saw a community where trade was a priority and capital was applied to productive use. What more could the millions of France not do when to her resources and the talents of her people was added the direction and financing of the state, acting as its own entrepreneur?

Urban man to his shoe-buckles, Colbert was little interested in the country's main occupation for its own sake. In this he was only typical. After the important work of Olivier de Serres at the start of the century little was written about agriculture.[12] Any benefits from improved practice would feed through slowly; manufactures promised more immediate gains. Colbert was aware, of course, that a poor peasantry would depress demand. He had a horror of famine, ensuing civil disturbances and the loss of taxable incomes. His main concern, however, was for manufactures of high quality and price, beyond the peasant purse. Drainage schemes were pressed forward, the scientific breeding of horses in stud farms was subsidised. To meet the needs of the navy forestry was accorded a high priority in the west. Contributions to peasant welfare were likely, however, to be incidental, occurring mainly where farming was ancillary to home industries; peasants in the Auvergne and Brittany found wider markets for fine lace. Industrial crops such as hemp and flax were favoured. Colbert looked grudgingly on the wine industry of the south and even tried to destroy some vineyards and grow corn in their place, since 'wine hinders work'. Agriculture responds most fruitfully to local initiatives. What farmers require from the state is not direction but the removal of obstacles and improvement of transport. The failure to remove local customs barriers outweighed gains from new roads and canals. The ideal of a self-supporting country could have harmful effects. In years of bad harvests, rather than import foreign grain, Colbert imposed restrictions on the movements of crops to keep down the price; in good years elaborate controls prevented exports and caused waste and loss. His measures leave a sense of irrelevance, even futility. No amount of well-meaning control could make up for the greater landowner's lack of interest and the crown's fiscal priorities. The former's generally untaxed rentals were rarely spent on estates which they might never see. Nor would peasants make improvements that might catch the eye of the tax collector.

Manufactures were 'subject neither to the seasons, nor the fickle elements'. Here, for Colbert, was the scope for human ingenuity, for new techniques, for forward planning. A memoir for Mazarin shows him to have been thinking ahead.

> We must create or recreate all industries, even luxury industries; a system of protection must be established by means of a customs tariff; trade and traders must be organised into guilds. Transport of goods by sea and land must be restored, colonies developed and bound by financial ties to France . . . the navy strengthened to give protection to our merchant shipping.

In power large views became more precise objectives. In 1664, the year in which the *conseil de commerce* was instituted, he was reminding the king of the success of the Venetians and Dutch in exploiting, first, the old Middle Eastern routes, then the seaways opened by the discovery of the New World, the new route to India and the Far East. France must break into the restricted markets of the world. She must manufacture for herself the goods that were at present bought from the English, Dutch and Hamburgers. The finer quality of French goods should attract buyers from abroad. In new manufactures, a million subjects of the king 'now languishing in idleness will win their livelihood', and as many find work in the ports and in the marine. The king had a part to play for he could 'show a special interest in the commerce of the nation and receive merchants at court'. Then – a favourite theme – he might reduce the number of the religious 'who not only do no work for the community but also deprive it of the children they should be producing'. Last, almost as if caricaturing his own dirigiste tendency and the persistent theme of glory, Colbert proposed the best of all possible French worlds: 'If Your Majesty could constrain all your subjects into these four types of professions, agriculture, trade, war by land or by sea, it would be possible for you to become the master of the world.'

In the real world of local interests, obstructive officials and harassed *intendants*, State action could take several forms. It could create new industries or revive old ones by lending capital and advisers; encourage wealthy men to invest; support research; finance importation of skilled foreign workers. It could protect from the rigours of competition by granting monopolies and imposing tariffs and embargoes. It could control from within by ordering standards of quality, methods of production, and enforcing the rules through inspectors. All these methods played a part. At the heart of the operation was the state factory. Privileged and protected, it was meant to be the model for lesser concerns.

'We must resign ourselves to do the people good, despite themselves.' The paternalist reformer could not resist the social challenge. Nor could he shed the outlook of the bureaucrat. 'The state must order the business of a great people on the same basis as the divisions of a government department.' The discipline ordained for state factories suggests that Colbert envisaged the translation of the monastic ideal into these secular workplaces. There was to be no swearing; only sacred chants were to be sung at work – in a low voice so as not to disturb neighbours. *Laborare est orare*. With such instructions on record Colbert has hardly needed critics to draw attention to naive aspects in his planning: his obsession with detail, insufficient allowance for the vagaries of human nature; and, the fundamental weakness, his ignoring the laws of supply and demand.

The entrepreneur would point out that Colbert was not risking his own capital. Colbert could reply that entrepreneurs were not coming forward with theirs. He was faced by the oligarchic exclusiveness of the craft guilds which controlled manufactures in the cities, and by the distaste of the domestic worker for factory life. His policy was to use the guilds as crown agents to enforce his regulations. It is the familiar aspect of the régime; absolutism qualified by concessions to the privileged and progress through compromise. At the same time – the radical aspect, the attempt to manoeuvre within limited space – the *manufactures royales*, sheltered and favoured, sapped the guild position. As the *corps d'élite* of the industrial army they suggest an analogy with Louvois's army reforms. They had the king as patron; their patents bore the *fleur de lis*; their workmen were often exempt from the *taille*. They were meant to provide an advertisement for the quality of French goods.

The tapestry industry was nearly extinct after earlier encouragement by Henry IV. Here patient skill and artistry brought slow rewards and called for long-term investment. Adorning the walls of the great and wealthy tapestries offered prestige and profit. They pleased the king.[13] So the Gobelins workshops in Paris, where his favourite painter Le Brun supervised the making of tapestries, was Colbert's cherished showpiece. With sixty apprentices and large commissions for royal palaces, the place was as much a school of arts and crafts as a workshop. The results brought France to the great houses and museums of Europe. The cost was high. Subsidies amounted to seven million *livres* in twenty years, when private industries received but half a million a year. But in Colbert's terms, as in his king's, the Gobelins was a triumphant success.

Colbert's policy can be tested by its effect on the production of textiles: mainly still a cottage industry producing low-quality cloth for local markets, it was vital to the peasantry but inadequate as a contender for the international market. It was an important field of experiment in which Colbert hoped to challenge the lead of England and Holland. Where there was no industry flax and madder crops were grown to supply materials or, as round Lyon, mulberry trees planted for the city's silk manufacture. Practical instructions were laid down for making and dyeing the cloth. A civic stamp was only issued by the inspector when he was satisfied that the finished article complied to the highest official standard. At Abbeville Van Robais, a Dutch capitalist, managed the most modern cloth factory in Europe. The local *intendant* was required to inspect bi-monthly to find 'the number of workers in each factory, the bales of cloth they produced and their quality' in order that he might make 'some monetary bonus to Sieur van Robais, to keep him up to constant improvements, these manufactures being of the greatest utility to the state'. In another of the *manufactures royales*, within the mediaeval walls of Carcassonne, the making of the finest cloth was supervised by Dutch experts. On his own estates at Seignelay Colbert saw to it that poor children became apprentices in his model lace workshop. Locke saw such child labour, and a fourteen-hour day, at a silk manufactory at Tours where 'a maid turns at once about 120 spools and windes the silk off them'.[14] It is a glimpse into the industrial future. Meanwhile most industries, including the linen of Brittany, were still dependent mainly on domestic work, peasant families ready to weave and spin to supplement their meagre incomes.

The importing of foreign specialists had a large part in Colbert's design: textile craftsmen and paper makers from Holland, glass blowers from Venice. Miners were recruited in Sweden to assist in the development of the copper and lead mines of the south; engineers in England to construct the new dockyards and arsenals at Toulon, Rochefort and Brest. Ambassadors acted as recruiting agents and were empowered to offer bribes. When a cloth manufacturer of Rouen was so ill-advised as to go to Portugal, the ambassador at Lisbon was told to harass the man and his family till he decided to return. It is as if Colbert saw economic development as a kind of war, in which no unit was too small to be neglected.

Workers could be found more easily than capital. Alongside the sponsoring of new projects went a stream of propaganda aimed at persuading financiers, magistrates, even bishops, to support the money campaign, to overcome 'the difficulties that merchants, by their own private efforts cannot surmount'. Royalist and militarist sentiment blend in the reiterated message: 'the trading companies are the armies of the king and the manufactures of France their reserves'. One effect was to release for industrial purposes some – not enough – of the capital that was locked up in the great commercial companies, notably the *merciers*, who had the right of selling certificates of mastery and controlled the corporations which monopolised trade in cloth, silks, gold and silver ware – all the crafts that Colbert wanted to promote. It bore fruit in capitalist enterprises without which many of his schemes would have been still-born. Formont was a lifetime collaborator with Colbert and cloth manufacturer; *receveur-général* Claustrier a manufacturer of gold thread at Lyon; Dalliez de la Tour had interests in armaments and mines; Jabach, from Cologne, financed the weaving of tapestries at Aubusson – it was men like these who did most to bridge the gap between Colbertism, as theory, and the creation of wealth which was its aim. Colbert could usually get a good response from Huguenots debarred by their faith from public office, as in reborn, bustling La Rochelle. Quite different was his experience of Marseille which obstructed his efforts to change trading patterns to export cloth from Languedoc to the Levant. The merchants of Lyon would only agree to subscribe to the East India Company on condition that one of its regional chambers be established in the city. Typical of France as a whole was Dijon, once the centre of a prosperous cloth trade and well placed for international commerce. Rich in land and vineyards, buying up offices for further security, its bourgeois had no time for new industrial projects.[15] Interest rates were a crucial factor, and they remained high. When it was possible to get 6 per cent in safe investment why risk money in trading companies? It is in such attitudes that we can see a crucial difference between Louis XIV's France and the maritime powers, and the way in which France and England would continue to evolve along the divergent paths that had already been marked out, in constitutional terms, by their political history.

Looking at high interest rates and low returns on most commercial investments, it is possible to judge Colbertism as essentially misdirected, even futile. If so it was not for want of effort. There is a heroism about the man, apparently inexhaustible and unbowed by checks and losses. Directives and memoranda flowed from his pen to the *intendants* and inspectors who had to carry them out. As well as the Inspectorate-general of Manufactures, with its travelling agents, regional committees were set up, on which sat industrialists and merchants. With the guilds they were given a double role: the maintenance of standards which would impress the world's buyers, and the enforcement of the social and economic discipline which was so dear to him. An edict of 1669 concerning textiles was one of a hundred and fifty such. It specified texture and dyes, with the number of threads to the warp and woof, the length and breadth of every piece. For offences against the regulations the manufacturer could be put in the pillory, with the offending article round his neck. Peasants in ragged homespun might be bemused to watch a bonfire of defective goods in the marketplace.

Such an example shows the process of state intervention in the worst light. The great Ordinance of Commerce of 1673 puts it into perspective. It established rules for apprenticeships, contracts and bankruptcies and swept away a mass of local customs. It was intended to be only part of a wider reform of the whole judicial system. The infinite variety of laws and customs and the overlapping layers of jurisdiction were anathema to the minister's rational and tidy mind. Reform was also a family interest and he was advised by a learned uncle, Henri Colbert de Pussort. Committees were set up to examine the situation and draw up codes. In 1667 an ordinance dealt with civil procedure; in 1669 another with the strategically vital areas of rivers and forests. In 1670 crime was the target. Altogether Colbert saw 'a great work which has been preserved in its entirety for Louis XIV' – but which, in the end, had to wait for Napoleon, despite all that was achieved in the Civil and Criminal Ordinances. The rhetoric, as ever, is grander than the achievement; the achievement overall should not be belittled.

It did not need comparison with the waterways of Holland to convince Colbert of the importance of improving internal communications. He ordered the repair of roads and bridges. Between Paris and Orléans the first road was completed with the *pavé* that was to become standard surface (and an uncomfortable memory for older twentieth-century drivers). For labour, *intendants* could exploit the *corvée* introduced by Sully. That enterprising minister, and Richelieu after him, had sponsored canal-building. The greatest enterprise of Colbert's time was the canal of 'The Two Seas'. Its principal engineer was Riquet. When completed, in 1681, 170 miles of waterway from the Garonne to the Aude linked Atlantic Bordeaux to Mediterranean Toulon. It marked 'the grandeur, abundance and felicity of his reign'. It also brought measurable benefits, reducing the cost of transport by three-quarters. It should be added that the main influence behind the scheme, without which it would have failed for lack of support from the Estates, was that of the enterprising archbishop of Toulouse. After all the projecting and planning of new enterprises action on the ground was almost invariably preceded by bargaining to secure the cooperation of local bodies – for which the minister needed the good will and patronage of the local grandee.

There were still only two other canals of importance, the Briaire and Orléans. Travellers still feared brigands, even as near to Paris as the forest of Fontainebleau. The transport of goods remained costly. The internal tolls of the country were so various and numerous, many of them mediaeval survivals, that only a specialist could know them. The river Rhône alone had more than forty toll stations. Some that could prove no right were abolished in 1664. In the 'Five Great Farms', the central provinces which approximated to the core Capetian domain and which were most amenable to direct crown action, Colbert did establish uniform rates. Outside this area many barriers to trade remained. Wine would be four days in transit from Paris to Orléans, bales of cloth a month from Rouen to Lyon. Throughout the reign the newly acquired province of Alsace could trade more profitably with German states than with France.

TRADE AND SEA POWER

In 1600 there had been only one colonial power deserving the name of empire. Reluctant partners for sixty years, Spain and Portugal were split after the revolt of Portugal in 1640. Spain kept most of her lands but the Portuguese lost the richest part of her eastern possessions to the Dutch. By 1661, though the English were challenging strongly, the United Provinces, having about three-quarters of the Europe's merchant shipping, controlled the external trade of Arabia and dominated Indonesia and Far Eastern waters. Queen Catherine of Braganza's dowry had given the English footholds in India, in Madras and Bombay. Their settlements in North America were more important, stretching, by 1664, from South Carolina north toward the St Lawrence. On the banks of the river French settlements had grown up early in the century, following the remarkable travels of Samuel Champlain. The struggles of the future between New England and New France could be foreseen. Opportunities beckoned. The Dutch absorption of the Portuguese Far Eastern Empire had taxed their resources fully and three trade wars with England (1654–74) brought grievous loss in ships and money. The early English Puritan impulse towards colonisation had passed. Neither Spain nor her maturing colonies were likely to produce any new *conquistador* initiatives. Sustained French effort in North America might therefore give her the lasting control of the virgin lands explored by her hunters and missionaries. The time was also ripe for a trade offensive into the ocean lanes where the *fleur de lis* was so rarely seen.

Colonies should serve the parent country exclusively by providing natural resources and a market for her manufactures: that was common ground. Spain looked to the silver of Peru, Holland to the spices of the east, England to the timber and furs of North America. England's Navigation Acts had already advertised her aggressive brand of protection. Colbert foresaw that future trade wars would be fought over the possession of colonies. Wearing the mantle of Richelieu Colbert went further than the cardinal, further indeed than any contemporary statesman, in working out a science of colonisation. Each colony was to be a 'Little France', reserved for Frenchmen, living under French laws, reserving its products for the homeland and accepting only French manufactures. Not for the French colonist the haphazard proprietary arrangements which were to remain a characteristic of England's colonies. Where possible the settlements were administered through monopolist companies directly under the crown. In 1664 the first two such companies were founded: that of the West Indies, based at Le Havre; that of the East Indies at Lorient. The Company of the North was founded in 1670 to challenge the Dutch grip over Baltic trade in timber and naval stores. More promising were the prospects of the Levant Company, formed in 1671, with businessmen in charge and the grant of a state premium on every piece of cloth. Trading from Marseille and Toulon this company could compete on good terms with its English rivals.

Colbert's economic imperialism faced problems so daunting that it commands respect for its vision and courage. There was no tradition of private commercial enterprise to compare with the enterprise of the merchant adventurers of Holland and England. There had been explorers like Cartier, Champlain and Roberval; bold and hardy fishermen and fur traders from Brittany and Normandy. The typical Frenchman was, however, a reluctant emigrant. There had been no community exodus to compare with those of the religious minority groups from England. The missionary activity of the religious orders had an unfortunate effect: it debarred Huguenots from the New World. It was also government policy. When the Huguenots left France in the 1680s they went to all parts of the world – except New France. The ethos of the nobility was unsympathetic to projects of trade and settlement and capitalists were reluctant to finance them. Louis was unconvinced of their importance. He might listen and subscribe dutifully to projects for new companies, but they were of little real interest to him. His vision of glory was framed by the Rhine and the Pyrenees and focused on more traditional military goals. Against this indifference Colbert could make limited headway. Glowing prospectuses were commissioned from the pens of academicians. A brilliant future, promised Charpentier, awaited the East Indies Company. Few responded and some objected. Colbert's insistence on monopoly and his apparent indifference to the experience of private merchants aroused irritation. The Chamber of Commerce at Marseille urged him to leave them alone, for monopolist companies were 'odious to God and man'. Yet the experience of Canada suggests, from what was achieved, what might have been: another kind of power than that which the king pursued.

In 1663 Canada had only 2,500 inhabitants. Its expansion was entrusted to the Company of the West Indies which was granted a ten-year monopoly of trade. He sent out Jean Talon to be *intendant* of the colony: he was able and ambitious. Emigrants trickled out. Before long the colony had its own law court, bishop, and royal troops at the governor's disposal. The lands of the Huron and Illinois Indians were explored and 'concessions' staked out by adventurers like Cavelier de la Salle. With the pioneers went the Jesuits, always at their best in raw missionary situations, courting martyrdom, teaching the gospel – and the benefits of the protection of the great king. Two years after his appointment, the end of the company's monopoly liberated governor Frontenac for more decisive action. Overriding Laval, bishop of Quebec, and the independent-minded Jesuits, he was unpopular but effective. At the end of his ten-year rule ten thousand Frenchmen were strung out in communities along the valley of the St Lawrence river, mainly in Quebec and Montreal, more thinly in missions and forts along the route of the Great Lakes. Military posts protected the frontier against Indians and English. With its superb natural situation Quebec was becoming an important port. New France was underpopulated but it was starting to look like an impregnable redoubt and base for the exploration and conquest of North America.

From a draft plan to a potent empire: one way forward was shown by La Salle's astonishing journey down the Mississippi. On his way down, with a handful of soldiers and friars, the indomitable Norman noted the confluence of the Missouri and Ohio rivers; for a month he was lost in a maze of lakes and islets before he found the main stream. It bore him through Arkansas to the Gulf of Mexico. There, in April 1682, he arrived at the river mouth in the Gulf of Mexico, where his men set up a cross, sang a *Te Deum* and declared possession of all the land they had traversed. All was done in the name of God and of the king, in whose honour they called it Louisiana. On the return journey, on an escarpment 600 feet high, La Salle built a new fort,

Saint-Louis. When he returned to France he offered Louis the prodigious prospect of an empire stretching from the Great Lakes to the Gulf of Mexico. Louis was impressed. He had already granted La Salle title of nobility. But to encourage more Frenchmen to settle, to provide resources for stronger forts, more soldiers and, above all, ships, there had to be more than the momentary interest of the flattered king. Nothing less was needed than a re-direction of policy, a re-ordering of priorities – and that at Versailles, emerging vast and grand from its scaffolding, its fresh paint and plaster dazzling courtiers with images of military triumph. The *réunions*, the Rhine frontier, Cologne, the Spanish Succession, were the preoccupation of king and court. Where in this scene was there room for a little wooden fort in the swamps and forests of the New World, a rough handful of settlers and missionaries planting their flags and crosses? Anyway, it was the *contrôleur-général*'s business. And in 1683 he died.[16]

It was only part of his business. It is subject to the criticisms that apply to his trading policies as a whole. He could be obstinate to the point of absurdity. He refused to allow the West Indian planters to trade their molasses with the New Englanders who wished to sell their provisions in exchange. He insisted on excluding foreigners altogether from French settlements. Imports of tobacco were granted to a syndicate which had a monopoly of the market. As a result neither state nor producer benefited fully. Is it fair, however, to blame the rigid application of state control for the later failure of French settlements? Colbert's views were typical of the xenophobic character of mercantilism, views which would suffuse the hundred-year colonial war that was to come. If he had overlaid enterprise with regulation, he has also fostered communities with the capacity to survive. At the same time he was creating a navy to match the English. One is left to guess what might have been if Louis had given to its further development a reasonable share of the resources that went into the land wars. In the last resort all was to depend on sea power. Intelligently applied by the British it would contribute to Wolfe's decisive victory at Quebec in 1759. Even so one may wonder what the verdict on Colbert would have been if the British soldiers had failed in their last throw, the risky climb up the Heights of Abraham. Would he have been seen as the prime creator, against the odds, of a North American empire that survived?

Another way of assessing Colbert's achievement is to look at the overall situation in 1714, the year peace was made after twenty years of war (out of twenty-five). It should be stressed that the fate of trading companies, though commonly used, is a misleading criterion. When traders had secured a foothold it did not matter if the company later failed. There had been a considerable increase in trade. Following vigorous action against pirates from Naples and the Barbary coast and concessions to the merchants, profitable trade links were established with Syria and Morocco. An entry had been made into the spice market of the Far East and a precarious base established, by the enterprise of François Martin, at Pondicherry. There was a profitable trade in sugar with the potential for huge growth as the *fleur de lis* flew over several Caribbean islands, Martinique, Guadeloupe, Saint-Christophe and Antigua. The Company of Senegal shipped black slaves to work in the plantations, while in France itself improved refining methods were creating a new industry. Sugar and slaves were carried in French ships. The busy wharves of Nantes and La Rochelle witnessed to the extent of this trade at a time when Liverpool and Glasgow were insignificant. In 1664 there were only sixty merchant ships of over 300 tons; twenty years later there were 700, to play their part in the 'money war', to carry brandy, olive oil and cloth to the colonies and French goods of high value to England, Spain and the Levant. At the end of Louis's reign, foreign trade was worth 200 million *livres* a year, of which two-thirds was exports. Given contemporary political and social attitudes it cannot be seriously contended that this had little to do with Colbert's policies. They contributed significantly to the wealth and power of the state.

An integral part of his overall economic strategy, the most quantifiable and, in some ways, most remarkable among Colbert's achievements, was the re-creation of the navy. Thinking along the same lines, and with a strong personal interest and base in the western provinces, Richelieu had made a determined start. He had resolved the crucial question of authority by abolishing the feudal admiralty and vesting authority in himself, under the crown. He had bequeathed a small Atlantic fleet. Galleys were used effectively against Mediterranean pirates. Improved facilities at Brest and Le Havre were part of the infrastructure without which no progress could be made in the huge task of a navy to compete with the English and Dutch. Inevitably, after 1635, the bulk of the revenue went to keeping the armies in the field. To Mazarin, struggling for his own political life and for the defeat of Spain, naval concerns were almost irrelevant. The king's ships rotted at their anchors. Meanwhile Dutch and English shipbuilders honed their skills and their seamen won experience in costly battles. The naval war of 1652–54 showed that, in a war of fleet actions, the converted merchantman could be no substitute for a regular navy.

Developments in the naval world were similar to those of armies: stricter state control, greater professional efficiency, more effective recruitment, more attention to support services and supply. In England, for instance, reforms culminating in the work of Samuel Pepys laid down tactical principles, disciplinary rules and standards for dockyards, which were to be the model for all subsequent advance. Progress among navies was stimulated by the intense commercial rivalry of England and Holland. Colbert saw from the outset that a powerful navy was essential to give effective backing to his trade initiatives and tariff wars. A measure of rebuilding was inevitable in any case for the appearance of sailing warships in the Mediterranean limited the use of galleys to pirate patrol. The larger task fired Colbert's imagination and taxed to the full his administrative talent. The importance he attached to the work can be seen in the care – and success – with which he groomed his son Seignelay to succeed him as naval minister.

Dockyards and arsenals were constructed at Toulon, Brest, Rochefort and Dunkirk, in order that the new fleets might be built and equipped entirely in France. Dunkirk was Vauban's first work and, to his patron, 'the most grand and beautiful design of fortification in the world'. Forests were laid low and others planted for ships' timber; an inventory was made of trees within reach of all rivers suitable for floating trunks to the shipyards. Sailors were recruited from coastal towns and villages from Bayonne to Dunkirk. From the haphazard injustices of the press Colbert turned to a regular system of conscription. Of course it was unpopular despite allowances, including exemption from the *taille*. A register was kept of all classes of seamen, a system so efficient that it has been retained to the present day. A path-breaking study of the *classes maritimes* has shown the strength and range of the resistance that could be mustered when absolutism was translated into hard practice.[17] It came not only from the fishermen, whose livelihood was threatened, or naval officers, now listed in seniority (introducing a principle wholly foreign to the ethos of the time) but from provincial *parlements*. The remaining galleys of Provence provided no problem, with the flow of prisoners to man the oars soon to be reinforced by Huguenots. Colbert applied himself restlessly to the smallest details. The commander at Le Havre was ordered to see that his ships were kept clean and brightly painted within and without so that merchants should be attracted by them. Prizes were awarded for naval construction and for gunnery; schools were started for naval cadets. With the help of the *Académie des Sciences* (founded in 1666), the reform of hydrography was taken in hand.

Like his English counterpart Pepys, Colbert found that his greatest problem lay in discipline: how to instil the regular notions of a department of state in place of the casual ways of the former traders, adventurers and amateurish noblemen who commanded the new ships? He was not helped by the independent attitude of commanders such as Châteaurenard or Duquesne. The latter was an accomplished seaman who had started life as a pirate. The solution, inevitably, was the *intendant*. As with the army, the factory or the distant province, the trained lawyer, commissioned to serve the state, came to ensure obedience and loyalty. At the same time, the formation of a regular officer corps, the *compagnie des gardes de la marines* helped meet the need. Parallel commands made for difficulties but the point was slowly made. Before Colbert's death his navy had won its first battles and was a fighting instrument ready to contest the seas with the established sea powers. Duquesne twice defeated the Dutch in running battles off the coast of Sicily, January to April 1676.[18] The great De Ruyter was killed in the second action. The ability and courage of Tourville made the navy, for a brief but glorious time at the start of the war of the League of Augsburg, a real threat to Anglo-Dutch supremacy. Colbert found some twenty ships. He left two hundred and fifty. After the death of his son Seignelay, who proved both devoted and competent, despite the best efforts of his successor Jérôme de Pontchartrain,[19] the navy was allowed to run down and reduced to the subordinate role of commerce raiding. In the hands of adventurous seamen such as Jean Bart it made a large contribution to the war effort as may be seen in the insistence of the English parliament on the destruction of the fortifications of Dunkirk. The port had commissioned eight hundred corsairs by 1713. Such men, and such a style of war, were far from Colbert's notion of a naval power to enhance the glory of the king.

Notes

1. For the prime example of the liberal, bourgeois progressive view, see Ernest Lavisse, most accessible in *Louis XIV*, 2 vols (Paris, 1983): a new edition, with introduction by R. and S. Pillorget (stressing Lavisse's political commitment to republicanism colouring his view of Louis XIV) of the main parts of his immense *Histoire de France depuis les origines jusqu'à la Revolution*. For economic aspects generally see Bibliography. A magisterial work which may still be a starting point is C.W. Cole, *Colbert and a Century of French Mercantilism* (New York, 1938). 'Cold, humourless, hardworking, narrow, devoted' is his opinion of the man he pursued through his two volumes: vol. I, p. 300. The most recent full study is J. Meyer, *Colbert* (Paris, 1981). A useful short account is A.P. Trout, *Jean-Baptiste Colbert* (Boston, 1978). The substantial catalogue of the 1983 exhibition, *Colbert* (Hôtel de la Monnaie, Paris), gives an idea of the extraordinary range of Colbert's activities.

2. Two recent articles in *Seventeenth-Century French Studies* have explored Colbert's patronage of the arts and sciences. R. Maber, 'Colbert and the scholars, Ménage, Huet and the royal pensions of 1663', VII (1985), 106–14, describes his methods.

D.S. Lux, 'Colbert's plan for the Grande Académie: royal policy towards science, 1663–67', XII (1990), pp. 177–88, discusses his vaulting plan for a single superior academy to encourage and exploit the various disciplines.

3. As portrayed in Paul Sonnino, *Louis XIV and the Origins of the Dutch War* (Cambridge, 1988). Among many examples, see p. 49, starting 'Louis was not an easy man to hold in check'.

4. See p. 187.

5. Barthélemy Laffemas (1545–1612) was author of the suggestively titled *Les Trésors et Richesses de la France* (1597), Antoine de Montchrétien (1570–1621) of the influential *Traité de l'Economie politique* (1615).

6. Accepted – but only after much lively debate which can be traced back to its major source, E. Hecksher, *Mercantilism* (1935). It may be followed, relatively painlessly, through the writing of Charles Wilson, an economic historian who also wrote well, as in 'Treasure and the trade balance: the mercantilist problem', *Economic History Review*, 2, 1949; or *Mercantilism*, Historical Association pamphlet, no. G 37 (1958).

7. For the periodic use of this instrument of financial recovery and political control, see J.F. Bosher, '*Chambres de justice* in the French monarchy', in Bosher (ed.), *French Government and Society* (London, 1973), pp. 19–41.

8. Quoted by R. Mousner, *La vénalité des offices sous Henri IV et Louis XIII* (Paris, 1971), p. 7.

9. W. Beik, *Absolutism and Society in Seventeenth-century France* (Cambridge, 1985), p. 119 .

10. See R. Bonney, 'Jean-Roland Malet: historian of the finances of the French monarchy', *French History*, vol. 5, no. 2, 1991, for the source and accuracy of his figures, on which most accounts of French royal income are based. He was a *premier commis* in the *contrôle-générale* under Desmarets from 1708, then, after his fall in 1715, served successive ministers till his death in 1736. His *Comptes rendu de l'administration des finances du royaume de France* was completed by 1720. It was intended as a justification of Desmarets's policies, but the sums are as reliable as anything available, for Malet was an a insider, with privileged access to the figures and an understanding of what they meant.

11. The main authority on the Breton revolts is Y. Garlan and C. Nières, *Les révoltes bretonnes de 1675* (Paris, 1975). For a short account see R. Mousnier, *Fureurs paysannes* (Paris, 1967), pp. 123–56.

12. Olivier de Serres (1539–1619), author of *Théâtre de l'Agriculture*.

13. *La Visite aux Gobelins*, the tapestry of Le Brun from the series, *l'Histoire des Rois* (*c.* 1670) shows Louis visiting a busy, perhaps somewhat flurried, studio–workshop.

14. Locke, op. cit., p. 217, 11 August 1678. This little subject worked 'from 5 in the morning till night, only rests twice in the day . . . and has for her day's work 5 s[ous], a small recompence for drawing such a weight 7 leagues, for soe much they say she goes in a day. The wages was formerly greater.' Locke, providing here a snapshot of the human toll of economic depression, has earlier commented: 'The workemen complain of want of worke, decay of trade & abatement of wages.'

15. The classic study of G. Roupnel, *La Ville et la Campagne au XVIIe siècle* (2nd edn, 1955) portrays this little world, relatively secure after the battering endured in decades of war: he estimates (p. 133) 1,200 office-holders in 1698, 889 clergy (priests, monks

and nuns). With massive evidence, pp. 199ff., he chronicles '*La conquête du Sol*', tolling the bell for the eclipse of the old nobility.

16. F. Bluche, *Louis XIV*, op. cit., pp. 135–6, 155–6, makes out a strong case for the close cooperation of Louis with Colbert. Moreover (p. 301), 'Louis XIV and Colbert had vision enough to foresee the longer-term interest which would develop in colonies on the American continent.' If Colbert had lived longer, or if land war had not consumed so much of the next thirty years would Louis had persisted in this vision?

17. E. Asher, *Resistance to the Maritime Classes: the Survival of Feudalism in the France of Colbert* (California, 1960) throws light on this and related aspects of government.

18. But a modern naval historian is sceptical about Duquesne's achievement. 'All the so-called glory of Duquesne comes down to two days.' D. Dessert, *La Royale: Vaisseaux et marins du Roi-Soleil* (Paris, 1996).

19. The reputation of Jérôme Phelypeaux, comte de Pontchartrain has been enhanced recently, mainly by the work of C. Frostin, as in 'Les Pontchartrain et la pénétration commerciale française en Amérique espagnole (1690–1715)', *Revue historique*, 498 (1971), pp. 307–36.

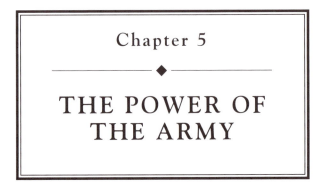

Chapter 5

THE POWER OF
THE ARMY

The most remarkable instrument of state power that Europe had yet seen.

MICHAEL HOWARD (on the French army)

A DEFECTIVE INSTRUMENT

For Colbert Louis had a steady respect. He was indispensable. He might make difficulties when expenditure was in question but he seemed to subscribe wholeheartedly to the overriding principle of policy. 'When your Majesty's glory is at stake', he once observed, 'what do the millions matter?' That the millions did matter to Colbert, and with them his say in the making of policies that would determine how they would be spent, can be seen, however, in his protracted struggle with the Le Telliers. Father and son, they were busy fashioning the most formidable instrument of power that the world had seen, a standing temptation to a sovereign avid for glory. For Michel le Tellier Louis had a deeper feeling, compounded of admiration and gratitude.[1] War minister since 1643, he had done as much as any one to ensure victory against the Habsburgs and the emergence of the crown stronger from the Fronde. 'I never had a better councillor', Louis wrote, 'and on all sorts of matters.' For Michel *fils*, marquis de Louvois, Louis had something like friendship. After the outbreak of the War of Devolution in 1666 a confident young man, groomed by his father to succeed, hungry for work and power, he was constantly at the king's side, as attentive and eager to please his master as he was brusque and arrogant with others. Meanwhile he channelled his own frustrated military ambitions into administration, determined to be tough on indiscipline and on its causes. More evidently than his father,

Louvois was determined to have a strategic role, to direct the movements of his cherished armies. Since Le Tellier *père* maintained his interest, and the process of reform was gradual, it is otherwise fruitless to distinguish between his role and his son's. Certainly the process was well advanced before Louvois took a formal part. It evolved out of the disturbing experiences of the Thirty Years War, its geographical spread and long duration, with an increase in the size of armies not matched by political control. It was made possible by the strengthening of royal authority.

There is still room for debate about the nature of the twin process. Was absolutism the product, essentially, of the growth in the size of armies and the consequent fiscal pressures enforcing administrative change? Or, the other way round, did stronger government make military reform possible since, for the first time, the sovereign could become, in reality, master of the soldiers who fought in his name?[2] Each view represents a way of looking at what was essentially a single process. After 1635 government under the cardinals was war government, first growing more ambitious in response to military demands, then, during the Fronde, improvising tenaciously to keep the war going. Louis XIV's reign would see completed the change from an army recruited by multiple contract to one commissioned by the state. The creation of a regular, in some respects modern, army in the personal reign of Louis XIV would not have been possible, however, without the unprecedented concentration of power in the hands of the king and his ministers.

In a century which saw only seven calendar years without a war somewhere in Europe, and in which there had been a steady increase in scale, France now led the way. Its military reforms cannot however be viewed in isolation, being part of the European phenomenon which historians have labelled the military revolution. Its main features are an increase in the size and cost of armies and navies, in the scale and sophistication of fortresses, developments in weapons and tactical changes and improvements in field discipline calculated to make the best use of them. In consequence there could be more ambitious campaigns with larger armies kept longer in the field. With significant changes in the ways in which armies were used went political changes. The state that could not raise or control a sufficient force, or find the means of maintaining it on a regular footing, became vulnerable. Here or there a province would be lost, eventually, in the most notorious case, a country. The partitions of Poland (1772, 1793, 1795) could hardly have been anticipated a century earlier: meanwhile, however, the condition of Spain was alarming enough. Those states that remained in the foreground, or forced their way to it, experienced a profound challenge to existing constitutional and administrative structures. However resolved, it could only lead to a larger role for the state and to a more strictly ordered society. That stronger state would be better positioned to develop its military power. In the eighteenth century the example of Brandenburg–Prussia would show what a relatively small state could achieve, becoming a leading military power through efficient mechanisms of finance and recruitment. The case is exceptional. In the 1690s the French army exceeded 1.5 per cent of the population, a ratio never again achieved.[3] It placed an intolerable burden on the economy and it was that, rather than the authority or administrative capacity of government, that determined the future size of armed forces.

Meanwhile society was profoundly affected. More men came directly into state service. At both ends of the social scale, for disaffected nobleman or destitute vagrant, military service offered a hopeful alternative to an empty life. Especially, in any family it was the younger son who was most likely to be drawn to serve for honour, bread or profitable adventure. Society became gradually more manageable when its victims and outsiders were drawn into the military machine. Many were indirectly involved in supply or administration. A few *munitionnaires* made great fortunes; at the humblest level many were harassed, even ruined, by demands for billets and food for men and horses – a further incentive to the peasant to enlist. As taxpayers, most of the community were affected; how seriously emerges from the experience of one province. In 1682 the residents of Bourg-en-Bresse, Coligny and Villars decided to abandon their homes 'since they could no longer bear the burden of billeting'. In 1694, after a disastrous harvest Bresse and Bugey were reduced to famine by the passage of 17,000 soldiers who spent five nights in the region.

The macro-economic picture shows another, more benign side of the growth of armies. Development was not confined to men under arms and the swelling world of officialdom. The state's activity as largest purchaser of food, textiles, metalware, gunpowder, timber and naval stores, and as largest employer in construction, for harbours, fortresses and roads, had a stimulating effect on demand. It undoubtedly helped to mitigate the effects of the long price recession. The military concerns of the state could also be, as in modern times, a stimulus to science and technology. Among economic effects should be included the evolution of credit finance (though France did not benefit, unlike England and Holland, because of the failure to create a central bank), and the refinement of management skills. At a time when most of those wounded later died, and more died of disease in camp than on the battlefield, medicine, particularly surgery, was promoted by the pressing need to conserve manpower. Not only was the military revolution at the heart of the development of absolute government; it affected profoundly, at all levels and in most activities, the evolution of society.

The French army which won the battle of Rocroi in 1643, the year of Le Tellier's appointment as secretary of state, owed little to training or discipline. Nowhere had amateurism and personal, local loyalties, relics of the feudal spirit, obstructed the state more than in France. Le Tellier's own description of the army was: 'a republic, composed of as many provinces as there are Lieutenant-Generals'.[4] The tactical improvements of Gustavus Adolphus, the technical innovations of Maurice of Nassau and those of Cromwell in uniform and discipline, had not reached France. The French were little used to the large-scale operations of armies which had advanced the art of war since 1618, nor the cohesive professionalism required of an army like the Spanish which had generally to fight far from home. Richelieu had so mistrusted French contingents, levied by traditional methods, that he had raised Swiss, Germans, Scots and Irish to swell his ranks. His posthumous justification was a great victory, but the soldiers' élan and the flair of the young Condé did not constitute military power. The high personal repute of Condé and Turenne and the way in which they exploited their position during the Fronde, highlighted the government's problem: its echoes can be heard, especially in the case of Turenne, in the policy debates before and during the Devolution and Dutch wars; but then the general's view was balanced by those of ministers, and all was firmly under the authority of the king. By then too the army was becoming more of a reliable instrument of state.

CONTROL, DISCIPLINE AND RECRUITMENT

In 1661, with the double advantage of peace and a strong king, Le Tellier was able to move from piecemeal measures to radical reform, starting with the crucial area: commissioning and recruiting. In that year, the duc d'Épernon died and Louis XIV assumed his post of Colonel-general of Infantry. Feudal in tradition, largely mercenary in composition, the army had not been, effectively, his army, but a medley of levies, for which the king was only chief among many contractors, biggest among many shareholders. His experiences during the Fronde had shown him that the enthusiasm of the soldiers for the idea that he should lead them was no guarantee that noble officers would not lead them into a dissident camp. Regiments were not his property so he had little political control. The Secretary for War had none beyond what negotiation could secure and his main concern was to keep the army at the front. Richelieu's war minister Sublet de Noyers had instituted *intendants de l'armée*. In the 1650s, with that experience behind him Le Tellier had started to build up a staff of *commissaires de guerre*, largely composed, typically, of his friends and relations.

The army was still an irregular and shabby force, with a high rate of desertion and discipline that depended precariously on floggings and hangings. A noble officer would view a military commission in a traditional but materialist light. War was his métier; his commission was a form of investment whose price rose with war, or preparations for it, and fell in peace or rumoured negotiations. Such insecurity encouraged speculation and provided no incentive to spend time and money on field training. When infantry officers held their commissions direct from the king and every commission was countersigned by the minister, the way was open to raise standards. Louis took the job most seriously, checking even minor appointments. He was not able to abolish purchase but tried to restrict it to the wealthy who would not rely on it as a speculation. For well-placed grandees there was scope for lucrative patronage in recruitment to the regiments of the *Maison du Roi*. Meanwhile, however, a new ladder of promotion was set alongside the old, with two new, unpurchaseable ranks, lieutenant-colonel and major. So even in the army, where noble privilege had the highest profile (and most obvious justification), the new man found room at the top. When in 1684 the king created twenty-seven new infantry regiments, there was not one colonel who had not been either major or lieutenant-colonel. A surprising number of rankers rose in Louis XIV's army, more than in the eighteenth century when there was reaction against this levelling tendency: two marshals, Catinat and Fabert were *roturier* in origin. Of all men, Saint-Simon could refer, without apparent disapproval, to one Boissieux, a fellow officer in the Royal regiment of Roussillon, who 'has started life as a swineherd, and risen by sheer merit; though old he has never learned to read or write'. The idea of 'a career open to talents' seems to belong to the 1789 revolution but it was, in a limited way, the principle on which Louis's government was based.

Some old abuses died hard. The *passe-volant*, or false muster, was a time-honoured fraud: a captain, drawing pay for a full company, might borrow men, 'faggots', from another company and present a full complement for inspection. Louvois encouraged soldiers to inform against a corrupt officer. A detected 'faggot' was flogged and branded; after 1667 he would be hanged. When the minister heard of a case hushed up by the governor of Belle-Isle, the governor forfeited a month's pay and the captain was cashiered. It was by such measures that Louvois gained his formidable reputation. When he first appeared at the front he had been treated with disdain by Turenne who used his prestige to block reforms. But he could rely on the support of the king, himself a stickler for detail, and he lost no chance to put down an insolent or idle officer. With one he concluded an interview: 'either declare yourself a courtier or do your duty as an officer'. The case of Dufay, defender of Philippsburg, shows that he had a long reach. He had had a soldier shot without reference to the minister who 'learned with surprise of the fact, so that it was necessary to remind the king of his past services to prevent his being dismissed and put into prison'.[5] Foreigners could not expect special treatment. In 1685 Lord Hamilton was criticised for the state of his regiment and retorted that he would go home to serve under James II. Louvois reported the matter to the king who declared that it was only out of respect for Hamilton's sister, comtesse de Gramont, that he had not had him sent to the Bastille.

The example of the king, and the expectations of women ensured that war would be the fashion at court and military service a social duty. Mme de Sévigné wrote on 10 August 1677: 'The news of the siege of Charleroi has sent all the young, even the lame, hurrying to serve.' A few days later she was 'longing to know if we had given battle' and was reassured after contacting Mme de Louvois: 'such a relief to be able to dismiss the war from one's mind'.[6] Military triumphalism was an all-pervading theme. It reflected but also appeared to justify, and therefore further influenced, the king's policies. Women played their part, responding to soldiering as an aphrodisiac, and echoing the traditional language of the tournament, when they proclaimed that they would give their favours only to those who fought. Sculptors and painters might wrap the theme in classical garb but courtiers read a contemporary message.[7] When there was no fighting on the frontiers, officers would press the king for leave to fight further afield: in 1685, for instance, in Poland against the Turks.

Reckless courage was expected of the nobleman. Professional year-round commitment was another matter. Training was haphazard or non-existent though an attempt was made, with some success, to establish cadet companies at frontier towns. Louvois bullied some incompetents to give up their commissions. Senior generals who questioned reforms might be sent to their country estates to reconsider their position. Inspectors of Infantry and Cavalry were appointed to stiffen discipline, one of the former, Jean Martinet, with a severity which has given his name to the English language. The creation of a regular reserve of officers seems to have been Louis's own contribution. It made possible the speedy mobilisation of the army in 1667.

In 1668 officers allegedly demobilised were secretly absorbed into permanent formations. Further war was clearly anticipated.

To recruit sound young men to the rank and file, Louvois sought to make soldiering respectable. A recruit was expected to sign on for four years, to be single, and physically fit. If destined for the *maison du roi* he should be a Catholic and, if possible, *gentilhomme*. Inevitably as successive wars of attrition strained the country's resources of manpower standards fell. Desertion was always a serious problem. Rounding up vagabonds in Paris the authority would find many young ex-soldiers. Of the 7,000 under marshal Vivonne's command in 1677 some 4,000 deserted; in ten days, in the following year, the crack regiment of Champagne lost sixty-five men. During this war Luxembourg complained that his troops were 'deplorable', half of them 'children whom I shall have to send back to France'. In 1689 Vauban urged a defensive campaign because the infantry differed in quality from that of the last war. By 1703 Louis was reduced to offering five years' exemption from tax to any man who would enlist for three years. Only hunger would tempt the average peasant to go soldiering. In 1707 the unpaid actors of Marseille opera house joined up. Significantly a high proportion of recruits came from war-seasoned eastern provinces, from the uplands, and from further afield, from Scotland, Ireland, Switzerland, and Savoy.

The Dutch, Nine Years and Spanish Succession wars fought against coalitions demanded an army of unprecedented size. Because he understood the discrepancies between the nominal and the available, and knew that about a third were dispersed in garrisons, Louis called repeatedly for a realistic assessment of numbers. Historians still seek it and realise that figures like the following can only be approximate.[8] Roughly in line with other continental countries, the trend is as important as the figures. Rising from around 85,000 in 1667 to upwards of 250,000 ten years later at the height of the Dutch war; further, after an inter-war dip, to an all-time peak of 340,000 in 1696 (the last figure includes the militia): such figures suggest both an administrative miracle and a crushing burden on the people. It was all achieved in a time of virtually static population.

There were many foreigners in the ranks: during the Dutch war, for example, there were Swiss (20,000), Piedmontese, Genoese, Germans, Irish, even Hungarians. Nor was the army of later years composed solely of professional soldiers. Waiting to be resurrected was the feudal *ban*. When convoked in 1636 it had produced such a motley array that it was found expedient to turn it into a tax. In 1675 the principle was revived and marshal

Créqui had received, with some consternation, a muster of *hobereaux*, armed with archaic weapons or with none. In 1688 Louvois went further in starting a local militia, drawn by lot from every village, armed, equipped and drilled by the parish. Later the parishes were allowed to send 100 *livres* in place of a man.

The militia also became a device for raising men for the regular army. Between 1701 and 1713, 260,000 were recruited in this way, nearly half the total number. Militia duty, moreover, was not confined to garrisons. At Malplaquet and Denain the militia played a heroic part. That has to be judged in the context of the country's crisis, Louis's appeal to his people and the spirit it roused.[9] It is, however, ironic, that after the labours of the Le Telliers to create a great professional army, the salvation of France should have come, even partly, from the spirit of professional soldiers. The ministers' legacy was to be found, however, in the resilience of the army's organisation under the most severe strain.

The armed forces were the sphere in which the absolutist state was most evidently effective, in which there was least distance between claim and accomplishment, between paper and practice. The army, in particular, was the state's spoiled child. Policies that called for its constant employment and enlargement, Louis's keen interest in the incidentals of soldiering and deep need to exercise control, the jealous vigilance of the Le Telliers (sharpened by Colbert's rival concern for the navy), all helped give it a special status in the community. Louvois did little, surprisingly, to encourage the use of uniforms, which can be shown to have a significant effect on discipline. They were compulsory for officers only after 1682, introduced for rank and file largely by the enterprise of individual colonels, and not standardised till 1700. But in small practical ways, and by small privileges, the lot of the soldier was improved. When Huguenots were being 'compensated' in the period of the Revocation Louvois negotiated special tariffs for soldiers. A private received twice as much as a peasant: that can be said to represent the values of the régime. The fact that the army was almost unique in being regularly paid made foreigners keen to enlist. A regular scale of pay was laid down. While its issue came from the captain, after 1670 it was audited by civilians, the *intendants de l'armée*. There were no decorations but tax exemption was offered to reward good conduct.

At one moment discussing allowances in billets, at another ordering extra pay for troops stationed in plague spots, or improved hospital services, Louis showed a personal concern for the soldier's welfare. It is an appealing side of the paternalism that appears otherwise as a desire to dominate. The Hôtel des Invalides, founded in 1674 for ex-soldiers, was the first regular establishment of its kind. Its magnificent dome did more for the skyline of Paris than for the well-being of the 800 pensioners whom Vauban portrays as being bored and listless in their grand surroundings. Ex-servicemen were given a monopoly of sedan-chair traffic in the royal palaces. Pioneering here, soon to be imitated elsewhere, the state can be seen, in these small ways, taking tactical measures to fulfil its responsibilities to its servants, those whom its policies most directly affected. At the same time, from its priorities in society and the prestige it gained from its victories, the army gained a certain *esprit de corps*. The troops who served under Vauban, Catinat and Villars anticipated in some ways the national and professional army of modern times. They were nearer to Napoleon than they were to Condé.

WEAPONRY, FORTRESSES AND SUPPLY

It needed more than intensive recruitment and improvements in serving conditions to make an efficient *force de frappe*. Le Tellier was shocked to hear that many of the soldiers sent to Hungary to fight the Turks in 1664 could not fire a musket. Infantry training had been neglected because social values promoted the cavalry as the favoured arm. The generals tended to be cavalry-minded; infantry existed to follow up the initial charge or to soften up the enemy lines before the decisive thrust of cavalry. This view changed slowly with the increase in the size of the army, the introduction of superior infantry weapons and the prevalence, in Flanders, of siege warfare. By 1691 there were 98 infantry regiments, of which 72 had regular names. Cavalry cost twice as much as infantry and there was a chronic shortage of horses.[10] The proportion of infantry to cavalry remained about four to one. The cavalry remained the smarter arm: it is the social history of armies till modern times. They were now carefully trained, their swords replaced by sabres. Carabineers were attached to squadrons. The annual camps held for field training were attended by the king, his family and attendant courtiers. Louis found the parades and manoeuvres enjoyable in themselves and gratifying as a display of power: how different from the ragged forces he had observed as a boy! From formal review it was a short step to attendance at a real siege, the assault timed to the hour, in the early years in Flanders a delusively easy performance and one relished by the king.

Cavalry tactics altered during the reign. The breeding of a lighter, swifter horse gave a new momentum to the charge, with heavy sabre thrusts from a galloping line. Most of the great battles of the reign were won, however, by the firepower of infantry fighting in line, with musket and *fusil*. In choice of weapons Louvois was conservative. The French infantry was still being given muskets after the introduction of the more serviceable *fusil*, with its flintlock mechanism. Until the end of the century a third of each company was still being armed with the pike, to form a hedgehog of defence. Yet it was already being rendered obsolete by the development of the *baionette à l'aiguille*, needle-shaped, which could be fitted into a socket, allowing free fire. Reports that the French soldiers threw away pike and musket and picked up *fusils* abandoned by the enemy, did not seem to shake the view of the authorities that 'to change is to disarm'.

Infantry had played an inferior part before the reforms of the Le Telliers. Artillery and engineers had hardly belonged to the army at all. Until Vauban's elaborate siege operations made the system impossible, artillery was a civilian affair, provided by contractors who were paid for every gun they brought into action. Louvois brought guns and gunners under straight royal control. Starting with two companies of bombardiers he rapidly increased the size of this arm until, by 1689, there were 24 companies in the now royal corps. With a maximum range of 2,500 yards (Vauban's estimate) and relative accuracy up to 500 yards, loaded with solid round shot, or canisters containing smaller balls or shot, the army's cannon, together with the mortars, whose high trajectory made them essential siege weapons, were a formidable instrument of war. The gun park assembled in Flanders for the siege and field operations of 1690 had 58 cannon, 38 mortars and a million pounds of gunpowder.

The increasing use of artillery meant more and horrifying wounds. Contemporary descriptions of trench conditions, the mud, claustrophobia and the sudden mutilations, might come from 1914–18. One such comes from the siege of Maastricht in 1673: 'Some lacked a leg, some arms. Here there was a soldier whose guts were pouring from his body and over there lay a soldier who had half his face torn away.'[11] Since amputation was the standard response to wounds there would be many *mutilés* among Louis XIV's subjects. But sepsis ensured that most wounded men died. That explains the general acceptance of high casualties in the killing fields of Flanders. 15 per cent of the victorious side, 30 per cent of the losing (and 20 per cent prisoners) was thought the norm. Given the relatively small area within which battles were fought, and the size of armies (80,000 altogether fought at Fleurus, 180,000 at Malplaquet) the dead and wounded would soon lie thick on the ground. The noble officer's thirst for renown, his readiness to die for his king and for glory, the royal chronicler's propaganda and the artist's gloss, should not delude us. The battlefield at the end of the day was as appalling a place as any that soldiers of subsequent centuries would know, as a Tolstoy or a Remarque might describe.

Because of its relevance to the permanent and overriding concern of foreign policy – the vulnerable frontier – and because of the sheer scale and magnificence of the achievement, the growth of military engineering is a major theme of the reign. It is inseparably linked with the name of Sebastien Vauban. Few men have been given such opportunity to leave their mark on landscape and history. Few successful soldiers have been less spoiled by success. A Burgundian, of impoverished noble family, Vauban would show to the end of his life that he was an honest patriot (for once the appropriate word), concerned above all with the security and well-being of his fellow-countrymen. Following Lipsius and his famous pupil Maurice of Nassau in the craft of scientific warfare, Vauban was endlessly ingenious. When he first served under Condé, then the governor of his province, the art of fortification, as taught at Leyden, was a normal part of a gentleman's education. He caught Mazarin's eye by his work on the defences of Stenay. He made his name at Dunkirk (bought from the English) where he turned the wretched fishing village, surrounded by sand dunes, into a fine fortified harbour. With his skilled team, his 'band of Archimedes', he perfected new ways of fortifying and besieging towns. He could claim eventually that he had laid siege to forty places without a failure and sieges, under his direction, became precisely scheduled operations. Louis was present at eighteen of them. Sometimes they were stage-managed for his benefit, with an orchestra primed to play at the moment the mines were set off, the breaches made and the royal party could expect a white flag to signal a sensible surrender. At the siege of Maastricht parallel trenches were first used. The trench system of the Great War was only Vauban's, brought up to date. At the siege of Philippsburg in 1689 he invented ricochet fire which was so deadly that the delighted king made him lieutenant-general on the spot.

Vauban's life work was the fortification of the bordering lands which were becoming the prototype of the modern frontier, conceived not as a patchwork of estates and areas of personal sovereignty but as a hard-and-fast line. In flat Flanders, geography could suggest no clear boundary, so Vauban had to make good, by his work, the defects of nature. When the frontier was still an imperfect sketch, in 1673, he wrote to Louvois: 'seriously now, the king ought to give some thought to establishing his meadow square. This profusion of friendly and hostile forts does not please me at all, for you are obliged to maintain three for the sake of one.'[12] Vauban planned an unbroken defensive line stretching from Lille to Briançon in the Alps; from Mont-Louis to Bayonne on the Atlantic frontier with Spain; and, on the coast, from Antibes to Dunkirk. After the Dutch War he was in sole charge and Louvois encouraged him to spare no expense. The result was a skein of fortresses, each with double or triple girdles, stone surmounting vast earthworks, deep ditches and steep slopes. There were angled forts and barbicans. Great doors gilt with the *fleur de lis* opened on to barrack buildings of severe splendour. Starkly utilitarian yet works of art in their classical precision, Vauban's forts – many still surviving – are as typical of the age as a play by Racine or sermon by Bossuet. At Strasbourg Vauban designed magnificent gates for the citadel. When Louis protested at the expense the general was adamant: was not Strasbourg the key to Germany and did not Germans respect display? They would judge the grandeur of the king by the beauty of these gates. 'True *gloire*', Vauban considered, 'does not flit like a butterfly, it is only acquired by real and solid actions.'[13]

Each fortress was adapted to its terrain. At Neuf-Breisach Vauban projected bastion towers over the river; at Mont-Louis, on a high escarpment, he placed an eagle's nest to overlook the valleys around. From the Rhine to the sea he divided the frontier into sectors, according to the dictates of ground and communications. The ever-vulnerable northern plain was covered by two lines of works; the first from Dunkirk to Dinant, comprising fifteen forts; the second from Graveslines to Charleville, with thirteen; from Dunkirk to Escaut, implementing the strategy of defence in depth, stretched a tracery of trenches and ramparts, strengthened by redoubts. It was no Maginot line of static defence, rather a fortified zone of manoeuvre. As defensive hedgehogs, his forts blocked the aggressor's path; as pivots for the defending force they covered its communications and guarded its supplies. The value of these works would be proved in the campaigns of 1702–13. After the defeat of an army in the field the enemy were deprived of their advantage by the presence around them of French garrisons straddling their communications. After the victory of Oudenarde, Marlborough, wishing to advance on Paris, had to spend five months investing Lille. The logistics of such an operation, with the financial strain imposed upon the allies, also put the costs of Vauban's operation into perspective. It took 16,000 horses to draw the 100 field pieces, 60 mortars and 3,000 carts required. Exploiting the power gained in the years of victory Vauban's constructions saved France in the years of defeat.

To his troops Louvois was 'the great victualler'. It was no longer enough for troops to live off the foreign countries in which it was hoped they would campaign. For their preliminary manoeuvres they needed regular supplies of food, clothing and ammunition. The amount required was prodigious. An army of 60,000 was reckoned to need 45 tons of bread, and meat from 2–300 cattle a day. Its animals consumed 90 tons of fodder, equivalent to 400 acres of grazing. Exact ration scales were laid down and varied to meet operational needs. By careful commissariat he was able to increase mobility on campaign. Destructive habits ingrained after years of living on the land could not, however, be wholly eradicated. In 1673 the whole of Luxembourg's army had their pay stopped because the soldiers had looted their own magazines. Faults in the contractor system, on which Louvois depended for food and carts, went unchecked by officers disinclined to undertake such clerkly work. Slackness and stupidity continued to frustrate the best intentions. When Boufflers surrendered Lille in 1708 he was forced to it by lack of food; he had throughout issued rations for the same number of men regardless of the garrison's heavy casualties.

The introduction of Louvois's magazine system so extended the operational range of an army that it is hard to realise that it was not used earlier. Well maintained dumps of forage and ammunition enabled French armies to discard the convention of winter quarters that had restricted western warfare since the time of Caesar. The army which did not need to wait for the spring herbage to feed its horses (fuel, as it were, for its tanks and trucks) stood at an advantage which was exploited in early campaigns. Condé invaded Franche-Comté in February 1668; in January 1675, Turenne operated audaciously and out-fought the Imperialists among the snowy hills of the Vosges. France, more than any other state, was responsible for the intensification of warfare during the second half of the century. Her example forced change upon the other states until, in the last and biggest war of the reign she became victim of the very advances in war she had done most to pioneer. Marlborough had been the pupil of Turenne.

Le Tellier was one of several ministers who had learned their trade as *intendants* attached to an army. He used them on a regular basis as the instrument of civilian control. As the *intendant* was in the province so the *intendant de l'armée* should be king in the army: under his authority officers and men should belong, not just by formal title, but absolutely and unquestionably, to the king. Of course his presence was resented and his mandate opposed by officers used to being a law unto themselves. He operated in a rough world, far from the civilities of the council chamber and the reassuring technicalities of the courts. Louvois expected his agents to be treated with deference by all officers but he was more likely to be regarded as a superior clerk, useful enough for the figures and reports demanded by government, or cold-shouldered as the minister's spy. The latter was near to the mark. In 1678 Louvois wrote to the *intendant* in Roussillon: 'your first duty is to let me know everything that is said, projected and done in the army'. It is the civilian case in the perennial conflict of modern societies. The civilian, be he Louvois relating to Luxembourg or Lloyd George to Haig, seeks to ensure that the policies of the state be accurately interpreted by generals, and faithfully followed. The soldier has the immediate responsibility and incurs the immediate risks: in question is his judgement; at stake is his reputation. Victories can only be won by the initiative of the general in the field.

As the reign proceeded, it is clear that Louis and Louvois could not stay content with administrative control but tried to order tactics in minute detail. Writing in 1688, Chamlay, Louis's personal military adviser, suggested that the sound strategic situation achieved by conquests means that 'the king finds himself able to grant command . . . without having anything to fear from the mediocre capacity of any to whom he may confide it'.[14] Luxembourg would show himself to be far from mediocre. But evidently Tallard and Villeroy were. Their heavy defeats would expose the flaw in the argument. It surely reflects the king's opinion and reveals – in a way analogous to the case of Jansenism, where control was also in question – an area where the king's early experiences influenced his mature conduct. In the fifties he had learned the personal pain, and the threat to security, of the semi-independent general. He was tenacious of such lessons long after they ceased to be relevant. Easy victories and the flattery of courtiers helped to convince him that he had a flair for soldiering. Indeed he would have made an admirable staff officer. Nor would he have failed as trainer of troops. He confided to his *Mémoires* his passionate interest in drill. 'Many more battles are won by good march order and good bearing than by sword blows and musketry . . . this habit of marching well and keeping order can only be acquired by drill.' If only his people could be controlled in this fashion!

There is much in Louis's distinctive style to show that war was a fundamental attribute of his sovereignty and of his idea of life and rule.[15] To impress his leading subjects he had to show that he was a true soldier. It was as much of a duty as presence in council and one that he was eager to perform. War, the greatest of professions, had a favoured place among the values of the court and it possessed a virtue quite apart from its necessity as the last argument of diplomacy.

It must be said (by contrast, for example, with the impressive record of Mazarin's campaign management) that there is little to show that Louis was anything of a strategist. Generals found his presence at the front embarrassing and assured him that he could exercise supreme command as well from his palace, and with less danger to his person. After the Dutch war and the permanent establishment at Versailles he tended to stay at home. Palace control became, inevitably, more strict and detailed until, in the last war, a general could hardly move from camp without sending couriers to the king to learn his pleasure. A large part of successful generalship, as illustrated notably by Marlborough at Oudenarde, is the ability to take quick advantage of a sudden development; risks do not look the same to the commander in the country as to the student of the wall-map. Remote control means time lags. Apart from some critical blunders by his generals, the later failures of French armies may be ascribed partly to the king's strategic activities. Significantly generals were in the end most successful in Spain, where they were allowed most operational scope. But towards the end Villars was given a relatively free hand – and he repaid trust with victory.

Notes

1. For the family and Michel *père*'s rise to power see p. 96.
2. For a résumé of the two-way process see Frank Tallett, *War and Society in Early Modern Europe, 1495–1715* (London, 1992), pp. 193–216. For the debate see Bibliography: 'War'.
3. For the size, nominal and effective, of the French army, see J.A. Lynn, 'Recalculating French army growth during the *Grand siècle*, 1610–1715', in *French Historical Studies*, 18 (1994) pp. 881–906. In the 1690s 65 per cent of royal revenue went on the army, 9 per cent on the navy: for which see A. Guéry, 'Les finances de la monarchie française sous l'ancien régime', *Annales, E.S.C.,* 33, 1978, p. 228, graph 4. Also, see below, p. 257, n. 10.
4. Quoted in L. Corvisier, *Louvois* (Paris, 1983), p. 80.
5. Did Dufay see an irony here? He had just informed Louvois that in the last two weeks he had 'burned 13 towns and villages' and 'there was not a soul left in any of them'. The discipline of the army was, of course, more important than the lives of German civilians.
6. Marie de Rabutin-Chantal, Marquise de Sévigné (1626–96), left a widow at 26 when her husband was killed in a duel, wrote letters to please herself, her beloved daughter, comtesse de Grignan, and her friends. Her letters reveal a cultivated, balanced, clear-headed woman, apparently casual in her portraiture but remarkably perceptive. They provide a commentary on Louis XIV's reign, seen from the angle of a woman on the fringe of the court, enjoying access to those in the know but never so close to events as to become blasé or to lose her sense of fun. From her lively pen we may learn about the first performance of a Racine play, the birth of a son to the Dauphin, the Breton revolt from the point of view of the Breton châtelaine, such an incomparable event as Mme de Sévigné dancing a minuet with the king, or – as here – war

from the viewpoint of the woman waiting for news of casualties. The most recent edition of her letters is that edited by Duchêne (3 vols, Paris 1972–78). An accessible and pleasing English selection, 272 letters out of 1679, in one volume, is that edited and translated by Violet Hammersley (London, 1953).

7. For this aspect of Versailles culture see also p. 189.

8. Lynn, 'Recalculating . . .', op. cit., pp. 881–906.

9. For the context of the king's appeal see pp. 280–4.

10. I know of no study of the warhorse in this period and the problems of finding and feeding them. Can one imagine such a gap in the story, for example, of the tank and armoured car?

11. Quoted by Tallett, op. cit., p. 108.

12. Much quoted as containing the essence of Vauban's thinking about defence. See R. Blomfield, *Sebastien le Prestre de Vauban* (2nd edn, New York, 1971), p. 73.

13. Quoted by Lynn, *The Wars* . . . op. cit., p. 31. Much has been written about Vauban and siege warfare (see Bibliography). For a good recent account of the archetypal siege, 'in the grand style', of the formidably strong fortress of Namur, with Racine in attendance as royal historiographer, see ibid., pp. 223–6.

14. Ibid, p. 23.

15. This is the central argument in Joel Cornette, *Le roi de guerre: Essai sur la souveraineté dans la France du Grand Siècle* (Paris, 1993).

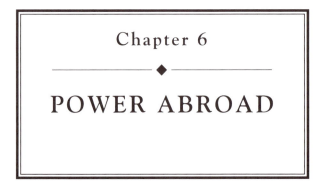

Chapter 6

POWER ABROAD

I made my enemies tremble, astounded my neighbours, and brought despair to my foes . . . France has demonstrated the difference between herself and other nations.

LOUIS XIV, 1672

THE WORLD OF DIPLOMACY

'The peace gained by the victorious arms of Louis XIV, the wise counsels of Anne, the august marriage of Maria Teresa, the diligent aid of Julius, Cardinal Mazarin': so ran the Latin inscription, with Louis's bust, above the arch erected over the Porte Saint-Antoine for the formal entry into Paris, in August 1660, of Louis XIV and his bride.[1] The peace of the Pyrenees had been a most notable achievement, full of promise for the future. The consequences of 'the august marriage' would be an issue, with recurring crises, throughout the reign. The crises would offer opportunities, but accompanying risks. The significant gains on France's vulnerable northern frontier, notably that of Artois, coupled with the evident military weakness of Spain, could be seen likewise as sufficient security or, as by Turenne, impatient for further conquest, as an interim settlement, a standing invitation to take more. Meanwhile the League of the Rhine, completed in August 1658, had extended 'the true frontier of France, that of political influence, beyond the territorial frontier, to the Rhine' (Hauser).[2] Never did France enjoy a greater degree of security than in the last years before Louis's personal reign, but it would see conquests and annexations that would further extend the eastern and north-eastern frontier, make stretches of the Rhine into a physical frontier, and make possible a coherent defence system. In bouts of aggression

and interludes of heavy diplomatic pressure, Louis can be said to have fulfilled Mazarin's territorial hopes – and more. Ironically the greatest prize,
succession to the entire Spanish Empire, came to his house unexpectedly.

Would Mazarin have approved of his pupil's achievement? Prolonged wars
of attrition, fought against the coalitions that formed to check his onslaughts,
resulted in the loss of much of the influence abroad for which Mazarin had
worked so hard. The severe economic and social costs, and serious, though
less measurable damage to the standing of monarchy, can further be seen as
an unacceptable price for territorial gains. They were indeed substantial but
we can only guess what Mazarin – or indeed Richelieu – would have thought
of the situation of France in the year of Malplaquet, when Marlborough
threatened invasion. Thus stated the verdict may seem to go against Louis.
Opportunities for lasting political influence, security and material progress
squandered in the pursuit of glory? It is a serious and familiar charge. To
review it fairly it is essential to place Louis in the context of contemporary
values and principles, of diplomatic theory and practice, and the state of
international law. Highly relevant is the troubled history of France during the
previous century, when the country had suffered repeatedly from foreign
invasion. Then one must reckon with the ambitions and actions of fellow
sovereigns, notably the Emperor Leopold (1657–1705) and Stadtholder
William of Orange, later (1689–1702) King William III of England.

Professionalism in diplomacy matched the growth in the power of states.
It was the product, at first, of the insecure conditions of Renaissance Italy,
the political laboratory of the western world: its frequent changes in and
between states led rulers to seek reliable information from representatives on
the spot. The advice of Ermaloa Barbaro would have been acceptable, two
centuries on, to one of Louis XIV's ambassadors. His duty was 'to do, say,
advise and think whatever may best serve the preservation and aggrandise-
ment of his own state'. The wars of the first half of the sixteenth century led
to the spread of resident diplomacy and the development of chanceries spe-
cialising in foreign policy. The process was checked during the religious and
civil wars of the second half of the century. The Reformation led to problems
of diplomatic immunity when envoys could demand the right to worship
God after his master's manner. As in recent periods of ideological conflict,
embassies became suspect as the centres of alien and subversive ideas. By
1600 only France, among Catholic rulers, held to the policy of exchanging
ambassadors with Protestant powers.

The virtual severance of diplomatic links between northern and southern
Europe was one casualty of this period of ideological conflict, reflecting the

morality that condoned religious persecution and political assassination. All the greater was the shock effect of Richelieu's treaty with Sweden, only twenty years after the assassination of 'the apostate' Henry IV. It stiffened attitudes among *dévôts* and can still be felt in the writing of Fénelon at the end of the century. 'Machiavelli', as much an epithet as the name of a thoughtfully realistic political philosopher, came to denote, as it did later about Mazarin, the absence of scruple, in particular religious scruple, in the conduct of foreign affairs.[3] For Richelieu, *polititique* as well as *dévôt*, as for the *'bons français'* that he employed to publicise his views, there was an overriding interest of state. As it had been for Francis I, threatened a century earlier by the Habsburg power encircling the realm, it was legitimate, in the interests of security, to come to terms with a Protestant power (and in the case of Francis, the Ottoman). For Mazarin's attentive royal pupil, therefore, there was nothing new about the kind of dilemma he faced when fidelity to religious principles sat uncomfortably with the needs of the state. He was heir to a distinctive French diplomatic tradition and to the commanding position in Europe which French diplomats had brought about. He was in a stronger position to discount the *dévôt* tradition – at least for as long as his policies were evidently successful. He would be most content, as in the case of Lutheran Strasbourg, when a strategic gain could be lauded as a blow for the church.

The prolonged conflicts of the Thirty Years War led to the gradual discrediting of the ideal – that which inspired the Emperor Ferdinand II and which also served his dynastic interest – of religious conformity as a good so absolute as to justify any force necessary to achieve it. A separate, but not unrelated, trend saw the fashioning of a new doctrine of international law and the emergence of shared conventions that enabled envoys to operate in a secure environment. The practice of holding congresses for the settlement of issues arising out of wars involving a number of states should take a high place among the civilising innovations of the age. One may point to the manoeuvres and squabbles over apparent minutiae that made the separate negotiations at Münster and Osnabrück such a long-drawn out affair as evidence of flaws in the process. Yet the resulting treaty of Westphalia (1648) marked an immense advance in diplomatic practice, a precedent for future congresses (which led to adjustments to rather than complete re-workings of the Westphalia settlement) and a basis for peaceful order in European affairs. It did not of course discourage rulers from pursuing further their own goals, as did those of France and Spain up to the peace of the Pyrenees. In its further gains, if Louis XIV needed it, was the encouragement to resort again to war; there too was the implicit warning that if he went too far he could expect concerted opposition. The natural development from the congress, with the relationships forged in formal dealings and the perception of common interest that it fostered, was the coalition.

The evolution of the congress was all the more important because diplomats worked now in a world which had come to mistrust projects of general reform and set little value on the mediaeval ideal of universality. That concept had left its trace in the use of Latin in diplomatic documents, but it was soon to go. At the peace of Rastadt, in 1714, French was used. Sully's *grand dessein* for a balanced federation of European states had been the product of enforced retirement when Henry IV's minister was left with no opportunity to influence affairs directly. It was, in any case, strongly tinged with ambition for France. It belonged, moreover, to the uneasy period before it was clear that the revolt of Bohemia would lead to a general European war. A product of that war was the plea of Grimmelshausen, in *Simplicissimus*, for an international peace plan: its author was portrayed as being out of his mind. A forlorn hope then – but born out of intense suffering. It recalls the entry in the diary of the German peasant Hartick Siert: 'God send that there may be an end at last; God send that there may be peace. God in heaven send us peace.' It was 1627. Twenty-one years later the German peace reflected the new spirit of disillusioned realism, the secular mood, the more moderate aims of rulers. The Emperor, important chiefly as a ruler of family lands, was forced to allow German states to treat for themselves. After Westphalia they had the right to send their own representatives to foreign states. The Pope condemned the settlement as 'null and void' because it took so little account of his views. At the peace of the Pyrenees he was not even represented. It was that retreat to the political margin that Mazarin had foreseen when he left papal service for that of France. He left behind him efforts to influence and offers to mediate; he came to wield power – and in the end to enhance it.

Mazarin offers us a paradigm: there was, post-1648, a political awareness less cluttered by traditions of what was possible and a resolve to exploit real resources and powers. Professors of law, like Grotius,[4] assumed that the sovereign state was subject to no human authority whatever outside itself. In *De Jure Belli et Pacis* (1625) Grotius postulated the existence of a fundamental law of nature, stemming from mankind's reserves of conscience and reason, and stationed above the interests of dynasty or nation. Accepting that war was inevitable he assigned to it a quasi-magisterial role, both judge and executioner. Wars of ambition, conquest and propaganda were unjust. Furthermore he asserted that no arrangement between rulers to provide stability could last unless they recognised that their acts must be governed by principles higher than mere expediency.

We need not be surprised that Grotius's book had only a limited effect on international dealings. The main factor then, as later, was the existence of separate states, with their own territorial claims and commercial interests. As in 1667 over Louis XIV's claim, by the law of devolution, to the Spanish Netherlands, a sovereign was more likely to look for local laws to suit his case than respect a rule in international law. The body of such law was, however, steadily enlarged. More treaties were concluded by which two or more powers agree to observe certain rules – though that did not lessen the scope for disagreement about how such rules should be interpreted. International law did not make the relations of states more legal, but it did provide a growing body of experience in the regular legal handling of disputes. It is against that background that Louis's *réunions*, based on supposed feudal rights, should be judged.

Inevitably war figured more prominently than peace in Grotius's treatise. There were agreed rules about its conduct. A country which was neutral, for example, might expect to be protected from its worst ravages, but usually had to allow combatant armies to cross its territory, as the French crossed Cologne and the Spanish Netherlands in their marches against the Dutch in 1672. The exchange of prisoners was normally conducted rank for rank, an officer counting for several soldiers. Belligerents had the right to exact contributions from the inhabitants in a theatre of war. Naval practice proved more contentious. Grotius's doctrine of *mare liberum* was no general statement of principle but an attack on the Portuguese claim, inconvenient to his Dutch countrymen, to exclusive rights in the Indian Ocean. There was dispute about 'coastal waters' as distinct from high seas. Colbert's naval ordinance of 1681 defined the *mer littorale* as 'that which the sea covers and leaves bare during the new and full moons and up to where the great tides reach on the beaches'. By far the most important question was that of the salute, the customary courtesies of salvo or dipping the flag: it was among the causes of the mid-century wars between the English and the Dutch. The English demanded that all salute their flag in the Channel. When the Danes refused, English diplomats were concerned whether the country 'would stand the affront without recourse to war'. Colbert wrote in 1677 that France claimed that 'all nations must bow to her at sea as at the Court of Kings'. In 1678 the Genoese learned that it was no idle boast when a French squadron, sent to demand the first salute, and being refused, bombarded the city. The English would never give way on this point so, even when the French were their allies, they had to avoid meeting at sea. When, in 1685, a Spanish commander refused to salute the *fleur de lis*, Admiral Tourville attacked his fleet.

That was no isolated incident, a mere display of arrogant temper. Like the overbearing conduct of Vatican ambassador Créqui which precipitated 'the affair of the Corsican Guards' (1662), the king's servant was behaving in a way that he believed would be acceptable to the king. Nor was Louis so different in his notion of rights from other sovereigns. At Vienna his representative enjoyed only the modest title and limited privileges of 'envoy extraordinary' because the Emperor insisted on according the right of ceremonial precedence to the Spanish ambassador as representing a fellow Habsburg. Indeed when he was sure that his honour was not compromised, or when the *bienfait* of the nation required it (the much used term reflects a key concern), he could be pragmatic and flexible. He was free in his letters with the much appreciated '*Frère*'. He encouraged his diplomats to expedite business by finding ways round issues of precedence 'as long as the royal dignity is not impaired'. It was not always possible to find so neat a solution as the choice of the Isle of Pheasants, midstream in the river Bidassoa between France and Spain, for the negotiations of 1659. He cooperated fully in the mathematical solution to the problem of precedence between France and Spain that threatened to hold up the signing of the peace of Nijmegen. A table, with two copies of the treaty was placed between doors which, at a signal, the two delegations could approach, so as to sign simultaneously, and each in the place decreed by protocol on their copy of the document. To understand Louis we have to realise that he would not have found the situation surprising, nor let it stand in the way of his diplomatic objectives. When Louis, or indeed any other sovereign, made an issue out of precedence there was likely to be a political motive. When received ideas are allowed for, and occasional braggart words (as likely to be found in ministers' drafts as in his) there is left a strong impression of common sense. The ideas were still potent, the rights were a resource, the words could convey a useful message.

When, moreover, it comes to proud assertiveness of rights at sea there is little to choose between the English and Dutch. It was more than a matter of an individual's, or government's pretension or temper. It expresses and complements the ever-more precise definition of sovereign rights by political theorists and the more rigorous application of sovereign authority within states. It also reflects the attitudes of a ceremonious age and the pervasive influence of a mature courtly culture. The intricate codes of Byzantium, the opulence of Renaissance Burgundy and the grave manners of Spain contributed to the formation of an international palace style.[5] It was marked by a strong awareness of being separate from the world outside, along with that characteristic of closed élites – intense preoccupation with rank and with what signified it: precedence, special privileges and marks of favour. Wherever men aspired to live nobly, and women to make the best of their supportive role, and in all countries – though most in Spain and in courts such as those of Vienna and Versailles where the Spanish influence was strong – honour was at a premium. On its points men fought duels. For its demands men bankrupted themselves. They assumed that they would be judged by appearances, by their dress, carriage and servants. At society's apex the presentation had to be very grand indeed. When Louis XIV went to meet his bride the procession was several miles long. Lower in the scale the *entrée* of a bishop to his see or a governor to his province represented the same concerns. The dignitary must show that he was conferring honour, the town that it was worthy of it.

Upon the same considerations of prestige an ambassador was expected to maintain high pomp. His arrival was an occasion for elaborate ceremony. Outside the city that housed court or government a procession of coaches, with soldiers, servants, liveried pages and musicians would form. The ambassador would be received in the city with bells and rounds of cannon. A few days later another procession preceded the presentation of letters of credence and a first audience with the sovereign and ministers. At Versailles such an occasion was invariably splendid.[6] Saint-Simon's account of the reception of the Persian ambassador in the last year of the reign, with a full parade of courtiers before the king and his family, is not, however, without pathos. The ambassador's credentials were found to be dubious; the frail old king was persuaded that he must endure that hollow ceremony. Are we looking at the end of an age? The 'age of reason' was to favour simpler styles. Diplomatic manners then came to reflect a more pragmatic outlook. Diplomatic practice became sharper, the military, territorial arguments more starkly opportunistic. To 'enlightened' minds of the next century, offered such examples as Frederick the Great's invasion of Silesia or the partitions of Poland, the respect for the letter of law and for corporate rights, with the significant concept of honour that characterised the diplomacy of Louis XIV, might look altogether archaic. Were not its forms pedantic, its values artificial, unrealistic, at worst hypocritical? After three centuries of realpolitik we may have a greater respect for the diplomats of the seventeenth century, the moral climate, essentially Christian, within which they worked, and the spirit of civilised moderation that informed their ceremonious manners. Something of it was to reappear, in reaction to the smash and grab of the Napoleonic era, at the Congress of Vienna. Louis XIV would have been at home there.

In 1661 the development of specialised foreign ministries was still far from complete. The reign saw the emergence of larger departments and more regular bureaucratic procedure. There persisted, however, the traditional idea that foreign policy was the special business of the king, a prerogative and a mystery. Louis XIV's practice should be distinguished, however, from that of his counterparts in eastern Europe where, notably in Brandenburg–Prussia and Russia, the state evolved as an extension of the power of the autocrat and policy depended largely on his will and personality.

THE GREAT TREATIES

No French ruler had possessed so complete a knowledge and understanding of the face of Europe, its recent history and present conditions; the terms of treaties and the interests of rulers. Louis took great pains to master briefs. He made his preferences clear and that could affect the advice he was given. Neither Colbert, in 1672, nor Torcy in 1701, were at first in favour of the policy, the king's, that was eventually adopted. Before they came round to acceptance, no doubt mindful of their own careers, they had the opportunity to express their view, and knew that the king would listen carefully. He listened to generals as well as to his foreign minister – but the minister had the advantage of almost daily access and a secure position. There was a notable continuity. There were only four in the reign, Lionne, Pomponne, Colbert de Croissy, Torcy, each uncommonly able. There was, at first, no formal establishment, only a handful of cipher clerks, secretaries and interpreters. In the 1700s Torcy carried out important reforms. An archive of diplomatic dispatches and memoranda was established. A pool of trained secretaries went some way to provide expertise and continuity in diplomatic practice. The *Académie politique* was founded as a school for prospective diplomats. Abroad the coverage was already ambitious, far beyond that of other powers. By 1685 there were formal embassies in all the more important capitals, beside special ministers resident in such important places as Heidelberg, Hamburg and Genoa, and consuls in the Levant where the French had long been to the fore since establishing the first European embassy in Constantinople in 1535.

The ambassador was expected to be fully acquainted with conditions in his destined country. Before departing he was meticulously briefed. He took with him letters of introduction, instructions and a cipher table: the cipher was used because letters were generally intercepted by postmasters who transcribed the most interesting bits for their own government. He might have to treat or bribe. Indeed few foreign princes failed to benefit at one time or another from Louis XIV's diplomatic generosity. Eagerly solicited, whether as aid to government, or to opposition as a way of disabling government, French subsidies were a permanent feature of English politics from 1660 to 1688. Faction, faithlessness and greed: all confirmed Louis's disdain for England – and led him, fatally, to underestimate its capacity to surprise.

The ambassador's prime duty was to glean and transmit information. He had to heed the customs of the court and the foibles of the ruler. Attendance at long and frequent religious ceremonies was required of the French envoy at Vienna. London was a more acceptable assignment but its politics could be baffling. The duc d'Aumont was advised that 'the English constitution is such that it is not regarded as offensive by the court of King James to have relations with the opposition. The duke need not therefore reject the society of the Whigs.' From the memoirs of François de Callières,[7] a leading nego-tiator of the peace of Ryswick, we can see what was expected of the men who served that exacting master. The ideal diplomat should be 'quick, resource-ful, a good listener, courteous and agreeable'. By studying history and by enquiring about institutions and conventions he should be able 'to tell in any country where the real sovereignty lies'. Like a banker, the good diplomat should build up credit by inspiring trust. A lie 'may confer success today but will create an atmosphere of suspicion which will prevent success tomorrow'. 'The secret of negotiations is to harmonise the real interests of the powers concerned.' It could have been Mazarin's voice, indeed Louis XIV's. The king would ask searching questions. Tallard, for example, reported every word of his audience with William III in 1697, with comments on his expression and gestures. The idiosyncrasies of a sovereign, the body language that could be observed, might matter as much as his words.

Louis would not have demurred at Richelieu's view that a treaty, once signed, was something to be observed 'with religious scruple'. He would know, however, that Richelieu had, on occasion disowned an envoy's com-mitment.[8] If a minister, then surely a king could break faith, under excep-tional circumstances, when, as in 1709, the safety of the state was in question? Where right was uncertain or a twinge of conscience stirred, the law could be useful. With *Parlement* at hand and an unrivalled store of legal expertise to draw on it is not surprising that Louis's foreign policy is tinged with legalism. He prided himself on close attention to the letter of a treaty but he added a significant rider: 'there is no agreement in any clause so watertight as not to allow some elasticity of interpretation'. He once, though uncharacteristically, compared treaties to compliments, 'absolutely necessary for co-existence but of little significance beyond their sound'. He could have been referring to the treaty of Ryswick to which, with William III he put his seal in 1697: it was to be 'a universal, perpetual peace to be inviolably, religiously and sincerely observed'. Within five years Louis and William were at war again. Though he did not want war, Louis had acted, first in accepting the Spanish Succession for his grandson, in ways which made it almost inevitable. When all sovereigns treated diplomacy as part of a continuing campaign to protect or further the interests of their states, as, maybe, the preferred alternative to war – but only when the state was not thereby disadvantaged – however punctilious in form it was to some extent dishonest in spirit. For most of his reign Louis was the prime mover and shaker among sovereigns. He was also, throughout, the zealous dynast. At times, as at the peace of Aix-la-Chapelle, he could be moderate, even magnanimous, without damage to French interests. At Ryswick, after a war in which great battles had been won, many Frenchmen were outraged at the concessions he made. In both cases he was looking to win time and credit, to create a favourable climate for future moves. If he appears a paragon of honesty and reliability, it may be by comparison with Charles II of England, author of the treaty of Dover, whom no politician at home or abroad would be wise to trust. If a hypocrite or cynic, it must be because, on occasion, he judged that the dynastic interest, the good of France as he saw it, legitimised sharp practice or evasion. The record shows that the issues were rarely simple, choice of policy correspondingly hard. When rational analysis offered no clear-cut answer, judgement could come down to the instinctive response, decision to the gambler's throw.

Underlying all decisions in foreign policy was, however, a sense of certain objectives; broadly they had remained unchanged since the rule of the Cardinals. They are revealed in the instructions of Mazarin to his envoys at Münster and Osnabrück in 1646;[9] essentially they were Richelieu's.[10] Mazarin had been brought forward by Richelieu as the man best fitted to carry them out. His men at the negotiating tables, notably D'Avaux, Servien and Lionne, were shrewd, tough and resourceful. They were to recover the Low Countries 'for an impregnable barrier' to Northern France for only then would Paris be 'truly the heart of France'. To secure the old county of Burgundy and Luxembourg they should be prepared to sacrifice Roussillon and Catalonia (where the French had established themselves after the Catalan revolt of 1640). They were to reach for the Rhine by acquisitions in Alsace and Lorraine. Apart from the Spanish succession which became a leading factor in the policy of Louis's personal reign, these instructions of the Minority serve as a summary of French policy for the whole reign. Mazarin himself brought the succession into play through the marriage conditions negotiated at the peace of the Pyrenees.

Though there were alarms along the way, with disturbing military failures in 1647, France was in a relatively strong position in the Westphalia negoti-ations and her overall gains were substantial, if less than Mazarin had hoped for. With possession of Metz, Toul, Verdun, Moyenvic, Breisach and the right to garrison Philippsburg, France was well placed to defend herself, or to exploit the divisions of Germany. In the settlement of Alsace there was an ambiguity which left the way open to further infiltration. France obtained the landgraviate of Upper and Lower Alsace, in full sovereignty, together with the 'provincial prefecture' of the 'ten Alsatian towns' which, like the nobility of Lower Alsace were to be left in full possession of their privileges. Did the landgraviate bring territorial or merely feudal rights? D'Avaux prophesied that these questions contained the seeds of future European wars. How many, or how terrible, he cannot have imagined. Meanwhile the emperor would not be reconciled to the loss of Alsace; Louis wanted to consolidate his position.

The same mixture of advantage, opportunity and hazard is to be found in the Peace of the Pyrenees (1659). Mazarin did now secure more of what he regarded as essential: in the north, Artois, with Graveslines, parts of Hainault and of Luxembourg; in the south Roussillon and much of Cerdagne. Behind the headline gains there were others less obvious. The status of Condé gave Mazarin a bargaining counter. The Spanish had incurred a debt of honour for his alliance; now that such a prominent defector wanted to be reinstated, the French were determined to exact a price but one which would not visibly embarrass Philip IV. So he was persuaded to cede Jülich to the duke of Neuberg. It was a small but strategically important duchy – and the duke was a French ally. Mazarin might have pressed even harder for concessions if he had not been intent on a larger prize. Spain's future was already a topic of speculation. Philip IV, aging, wanting a male heir from his second marriage, was sufficiently concerned to ensure that a clause be inserted into the treaty by which France renounced Maria Theresa's rights to the succession. Mazarin accepted it, but required an exception for the Netherlands. The clause concerning the dowry referred also to the Infanta's rights, and so her husband's. A large sum was agreed upon, 500,000 *écus*, to be paid in three instalments. Lionne was responsible for its drafting. He saw to it that one word, *moyennant*, implying that the renunciation was conditional on payment of the dowry, was slipped into the marriage contract. In November 1661 a male heir was born to the Spanish throne. The frail, retarded child, the future

Charles II, did not look set for a long life. Meanwhile the Spanish had fallen behind in payment of the dowry. With his queen, Louis XIV had received a dowry of expectations, arguably more valuable than the money and certain to cause more trouble.

TRIALS OF STRENGTH

The War of Devolution started in May 1667 with a straightforward act of aggression. The military reviews and diplomatic exchanges that preceded it had already conveyed a clear message. The king intended to defend the queen's rights. Two diplomatic incidents had already set the tone. In October 1661 a fracas in London between the rival staffs of the French and Spanish ambassadors in which several people were killed tested Louis's nerve and provided him with an opportunity to make his mark. He described the affair and its aftermath in his memoirs with care and evident relish:[11] that he thought it important is borne out by Colbert's letters. At the outset of his personal reign, and in relation to the rival power so recently an enemy, his prestige was at stake. The Spanish ambassador in France was expelled. A note to Madrid called for a complete apology. He required that Spain accept the precedence of French ambassadors in every court. In February 1662, adding the note of menace which Europe would come to recognise, he demanded an advance payment of the dowry in the shape of Franche-Comté, Luxembourg, Hainault and Cambrai. The Spanish ambassador then announced, at a special royal audience, that his master conceded Louis's first demand. The affair of the Corsican Guards was used to reinforce the message.

A feud between French embassy staff in Rome and the Pope's Corsican guards, a bloody skirmish; an attack on the embassy and insult to the ambassador's wife: stated thus the affair can look trivial. When, however, the background is taken into account, then the intense diplomatic activity over two years, with Louis's personal commitment to a satisfactory outcome, it is seen to be important. Fabio Chigi, from 1655 Pope Alexander VII, had been nuncio at Münster and critical of Mazarin's tactics there, designed, as he saw it, to delay peace so as to secure further gains for France – and power for the cardinal. Mazarin scorned Chigi's moral tone, viewing him as a hypocrite and a Habsburg partisan. With his own interest – and alternative candidate – he had unsuccessfully opposed Chigi's election. Lionne had then been his agent in Rome. After his escape from France, the Cardinal de Retz won the support of the Pope for his claim to be archbishop of Paris. The Pope had not yet allowed that formerly Spanish territories, now French, were subject to the Concordat – so that Louis could appoint to bishoprics. So the king brought preconceived notions and immediate concerns to colour his view of the proper relationship between Rome and France: the one an ecclesiastical authority of tarnished reputation and a weak Italian state, inherently corrupt, a prey to nepotism and to foreign pressure; the other a great power under the foremost Christian king, *fils aîné de l'Église*. He seized the first chance to put his views to the test.

The duc de Créqui had extended the diplomatic privileges, already a contentious issue, beyond the embassy in the Palazzo Farnese. Street brawls left the papal authorities powerless when they were met by French claims of immunity. One day in August 1662 the Pope's Guards, bent on avenging insults, attacked the embassy. They killed several Frenchmen, and tipped the ambassador's wife, returning from Mass, out of her carriage. Urged on by his Gallican-minded ministers, notably Lionne and Colbert (the latter wrote a full account of the affair and its origins), Louis sent troops to occupy Papal Avignon with the threat that they would march on into Italy. From the outset Louis had to balance conflicting aims. Protracted negotiations showed 'the insecure and intense young man' portrayed by Sonnino to be less sure or consistent than the outcome might suggest. He intended to advertise to the world the insignificance of Papal power. He wanted '*une très grande et forte éclatante satisfaction*'. He also wished to find a way of supporting the Portuguese rebels by depriving the Spanish of their recruiting grounds in North Italy. The presence of French troops might achieve that, but might also antagonise the other Italian states. It would be better therefore to persuade the Pope to authorise their presence. He also needed the Pope's theological authority to deal with Jansenism. Yet he was reluctant to accept the principle of Papal infallibility. He had to consider the Gallican mood in *Parlement*. So he gave support to *Parlement* when it intervened to stop the Sorbonne approving a Jesuit work defending papal infallibility. Eventually Pope Alexander VII sent his nephew, cardinal Chigi, to make a qualified apology. Louis held on to Avignon and embarrassed the Pope by calling for reform at the Vatican. The French seemed to have won the trial of strength when, in February 1664, by the Peace of Pisa, the pope agreed to terms. He had to disband his Corsican Guards. He also had to erect an obelisk, recording the insult to the king and its sequel. Louis took a personal interest in its design and insisted on the lettering being large enough to be read by the passer-by. The political lesson had been taught, with the mixture of finesse and insensitivity, serious conviction and provoking self-righteousness that would become familiar. It left resentment at the Vatican. Louis believed that he was strong enough to ignore it. One day he would be less favourably placed and an upright and determined pope would stand up to him. There would be a price to pay.

When Philip IV died in 1665 he specifically excluded Maria Theresa from all or part of the inheritance. The four-year-old Charles II was backward and frail. If there were ever to be an heir it was a distant prospect. Louis's reasonable concerns pointed to two lines of policy:[12] negotiation with the other interested party, the Emperor, about some kind of partition, and a military strike to secure at least part of his wife's inheritance. Louis did not see that the first need rule out the second. For him it was a question of the queen's rights. To provide further justification his lawyers offered the law of Devolution, which gives the war of 1667–68 its name. According to a law of Brabant, property devolved upon the children of the first marriage, to the exclusion of those of the second. Ignoring the fact that as private law it had no relevance to Louis's claim, a French pamphlet asserted that Louis was duty-bound, as king, to prevent injustice; as husband, to oppose usurpation; and, as father, to assure the patrimony to his son. The real argument was about security and the nature of the frontier. As is so often the case it derived force from the past, with its periodic Habsburg invasions, rather than from any realistic assessment of present danger. The campaign of 1667 showed that the Spanish forces, around 22,000 dispersed in garrisons, were unable to put up much resistance to Turenne's concentrated force of 30,000. The many-sided nature of Spain's decline was not, however, so plain as it has been to historians; nor was that decline irreversible. Nor indeed was it certain that the preoccupation of the Habsburgs with their eastern frontier and the consolidation of the family lands was bound to continue. The French thought always of the Habsburg family interest, and its encircling lands, rather than just of Spain. Meanwhile those, like Vauban, who argued that it was essential to establish for all time a defensible frontier and ministers who found that it was impossible to administer the area effectively, found Louis eager to listen. The frontier, after recent acquisitions, comprised an irregular, discontinuous patchwork of towns and estates lying just beyond the rivers, Somme, Meuse and Aisne. Running through the open country of plains, downs and gentle hills that was to become so familiar to soldiers of 1914–18, the slow-moving rivers were more lines of advance than barriers to an enemy.

By comparison with its later size, the French army was not large. It had, however, been maintained in a state of war-preparedness and the élite regiments were at full strength. In effectiveness related to size, and in the resources available to the engineers for siege warfare, it compares favourably with the swollen, less manageable forces of later wars. It also enjoyed the advantage of shock. The Dutch, lulled by Louis's earlier treaty of alliance (1662) were still fighting the English; the Emperor could do little because the Rhineland states would not cooperate. Mazarin's patronage of the Elector of Mainz's Rheinbund, proved its worth. Turenne's invasion became a procession, with short stops to besiege towns along the way. With his base, and much of the court, at Compiègne, the king went on from holding formal reviews to active campaigning. He left the overall direction of the army to Turenne but took charge of particular operations. Typical was the siege of Tournai, in June: it surrendered four days after the first breach in the walls. It was a similar story at Douai. Louis's most gratifying success was the capture of Lille, an important and strongly fortified city. Here fifteen miles of circumvallation were dug; the siege lasted a month. Riding exuberantly to war, accompanied by his wife, brother, La Vallière and her successor, Montespan; quite above conventional manners, in his Olympian world apart from ordinary mortals; watching the assault, listening to the fiddles and oboes of his orchestra, receiving the surrender and making formal entry – Louis was in his element. 'His army and its conquests', wrote Saint-Maurice,[13] 'occupied his whole mind.' He went around trench positions within cannon range. The troops were no doubt heartened by the presence of a king who seemed to revel in 'the tackle and trim' of war. Overall the campaign was no remarkable military achievement. Spanish resistance was sometimes mere token, never prolonged; surrenders came as soon as honour permitted. There was an ample haul of towns, valuable counters for the diplomats to play with. The campaign encouraged the young king, now graduate *cum laude* in the military arts, to see war as an honourable, enjoyable and entirely proper exercise of power.

'DESIRE TO ATTACK THE DUTCH'

The Dutch had not been disturbed by Louis XIV's purchase of Dunkirk from England in 1662 but they now saw, in the invasion of Flanders, the possibility that Antwerp, if revived under French control, would again become a competitor in trade. In January 1668, Louis's envoy in Vienna, Grémonville, negotiated a secret partition treaty. Young and inexperienced like his Bourbon cousin but less confident about the future, shaken by the death of his infant son, Leopold chose the option which, in the event of Charles II's death without heir, would give him, or a future son, the Spanish kingdoms, with Milan and most of the colonial empire, leaving, for Louis, the Netherlands and Naples. 'I would not mind dying the day I signed such a treaty', wrote Lionne.[14] From now on it would be his main argument as he sought to restrain Louis's impatience for more gains in the hand. In February, nonetheless, Condé was ordered to proceed with the carefully prepared invasion of Franche-Comté. It was completed within a few weeks, by the capture of the capital, Dôle. Louis intended, by this bold, unseasonable operation, to forestall a possible Spanish attack and to strengthen his negotiating hand. For now he had to contend with the Anglo-Dutch entente of January which would become, in May, with the inclusion of Sweden, the Triple Alliance. Deadly enemies at sea, with unresolved issues to be decided, the English and Dutch had made peace; they now served notice on Louis that he should make terms. With Franche-Comté as his major counter, he secured most of what he had aimed for in the Netherlands. By the terms of the peace of Aix-la-Chapelle he gained Bergues in Maritime Flanders; Charleroi took him into Hainault; most of his gains were, however, in French Flanders (where, ironically, the devolution law did not apply). Armentières, Menin, Oudenarde, Tournai, Courtrai were the most considerable Flemish towns which were now to become the vital links in Vauban's defensive chain. Louis had listened carefully to the hawkish submissions of the generals and the young Louvois. They saw little potential resistance to a further push. As Louis confided to his *Mémoires*, enraged by the Dutch action, he was tempted: 'their insolence struck me to the quick'. But he 'wanted to profit not merely from present circumstances but from future ones'. In council he came down emphatically on the side of Lionne and Colbert. Handing back Franche-Comté he was able to gain credit for moderation and a breathing space to make diplomatic preparation for a greater onslaught. Meanwhile, significantly, the Rheinbund disintegrated. The German members would not renew their association.

At this point in the reign, when the question of another war was not so much whether as when, Louis might seem to be behaving as a completely free agent. If he hesitated it was surely only over timing and tactics; if he doubted, only as to which course would bring the greater advantage. In reality, so far from pursuing a consistent and cold-blooded line towards war, he seems to have listened anxiously to advisors and their conflicting advice. He was intelligent enough to see that the diplomatic cost of premature aggression might outweigh the plain military benefits urged by Louvois and Turenne. The environment in which he worked, the personalities and aims of those closest to him, and the simply fortuitous – the actions of other interested parties, notably English, Dutch and Imperial – swayed the outcome. Undoubtedly he relished the prospect. A heading in his *Mémoires* (January 1670) reads simply: 'Desire to attack the Dutch'. Nor need we think that he had misgivings about his motives. 'I have made it my rule to consecrate the fruits of my conquests to the repose of Europe.' Was he not honestly expressing what Frenchmen have tended to think over the years, that what was good for France was self-evidently good for Europe?

The king of France was the principal, its acclaimed hero, in a court that buzzed with military talk. At present the royal life was neither stable nor decorous. Versailles was a building site. Earthworks and scaffolding, vast piles of stone, thousands of workmen, teams of craftsmen and artists, meant clamour, confusion and discomfort before Le Vau's elegant design could take shape and Mansard's grand frame be imposed to provide a final, formal setting for court and government. Meanwhile the court was itinerant, the atmosphere febrile; constant shifts brought irritation and bred rumour. The perennial question among courtiers, ineffectual spectators of the power game, was: who was in, who out? Advancement or special favour to a minister was noted. The king was at Saint-Germain in the autumn of 1669, closely attended by Louvois, Turenne and several senior generals: so it was declared that Colbert was disgraced. Louis made it clear that his private relationships did not affect policy. Even so the ascendancy of a new mistress, Mme de Montespan, the discomfiture of Louise de la Vallière and her retreat to a monastery can be thought to have affected, or reflected his mood: there was the new incentive to show himself in the best light. Coping with the moral implications of the king's ambiguous position was a new confessor: Père Ferrier replaced Père Annat, who had known him since boyhood.

A change of ministers was a tantalising prospect, accompanied by much calculation of client prospects. Lionne, holding tenaciously to the argument that the king should be patient, was a sick man. Colbert was in a delicate position. His protectionism and need to maximise revenues led him to impose tariffs and to try to restrain the Flemish cities that were now French from trading with their old partners in the Spanish lands. Spanish counter-measures included an embargo on the coal that was essential for the brick kilns on the fortress construction sites.[15] It was one of several issues that gave an edge to his rivalry with Louvois. Another was the cost of the new fortifications and of the enlargement of the army, 'with the taxation required, the true cause of the diminution of commerce in the kingdom'. He was a realist, with his own career to consider. The king's firm rebuke after one celebrated outburst in council reminded him that he had nothing to gain by plain speaking.[16] He began to trim. If the army was to be maintained on a war footing and if war was inevitable anyway, would it not be better to have it over quickly? Indeed, would not war with Holland damage its economy more effectively than the punitive tariffs of the trade war? So even the *contrôleur-général* began to contemplate the more brutal solution. He seemed to hope for an indefinite postponement. But war might be 'the only means by which His Majesty can put an end to the insolence of this nation'. Meanwhile, rather than oppose the king's demand for extra money for the war he began to think the hitherto unthinkable: he would raise the money through *affaires extraordinaires*.

The little king of Spain recovered from a severe illness. Perhaps he might live longer than had been anticipated. Louis from impatience, Leopold from family pride, turned away from the idea of partition. He dismissed his pro-French minister Auerbach. No one was more sensitive than Louis to the message intended by commemorative medals.[17] Medals conveyed special messages. One was struck in Holland depicting Conraad van Beunigen, architect of the Triple Alliance, as Joshua stopping the sun in its course. 'Who will divert its course?' was the wording. It was probably unauthorised, but it hit home. Even Lionne caught the royal mood: it did not belong to 'a nation which has exhibited such extreme ingratitude towards its founders' to set itself up 'as sovereign-arbiter over all the other powers'.[18] One of them was now playing a significant part. Charles II of England was drawn by instinctive preference and family feeling towards alliance with France. Henrietta of Orléans, his sister and Louis XIV's sister in law, was one powerful advocate. Another was his ambassador in Paris, Ralph Montagu, whose cousin was spiritual adviser to Louis's aunt, queen Henrietta Maria. With the king's Catholic ministers, they planned a daring religious coup. In exchange for a subsidy, Charles would put Catholics in key places and issue a Declaration of Indulgence; attached was an undertaking to go to war with Holland. This was the substance of the secret treaty of Dover of 1670. Its open clauses, creating a formal alliance between England and France, were sufficiently alarming to the Dutch.

Diplomatic efforts, notably those of Pomponne in Sweden, and the tireless intrigues of Fürstenberg,[19] Louis's unofficial agent for German business, alerted Europe to the likelihood of war. The invasion of Lorraine suggested that it was imminent. There was a sound precedent and some justification. Richelieu had acted in the same way in 1632 after Lorraine's duke, Charles IV, had given shelter to rebels. Charles had enjoyed a brief revenge during the Fronde, with his destructive, ultimately futile invasion. Now he meddled with Fürstenberg's efforts on Louis's behalf to create an offensive alliance out of the west German princes. Lionne would have preferred the diplomatic course: his project was to secure Charles's abdication in favour of his nephew and heir, Prince Charles: thus to secure Louis's flank without alienating the Emperor. In the events of August 1670 we can see Louis's impatience with such cautious counsel – he later confessed to his constant irritation and sense of being thwarted – and also the hand of Louvois, never one for diplomatic niceties. As French troops moved in to secure key towns, Charles was to be kidnapped. He escaped, leaving the French to raze fortresses and to take over the duchy's administration. In one exchange which reveals the tensions between Louis and his older ministers, even Le Tellier *père*, they persuaded Louis to revoke his order to send captured Lorrainers to the galleys. A sign of Louvois's strength, however, was Louis's order (November 1670) to place the courts of Lorraine under the jurisdiction of the *parlement* of Metz (under Lionne's department). This, and other departures from received administrative practice, provoked Lionne to a strong memoir. Louis professed to be indifferent to rivalries and disputes between ministers since it reinforced his idea of rule, above faction and independent in judgement. That did not mean that he was not vulnerable to a pressure group, particularly when its advice supported his own inclinations. The sheer confidence of the war party was persuasive.

Turenne, now Catholic and with a convert's fervour, was bent on completing his work. He had no qualms about fighting the Dutch. The king now listened again to Condé who brought all his energy and expertise to planning the great onslaught. Among the detailed lists of supplies to be provided, ammunition, forage, boats and siege equipment, there is a significant request. One of the places designated for supply dumps was well within the Spanish Netherlands. Were not Condé and the king confident that their attack along the Rhine would bring Spain into the war? There was no plan to go far into Holland, let alone to Amsterdam. The Dutch were expected to collapse. More than chastisement of the Dutch for their retaliatory tariffs and other provocations, or the underlying religious motive which was to surface when peace terms were offered, or his own thirst for glory, the extension of the frontier into the Spanish Netherlands was emerging as Louis's main objective.

The death of Lionne, in October 1671, removed the only minister who had any chance of restraining him. 'A capable man', wrote Louis, 'but not without his faults.' Was it a main fault that he pursued to the end a strategy for keeping the Dutch apart from the Spanish when he, Louis, wanted to have the Spanish intervene so that he could attack their lands? With Lionne died the foreign policy of Mazarin, what has been called 'the natural policy of France'. His successor, Arnauld de Pomponne, was another diplomat. Successful in Sweden, and instinctively moderate, he lacked the authority to counter the influence of Louvois. 'The young minister who is out for his own glory',[20] as Fürstenberg called him, Louvois took his place in the *conseil en haut* in February 1672. He had earned his prominence. Standing in as foreign minister in the interval following Lionne's death he had finalised arrangements with the crucial allies, the Elector of Cologne and the duke of Münster. French troops slipped into Cologne, nominally in the Elector's service. The troops were paid and morale was high; the magazines were stocked for six months; he was involved in tactical planning as well as in the army's administration. Civilian control of the army was coming to be a reality; with the death of Turenne in 1675 and retirement of Condé in 1676 it would be complete. Louvois had set an indelible stamp on the reign. What was done between 1668 and 1678 would have consequences for the rest of the reign.

THE DUTCH WAR

Charles II started the war, in March 1672, by ordering his admiral to attack the Dutch Smyrna convoy. Louis followed suit by declaring war on the United Provinces. The wording of the declaration, on 6 April, is revealing. He could not specify the main offence of the Dutch, that they had opposed his efforts to annex the Spanish Netherlands, without exposing his own motives. So there was heavy stress on Dutch ingratitude after 'great favours', something which he could no longer ignore 'except to the detriment of his glory'.

The campaign began with heady successes as the fall of Rheinberg and other strongholds on the Rhine was followed, in June, by the crossing of the river. For Bossuet it was 'the wonder of the century and of the life of Louis the Great'. Actually the troops waded across at a shallow point and the Dutch fled. But it was a tactical coup and a propaganda triumph. With one army mopping up fortresses to their front, another advancing from the flank, the Dutch situation appeared to be desperate. Condé advised sending on the cavalry to take Amsterdam. Louis delayed, believing that he had already done enough for glory and a good peace. 'It is a good thing that I have prepared for so long for nothing has been lacking. . . . I am in a position to instil fear into my enemies, astonishment to my neighbours and fear to the envious.' Thus invited, Nemesis struck. While Dutch envoys gave teasing assurances of willingness to treat, the French army was outrunning its well-stocked frontier magazines. Faithful to their traditions the Dutch then opened the sluice gates and flooded the polders around the capital. Amsterdam was safe. Their army took heart. Offended by France's alliance with Sweden and alarmed by the threat to his Rhineland estates, the Elector of Brandenburg undertook to send 20,000 troops. The Emperor offered aid. The Dutch wanted peace – but not at any price. Their emissaries offered much – but not enough for Louis. He demanded all lands already occupied, with Maastricht and Bois-le-Duc, compensation for his allies, suspension of tariffs, an indemnity of 24 million *livres* (about the cost of the French war effort to date) and toleration for Roman Catholics. Louis was not reluctant to see the war continue till Spain came in. The Dutch too were playing for time. On 8 July, aged 22, William of Orange became Stadtholder. Still to be tried in war, he spurned the commercial values of the Amsterdam oligarchs, detested Roman Catholicism and saw Louis as his personal enemy. On 20 August an Orangeist mob, spurred on by the *predikants*, lynched the brothers de Witt. William's political authority, in essentials that of a military dictatorship, was now to be stiffened by orthodox Calvinism and its tradition of resistance to the foreign invader. It was to prove a formidable combination. The Emperor decided that inaction would be more dangerous than intervention. The Dutch had won time for a coalition to form and come to their aid. It would be six years before the peace of Nijmegen brought Louis the substantial gains for which he was prepared to prolong the war.

The campaign of 1672 ended disappointingly but then, and during the next five years, there is little sign that Louis regretted its continuance or feared failure. In December 1672 he confided in Louvois that he thought of establishing himself at Lille 'to fall upon wherever I might think I could do something'. His instructions and memoranda show him absorbed in the exercise of his *métier*, personally drawing up marching orders, consulting much with Louvois, but increasingly too with Chamlay who became his personal military advisor and compiled his *Livre du Roi*, recording the marches, sieges and other details of the campaign. The analogy of a game book is not inapt for Louis went to war in the spirit of the chase, intent on the prey but as near as his nature would allow to being light-hearted about it. As intended, the *Livre* shows Louis, neither armchair strategist nor parade-ground general, but active in the field, travelling much and present at several sieges and other actions. If generals had misgivings they criticised Louvois, not his master. He could rely on the praise of sycophantic courtiers. It has to be said, however, that he did much to earn it. Occasionally in danger and often in discomfort, Louis was plainly seen to be striving, as the most energetic of his forebears had done, to win glory and to enlarge the realm. He represented, to his entourage and, through the medium of commissioned writers, poets and painters, to a wider public, a chivalric warrior tradition that could still rouse deep emotion. 'I would think it grand', he wrote, 'if while the Emperor, Spain and Brandenburg try to stop my projects, one saw M. de Luxembourg enter Holland over the ice, M. le Prince [Condé] take part of Burgundy and me in Flanders clearing away all their troops and taking some strongholds. . . .' A snapshot from the *Livre* shows us the king, leaving the war theatre for Versailles, 'with his musketeers . . . and the quarter of the guards, gendarmes and light horse that he ordinarily keeps at his side'.

The war brought setbacks like William's capture of Naarden in August 1673. It exposed strains, the long-standing rivalry of Condé and Turenne, the hostility of the older generals to Louvois. Fortunately for France the coalition was weakened by divided aims and personal jealousies. Only hostility towards France could bind Austria and Spain to Holland and Brandenburg. Montecucoli, the leading Imperialist commander, was constantly at odds with William. The French generally retained the initiative. After Turenne had driven the Elector of Brandenburg back to his homeland (February 1673), Vauban – with Louis in attendance – besieged the great fortress of Maastricht. Here, using parallel trenches for the first time, with a large civilian force to dig them, Vauban showed how lives and time could be saved by a scientific approach. Twenty-five June days were sufficient to secure one of Europe's most powerful fortresses. In the spring of the following year Louis ordered a second invasion of Franche-Comté and personally directed the siege of its capital, Besançon. In August Condé was master of the field after a hideously bloody battle at Senef. The Dutch and their allies lost 15,000 men, the French 10,000. Condé sent back over a hundred captured standards but the battle decided nothing. Vauban pointed the moral. 'The enemies', he told Louvois, 'ought to seek a battle and we to avoid one, since to avoid fighting is the sure way to beat them.' Two years later Condé retired.

In July 1675, while reconnoitring the Imperialist lines, Turenne was killed by a stray bullet. 'Today', said their general Montecucoli, 'died a man who did honour to mankind.'[21] His reputation had been enhanced by his masterly winter campaign among the slopes and snows of the Vosges, itself an indication of the new approach to warfare. Like his veteran adversary Monteccucoli, the victor of St Gothard, his career spans the two military worlds. That of the Thirty Years War, which saw semi-independent war lords like Wallenstein or Bernard of Saxe-Weimar striving to create independent principalities, was the world in which Turenne learned soldiering. It was the world in which Richelieu and Mazarin had to operate, buying the loyalty of the generals and unable to make significant reforms. Turenne, whose own *vicomté* enjoyed virtually independent status within France, had found it hard to accept the political control of the new military régime of Louvois. He had realised, however, that the stronger central authority, backed by ample resources, brought him new opportunities. His eventually supportive role in the Fronde, his successes in the War of Devolution, his conversion to Catholicism, his weighty voice in council, and the respect of a younger generation of soldiers, combined to give him unique status. It was sustained by the respect of a younger generation of soldiers, the militarist atmosphere at court and the brilliant victories of his last campaign that pushed the Imperialists across the Rhine. It can all be read in the unmeasured effusions of Bossuet's *oraison funèbre*. The marshal's body was brought back past distressed crowds. 'Everywhere', wrote Mme de Sévigné, 'there were tears, emotions, crowds, processions, forcing them to travel by night.' Louis XIV decreed that the body should be interred at Saint-Denis, the resting place of kings. In a subsequent oration by Fléchier, in the church of Saint-Eustache, Parisians were told that Turenne 'embodied the glory of the nation', having 'embraced the cause of the glory of the king, the desire for peace and zeal for the public good . . .'. In life he might have embodied typically brutal aspects of soldiering as well as some of its finer traditions; in death, his example helped nurture the Frenchman's growing sense of nation and of a glory in which all could share.

In the fast-developing myth Condé and Turenne were the great captains, irreplaceable. In fact there were competent successors, notably Luxembourg, who first showed his ability in this war, and Villars. The latter saw Condé lead a charge at Senef. 'Now I have seen what I most longed to see – the great Condé sword in hand.'[22] But now Condé retired, to nurse his gout and improve his mind at Chantilly. The age of easy victories was gone. The balance of strength had become more even with the intervention of Austria and Spain and, in 1674, the defection of England. Louis found himself engaged in a war on two fronts, Flanders and the middle Rhineland, to defend his gains against a coalition which included, at different times, Lorraine's aggrieved duke and Brandenburg's ambitious Elector. With Sweden engaged mainly in defending its North German lands – but keeping Brandenburg engaged – and her German allies, Münster and Cologne, falling away after their initial support, France bore the brunt. The strategy of Lionne was in tatters and Colbert was reduced to increasingly desperate efforts to maintain the revenues. Yet Louis was buoyant and unperturbed by the hostile propaganda. The war of words for the mind of Europe, of Germany in particular, was to become more intense with the years. Already it was creating new images: Louis was 'the Christian Turk'. There were military setbacks, like the defeat of Créqui, after Turenne's death and the loss of Philippsburg to Lorraine in 1676, but Louis's armies did not usually let him down.

In 1676 caution prevailed. It was Louvois, not Louis, then covering the siege of Bouchain, who urged caution when the chance came to attack the Dutch near Valenciennes. Chamlay managed to improve the occasion in the *Livre du Roi*: 'Orange must have been most upset to have stood in the presence of his enemy for three days, only to be the witness of his glory.' When Luxembourg won his timely victory over Orange at Cassel, in April 1677, Orléans was nominally, and courageously, in command; otherwise it might have been trumpeted more loudly. For the Dutch lost heavily and French casualties were light. There was no reticence about Louis's strenuous part in the bold thrust of March 1678 that led to the siege and capture of first Ghent, then Ypres. With the Spanish governor at the end of his tether and William reluctantly accepting that peace was inevitable the way was clear for peace talks at Nijmegen.

'I FULLY REJOICE IN MY CLEVER CONDUCT'

Louis had advertised the tiger's strength and its smiling face when he launched his last campaign, took Ghent, published his proposals for peace, and threw Messina[23] on the board as proof of his desire for peace. Two positions were staunchly held. The Dutch wanted to retain a barrier of frontier fortresses; the French refused to sacrifice their ally Sweden. Louis and Pomponne, who had been ambassador in Stockholm and negotiated the alliance, saw that it was important that other powers should see the king as an honourable and reliable ally. Louis insisted that Brandenburg should return to Sweden the lands they had won since the battle of Fehrbellin in 1675. The Dutch then made an alliance with England and threatened renewal of war if the French did not evacuate the Flemish towns without waiting for settlement of the Swedish question. In August Luxembourg easily repelled an attack by William at Mons. The Stadtholder was already in trouble with the trading community as its losses rose. Louis, too, was aware of strains at home. In 1675 Vauban had complained about the state of the army, 'its garrisons defended by children or poor little wretches, the officers as bad'. That year had seen the serious Breton rising and the diversion of 6,000 men to put it down. So long, however, as the army could take towns and win battles, France was plainly dominant and could make large claims. The French diplomats, expert and resourceful, working to a clear brief, held the initiative. The allies were divided. The Dutch were primarily concerned about their security. The Emperor wanted to return to the situation after Westphalia, the Spanish to that after the Pyrenees. Charles II of England was mainly concerned to preserve the succession of his brother against Whig attempts to exclude him that had their origin in exposure of the secret Treaty of Dover.

Peace was made possible by deferring the Swedish settlement. Offered generous terms, and indifferent to the interests of Spain, the Dutch promised not to help Brandenburg. So Louis was left free to bargain from strength for the Spanish possessions which he really wanted. The peace of Nijmegen comprised, in fact, several separate treaties, in which France settled matters with Holland and Spain, in 1678, and with the Emperor, Brandenburg and the Danes in 1679. Significantly, the language had changed since 1672. There was no mention of religion or of 'tokens of submission'. Colbert's policy was abandoned, with his tariffs. All was pared down to France's essential, permanent interest. The vulnerable north-east frontier was strengthened by the acquisition of a line of strong places through Spanish Flanders. Chief among them were Ypres, Cambrai and Valenciennes. For Vauban's defensible line Ghent, Courtrai, even Charleroi (gained at Aix) were given up. Louis could justly say that his prime interest now was security. To the relief of Burgundians, Franche-Comté was now retained. It had long been the source of border unrest. The Emperor restored Breisach to France and ceded Freiburg as well. By the treaty of Saint-Germain, Brandenburg was compelled to give back to Sweden her conquests in Pomerania. This act of favour to a disappointing ally was a powerful advertisement of the value of the French alliance. Its bitterness was palliated for Elector Frederick William by a present of 900,000 *livres*. Louis could still afford to be both honourable and generous.

Louis put a characteristic gloss on the difficulties he had experienced: it was the successes of the French armies 'that excited the hatreds and jealousies of neighbours'. He was apparently untroubled by decisions which had prolonged the war for 'ambition and glory are always pardonable in a prince so young and blessed by fortune as I was'. He did not undervalue his overall achievement. 'I fully rejoice', he wrote in his *Mémoires*, 'in my clever conduct whereby I was able to extend the boundaries of my kingdom at the expense of my enemies.' He had indeed shown political skill in his grasp of what was relevant and vital, and in his timing. Circumstances were, however, exceptionally favourable. Spain had proved to be unable to impose upon events. Her soldiers could barely keep the Moors from her African forts. Her Mediterranean fleet had been defeated by Duquesne. The security of her possessions depended mainly on the sufferance of stronger states, each jealous of the gains another might make. Her very existence as a state was soon to be a matter for bargain and contract between the powers. Though a peasant rising in Bohemia was easily suppressed (in 1680), Austria was virtually paralysed by mounting pressure from Hungarians and Turks.[24] Leopold had not reconciled himself to the loss of Alsace but his hold over his remaining lands there was merely nominal. The Dutch had preserved their frontiers at the cost of much trade, shipping and capital. England was sunk in the near-revolutionary disorders of the Popish Plot. Charles regained the initiative in 1681 but his main interest was to survive without calling Parliament. So he held out his hand for a French pension and remained tactfully neutral. The German states had shown that their interests were local and that, even if they could be roused against France, they would be useful only as auxiliaries to a great alliance. There were smouldering resentments. Lorraine's duke preferred to wander stateless than to accept terms he thought degrading. The Elector of Brandenburg was not reconciled to Sweden's presence in Pomerania. Yet, for such interests and grievances to be fused in a common cause, there needed to be some great provocation. Only if Louis showed that he had further territorial ambitions, such as might threaten further the integrity of the Empire, would the interested powers ally; only by such an alliance could he be defeated.

Louis was pre-eminent in 1679. Ten years later he was fighting again, on several fronts, against a coalition, more determined and far more formidable than that of the Dutch war. There would be considerable victories, but it was essentially a defensive war. The effort, in terms of numbers engaged, and overall cost, was beyond anything conceivable even twenty years before. It is not hard to establish that Louis and his ministers were, in some degree, responsible for the outbreak of the War of the League of Augsburg and its prolonged, destructive course. It is mistaken, however, to assert that they were solely, or even mainly responsible, or that there would have been no war if they had acted differently. It is to overlook the unforgiving obduracy of the Emperor, hardening with every victory against the Turks; also the mortal enmity of William of Orange. Pursuing the personal mission that had begun with the French invasion he regarded his elevation to the English throne mainly in the light of the extra resources it would bring to his war.

The mood and opinion of the time should be recalled. Detached observers and committed policy makers shared certain assumptions, realistic in the light of experience, or plain pessimistic about human nature. War was normal, peace an interlude. States had certain interests, sovereigns, human ambitions;

a position of relative strength was one to exploit while the going was good. The opportunity might not recur. To seize it was a duty. Montecucoli had said, in 1668, that within living memory there had been no peace that had not been unreliable or suspect. Thoughtful students of the international scene, like Leibnitz, could think of no better solution than to unite Europe against the Ottoman and divert militancy to crusade. 'Turn against the Holland of the east' was one German's plea to Pomponne in 1672. 'They [holy wars] have been out of fashion since St Louis' was the minister's dry response.[25] Chief architect of the peace of Nijmegen, Pomponne was perhaps the most reasonable and humane of Louis' ministers. In 1679 he was dismissed, supposedly for Jansenist sympathies. The chief effect of his disgrace and the appointment of Colbert's brother, Colbert de Croissy, was to give Louis even closer control of foreign affairs. In terms of policy France, more than ever, was the king. His character, and the milieu in which he worked, were of crucial importance.

Louis worked as methodically as ever, and with a new intensity of interest in state affairs and serious-mindedness that can be seen to have coincided with a change in his private life as he repudiated Mme de Montespan[26] and turned for consolation to Mme de Maintenon. He took more on himself, claimed more for his experience, and insisted more firmly on his authority. Even routine requests by ministers were liable to be refused 'to show that he . . . would not be governed'. Ministers accordingly showed less independence than those of the first generation. More serious in this respect than the downfall of Pomponne was the decline in vigour, then the death, in 1683, of Colbert. It left Louvois the leading figure. He had shown himself a superb administrator, but his political ideas were limited. The good of the army was, for him, the good of France. How to improve it, how best to use it, were his daily concerns. Perhaps he had risen too fast and settled too quickly into the affairs of a department. His belief in force as the solution to political problems was always at hand to support Louis's grand notions of what was right and due. After 1683 Louvois secured the exclusion from the *conseil en haut* of Colbert's son Seignelay, the efficient Secretary for the Navy. He himself took over Colbert's responsibility for *bâtiments*, while his friend Le Pelletier was made *contrôleur-général*. Since his father had been made chancellor in 1679 the Le Tellier faction could rely, in council, on three voices out of the usual four. But its influence should not be over-stated. Louis was his own master. He was settling on Versailles as his permanent abode. The main quarters of the palace were complete by 1682. Everything about the palace spoke of glory.

Notes

1. For this occasion, and significance of the tableaux, arches and inscriptions, see pp. 34–5. Also V.L. Tapié, *The Age of Grandeur* (London, 1960; orig., Paris, 1957), pp. 94–102.

2. H. Hauser, *La Prépondérance espagnole* (1934), p. 393. At the beginning, in 1658, under France's patronage, the League included the archbishop Electors of Mainz and Cologne and several Imperial princes, duke Philip-William of Neuburg, three Brunswick dukes and the Landgrave of Hesse-Cassel. During the next few years it was joined by Württemberg, Münster, Trier, Hesse-Darmstadt and – crucially – Brandenburg.

3. For the standard case against Mazarin (through the mouth of Richelieu in Fénelon's imaginary dialogue) see B. Jullien (ed.), *Fénelon, Dialogues des Morts* (Paris, 1900): 'You were only subtle because you were feeble and lacked fixed principles.' The dialogue is worth studying for the way in which the two Cardinals' claims and sallies are made to convey the revulsion of *dévôts* from the violence and deceits which they held to have stained the policies of the Cardinals and, by inference, the ways in which they thought that Louis had erred latterly in the same direction.

4. Huig van Groot (1583–1645), an exile from his native Holland because of his opposition to its prevailing hard-line Calvinism, long-term resident in Paris and representative there of Sweden, was one of the most influential writers of his time, drawing, for his theories, on a fund of political and diplomatic experience.

5. For court manners see also pp. 190 et seq. Also Olivier Chaline, 'The Valois and Bourbon courts', in John Adamson (ed.), *The Princely Courts of Europe* (London, 1999) pp. 67–93.

6. Especially after the construction (1677) of the magnificent Escalier des Ambassadeurs (see p. 189).

7. For François de Callières (1645–1717) see S.D. Kertes (ed.), and A.F. Whyte (trans.). *On the manner of Negotiation with Princes* (New York, 1963).

8. As notably, in 1630, after the Diet of Regensburg and Father Joseph's commitment to the almost complete evacuation of North Italy.

9. The text is reproduced in *Recueil des Instructions donnés aux Ambassadeurs et Ministres de France depuis les Traités de Westphalia jusqu'à la Révolution française* (Paris, 1884). For a revealing account of the negotiations before Westphalia, see D. Croxton, *Peacemaking in Early Modern Europe, Cardinal Mazarin and the Congress of Westphalia, 1643–8* (New York, 1999).

10. In an important article on Richelieu's foreign policy, 'Une bonne paix', J. Bergin and L. Brockliss (eds), *Richelieu and his Age* (Oxford, 1992) pp. 45–69, H. Weber contends that Richelieu saw the making of peace as a moral duty and that he envisaged the interests of France as combined with those of Christendom, not because of Machiavellian *raison d'état* (as *dévôts* contended) but because 'the kingdom of France had a divinely ordained function in respect of both France and Christendom'. Though neither Mazarin nor Louis XIV would disagree with this, the tone and content of Westphalia and the way it was subsequently exploited represent (in Weber's view) the failure of Richelieu's peace policy and ushered in a period where the self-interest of states was dominant. One is left with the question: if Richelieu had lived,

would he have made the concessions (in Alsace for example to the Emperor, in Flanders to Spain) conducive to a quicker settlement but not one so plainly in the interest of France with her paramount need for more secure frontiers?

11. P. Sonnino, *Louis XIV's View of the Papacy* (California, 1966), gives an account of the quarrel which, drawing heavily on the *Mémoires*, is also a character study of the young king.

12. Use of the word 'reasonable' may surprise. But the notable Dutch historian, Pieter Geyl, analysing Louis's policies in the sixties, saw reason and caution. Louis was, for example, 'surprisingly moderate' in negotiations with the Dutch and Geyl stressed that it was domestic struggles in Holland that prevented a Franco-Dutch solution of the problem of the southern Netherlands. P. Geyl, *The Netherlands, 1648–1715*, pp. 42–3, 99.

13. Quoted by Bluche, op. cit., p. 242. Further observations of the marquis, the Savoyard ambassador, add up to an impressive picture of committed soldiering. 'He spent the whole night under canvas and only went to bed as dawn broke.' In councils of war, 'he issued his orders very deftly'. 'He was decisive in danger and as poised as a dancer at a ball.' Pressed by his officers to keep clear of danger he said: 'Since you want me to take care of myself for your sakes, I also want to make sure that you look after yourselves for mine.' See also J. Wolf in J.C. Rule (ed.), 'Louis XIV, soldier-king', in *Louis XIV and the Craft of Kingship* (Ohio, 1969) pp. 196–220.

14. In P. Sonnino, *Louis XIV and the Origins of the Dutch War* (Cambridge, 1988), p. 20. Up till his death, Lionne is the central figure in this important study; a good example of how enlightening diplomatic history can be – about personalities as well as policies,

15. The new fortress of Lille required 60 million bricks, $3\frac{1}{2}$ million pieces of stone. In 1708 Marlborough would realise they had been well used. The story of these two sieges is that of the 'Military revolution' in a single embattled place.

16. See also p. 138. Undoubtedly Colbert preferred the 'perpetual and peaceable war [commerce] of wit and hard work.' He insisted (Sonnino, op. cit., p. 7) on 'burying his head in the sand until it was too late'.

17. For the value attached to the issue of medals, see P. Burke, *The Fabrication of Louis XIV* (Cambridge, 1992), in particular pp. 115–22.

18. See also P. Sonnino, op. cit., p. 62.

19. Wilhelm, Prince von Fürstenberg, Mazarin's client and friend of Lionne, German by birth, French by naturalisation, was well placed to serve France, having brothers as chief ministers to the Catholic Electors of Cologne and Bavaria. He had 'no trouble believing that what was good for his family must be good for the princes of the Empire, and that was to collect subsidies from France while restraining the power of the House of Austria'. (ibid., p. 15). He could only operate effectively, however, if Louis were seen by other princes to be acting with restraint.

20. Ibid., p. 166

21. Quoted Lynn, op. cit., p. 141.

22. E. Godley, *The Great Condé: A Life of Louis II de Bourbon, Prince de Condé* (London, 1915), p. 564. Claude, duc de Villars (1653–1734) would come to represent, in a dark hour for his country, enduring traits in the cult of glory when it was infused with

devotion to French soil. Here his hero-worship evokes Condé's renown and another aspect of *la gloire* – that of which Mme de Sévigné wrote (to Bussy in 1683) that it was a prime element in the upbringing of young nobles. She understood the role of women in fostering it: 'since one constantly tells men that they are only worthy of esteem to the extent that they love *gloire*, they devote all their time to it'. She also felt the cost, after the battle of Senef, for example: 'We have lost so much by this battle that without the Te Deum and some flags [107] brought to Notre Dame we would believe we had lost the battle.'

23. The rebellion of Messina against Spanish rule had allowed France to mount amphibious support operations from 1675. While the French proved the worth of Colbert's navy in sustained operations, and even saw off the great De Ruyter it seems that their main interest was not in securing Sicily but in a diversion which would limit the force they could send to Catalonia and Rousillon.

24. The main projects of Louis's anti-Habsburg diplomacy were an alliance between John Sobieski of Poland and Prince Apafi of Transylvania, and support for the ambitious Imri Thököli. French officers advised the latter and his soldiers called themselves 'the soldiers of France'. His coins carried the slogan: *Ludovicus XIV, Galliae Rex, Defensor Hungariae*. It was his successes after 1678 – he had overrun most of Hungary by 1680 – that persuaded the Turks to make their great assault on Austria. However the Turkish threat was enough to bring John Sobieski into line with the Emperor. Louis might have done better to have secured his friendship. In Poland French diplomacy had a costly failure.

25. Leibnitz then served the Elector of Mainz and no doubt inspired this suggestion. The text of his *Project for the Conquest of Egypt* (1672) can be found in O. and P. Ranum (eds), *The Century of Louis XIV* (New York, 1972) pp. 253–8. It is interesting as an example of a profound and wide-ranging thinker's ideas about the interests of European states: hardly objective though, since Mainz was uncomfortably open to French troops. Pomponne took Leibnitz sufficiently seriously to invite him to Paris, but Louis was not impressed and did not give him an audience.

26. For his relations with Montespan and for her situation see p. 107, n. 26 and 184. For Maintenon see pp. 325–6.

Chapter 7

◆

VERSAILLES: THE DISPLAY OF POWER

The people of the court are like a foreign nation within the state.

ABBÉ DE SAINT-RÉAL, *c.* 1705

In opening our hearts we should retain the mastery of our minds.

LOUIS XIV

'GREAT BUILDINGS, THEIR MAGNIFICENCE'

At Versailles Louis practised the art of government by spectacle and through ritual. In Cannadine's striking phrase: 'Power is like the wind; we cannot see it, but we feel its force. Ceremonial is like the snow; an insubstantial pageant, soon melted into thin air.'[1] Here, however, power was visibly displayed and the ceremonial aspect was vital to its acceptance. In Montesquieu's retrospective view 'the magnificence and splendour which surrounds kings form part of their power'.[2] Here Louis was in his element. The palace was his creation; its routines suited his needs; its manners reflected his personality. When in his *Mémoires* he reflected on the value of display as a means of enhancing a monarch's standing he did not omit architecture and one note reads simply: '*Grands bâtiments, leur magnificence.*' Versailles was an explicit statement about the king's authority. In Bossuet's words it was meant 'to make the people respect him'.[3]

The idea was not novel but it commanded more resources and it was more ambitious in scale and in patronage than any previous sovereign could have envisaged. It was master-minded by Colbert as part of a wider programme for impressing Europe with the superiority of French culture. In aspiration it was nearer to Philip IV's Buen Retiro than to Louis XIII's Louvre. In conception it was a natural development from the cardinals' palaces. Both Richelieu and Mazarin had used architecture and classical imagery to convey a message of legitimate power. How much stronger the message – and more authentic – when the king was lord and master.

Versailles meant a way of life of a privileged nobility. It was also the centre of royal government. Saint-Simon[4] stressed an important fact when he noted 'the incredible advantage' gained by Louis's settling in a single residence outside Paris: 'it imposed orderliness on everybody and secured dispatch and facility to his affairs'. Unprecedently grand, Versailles came to embody a form of court and government that would be widely admired and copied. The Emperor Leopold built Schönbrünn in imitation; scores of German princelings planted out miniature Versailles to impress their authority on their subjects.

The wisdom of posterity has tended to condemn the palace. Was it not irrelevant to the needs of the people? Did it not isolate the king from his people? A school for sycophants; a place of artifice and pretence; encouraging in the king pomposity, egotism and – the most serious charge – false values and goals: such are the notions and images that Versailles has conjured up. In different ways they miss the point of the place and misrepresent the achievement. 'Who could help being repelled and disgusted by the violence done to nature', asked Saint-Simon. He disliked the damp of gardens insufficiently drained from the original swamp; he flinched, as might we, from the smells of a palace where grandeur was more important than plumbing (ironically one of Colbert's main complaints about Bernini's rejected design for the Louvre). His main objection, however, was to the idea of the place, exactly what most impressed contemporaries. Imposing rule over unruly nature Versailles symbolised Louis's mastery over unruly subjects; praising his achievements, it stood for absolute power and the abundant patronage which drew men to court. Bossuet's genius was to elevate and cense the notions that ordinary men might struggle to express: his prayer was that 'the glorious dignity and the majesty of the palace might blaze out, for all to see, the splendid grandeur of royal power'. And Saint-Simon stayed there for most of his life and became its most notable chronicler.

So completely has Versailles come to be associated with Louis XIV that it may seem that it was the logical outcome of a deliberate design from the outset of personal rule. Its story is less even and chance played a part. The timing of building operations, with their greatest surge following the peace of Nijmegen and a tailing off after 1689, was linked to Louis's fortunes in war. Yet a number of factors were consistently at work. Louis's disagreable memories of Paris meant that he was unenthusiastic about Colbert's plans to develop the Louvre. He certainly felt the need for a grander setting for government and for a court more formal than that which he had inherited. Looking to the Spanish way and his uncle Philip IV's example of calm dignity (though not his remoteness) he was deliberately marking a break with the French past: the relatively *nouveau* Bourbon with the ancient, if latterly unfortunate Valois. It was as much a question of putting *les grands* in their subordinate place, of ensuring that there would be no social embarrassment, as of implementing a new form of government. Of course the one went with the other – but the deep need of Louis lay at the heart of the process. Permanently scarred by his early experiences, he associated political disobedience with the casual manners of his cousins and peers. He needed the routine of days so regular that courtiers could tell the time by his movements, and the conventions which kept subjects, however grand, at a distance. At the same time he realised the importance of being visible and, through formal channels, accessible to the largest possible numbers of those subjects. In this he was faithful to French tradition, rejecting the Spanish 'in which the majesty of kings consists largely in their not being seen'. He was also entirely in tune with contemporary practice in a society obsessed by ritual, as would be recognised, for example, by representatives of Estates at the opening of a session, or envoys involved in the preliminaries to treaty-making.

THE PROBLEM OF PARIS

At the outset it was important that Louis actually liked Versailles and his father's simple brick hunting box, his 'little house of cards', with its pleasant garden surrounded by waste and swamp. He associated it with carefree and enjoyable days and his love for Louise de la Vallière, in whose honour was mounted the memorable fête of 1664, *les plaisirs de l'île enchantée*. The idea of an island, spell-bound by the magician Alcide, sufficed for spectacular tableaux, dances, jousts, processions, plays, music, banquets, fireworks: all, for the world's admiration, graphically described in the *Gazette*.[5] In the first decade of the reign Versailles was developed as a country seat for such occasions, and otherwise for excursions of small intimate groups. An important early addition was a menagerie.[6] The king then travelled from one royal château to another and, when unavoidable, to the Louvre or the Tuileries.

The experience, with its attendant discomforts, stiffened his resolve to settle in one place splendid enough to represent him adequately, but convenient for the needs of government. Bernini[7] was summoned from Rome: Europe's most renowned architect for Europe's greatest king. Deeply religious himself, a passionate artist and a perfectionist, Bernini was struck by Louis's interest and by his ability to read plans. The portrait bust that he left as the single fruit of his mission suggests that the Roman recognised power when he saw it. Just as his *Ecstasy of St Teresa* draws the spectator into a religious drama, so his portrait invites reflection on the very idea of royal majesty. Louis was impressed by Bernini's baroque designs for the Louvre but a conservative instinct put him on his guard against the exuberant Roman. He had 'some inclination to preserve what his predecessors had built' – and Bernini would have pulled down a whole *quartier* to create his baroque masterpiece. So it did not need rejection by Colbert, in his capacity as *surintendant des bâtiments* and his insistence on a more sober, regular and wholly French design to make him opt for Versailles.

Another factor was Louis's own passionate interest in architecture and in gardens. Even while he was turning against the city as residence he was supporting Colbert's ambitious programme for improving the city's appearance and amenities. Up to 1670 annual expenditure on the city's palaces was double that on Versailles. Their grandeur only emphasised the surrounding squalor. As the city's population approached the half million mark its mediaeval streets, congestion, stench, disorder and criminality called for a new police. A first step was La Reynie's appointment as *lieutenant-général* in 1667.[8] Like his successor D'Argenson (1697–1715), he exploited the possibilities of his office to the full and, through his reforms, illustrated the potential, within an absolutist régime, for improvement when the objects were generally held desirable and the king was directly concerned.

The *lieutenant-général* was briefed directly by Colbert and his successors as secretary for the *maison du roi*. He saw much of the king who was concerned with several aspects of police work, and took a paternal interest in the behaviour of his more prominent subjects. A young nobleman, La Motte Aignan, was warned that if he could not behave himself in church he would be deported from the city. More serious were the investigations into the poisonings allegedly carried out by Mme de Brinvilliers that led to her trial before *Parlement* and execution in 1676. Disturbing revelations and rumours then came out of the prolonged efforts of the tribunal established in the Arsenal's ill-omened *chambre ardente*, charged to look into the sorceries of Catherine Deshayes, known as la Voisin, and her associates. 367 suspects were tried, 34 of them were executed. Doubt was cast on the judgment and morality of some prominent personalities. Colbert could point out that it was absurd to suppose that Mme de Montespan should seek to hurt her royal lover. Louvois's zeal for investigation and the high proportion of Colbert's clients among the accused no doubt increased the latter's justifiable scepticism. The gullibility of La Reynie and of some leading lawyers was furthered by the way in which benighted, malicious or simply hysterical witnesses insinuated or charged in the way expected of them. The atmosphere was oppressive and the king was increasingly upset by the travesties of legal process which titillated Parisians, gave a new edge and spice to foreign propaganda and damaged the image of the régime. It is to his credit that he did not react by turning on the unfortunate Montespan. The line he habitually drew between his private life and public duty proved its worth.

The 'affair of the poisons' would recede into insignificance. The solid achievement of La Reynie remained. Only the criminal could deplore the way in which the police, supported by a body of eight hundred sergeants and archers, worked to cleanse and light the city and safeguard its inhabitants. La Reynie's responsibilities included the water and food supplies of the city, the regulation of markets, the paving of streets, construction of fountains, fire-fighting, measures against prostitution and beggary, oversight of the vast *hôpital-général*.[9] In the 5,500 reflecting candle-lanterns that made Paris the best lit of European capital cities it may not be fanciful to see a sign and metaphor for the Enlightenment and the rational mentality, favourable to practical improvements and hostile to superstition, which is exemplified in Colbert's reforming codes of law. Another message comes, however, from efforts to tighten censorship of 'subversive' ideas. The *lieutenant-général* had to watch books printed in France as well as those printed abroad. Until about 1680 the government was reasonably successful. In the less favourable climate of the eighties and in face of Huguenot propaganda there was a growing market for banned books.[10]

The moulding of opinion through censorship might prove an elusive goal. Where twentieth-century dictatorships have struggled, eventually failed, the seventeenth-century monarchy could not hope to insulate itself from criticism. Where it could enhance its standing and create a positive – and lasting – image of responsible power was in the field of architecture. Improvement in the conditions of life in the capital was bound to be a slow business. Meanwhile the face of the city, and the image of monarchy, could be enhanced in more positive ways. The main work was the enlargement of the Louvre with the great eastern colonnade and its Corinthian order of columns by Le Vau and Perrault, and Perrault's more severe single pilastered south colonnade which is today's most familiar view of the palace. The building was young Christopher Wren's 'daily object' and 'a School of Architecture, the best probably, at this day in Europe'. The *Cours de Vincennes*, approaching Paris from the east, to culminate in Perrault's *Parc de Triomphe du Trône*, like the confident destruction of the old ramparts and the rebuilding of the *Portes* into the city, was as significant a pointer to the king's interests as Versailles. The *hôpital-général* brought the notion of central control and good order to the problem of the poor; the *Observatoire* (started 1667) enhanced his reputation (though again owed largely to Colbert) as a patron of science; it would not have displeased him that it was the finest in Europe. The need to house old soldiers would give him greater scope. The *Invalides* was begun in 1677. Its tremendous dome would show that its purpose was not merely functional. But it was the progressive enhancement of Versailles that would best promote his glory.

A NEW PALACE

Versailles was envisaged as theatrical space. Spectacular *fêtes* were held, typically to celebrate conquests and the extension of the realm, as after the peace of Aix in 1668 and the conquest of Franche-Comté in 1674, and to associate it with the best that Molière and Lully could offer of French drama and music. The gardens were also ideal for the ballet in which Louis was sometimes a principal performer. That he excelled as a dancer can only have enhanced the magic of ballet, with backdrop of lawns, statues, pools and fountains for the dancers' stately minuets. We may see a social metaphor in its control and balance, obedient to the music, precise and unhurried, with all participants held in the ordained relationship to one another. Did they too receive an impression, implied if not intended, of the harmony of Louis's ideal universe; of the subjection of all, dancers and spectators alike, to Apollo, god of the sun, music and poetry – and so to him?

The palace of Versailles and its artefacts were a deliberate working out of themes of his kingship in terms that could best be appreciated by its occupants and visitors. Through the iconography and ritual there is one all-pervasive idea: the fusion of the king's imaginary, symbolic body, with his real body: the state with the person. The idea can only be understood in the context of contemporary culture: outside it the palace appears not merely, as to some of Saint-Simon's generation of courtiers, dreary and stifling, but virtually incomprehensible. In some respects distinctive, epitomising under Colbert's orchestration the Age of Grandeur and reproduced throughout the country, the pervading style in art and architecture was still essentially conservative: a climactic moment in the classical culture of the Renaissance. Already, however, the lines were being drawn for the battle of Ancients and Moderns which was to be fought out so publically in the eighties. The central issue was the superiority or otherwise of classical writers over contemporaries. Though essentially about literature the contentions of Boileau and La Fontaine (for the classics) and of the Perrault brothers and Fontenelle, for the moderns, had wide artistic, therefore political implications.[11]

Meanwhile, even if they had not had the advantage of education at a Jesuit school[12] or one of comparable standard, even if they fell short of the ideal of *honnêté* which owed so much to Rome and Greece, most courtiers would have been at home with the classical myths and fables and with the main texts from which they were learnt. Running through many editions, Ovid's *Metamorphoses*, for example, was one of several influential texts. It came naturally to painters and sculptors to use classical models and stories since they could be sure that their allusions would be understood. On the authority of the *Annales* of Ennius it was still held (though taken less seriously than by Roman Emperors and become more of a pleasant conceit) that exceptional human beings, sovereigns or soldiers, revered in their lifetime, had become gods. Also to be reckoned with is the Neoplatonist convention that divine truth had to be hidden in a coded pictorial language. Artists, with perfect integrity, doing for Louis XIV only what they would for any other patron, employed symbolism to convey an acceptable message. In an early painting of Lebrun,[13] *The Family of Darius at the Feet of Alexander* (c. 1660), courtiers would not have been surprised to see Louis as Alexander. What is most off-putting to the modern eye, as for example in Lebrun's vast ceiling painting, *The king governs for himself* (1681), is just that which revealed most, and most forcibly, to Louis's contemporaries. They saw the king, holding a rudder, being crowned by the Graces while a France-figure deals with Discord under ominous storm-clouds. Hymen, goddess of marriage, offers Louis a cornucopia, signifying plenty. Minerva, goddess of wisdom, guides him to glory. In their 'firmament on high' attendant gods offer assistance: one sees Neptune's trident and Vulcan's hammer.

It was with such ideas and conventions that Louis set out to show 'what a great king can do when he spares nothing to satisfy his wishes'. Colbert later expressed misgivings: the place was 'more concerned with Your Majesty's pleasure and diversion than with your glory'. Yet he embraced the underlying principle whole-heartedly: 'Your majesty knows that apart from brilliant military exploits, nothing testifies more to the grandeur and spirit of princes than buildings; and all posterity takes the measure of princes by the proud mansions that they have constructed in their lifetime.' As with the ministers he inherited from Mazarin Louis was fortunate to have at hand an experienced team. Louis le Vau[14] as architect, André le Nôtre[15] as landscape gardener, and Charles le Brun as painter, had created Vaux-le-Vicomte for Fouquet.

When, after the peace of Aix, Louis decided to create a virtually new palace, pavilions had already been added to his father's château and a prodigious work of landscaping was creating the frame for Le Vau's construction. The eye would now travel down vistas of grass and stone, set with fountains and pools and adorned with sculptures, with here and there little classical temples, to the great canal which stretched to the horizon. All around trees were being planted, some mature and brought from distant parts. The waterworks which drained the unhealthy marsh and fed the fountains were a *chef d'oeuvre* of engineering. Le Nôtre brought to perfection the art of gardening as an extension of architecture. His *jardin de l'intelligence* eased the shock of transition from art to nature; the heath and marsh were transformed into a pattern of lines and spaces which exemplified the victory of rule over disorder. The classical symmetry of terraces and avenues, clipped yews, gravelled and grassy walks is as French, of its time, as the economics of Colbert and the plays of Racine. In illusion as in reality, this garden was about power. Fading into the distance the grass walks would seem to join the sky; flanking statues portraying mythological scenes would strengthen the theatrical impression of being in an Olympian world. The narcissist could find mirrors in the grotto of Thetis. There was a price to pay for his sovereign's glory and his enjoyment. On any day there might be twenty thousand working on the palace, surrounding buildings and grounds (in 1685 Dangeau reckoned 36,000). They died in hundreds of malarial fever and were taken away by night so that no one should be disturbed.

The building was a near continuous operation and the pace was maintained till the last twenty years of the reign. During the 1670s and early 1680s the annual cost averaged two million *livres*; from mid-1680s to early 1690s four million, for it was then that Louvois, Colbert's successor as *surintendant des bâtiments*, loosened the purse strings. It was in those years that Marly, designed for light relief for a favoured few (built between 1679 and 1686), and the Grand Trianon, most elegant of summerhouses (1687–89), came into the reckoning. Expenditure had rarely risen above 4 per cent of the state budget but even a lower proportion in later years looked like extravagance in a period of wartime deficits and dwindling enthusiasm for the régime. Against the cost should be set the value to a sluggish economy of this vast artistic enterprise: demand stimulated, employment created, skills fostered and standards raised. There was constant work for masons, carpenters, tilers and glaziers; for gardeners and grooms. A flow of new sculptures swelled the host of amazons, bacchants, tritons and naiads around grove and fountain. Continuous demand for tapestries, paintings and bas-reliefs, for mirrors, chairs and chandeliers, challenged the workshops of Le Brun. Patronage on such a scale cannot be valued merely in accountants' terms. If Colbert came to be genuinely committed to the enlargement and embellishment of the palace it was not simply to keep a step ahead of the ever-thrusting Louvois. He saw it as the showpiece of his grand plan for the economy, providing patronage on an unprecedented scale and advertising to the world the supremacy of his country's arts and crafts.

In all its forms, building, art or literature, the celebration of royal strength and virtues was propaganda for the country; and it worked. It was of a piece with the war of ideas under Colbert's generalship. (It is unlikely that he would have quarrelled with use of the word 'war', as applicable here as to his trading policies.) The greater the artist or scholar the more vital it was that he should accept the king's commission. Foreigners could play their part. Huygens was pensioned to promote the country's reputation as a pioneer in science. The patronage list of 1664 shows 6,000 *livres* going to him, 9,000 to the astronomer Cassini. The historian Mézeray rewarded royal support with his much-praised history of France. Racine was commissioned as historiographer specifically to write about the king's performance in the Dutch war. Praising the king, the great playwright was inviting the world to applaud the state; also those, like himself, its favoured sons. A lesser figure, Félibien,[16] wrote obsequiously about Versailles. But the palace spoke for itself.

The first château of 1668 was Le Vau's masterpiece, a three-storeyed façade of twenty-five bays with coupled columns enveloping the Louis XIII château. Le Vau died in 1670, and his work was completed by his pupil D'Orbay. When Louis decided to celebrate the peace of Nijmegen by a great extension of the palace he commissioned the versatile Mansard[17] who had just completed Clagny, the exquisite château ordered by Louis, in the tradition of royal lovers, for Mme de Montespan. Externally Mansard's Versailles may be faulted for, by linking Le Vau's two pavilions to make his *galérie des glaces*, he reduced the effect of Le Vau's Ionic order which had been rightly proportioned to the original height and length. The total length was now 550 yards, monotonous to some eyes, to others incomparable in its disciplined expanse. Undeniably it was successful in its main purpose. It was – and would remain – Europe's greatest palace.

In the *grands appartements* of the king and queen ceilings of stucco and paint crowned panelled walls of patterned velvet or marble. The central inspiration was that of Apollo: his domain, the Sun, was the theme, original only in its all-pervasive use. The king's seven apartments were named after the seven planets, their attributes displayed in flattering allegory: in the *salon de Venus* the influence of love on kings; in the *salon de Mars* the warrior kings of antiquity. There were other magnificent suites for the queen, Mme de Montespan and the Dauphin. State rooms were approached by the *escalier des ambassadeurs*, 'worthy', wrote Félibien, 'of receiving this great Monarch when he returns from his glorious conquests'. Above it a frescoed ceiling showed the four continents, with representative Indians, Africans and Americans, all subject to the power of the king: so shamelessly did the vision exceed the few forts and trading posts that were the modest reality of colonial power. The line of tall mirrors gave light and grace to the strict rectilinear design of the *galérie des glaces*. Extravagant detail was not allowed to get out of hand and, as in the best of French art in this period, baroque decoration was subdued to classical design. This wonderful creation was generally seen by the light of thousands of candles, set in silver chandeliers, softening hard, bright colours and reflecting upon crystal and glass and on Louis – Roman armoured but mantled like a French king – in Le Brun's ceiling centrepiece. In the *salon de guerre* leading off it, Louis appears again in Coysevox's white plaster panel triumphing over his enemies.[18] Commissioned art and the prevailing use of allegory achieved in Versailles a comprehensive image of power. Viewed out of its time, and far from the message so deliberately fabricated, its effect today may be merely stupefying. Even if it does not offend the mind, its art bullies the senses. Fresh created to honour and serve an admired sovereign, a busy, indeed uncomfortably crowded vehicle for the life of some five thousand of – in their own estimation – his most important subjects, Versailles inspired awe in courtiers and visitors alike. Its worth and effect cannot be realised without the king for whom it was built.

SIGNIFICANT RITUALS

Louis XIV thought of Versailles as his creation. There is evidence for his constant and informed interest, and occasional interventions in its planning.[19] From the unlucky Bernini to the triumphant Mansard architects testified to his understanding of their profession. Every day he conferred with architects and gardeners. Le Nôtre may have had first claim on his time. One of the few men who could talk informally to the king, one of the few indeed (another was his personal valet Bontemps[20]) who enjoyed an intimacy which can be called friendship, Le Nôtre knew that the king had a long purse; he soon discovered that he was a fellow gardener, enthusiastic and know-ledgeable. Louis used to conduct tours around the gardens whose main beds were changed every day so that they glowed with colour even in winter. He wrote a guidebook with crisp instructions as to where to stand for the best views. In the palace he seemed to relish the building process, stepping past scaffolding and buckets to show off his artists at work to admiring visitors. They were confronted at every turn by the king in some edifying guise. Here observing the crossing of the Rhine in Le Brun's ceiling painting; there, as seen by Mignard, presiding over the siege of Maastricht, on a prancing horse *à la Romaine*; here Coypel has him resting after peace-giving labours at Nijmegen; there, depicted by Garnier, he is 'Surrounded by Attributes of the Arts'; there again (by Testelin) 'Protector of the Academy of Painting and Sculpture'. Nor was this projection of the king as hero and *patron* only for Versailles. Visiting the 'hangings at the Goblins' (*sic*), in June 1677, Locke was impressed but caustic:

> In every peice Lewis le Grand was the hero, and the rest the marks of some conquest etc. In one was his makeing a league with the Swisse, where he lays his hand on the booke to swear the articles with his hat on & the Swiss ambassador in a submissive posture with his hat off.[21]

Frenchmen would expect nothing else. The craftsmen of the Gobelins received orders for tapestries to fill royal châteaux and nobles' *hôtels*, and for statues for provincial *intendants* to set up in town squares. Through commis-sioned statues the royal majesty could impress the townsfolk of Marseille, Grenoble or Caen. Through the regular issue of commemorative medals and the mass production of engravings the image could become part of the domestic scene.

In the palace, Apollo was everywhere, the very statues being placed, not haphazardly, but in relation to that deity. Over the doors the motto, *pluribus nec impar*, set the tone. Versailles witnessed heavily to the cult of roy-alty: Christian in profession, but largely pagan in imagery of ancient myth and history. Every act in its rituals was designed to emphasise Louis as the personification of royal power. Those who came to serve, petition or simply stare, had to conform to a discipline which was akin to a religious observance in its minute and ordered proceedings. He played his part with something of the intent concentration of a priest at the altar, remote, above the flux of events, dignified and serene. He was high enough to be polite to all. Those who surrounded him – the congregation as it were – amplified by their presence, words and gestures the image of royalty. They were not so much domesticated – a misleading word for the process by which nobles were drawn to Versailles – as conditioned to accept a distance between king and subject in a relationship of reciprocal value. He was the animating heart of society from which its members took life.

'Sire, it is time.' At eight o'clock the duty valet drew aside the curtains of the king's great bed (whichever other bed he had visited he would always be there, alone) and introduced the royal day. The king then ceased to be a private person. Starting with the *première entrée* of the royal doctor and bedroom functionaries the court entered in waves according to strict rules of precedence. To attend the king in the first intimate moments of the day, to see him rubbed down with rose water and spirits of wine, shaved and dressed, and use the *chaise percée*, was the privilege of the highest in the land. In a typical year, 1687, the Great Chamberlain, whose duty was to wrap a dressing gown round the king, was the duc de Bouillon; his father, lord of Sedan, had been an inveterate rebel. The Grand Master of the Wardrobe who pulled on his breeches was the duc de la Rochefoucauld:[22] the very name epitomises the Fronde. Some of Louis's family would be expected to be present and Monsieur himself might put on his shirt. An apparent trend of the time was the weakening of high nobles' clientage and the dilution of power in the provinces. But these grandees may not have thought themselves hard done by. The expansion of the army actually enlarged the scope for patronage in the military sphere.[23] Since these domestic moments were the recognised time for confidential requests they were uniquely well placed to improve family position and fortune. Saint-Simon, wishing to receive his late father's title, arranged that the duc de Beauvillier, acting gentleman of the bedchamber, should speak for him. Beauvillier 'assured me of much good feeling on the part of the princes and promised that when he drew the king's curtains he would ask the king to grant it'.

Gradually courtiers entered, passing ushers who asked the name and qualifications of any unknown to them, bowed deeply and stood outside the balustrade to watch the king receive the Holy Water, say his prayers, put on his wig and tie his cravat. He would announce his plans for the day, then perhaps retreat into a small study to consider some urgent matter of government or look at plans of building or garden. Before Mass came one of those long processions along the gallery which were so important in the courtiers' day. Then the king could be seen at his most majestic, equable, smiling often, but never laughing, or pausing for informal conversation. Since he usually reserved private audience, the *derrières*, for ministers, or a few particular friends, ambassadors returned from mission, or generals from campaign might be among the throng of courtiers, competing for a royal look, murmuring petitions or just watching others and gossiping. Faithful to Mazarin's training the king would give little away. 'I will see' had to satisfy most courtiers; for some there was the feared rebuff. Louis had a keen memory so 'I do not know him' meant that the petitioner was out of favour or not usually seen at court. Part of his skill in personal manipulation was to make it known that advancement required service: to be present was its prerequisite. In council the king might be less formal, at times jovial, impatient or cross. If, however, he was irritated or flustered in public courtiers knew that there was some major crisis of state – for then, indeed, he was the state.

Louis was less emotional and intense in pious observance than was his mother, but he reflected her influence in his daily attendance at Mass. It was a focal point of his day. It is surprising therefore, but only reflecting the worsening financial conditions, that Mansard's new chapel, projected in 1688 was not completed (though used before) till 1710. It had to consist of two storeys, the upper and royal being more important. So Mansard designed a low arcaded ground floor for the courtiers and a high colonnaded upper storey with the royal pew at the west end leading directly to the king's apartments, and a spacious gallery for his suite. Antoine Coypel's rich baroque ceiling capped the chapel in which, La Bruyère had earlier written, 'this people seemed to worship the prince and the prince to worship God'.

Adulation could go to extremes, but it was grounded, and so saved from absurdity, in genuine respect. Here was a great show but at its centre was a man, not only dignified, but level, sensible and, on any material consideration, successful. If Versailles represented a system, then the system, in terms of what it was designed for, surely worked. That said, it is important to make several qualifications. As the reign proceeded, the king aged, checks and defeats entered the reckoning, and the court proceedings lost some of their meaning: the forms were rigid, but the spirit, so proud and self-congratulatory, could not be sustained. Before the end of the century a change in the intellectual climate became apparent. The idea of Divine Right began to look old-fashioned. Meanwhile the attendant musters of the court, its studied modes of speech and conduct, the recurring rites within a fixed timetable and the constant focus of attention on the royal person, all helped create an enclosed world unfriendly to disinterested advice or honest criticism. The king would have been remarkable indeed if he had been wholly unaffected by the Caesarism of Versailles and the complementary, though more restrained, philosophy of Divine Right, when both seemed to be acted out so seriously in the daily round. It should therefore be stressed that the day included many hours, at least three every morning, of work in council: then reality had a chance and sober calculations had to be made. The line between business and pleasure, which the king passed so easily, was, for even the grandest courtier, fixed and impassable. All that he would see of the workings of government would be the comings and goings of ministers and secretaries. It was a solecisim even to talk about politics. The price he paid for his privileged lodging, an attic perhaps or apartment in one of the flanking buildings of the new town, was exclusion from affairs of state. Was it sufficient compensation that he might catch a glimpse of his sovereign at dinner, when Louis ate heartily, usually alone and in silence broken only by a few words between courses to some grandee standing behind his chair?

The king's afternoon might be spent in hunting or driving out; or he might walk briskly in the gardens, followed by droves of courtiers. A fine day might see him sailing on the Grand Canal in – one of the miniature warships that were a minor wonder of Versailles. Replicating ships of the line or galleys in every detail, this fleet was maintained by a corps of some fifty, having their own lodgings in '*La petite Venise*'. Usually further business occupied the early evening, hearing ministers' reports and signing those despatches that were too important for a secretary's hand. In the evening there would be *appartements*, assemblies of the whole court in the *salons* which fanned out from the *galérie des glaces*. Here they might dance or take their chance at the gaming tables. Or there might be a play or concert. At ten supper was served for the court at separate tables, the king supping in state with the 'sons, daughters and [as they grew up] grandsons and granddaughters of France'. The curtains closed theatrically on the royal day, with the *couchée*, a bedroom masque in which the procedure of the *levée* was re-enacted in reverse. While the high officers undressed their master, the king's candlestick was solemnly passed from the king's chaplain to the nobleman privileged to hold it for the night. Louis was happy to see great nobles thus employed and he understood perfectly the politician's art of putting a premium on empty favours. Aristocratic notions of precedence, reputation and honour, potentially so anarchic, were made to serve the crown. Nobles lived under a discipline which would have astonished their forebears. Exile to one's estates was a dreaded punishment for the ambitious noble: away from the fountain of honour, he was worse than poor; he was ridiculous.

Byzantium, Burgundy, Spain: several lines of ancestry may be traced from Versailles. Its manners also reflected, however, a contemporary, native influence, that of the Parisian *salon*, where a cult of civility was well established, with firm rules about deportment and conversation. The *salon* invited the kind of pretentiousness and affectation mocked in Molière's *Précieuses ridicules*. Yet its manners helped make a hard world more tolerable and rewarding to women who had generally to make what they could of an arranged marriage – or retire to a convent. Restraints imposed by strong-minded women, like the marquise de Rambouillet,[24] and the polite expectation that a man should listen attentively as well as speak cleverly, had created a milieu in which ideas could flourish and men of letters and science find a receptive audience. The courtier could aim to be an *honnête homme* and Versailles was, in the main, a decorous place. Louis was personally sympathetic to the ideal of a 'man of quality', distinguished in talents and achievements without necessarily being well born. The king who befriended Lully, admired his innovative genius[25] and forgave his misdemeanours, and supported Molière when he mocked hypocrites and social climbers, prided himself on being superior to vested interests and capable of independent judgement. He would have approved of père Bouhours, author of a manual on manners, who declared that 'the enquiring mind was no longer the preserve of men of letters; it was also required of men of the sword and even found in personages of the highest quality'. Inevitably having more of the sword than the gown about it, Versailles stood at a tangent to the culture of the *salon* and brought its own flavour of superciliousness to its notion of the *honnête homme*. The *salon* was concerned with mind as well as manners; the courtier's art was to be correct in externals. Every word and action must emphasise his esoteric status and the gulf that separated him from his country cousin. Spontaneity was at least possible in the *salon*; it was wholly missing from the punctilious ceremony of the court.

AN UNHEALTHY DEPENDENCE

It was inevitable – though precise connections are hard to determine – that the ethos of Versailles would have some effect on the judgement of king and ministers; also that this would become more apparent with the departure of the elder statesmen nurtured in a more independent school. No less significant for the future was the way in which Versailles affected the nobility. There had always been a gulf between Paris and the provinces. Politically this was less dangerous, in the long run, than the new gulf that was opening up between the élites of court and capital (and provincial capitals) where *bourgeois* wealth, open minds and professional expertise informed a separate, more dynamic culture.

The nobleman's life at court offered moments of luxury, amusement and the sense of proximity to greatness. For the soldier – most young men were – it was being off-duty at the fount of honour (and promotion) where his service was clearly valued. For some women there was the enchantment which Mme de Sévigné breathlessly conveys: 'all is great, all magnificent, music and dancing are perfection. . . . But what pleases me most is to live for four hours in the presence of the sovereign, to be in his pleasures and he in ours; it is enough to content a whole realm which passionately loves to see its master.' Mme de Sévigné was not an habitué. Madame Palatine was. For the gradual disenchantment of one who was brought by marriage into the inner circle, her letters[26] are a prime source. She is shrewd, sometimes poignant, increasingly grumpy and caustic. But Mme de Sévigné was neither naive, nor unobservant. Her uninhibited enthusiasm says much for Louis's achievement. It is the social element of power which should not be underestimated. The Englishman John Covel bore independent witness to one aspect of the king's winning ways. Describing the royal family at dinner he relates how a petition was presented to the king: 'Then came a poor gentlewoman (with three sons) and presented a petition to the king at table about her Husband lost in the warres; he received it with an abundance of sweetness mixt with majesty.' Covel came down to earth when he was warned to take care of his pocket: 'though the same person, before he stirred out of the chamber, had six or seven guineas & a *louis d'or* taken out of his'.[27]

A greater threat to most pockets was surely the gambling, not discouraged by the king, avidly pursued in the evening *appartements* by his leading subjects.[28] That, as ever, witnesses to boredom, also to an unhealthy aspect. Underlying the ideal and the splendour and, for some, the gaiety, were sordid material considerations, creating an unhealthy dependence. Versailles was about service, often sacrificial, and loyalty to a master who set the highest example of conscientious work. It was also about uprooting, subservience, intrigue and scrounging. The ideal and the sordid are two faces of the same coin. We see both in the journals of Saint-Simon.

His journal is invaluable because he was both involved and detached; passionately involved as a nobleman whose life was centred upon upholding his rights as *duc et pair*. The apparent detachment of a literary artist is deceptive. This acutely perceptive critic had the time and incentive to describe what he saw as the disaster of his class. He occupied one of the best garrets in a palace

of draughts and discomforts. He was often near to the king and he sometimes held the candlestick. He could be nowhere but at court. He might
nibble at the hand that fed him (he thought Louis 'an ordinary man', though
he conceded his politeness) and he certainly resented upstart ministers who
had the real power, and *la mécanique*, which was their business. Up to a point,
however, he accepted the régime that provided him with so congenial a
subject. It mattered greatly to him who should have the right of the *pour* (that
is, to be selected to accompany the king to Marly: *pour Marly* would be the
looked-for signal), what ladies should be allowed to sit on *tabourets*. We may
see why the wars of etiquette that he chronicles appealed to this subtle student of human behaviour. But why did it matter to so many others?

Trapped by the effects of earlier inflation on static rents, then by the
current agricultural depression, the sword noble had a choice between a
restricted life on his estates – which many accepted – the church, and a career
in the king's service, as soldier, diplomat or professional courtier. For most
the profession of arms brought more honour than gain; thanks to Louvois's
reforms it was harder than ever to recoup the price of a commission, and it
was a point of honour to have an expensive equipage. So we see the vicious
circle of many lives. Men came to court because all favours came from the
king, in the form of commissions, sinecures and pensions. But the cost of
keeping up appearances – and a wife's – in the world's centre of fashion in
clothes and jewellery, and gambling for high stakes, might reduce a family to
humiliating dependence on the hospitality of the king and, worse, on the
loans of some *bourgeois* financier. Here was subject indeed for the moralist.
What a contrast he may see between the heroic spirit of the building and the
mean shifts of so many of its inmates, hanging on from daybreak, through
anxious, slow hours in surroundings of gilt and profusion, hoping for some
morsel of royal favour, a free supper, and luck at cards! Some specialised
in broking: appointments, pensions and even, towards the end of the reign,
titles and membership of a chivalric order – and, of course marriages. A
mésalliance might be a matter of necessity, like that arranged for Mme de
Sévigné's grandson, married to the daughter of a tax-farmer who then paid
off half the family's debts. Reports made by *intendants* to Colbert reveal that
the costly life at court was a main cause of the widespread poverty among the
nobility. (He knew something of it since all of his daughters married *ducs*.) At
the foot of the ladder were the *gentilshommes indigents* who figure in Treasury
accounts as receiving grants of 15 or 20 *livres* to keep them alive. They may
have been old soldiers. Others were no doubt the casualties of a life that, for
all its high notions, was full of hollow pretence. 'Speak well of everyone, ask

for everything that falls vacant and sit down when you can.' That veteran's advice to a newcomer might have been given at any court. Is it one of the blessings of English history that the court did not develop as the Stuarts might have liked but remained impoverished and became so dull that gentlemen preferred to live in the country?

Notes

1. David Cannadine, 'Introduction; divine rites of kings', in D. Cannadine and S. Price (eds), *Rituals of Royalty: Power and Ceremonial in Traditional Societies* (Cambridge, 1987), p. 1.
2. In his *Esprit des Lois* (1746, but reflecting the trends, in particular the aristocratic reaction of earlier years after Louis XIV's death). Writing about monarchy in the first ten books, Montesquieu has the French monarchy chiefly in mind. It is plainly France that was 'degenerating into despotism'. The great kings of France had ruled constitutionally, retaining the services of the nobility and *Parlements*. They kept the love of the people by ruling moderately: the myth would be potent.
3. For the part of display, ritual and imagery in the presentation of the monarch and enhancement of his status, see particularly P. Burke, *The Fabrication of Louis XIV* (Cambridge, 1992).
4. For the duc de Saint-Simon see p. 37 note 6. Also pp. 195–6.
5. Published twice a week, the state-controlled *Gazette*, largely factual in reporting, gave much space to the king's actions in peace and war. So did the more effusive *Mercure galante*, published monthly. They had an essential part in linking king and court with the provincial élites, so broadening the support base of monarchy.
6. Since the time of Charlemagne French kings and those like the Angevin Henry II of England influenced by French example had maintained such menageries. A lion or leopard was an appropriate gift between rulers. Inherent interest and aesthetic value apart their possession can be seen as a statement of power: king as master of the natural world represented by its most splendid, and dangerous, creatures.
7. Giovanni Bernini (1598–1680), architect, sculptor and painter, author beside so much else of the Grand Colonnade enclosing the piazza before St Peter's, was the most versatile, if not indeed the greatest of Roman baroque artists.
8. Gabriel Nicolas de la Reynie was an influential figure who worked closely with the king. He was unrelenting in the exposure and suppression of immoralities and dissent: in the seventies, for example, providing evidence for the special tribunal investigating charges of poisoning and sorcery, later rigorous in the application of censorship. Marc-René de Voyer d'Argenson was another tireless administrator. There was nothing superior (or in England remotely comparable) to the scope of policing in Paris and its mechanism for social control. Given the importance to the régime of good order in the traditionally turbulent capital it is an aspect of royal absolutism that should have greater prominence than it usually receives. See L. Bernard, *The Emerging City, Paris in the Age of Louis XIV* (Durham, NC, 1970).
9. The idea of the *hôpital*, a place of refuge for the old, crippled and destitute and orphaned was taken over by the state in a way that reflects Colbert's utilitarian

approach to social problems. He wanted to clear the streets of beggars. In 1662, by royal edict, the institution was merged with other places of refuge and care to become part of a chain covering eventually the whole of France with 2,000 houses. For all the dilution of the original Christian purpose of the houses founded by Monsieur Vincent, voluntary and purely charitable, the system represents the most impressive effort in pre-Revolutionary Europe to mitigate the plight of the poor and afflicted. There is an interesting analysis of the subject in Olwen Hufton, *The Poor of Eighteenth Century France* (Oxford, 1974), pp. 139–76.

10. For the topic of censorship see J. Klaits, *Printed Propaganda under Louis XIV* (Princeton, 1976), specially pp. 35–57. Also R. Mandrou, *Louis XIV en son temps, 1661–1715* (Paris, 1973), pp. 161–8.

11. The dispute started in 1687 when Charles Perrault, brother of the architect Claude, read to the *Académie Française* his poem '*Sur le siècle de Louis le Grand*' in which he criticised 'ancient' writers and saluted the reign of Louis XIV (and contemporary writers and artists) as superior to that of Caesar Augustus. The eulogy would have passed with little notice had not Nicolas Boileau (1636–1711) taken umbrage at Perrault's disparaging comments on classical writers. The author of *l'Art poétique* (1674), with its first commandment, 'Think well if you wish to write well', used his deserved reputation as critic, and self-constituted role as arbiter in matters of literary style and taste – *législateur de Parnasse* – to mount a campaign against subversive elements. The ensuing quarrel has something in common with that between Jesuits and Jansenists (see pp. 316 et seq) and the later clash of Bossuet and Fénelon over Quietism (see pp. 324 et seq): it engaged a wider audience than that of writers, artists, their patrons and coteries, and it raised larger issues than the technical ones of interest to the specialist, be he concerned with the Dramatic Unities, Augustinianism or Mysticism. Before it subsided in the mid-nineties it had become part of a general critical tendency challenging orthodoxies, the values, artistic, religious and political, associated with them, and the authorities that defended them. Jean de la Fontaine (1621–95), author of pleasing fables in neat and pithy Horatian style, prime subscriber to the cult of *honnêteté*, was a natural supporter of classical rules. Proposing that modernism could start where classicism left off, Bernard de Fontenelle (1657–1757) was certainly no radical. But the fashionable author of *Dialogue des Morts* (1683) and *Entretiens sur la pluralité des mondes* (1686) was dealing with ideas, methods and discoveries that had radical implications. His belief in the order and precision of the geometric method of reasoning, his law, 'Make sure of the facts before you bother about their cause', and his commitment to the popularising of science, make this cautious and self-indulgent man an important link between the age of Descartes and that of Voltaire, indeed a precursor of the Enlightenment.

12. By 1715 there were over 100 colleges run by the Jesuits, outstripping their nearest rivals in influence and methods, the Oratorians, who had a quarter of that number. At a time when the discipline, scholarship and teaching at most French universities was at a low ebb, the quality of Jesuit colleges ensured their continuing influence. The Collège de Clermont was prominent in the University of Paris; that of Bordeaux had over a thousand students, Rouen two thousand. Besides classical languages,

philosophy and rhetoric, they taught modern literature, drama, mathematics and physics.

13. Charles le Brun (1619–90) was the king of decorators and artistic foreman of the Gobelins and Versailles. In the large canvas, *Louis XIV Adoring the Risen Christ*, discreetly placed, appears the small figure of his patron, Colbert. After his death Le Brun's supremacy was at an end for Louvois naturally supported a rival, Pierre Mignard (1612–94).

14. Louis le Vau (1612–70) was bequeathed, involuntarily, to Louis by Fouquet, whose palatial Vaux-le-Vicompte (see p. 41) was the talented architect's most important work to date.

15. André le Nôtre (1613–1700) had studied, as a young man, at the Grand Galérie du Louvre. Gardening as executed at Versailles was high art as much as earthy craft. With a labour force running to thousands his was also a managerial role.

16. André Félibien was appointed by Colbert in 1662 to be historiographer of the royal buildings. His work, shows the same mixture of history, factual recording and propaganda which is to be seen in Racine and Pellisson's accounts of war. To this he added artistic criticism. See Burke, op. cit., p. 53.

17. Jules Hardouin Mansard (1646–1708), responsible for Montespan's Clagny, the extension to Le Vau's Versailles and the *Galérie des Glaces* and Marly, added the suffix Hardouin to distinguish him from his distinguished great-uncle François.

18. Antoine Coysevox (1640–1720) was, with François Girardon (1628–1715), the leading sculptor engaged on the Versailles project. His *Louis XIV*, remarkable, typically, for its freedom and technical brilliance, may be seen in the Wallace Collection.

19. For the role of Louis in the great building enterprise, see R.W. Berger, *A Royal Passion: Louis XIV as Patron of Architecture* (Cambridge, 1994).

20. Alexandre Bontemps was also *intendant* of Versailles, until his death in 1701. His relationship with the king 'constituted in all conscience, forty years of connivance, a complicity which approached symbiosis' (Bluche, op. cit., p. 464).

21. Locke, op. cit., p. 150. The tapestry was part of a series designed by Le Brun.

22. François de Marcillac, duc de la Rochefoucauld (1613–80) was severely wounded at the battle of the Porte Saint-Antoine but survived to bring to perfection the *salon* fashion of penning *Maximes*. His polished sentences present a way of life that could see nothing but *amour propre* at the heart of social behaviour: a melancholy commentary perhaps on a lost cause.

23. See p. 138.

24. Catherine de Vivonne, Marquise de Rambouillet (1588–1665) was perhaps the most influential of hostesses. Virtuous and spiritual, she sought for fifty years to gather together the talented, witty and well-born. For women in the cultural sphere, see Gibson, op. cit., pp. 171–92.

25. See p. 38, n. 8.

26. See p. 257, n. 2.

27. Quotations drawn from J. Lough, *France Observed in the Seventeenth Century by British Travellers* (Stocksfield, 1985), p. 147. It is a valuable and entertaining collection.

28. Lansquenet, Trictrac, piquet, l'hombre according to Madame, who often referred to gambling in her letters, with increasing disapproval.

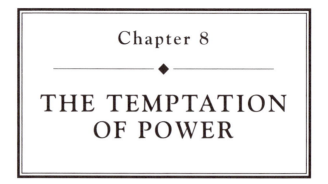

THE TEMPTATION
OF POWER

To the east, France has no other limits than those imposed
by her sense of moderation and justice.

FREDERICK THE GREAT

'THE GRAND DOGE'

At the heart of the palace were the *salons de Guerre* and *de Mars*. They were pagan temples, dedicated to the cult of war and the triumphs of the royal warrior. Outward appearances were of allegory and myth but the message was plain. Flattery enveloped the king. It might be absurd but – more harmfully – it was often sincere. The attendant musters of the court, its studied modes of speech and conduct, the recurring rituals within a fixed timetable and, throughout the day, the constant focus of attention on the royal person, all helped create an enclosed world unfriendly to disinterested advice or honest criticism. Louis would indeed have been scarcely human if he had not been a little affected by the ideas of Divine Right when they seemed to be taken so literally by lay and clergy alike.

Of course the mantras of absolutism did not absolve Louis from the need to act responsibly. Even in theory Louis's authority was fenced about with moral restraints: the obligations derived from his lieutenancy under God. He was also well aware of practical restraints on his freedom of action. No European government had more regular and reliable information. The messages that came from the provinces to ministers in their daily engagement with reports, pleas and memoranda were all about limits and obstacles. He took them seriously. But there were always influences working on ministers to undo these restraints, and to persuade them to play down difficulties.

When the ultimate responsibility was the king's it was tempting for a minister to advocate firm and forward policies. Louis was innately cautious but he had a natural weakness (is it less marked in the democratic politician?) for the 'decisive' stroke, that which brings tangible, instantly recognisable reward. His strokes and gestures were performed before a captive audience and their applause smothered independent views. The grand façade of Mansart's Versailles has become so familiar, its style so much imitated, that it is easy to forget the impact it had on contemporaries. Much of what was performed here, music and drama of lasting value, was overtly political, directing thoughts and feelings to the king's majesty. For all its civilised splendours Versailles was a constricting environment, heavily demeaning to individuals. It lacked the draughts of free discussion that freshened the air at Whitehall and The Hague. It housed a régime of institutionalised deference. Proceeding through gorgeous *salons* or immaculate paths and terraces, accompanied always by people who needed to please him, it was seductively easy for the king to see himself as being in control of events. It was increasingly hard for him to look imaginatively into the mind of other princes, or to weigh accurately the pressures under which they operated: that of Parliamentary debate, for example, on the English king, prices on the Amsterdam bourse on the views of the Regents, the looming Ottoman threat on the mind of the Emperor.

The mood in the early days of Versailles was militarist and triumphalist, matching its art. It was all too likely that the king, confronted by an issue of foreign policy, would see it exclusively in French terms, treating too lightly the possibility of hostile reaction. Louis's well-advertised principles and scruples then tended to make matters worse. He was perfectly sincere in rejoicing that the capture of Strasbourg had restored it to its Catholic faith, but Germany could only see French soldiers on the Rhine. As a domestic issue the Revocation of the Edict of Nantes could be justified, as it was by nearly everyone around him, as the logical completion of policies designed to reduce the offending presence of 'a religion which was false, disloyal and hostile to the monarchy' (La Bruyère). If, however, the Pope was less than enthusiastic about this mode of winning souls it was because Louis was engaged in an increasingly bitter struggle over the *régale*. Throughout the eighties we see Louis pursuing policies which, if not downright incompatible, were likely to be self-defeating. The overall impression is of incoherence, with the loss of that realistic sense of priorities that had characterised the policies of the cardinals. That does not mean that there was no justification for the *réunions*.[1]

Legal and diplomatic expertise there was in plenty; subtlety in method was not wanting. In those aspects the process of *réunion* was masterly. Where the argument came down to military strength it was deployed boldly, without qualm, and to immediate effect. Political foresight was less in evidence. When success was so confidently expected, whether measured in land gained or Huguenot souls won, ministers and officials were unlikely to play down achievements, or warn against unfavourable reactions, let alone the possibility of failure. Neither the king's thinking, nor the impressive machinery at his disposal, was well adapted to the situation created by the successes of his armies and diplomats. It may be argued that two events, with especially adverse consequences, might not have been predicted. Good fortune played a part both in the Emperor's deliverance from the Turk after the siege of Vienna and William III's seizure of the English throne. But the actions of France (inaction in the case of the siege of Vienna), before these crucial events, did ensure that they had the maximum impact.

Even before the treaty of Nijmegen Temple[2] observed that he was 'of the prince's [Orange's] opinion that he [Louis] will make with a design of a new war after he has fixed his conquests'. He was right about the aggressive intention, wrong about the method. The Dutch war taught Louis that a simple military offensive would force his rivals to unite against him. Forward policies therefore required a more subtle approach. The systematic expansion to which Louis committed his military and diplomatic resources proceeded under a camouflage of legalism. The *réunions* were carried out after exhaustive enquiry into juridical rights. Because no state was in a condition to challenge Louis's armies, the annexations were, at first, peaceful. They were none the less alarming. By his encroachments Louis appeared to be trespassing over lines of conduct that might be understood by treaty obligations, 'the balance of power', even 'international law'. Altogether they created an impression of insistent menace, of ambitions in Germany extending, perhaps, to the Imperial crown; an opportunist process not to be appeased; only to be met by an armed force that was not yet available. 'The grand doge, if we allow him, will soon leave to the German princes no throne but a tomb.' Sophia of Hanover was typically outspoken. Was she being fair?

A DEFENSIBLE FRONTIER

The policy of the *réunions* was, essentially, a simple one. It amounted to unilateral action to draw further advantage from the recent gains; to bring order to a medley of conflicting rights. In one aspect it exemplifies the passion for order that is a cultural hallmark of the age, and the centralising principle, its prime political trend. The *réunions* may therefore be seen as an operation to extend the control of the crown; when successful, the lands transferred could be called French. It was the intensification of a long process, the crown mopping up the loose pieces of a feudal society around its borders which its advance within the kingdom had already rendered largely obsolete. To meet the criteria of the modern state, feudal custom was invoked.

The policy was also driven by the lawyers who wanted to extend their jurisdiction and by the military, bruised by their recent experience of making war in march lands of patchy and uncertain allegiance. The war minister would be keenly aware of their concerns. At the heart of the process was the single-minded determination of Vauban to round off 'the meadow square' and create a defensible, if not strictly linear frontier. He, Louvois, Colbert de Croissy and the king were of a mind. The Dutch war had exposed the vulnerability of France to German invasion. The drive to establish a Rhine frontier from Philippsburg to Switzerland did not arise from some idea that it would be a 'natural frontier' but from considerations of military advantage and administrative convenience. Such a frontier, like those aimed at the Alps and Pyrenees, would be more defensible than the existing patchwork. Two important cases reveal government thinking. The county of Montbéliard linked the Franche-Comté with Alsace and allowed an enemy to invade both. Similarly Spanish-held Luxembourg, the scene of bitter fighting for possession of its citadel in 1682–83, provided a powerful base for raids into northern Lorraine and southern Flanders.

By the treaties of Westphalia and Nijmegen territories had been ceded with their 'dependencies'. They were among the loose ends commonly left by a treaty. Indeed the Westphalia settlement might never have been attained without some fudge, some contentious issues simply being left to be resolved between states. That did not necessarily imply unilateral action. After Nijmegen a Franco-Spanish commission was set up to resolve several questions of ownership. But Louis soon showed that if he did not get what he felt was his due he would take it. Allowed a choice between Charlemont and Dinant he took both. It was the French assumption that their interpretation of law was sufficient justification for annexation that most shocked German princes used to the conservative procedures of Imperial diplomacy and justice.

In the case of Alsace, Louis had gained a scattered holding, more like a landowner's estates than a province. There was genuine confusion about law and ownership. In 1789 certain landowners would claim that, as vassals of the Emperor, they were exempt from the revolutionary law abolishing feudal dues. The Ten Imperial Towns had presented a serious problem to French generals during the Dutch war.

Sedan had already provided the classic case of a problem of this kind, where political and military considerations had pointed the way to Mazarin's solution. It was a vital place, at a crossing of the Meuse, a centre from which roads went to Paris and Dijon, and into Germany, to Aachen and Strasbourg. Nominally a sub-fief of France, it had come under the lordship of the duc de Bouillon, Turenne's brother; he also held land from the bishop of Liège – who was a prince of the Empire. It was secured for France in 1651, in exchange for other estates within France. It is revealing that some writers have referred to this act as an annexation of foreign land, some as an addition to France. In truth the word 'foreign' is unhelpful in this context. Should Orange, the principality in southern France from which Louis's principal enemy took his title, be called 'foreign'? William saw Louis's seizure of his family land as outrage and a provocation. And what of papal Avignon?

The antiquarian Denis Godefroy had long been working on the charters in which the claims concerning feudal 'dependencies' were recorded. In 1678 Pomponne had 2,000 such claims examined. Before he became a full-time diplomat, Colbert de Croissy, Pomponne's successor, from 1679, had been *intendant* of Alsace and a councillor in the *parlement* of Metz. Even if he had not been working on the plan before it was adopted by Louvois he was well prepared to implement it. The choice of targets for *réunion* reflects mainly, however, the stated priorities of Vauban and the brutally direct approach of Louvois. In 1678 he had taken over the supervision of the frontier provinces of Alsace, Lorraine and the Three Bishoprics, in place of quieter provinces in the interior, Saintonge, Limousin and the Dauphiné. Here he directed the researches of Roland de Ravaulx, *procurateur-général* of the Metz *parlement*. Travelling tirelessly, consulting mainly with soldiers, he approached the problem in stark military terms. The line that had been achieved in Flanders should be extended to eastern France. Unlike contemporaries who were preoccupied with Spain he believed that 'the Germans ought now to be considered as our real enemies'. And he envisaged a defensive war. Each of the places 'reunited' in Alsace had some military value: such was Trarbach, commanding a loop of the Moselle, near which Vauban built his fortress of Mont-Royal. Strasbourg had shown Imperialist leanings during the Dutch war, giving Imperialist troops passage over the river, even entering into alliance with Lorraine. Where the lawyers' researches could find 'dependencies' in musty folios, and where, however vague the traditional tie, they comprised towns or lands of strategic value, they should be proved to belong to the king of France. That was to be the work of the *chambres de Réunion*.

The treatment varied. At Besançon, Breisach and Douai, ordinary courts were given the power to decide questions of sovereignty. At Metz a special tribunal was set up. At Strasbourg there was no question of legal form. In all the courts the decision could be anticipated for the judges knew what was expected of them. In the first two years there were large annexations: the province of the Saare up to the Moselle, the principality of Montbéliard, the county of Chiny and most of Luxembourg. Many places in Flanders were held under the pretext that they were still occupied and that their restitution was not specifically required by the terms of Nijmegen. Orange was a predictable acquisition. In Upper and Lower Alsace only the Imperial free city of Strasbourg was left to await its fate.

The territories of several German princes were affected, among them the Elector of Trier and the duke of Württemberg. When the French went into Zweibrücken they touched the interest of the king of Sweden: so recently supported over Pomerania, he now looked for an alliance with the Dutch. Louis thought that he could ignore this because he had made useful terms with Brandenburg and Saxony. In October 1679, in the second treaty of Saint-Germain, the Electors Frederick William and John George II promised their vote for Louis at the next election. Bavaria was already secured for the cause by the marriage of the Dauphin to Max-Emmanuel's sister. Did these princes privately hope that an election was far enough away for safety? It would not come until 1705, by which time Brandenburg – the kingdom of Prussia – was in the Imperial camp while Bavaria, France's only significant ally, had been crushingly defeated at Hochstädt. In any case too much should not be read into these treaties. Electors traditionally rallied to the Habsburgs when it came to the vote. They could rely on them to maintain defence against the Turks in critical times; to provide arbitration on disputes, to ask little in taxes, at most times to be undemanding. Meanwhile, they would extract as much as possible from the quarrel of the dynasties. With evidence of such disunity in Germany it is not surprising that Louis thought that he could go ahead with his most daring raid.

Without Strasbourg Alsace was worth little to Louis. It was like an independent republic, more like a Swiss town than any other of the Empire's Free Cities. Through the summer of 1681 the burghers negotiated with Louvois to preserve their free status under French patronage. But it became clear that they could not expect from France the Emperor's past policy of laissez-faire. A deputation to Versailles left without satisfaction. Meanwhile the Imperial Diet voted to raise an army of 40,000 and it was rumoured that Leopold planned to put troops into the city. Louvois did not wait for it. Accompanying in person the army that seized the vital bridge, he presented the citizens with a stark alternative: to surrender their privileges or be put to the sword. They assumed that he meant it. On 30 September 1681, the city surrendered. It was allowed to keep civic privileges and its Lutheran religion, but Egon de Fürstenberg,[3] brother of William and Louis's assiduous agent in Germany, long bishop *in partibus*, returned to his cathedral – and the cathedral to the Roman rites. Louis crowned the event by a solemn entry in October, with the queen and dauphin, to the pleasing music of massed artillery. Some burghers who attended the *Te deum* boasted that they had returned home to sing '*Super flumina Babylonis*'. They might weep – but the French entry was popular with many of the citizens who hoped for more rights than they had enjoyed under an oligarchic régime, for more work and prosperity. Already four hundred barges had arrived laden with stone for Vauban's new fortifications.

Inevitably a medal was struck. *Clausa Germania Gallia*; its inscription reveals the intended message to Europe, indeed the main significance and point of the *réunions*. The French frontier had been brought to the Rhine, in French eyes a strategic necessity. But would that be all? The Imperial commander, the Margrave of Baden, expressed natural fears. 'For Germany, possession of this city means simply a guarantee of peace. For France, it is a door through which she can invade German soil as often as she wishes.' Privately Louis thought the same: 'Alsace was a passage for our troops to Germany'. Given that troops could be maintained more easily on foreign soil, it was unrealistic to suppose that in a future war French troops would be confined to operations within the frontier. Meanwhile the Emperor had to abandon Alsace to deal with more urgent calls from Hungary. It was his correct assumption that Leopold would be unable to help Spain that led Louis to attack the fortress of Luxembourg.

It was first blockaded. Then after the Spanish commander had made a sortie to relieve the starving garrison, it was subjected to mortar bombardment. Finally Louis, directing operations from Valenciennes, decided on the full-dress siege which, with Vauban in charge and overwhelming French superiority, could have only one end, though delayed by a spirited Spanish resistance. Luxembourg's fall, in June 1682 was the prelude to the truce of Ratisbon (August 1684), prepared for realistically by Louis with the cession of Tournai and Dixmude.

If Louis hoped that his peace offerings would be enough to convince German opinion that he was thinking only of defence, he would soon be disappointed. Meanwhile, lacking a strong lead from Leopold, German rulers had to wait to see what France would do next. Questions simmered. If a long stretch of the Rhine was to be France's frontier where did the Palatinate stand? Or Cologne? If peace were to last it was essential that Louis should do nothing to provoke or alarm. It is by that test that his Italian policy should be judged.

The day Louis's troops entered Strasbourg, others entered Casale, capital of Montferrat, on the Po, near Turin. A key target of Richelieu's Italian policy, another vital *porte*, it had long been in Louis's sights. Richelieu had sought to counter Spain's power in North Italy, based on Milan; in different circumstance Louis wanted to advertise the dominance of France. Yet that was plain enough. Victor Amadeus II of Savoy had been left by his father virtually in the guardianship of Louis and he was married to Louis's niece, Anne of Orléans. The weak duke Cosimo III of Tuscany would take the line of least resistance. The absentee duke of Mantua, having no male heir to succeed to Montferrat, was prepared to sell its capital. The first deal miscarried when Mattioli,[4] the duke's agent, after taking his commission, betrayed the scheme to Venice and Vienna. At last, by a second treaty, the duke handed over the town and took his pension. It is questionable whether the military value of this base was enough to justify the resentment felt in Italy – and nowhere more than at Rome – for this high-handed action. D'Estrées, Louis's minister in Savoy, told him that 'there are few countries where the French are less loved than this one, or where Your Majesty's power causes more alarm and distrust'. It is borne out by Savoy's later defection to the League of Augsburg (1689). Meanwhile, awkward questions were being asked. Was Italy to be the stage for the next war? Was Louis going to revive the Valois policy of direct intervention in Italy? Did his persisting quarrel with the Pope show that, at heart, he shared the Frenchman's scorn for Italians?

In his handling of Italian affairs Louis was undoubtedly at fault, to say the least insensitive, neglectful of the normal diplomatic courtesies, and oblivious to lessons of recent history: that Italians might welcome the French as allies but would spurn them as invaders. The line was a fine one – and Louis appeared to cross it. In Savoy he played off the young duke against his mother and compelled him finally to accept the 'protection' of 3,000 French troops. After the Revocation of the Edict of Nantes he attacked the Vaudois in their Alpine valleys and ordered the duke to help him on his side of the valleys. Victor Amadeus hid his real feelings and bided his time. Later he would show himself a resourceful enemy and play a significant role in hostile coalitions.[4] The Vaudois would fight valiantly for him against the French.

The story of Genoa is even more revealing. Its old alliance with Spain had long ceased to be effective. Its prosperity continued, however, to be provocative since it was the chief trading rival of Marseille. It was said of Colbert that he could 'scarcely contain his anger when he heard that a rich [foreign] fleet had arrived at Marseille'. In May 1684 Genoa armed galleys and allowed Spanish ships to refit in her port. Louis ordered them to desist. They refused and he sent Duquesne to bombard the port. Again, as at Strasbourg and as if to emphasise the political point, a minister, Seignelay, was present. After ten days and great destruction the fleet withdrew. To emphasise the lesson, the doge was required to go to Versailles to ask the king's pardon. It was graciously granted and the Genoese were sent home with diamond-studded miniature portraits of the king.

Unfortunately such aggression diverted Italian opinion from more beneficial uses of France's now formidable naval power. The Barbary corsairs had long terrorised the western Mediterranean. They had benefited from the decline of Spain's navy and the recent war between France and Holland. Since 1678, under Colbert's direction, squadrons based on Toulon policed the Mediterranean. Duquesne actually sailed as far as the Dardanelles, but Louis cautioned him, not being prepared to offend the Sultan himself. Local Muslim rulers were his target. The sultan of Morocco had already conceded France commercial privileges when, in 1684–85, Duquesne and D'Estrées bombarded Algiers, Tunis and Tripoli, treated with the local rulers for the release of Christian captives and bound them to future good conduct. Here the legitimate pursuit of French interests could be shown to be for the general good.

VIENNA: A DECISIVE MOMENT

Of greater significance in the overall European scene and fateful for the future were the events in Eastern Europe culminating in the siege of Vienna by a huge Ottoman army. Two elements were here involved: the militant revival of the Turks under the Köprülü viziers and the persisting efforts of the Magyars, drawing strength from the unruly haven of neighbouring Transylvania, to free themselves from the rule of Vienna. That was a chronic problem for the Habsburgs. When Thököli allied his Magyars to the Grand Vizier Kara Mustapha, in return for the title of king of Hungary, the two elements fused in a single threat to the Empire and Christendom. Louis's position was equivocal. Early in his reign he had sent a contingent to aid the Emperor but its grudging reception in Germany after the victory of St Gothard in August 1664 had convinced him that he was mistaken. His policy thereafter should be viewed in the context of the persisting enmity of Leopold and his intervention in the Dutch war. Louis was sure that the Emperor would continue to work for the whole of the Spanish Succession and if necessary fight for it. Without committing France by treaty, Louis favoured the Hungarian rebels. After Nijmegen, he aided them.

Pomponne had expressed, in 1675, the intended vagueness of this policy, 'to encourage the rebels by some hope of aid and to force the court of Vienna to give greater attention to the revolt'. In 1677 Imre Thököli secured a small subsidy and his soldiers called themselves 'soldiers of France'. He advertised his client status. His coins carried the slogan: *Ludovicus XIV, Galliae Rex, Defensor Hungariae*. A stronger ally than Thököli might have been the doughty, ambitious John Sobieski, elected king of Poland, in 1674, with French support. But French diplomacy in Poland relied on personal links and vague promises and failed to get to grips with the realities of Polish politics, and so understand the aspirations of its kings. In 1677 John signed a treaty of neutrality with the Emperor. In Poland French diplomacy had a rare failure. John's significant move prompts another reflection. His ambitious French wife Marie Casimir, had importuned Louis XIV to promote her father to the status of *duc et pair*. He refused, she felt slighted and her husband – the future saviour of Vienna – turned to the Emperor. It would not be the last time that Louis's idea of status, and his honourable consistency in such matters, affected the fate of nations.

Prompted by Pope Innocent XI, in 1681, the Emperor restored to the Hungarians regular Estates and several of their traditional liberties. When Thököli offered soldiers to Kara Mustapha, Leopold countered with an offer of all of Hungary east of the Hron. It would mean little unless he could recover that land. While Louis XIV's troops were moving into the 'reunited dependencies', the pope's envoys worked to construct an alliance for the defence of Christendom. Germans noted the contrast. A threat became a crisis when, in March 1683, the Turkish horde began its historic march from Adrianople. Apafi of Transylvania joined it, Thököli provided a diversionary attack in Slovakia, and the Imperialists abandoned Hungary and fell back on Vienna. In July the Turks invested Vienna. The Pope called on Christian princes to go to its aid. At Versailles Bishop Bossuet spoke of the trials of Austrian Christians and urged his listeners 'to do penance, to appease God by your tears'. His king took a cooler view.

Leopold was still a member of a league against him. If Vienna fell, then he could march against the Turks, the undisputed master of Europe, protector of Germany. He was careful not to embarrass Leopold by any public move. His private thoughts can be deduced from his dealings with Turkey where French merchants had long enjoyed a privileged position. Louis had recently assured the Sultan of his friendship and curbed the actions of his navy in the Mediterranean. His ambassador Guilleragues was urged to be 'careful above all things, to give these assurances in our name, and still more not to put anything in writing'. Such hints and nudges may have been the deciding factor in the Sultan's decision to mount his campaign. It is not hard at this juncture – Mazarin would not have found it so – to make out a 'European' case against France.

The siege of Vienna was a savage affair. Christian captives were massacred outside the walls, as if to emphasise the importance of holding the city. Each day of early September brought nearer the final assault. Had Kara Mustapha been prepared to accept the loss of life that an assault would have entailed, had he even taken precautions against a relieving force, Vienna must have fallen. The walls had already been breached when, on 12 September, the Polish and Imperial troops swept down 'like a stream of black pitch' from the Khalenberg heights and swept the Turks before them. A terrible threat, a tenacious resistance, suspense, then a seeming miracle of deliverance: the event could not have been more dramatic. A historic victory had been won, but no French troops had been there. The Pope who had summoned the powers to defend Christendom and now saluted John Sobieski as 'the man sent from God' was at loggerheads with Louis. Sobieski's fellow commander was Louis's confirmed enemy, duke Charles of Lorraine. The Austrians surged on to further victories. Budapest fell in September 1686. The revival of their military power engendered confidence and impressed the German princes. Louis's decision not to respond to the Pope's call to arms turned out to be a misjudgement of historic proportions.

In retrospect the relief of Vienna can be seen as a critical moment in the reign of Louis XIV. It lifted from the consciousness of Germans, particularly those of the south and east, the overshadowing fear of a Turkish penetration into the heartlands of the empire. In the Habsburgs it induced the sense of triumph which permeates the Austrian baroque. It confirmed in the Hofburg the values of 'confessional absolutism'. It offered new lands, sources of revenue and at least the lineaments of massive territorial power. The lands would never become a unified territorial state. But they provided the basis for a new European balance of power. Louis would have to operate in a new framework. In the short term, of course, the effect was less perceptible. The Emperor was keen to follow up his victory and to secure peace in the west. Louis hoped to convert to a lasting peace the twenty-year truce of Ratisbon (August 1684) which ended his war with Spain and to secure Strasbourg, Luxembourg and the substantial areas gained by the *réunions*. Did he also hope that his measures against the Huguenots would convince the Pope – and more importantly, the German Catholic states, that he was as good a Catholic as the Emperor?

Notes

1. Among recent accounts of the *réunions*, Lossky is notably unsympathetic: they were 'indiscriminate' and 'an abandonment of the sensible aim of seeking a defensible frontier.' (A. Lossky, *Louis XIV* (New Brunswick, 1994), p. 11. Does this do justice to the strategic logic? For example, Strasbourg had been a regular gateway to France for Imperial troops. Montbéliard lay between Alsace and Franche-Comté. For the matter of boundaries see 'Frontière; word and concept' in P. Burke (ed.), *A New Kind of History from the Writings of Lucien Febvre* (London, 1973), pp. 209–17.
2. Sir William Temple, architect of the Triple Alliance and for many years ambassador at The Hague, was usually well informed.
3. Brother of William (see p. 178, n. 19) and Louis's assiduous agent in Germany.
4. A possible candidate for 'the man in the iron mask'.
5. See, for example, p. 271.

Chapter 9

◆

POWER AND
CONFORMITY

Great designs are rare in politics; the king proceeded empirically
and sometimes impulsively.

C.G. PICAVET

Sovereigns have no other law than their will.

PASTOR MERLAT, 1685

THE HUGUENOT QUESTION

On 22 October 1685, *Parlement* registered the Edict of Fontainebleau. It
brought to a formal end the special and tolerated place in the realm
enjoyed by Huguenots since Louis's grandfather had signed the Edict of
Nantes in 1598.[1] It was presented as the legal confirmation of 'an already
established fact': since so many Huguenots had become Catholic there
was no need to allow the rest any special legal status. The Edict banned the
public exercise of the R.P.R., as it was known in official documents: *réligion
prétendue réformée*. All *temples* were to be destroyed; ministers exiled unless they
accepted conversion. Laymen were forbidden to leave the country. Their
children were to be baptised and brought up as Catholics. The Edict can be
seen as the logical conclusion of a five-year process of constraint and curtail-
ment, intensifying to the point of downright coercion, following a period of
inconsistent policies when the Huguenot question was lower on the royal
agenda.

It must be stressed how exceptional, and to many Frenchmen how shame-
fully unacceptable, were the conditions under which Huguenots, since 1598,

had enjoyed their privileged and protected status. Nantes had been the last of a series of edicts of pacification which had punctuated the civil wars. It did not propose, let alone sanction toleration. Catholics who, in some southern communities, were the oppressed element, won two significant concessions: the restoration of the mass to all places where it had been abolished, and the return of church property. That could not fail to provoke local conflict. They still did not accept as satisfactory, or anything but a temporary position, the rules and provisions that protected Protestant belief and practice. The Huguenots might later see the edict as 'closing in on them like a tomb'. At the time many were militant, looking to convert, and ready to fight, if need be, for their faith. Even for Henry IV, ex-Huguenot, *politique*, battle-weary soldier, Nantes had not been a free act of grace. It was exacted, under duress. During the siege of Amiens, in 1597, the Huguenots had come close to betraying their king to Spain. They had taken advantage of Henry's commitment to the siege to bargain hard with his emissary Schomberg. A king who did not bear grudges (and understood the Huguenot mentality) was made to pay a high price for the freedom to rule effectively. His subsequent reign showed that he was justified. Events after his death, culminating in the serious revolt of 1626–29, showed that many Huguenots remained far from loyal. In 1598, they did not see themselves as a defeated faction but as a strong force, having some sixty *places de sûreté*, powerful magnates and soldiers to whom their *seigneur* meant more than the king. Their cause was nourished by the faith of many others, men and women of the Bible. A relatively high proportion of these were *bourgeois*, literate, educated in the faith. Many of them were, indeed, beginning to put the blessings of security before the urge to evangelise. But they would show, under pressure, as in the siege of La Rochelle, a formidable ability to resist. So Huguenotism was still dangerous to the crown after 1598. Its leaders knew that the dominant opinion in the church and at court was hostile and unforgiving. They were suspicious of the king's generosity to that other potentially subversive element in the state, their committed foe, the Catholic League. Meanwhile they had secured terms that did not so much protect their weakness as confirm their strength.

In the preamble to the Edict of Nantes its purpose was declared to be the provision of a general law regulating the differences between those of the two religions. It actually reaffirmed the ideal of a universal church. Did that mean that the ultimate objective was unity? Or was it for the consumption of the Pope? His support for Henry IV was at this stage crucially important. The Edict was a realistic political exercise: an acceptance of the fact that the crown could not muster sufficient force to defeat the Huguenots.

Inevitably it conceded most to the nobility. Specified places where the cult was authorised included 3,500 châteaux. A presbyterian church organisation was allowed by one article; another one forbade general assemblies. The Huguenots secured privileges that fostered their cultural separatism, law chambers attached to certain *parlements*, for example. They had their own academies, by 1660 more than thirty, ensuring a flow of well-educated men to be pastors and to pursue other professions. They held on to a strong position from which to bargain, but they were not a state within a state. They were a special case because of the deep religious passions and social animosities that were the legacy of civil war. Yet they should still be counted among the many privileged situations: feudal, fiscal, secular official and ecclesiastical, corporate and individual, which were the flawed reality of royal 'absolutism' and natural targets for its attack. That is the significance of Richelieu's successful siege of La Rochelle, and the subsequent Grace of Alais (1629). It was a milestone in the rise of absolute monarchy.[2] To the chagrin of *dévôts*, it did not turn out to be a conclusive triumph for Rome.

For Richelieu in the short term, the defeat of the feudal magnates, Rohan and Soubise, and the example to others, was as important as the check to Huguenot aspiration. The situation of the Huguenots was, none the less, transformed. They were effectively disarmed. Their fortifications were systematically demolished, in some cases under Richelieu's personal supervision. Ruined town walls everywhere displayed the end of Huguenotism as a political force. The cardinal remained wary in the face of the extreme demands of Catholic zealots. In his delicate diplomatic position (he was at war with Spain after 1635), he did need to display his own orthodoxy. In that year, under fire from church leaders, he promoted a decree forbidding Protestant teaching in ecclesiastical lordships. The council tended to back Catholics in local disputes. The *Compagnie du Saint-Sacrement*[3] maintained its intrusive watch, taking advantage of ambiguities in the Edict to sap at the Huguenot position. Yet it appears that the total number of Huguenots, around one million,[4] remained constant. Richelieu was concerned. We know that he spent hours pondering the question. Posthumously, his preferred approach, that of mission and debate, was revealed in his treatise on 'the easiest and most sure' methods of conversion of those whom, like Vincent de Paul, he called 'the separated brethren'. Meanwhile, in most respects, their rights remained intact. But the balance of power had shifted. It might be politic, as Mazarin saw during the crises of the Fronde, to show good will through conciliatory gestures. Nothing could alter the fact, the point from which Louis XIV started, that they owed their continuing security, not to the edict, not even to the influence of prominent Huguenots, but to the good will of the king. All therefore, depended on his view of them and, at any given time, his reading of the situation in which they found themselves.

That they had been for a century rebels as well as heretics was plain enough. Their separate existence was an affront to Louis's idea of rule and the relation of the subject to his ruler: an obstacle to the unity of the realm. The teaching of his mother, tutors, preachers and confessors left no room for doubt: heretics were bound for hell and it was a Christian and royal duty to save them. Was all that enough to justify a programme of repression? Until 1679 it seems that it was not. The flurry of measures at the start of his personal reign seem to have been designed to draw lines, to convince them that they could expect no extension of privileges. Meanwhile existing rights were confirmed. In Louis's *Mémoires* the Huguenots are not mentioned among the serious disorders that he found on accession. In the years of Colbertist reform and war in Flanders their case did not have priority. The contrast between years of seeming indifference and, after 1679, intense royal concern and whittling away of Huguenot rights is therefore striking. From 1661 to 1679 there were ten edicts, in the next six years eighty-five aimed at the R.P.R. of official parlance.

Superficially that mounting persecution may be seen as a natural follow-up to the peace of Nijmegen, as a peacetime exercise in the politics of glory, translating into religious terms the spirit of the *réunions*; or as an aspect of absolutism, a further effort to capitalise on royal prestige and extend the authority of the state. That may go some way to answering the question: 'why then?' It does not deal with the underlying question: 'why at all?' It does not account for the spiritual dimension, that of seventeenth-century man's relation to God and his notion of religious duty. For further explanation we need to look first at the changing condition of Huguenotism in the context of Catholic revival.

In May 1652, at a critical juncture of the civil war, when there was anxiety about the south, Mazarin praised the Huguenots for their 'devotion and loyalty, notably in the present circumstances', with which the king was declared to be 'highly satisfied'. As a measure of the crown's gratitude – or fear – it annulled all judgements made by *parlements* since 1629 contrary to the Edict's letter and spirit. In 1656 a cooler document projected the appointment at a future date of two commissioners for each province, one Catholic, one Huguenot, to enquire into breaches of the edict. It was the start of harder attitudes. In 1659 Mazarin gave leave for a national synod to meet at Loudun – but warned that it would be the last. Until then he had needed to appear to be conciliatory because of his alliance with Cromwell. By 1661 the Declaration of 1656 was being put into effect, with the destruction of a number of Huguenot temples.

How justified was Mazarin in his anxiety during the Fronde? The question is relevant because events of these years, as, for example, those relating to Jansenism, had such a profound influenced on Louis's later views. For him, as for many Catholics, the very existence of the Huguenots was a sort of treason. If there had been substance behind the idea, if Huguenots were more likely to rebel, soldiers to desert, then Louis's later actions are more readily explained. Only a few incidents suggest the tensions of the time – but they are significant. In May 1643 rumours, false it turned out, that a Parisian mob was on its way to burn down the temple of Charenton, caused the congregation to panic and noblemen to draw their swords. In 1653 a conflict over the rebuilding of a temple at Vals, above the Rhône valley, led to the establishment of an armed camp of some 6,000 men: Cromwell's soldiers would have recognised the mood as the Huguenots sang their militant psalms. A Huguenot nobleman, Bonneson, was a ringleader in the noble assemblies and the rising of the *Sabotiers* that troubled Mazarin in the late fifties. In the first years of the Minority *intendant* Balthasar believed that a revolt was hatching in Languedoc. His proposal, to exclude Huguenots from office, might well have precipitated it.

If during the Fronde, any incident had triggered a major Huguenot rising, the course, possibly its outcome might have been different. The Rohan family had been leaders in the rising of 1626–29 but had subsequently been treated with politic generosity; yet the duc de Rohan joined Condé in rebellion. In 1660 Turenne was surprised to find him still treated as a folk hero in the south, inspiring talk of rebellion. The provinces where Condé found most support were also those where the Huguenot population was relatively dense: about a third lived in Poitou, Saintonge, Angoumois and Guienne. There was another sizeable group in Normandy, a province that gave the Fronde some early support. Most Huguenots, however, lived in the southern provinces, those, notably Languedoc and the Dauphiné, most remote from Paris. It was there, with the influence of mountainous Dauphiné's Swiss neighbours in mind, that the government was haunted by the fear of separatist movements. There the atrocious experiences of civil war lived on in communities who still feuded over Huguenot rights, contested by lawyers and denounced by the church. There could be seen the power of ancestral memories to affect current attitudes. Significantly Bâville, *intendant* of Languedoc, would be one of the few to be sceptical about the Revocation:

he was prepared to be tough, but he knew his people.[5] Ecclesiastics were generally less restrained.

At the periodic church assemblies the militant rhetoric could be discounted as the norm at such gatherings when speakers bid for notice and are unconstrained by such mundane questions as how such a policy might be implemented or at what financial cost to the state. Successive speakers at the assembly of 1651 had expressed concern about Mazarin's apparent lack of principle. They voiced the fervour of resurgent Catholicism; they expressed a sense of the spiritual unity of the realm; most importantly, when it came to government's reading of the situation, they represented the real grievances of ordinary Catholics in those communities where Huguenots were in the ascendant. At the assembly of 1675 a bishop touched a sensitive nerve when he urged the king to recognise the favour of God, as revealed in his victories, by extinguishing heresy. 'Freedom of conscience is a . . . trap prepared for their simplicity and licence. Remove, Sire, this deadly freedom.'[6]

As with nonconformists in England, it was the prosperity of many Huguenots that attracted odium. In many communities they had a weight disproportionate to their numbers. The reasons become clear in the light of the later emigration and the remarkable adaptability and success of Huguenot expatriates: they may be said to lie in education, rules of life grounded in the Bible and a wide range of skills. There was, typically, a sober purposefulness, and that sense of spiritual privilege which seems generally to have outlasted, among Calvinists, the strict doctrine of predestination and of salvation limited to God's elect. Such élitism was specially provocative to those outside the cult when accompanied by material well-being.

HUGUENOT CRISIS; CATHOLIC ASCENDANCY

Many individuals and families were staunch for the faith but Huguenotism as an institution was experiencing a deepening crisis. Its external aspect was plain: steady hostility and pressure on government to take decisive action. Less obvious, at least to those outside academic and theological circles, but no less insidious, was the questioning of core beliefs. It was not peculiar to France. At the start of the century followers of Arminius,[7] Remonstrants, as they were called in Holland, had given up predestination and accepted the right of the ruler to control religion. So doing they qualified Calvin's essential tenet: the single and absolute nature of God's sovereignty. In France, the scholarly humanist Moise Amyraut, director of the Huguenot seminary of Saumur, came close, in language and argument, to the gentler and more reasonable of Catholics. When he wrote his *Apologie pour ceux de la réligion* in 1647, arguing that the Huguenots had never intended to set up a separate state, he strengthened the case of the absolutists. Indeed from one of them, Guez de Balzac, he earned the telling compliment that he showed qualities more of the court than of the consistory. The consistory fought back, led by Pierre du Moulin, pastor of Nimes, who spurned Amyraut's 'deviationism'. The issue remained unresolved.

Within European Calvinism generally the issue of authority reflected the harrowing experience and disillusioned aftermath of the Thirty Years War which had started with a Calvinist challenge to Imperial authority but degenerated into a medley of conflicts, having more to do with land than with religion. There were two special factors in the French dispute arising out of the distinctive experience of Huguenots and the exceptional growth in royal authority. Huguenots were confronted by specially painful questions. If Reform had been a providential act of God (which no Protestant should doubt) why in France should it have had such grave consequences? Was it true, as Catholics asserted, that to be a Huguenot was to be a bad Frenchman? St Paul had written in his letter to the Romans (13: 12): 'Every person must submit to the supreme authorities. . . . Anyone who rebels against authority is resisting a Divine institution.' Could the people of the Bible disregard the injunction?[8] These questions sapped Huguenot morale and, for some, pointed the way to conversion.

One aspect of the crisis in Huguenot morale was the movement for reunion. Prominent among Huguenot intellectuals was Isaac d'Huisseau of Saumur who proposed an ecumenical strategy based on the distinction between those fundamental beliefs he held necessary for salvation and those inessential, not revealed in the Bible and reflecting 'the faults and imperfections of the human spirit'. With astonishing audacity, anticipating in this respect the analytical spirit of the Enlightenment, he strove, by concentrating on what could be regarded as essential, to counter the view that to be tolerant meant to be indifferent. It was raised, nonetheless, and notably by Pierre Jurieu,[9] later to be Louis XIV's most outspoken and influential critic. D'Huisseau was excommunicated by his consistory but continued to press his case till his death (1671). With crucial issues, strong personalities and a public war of words, the dispute threatened the coherence and confidence in clear-cut beliefs that had been one of Huguenotism's greatest strengths – and which, ironically, it would recover under persecution.

On the Catholic side there was no indifference, little tolerance. If Catholics needed proof that they were in the right, that Huguenots were lost souls, they could find it in this spectacle of a house divided against itself. It offered an example to Bossuet[10] of the fissile tendency within Protestantism that was, as developed in his *Histoire des Variations*, a prime argument against it. For French Catholics there was no difficulty in subscribing to high notions of royal authority. Bossuet found in history and theology arguments for the validity of Divine Right monarchy that would hold the field until rationalist approaches to Scripture and relativist studies of other cultures began to undermine it. His synthesis was acceptable to Gallican and ultramontane alike. In the seventies and eighties it was Huguenotism, not Catholicism, that was in crisis. For French Catholics these were confident times (the last, it would turn out). During the past century there had been a notable revival. Never had lay men and women been so devout, priests better educated, bishops more conscientious. Disputes between the king and Rome did little to shake faith. The Jansenist issue which, eventually, would prove so destructive, witnessed more to an excess, or narrow focusing, of religious fervour than to its absence. Lives of prayer, pastoral care and missionary enterprise were anchored to the dogmatic certainties derived from the Council of Trent. It was from that secure position that thoughtful Catholics, notably bishop Bossuet, approached questions of reunion.

In the correspondence between Bossuet and Paul Ferry, pastor of Metz, on the project of reunion, it was the Council's categorical defiance of heresy that stood in the way of compromise. At the same time, in the work of men as different as Bérulle,[11] founder of the Oratory, and the Jansenist Antoine Arnauld,[12] there is apparent a concern for the individual soul, and an exploration of the implications of God's love, as strong as that of the first reformers. What Calvin's *Institution Chrétienne* was for the sixteenth century, Bérulle's *Traité de l'Amour* and Arnauld's *Fréquente Communion* were for the seventeenth. The position of Catholic and Protestant confessions had changed radically since the Reformation. The Catholic view of the Real Presence[13] and insistence on the authority of the Pope – not, in the view of Gallican bishops, infallible – were the only fundamental differences left. The first episodes in the Jansenist affair revealed how close Protestant and Catholic positions had become concerning what was necessary for salvation, when Dominican, Jansenist and Calvinist could all offer similar interpretations of St Augustine's writings about Divine Grace and human will. The papacy had already granted local concessions, notably the lay right to communion in both kinds. Even in the matter of the Real Presence, the Cartesian theory of extension seemed to offer a hope of conciliation. Meanwhile the church which had recently been adorned by men as impressive and appealing as François de

Sales, Jean-Jacques Olier and Vincent de Paul, the church now of Le Camus, Bossuet and Fénelon, offered a tolerable refuge to those Huguenots who were uncomfortable in their isolated position.

Among them the case of Turenne is especially significant, as it undoubtedly was to the king. He had acquired a position of moral leadership in international Protestantism similar to that of Coligny in the sixteenth century. His conversion, in 1668, had its political aspect. He was concerned for the unity and discipline of the nation. It was the soldier's view, hardened by his experience of the Fronde. Yet, in 1661, he had refused the Constable's sword rather than abjure. He was conscientious and supported by a devout wife. He became persuaded, however, that Protestantism, in which 'every individual wishes to found a faith after his own inclinations', was without theological justification. He was not alone in thinking so. After 1648 there were many abjurations in Germany and talk of reunion became fashionable. England's history ensured an eccentric course: hatred of Rome was balanced there by persecution of sects who would not conform to a strictly defined Anglicanism. Elsewhere a few enlightened spirits searched for a more broadly based Christianity, less in tolerance arising from a positive view of human rights than from distaste for the bigotry that led to war.

So Grotius,[14] brooding over the wasteland of the Thirty Years War and the sectarianism of his native Holland, had envisaged a reunion of the national churches of France, England and Scandinavia. He misread Gallicanism, perhaps Anglicanism too. However, he was able to assure archbishop Laud that there were in France many wise bishops who greatly approved the line of conduct of the Anglican church. Of greater importance, and more timely, was Leibnitz's work for reunion.[15] He thought it a duty of Protestants to negotiate as a body to end schism. Under his influence some Lutherans of Hanover signed articles which began by acknowledging the pope's claim to be head of the church. Bossuet, whose *Exposition de la doctrine Catholique* was so reasonable in tone that he was accused of watering down Roman doctrines to suit heretic taste, responded for moderates. In his correspondence with Leibnitz, we see that even his rational approach could not construct a bridge between Rome and the Lutheran confession which all could cross. If Augsburg were difficult to approach, how much more would be Geneva.

Louis respected Bossuet and made him the Dauphin's tutor. He would note his efforts and views as he did his grandiloquent sermons, appealing to his royal sense of duty. When even Bossuet came to think that the future lay in conversion, not compromise, then those advisers who had neither scruple about doctrine nor qualms about force were encouraged to advocate a harder line. Given their theology, from persuasion to compulsion was a logical step. Had not St Augustine, dealing with the Donatist heretics, advised the use of force: *compelle intrare*? In 1682 Louis approved the special publication of his letter. Bossuet noted that Protestants subscribed to the principle when dealing with Anabaptists.

One consideration for Louis's advisors was the increasing cost of implementing schemes of 'compensation'. A scheme piloted by Le Camus, bishop of Grenoble, in 1676, backed conversions among the Vaudois by a fund, the *caisse de conversions*, to compensate ministers for their loss of livelihood. It was managed by Paul Pellisson, using the revenues of abbeys of which he was treasurer during their vacancy through the *régale* dispute between king and Pope. His career reveals interesting links. Like many Huguenots he had held financial office before being disgraced and imprisoned after the fall of Fouquet. Converted under Jansenist influence, he became royal historiographer and pledged to give his life 'to the king and to God'. He was allowed to extend his fund until he was director of a network with agents in every province and a set tariff for payments ranging from six *livres* for a peasant to 3,000 for a nobleman: no small inducement to the poor in either category. He prepared regular statistical reports for the king. One entry in the *Gazette* of April 1678 speaks volumes: 'We have viewed with admiration the triumph of Louis over the Vaudois who have for centuries banned the Holy Church from their mountains.' Bossuet and Fénelon approved of the system as preferable to physical violence, material inducements preparing the ground for the operation of God's grace. Arnauld championed the purity of Pellisson's intentions in his *Apologie pour les Catholiques*: a Jansenist arguing that the end justified the means! But the Jansenists led in missionary effort, with translations of the liturgy and manuals of devotion to offer spiritual comfort to raw converts.

Here we see a new strand in the complicated pattern: the mutual mistrust between Jansenists and Jesuits.[16] The moderate stance of Port Royal, its vulgarisation of Holy Writ, and the ample resources it could command, alarmed the Jesuits. They had fought to check the growth of a church within the church. They were still smarting under the strictures of Pascal: 'The Jesuits have tried to combine God and the world and have only succeeded in gaining the contempt of both.' Were his successors now to be allowed to interpret the truth to Protestants in their own way – and so extend their influence? Through archbishop Harlay and the king's Jesuit confessor, Père La Chaise, on the *Conseil de Conscience*, they were well placed to influence the king. The Pope's nuncio in Paris wrote: 'The king, who has never read or studied a book, lets himself be misled ... and never lends an ear to anybody beyond these people.' After their secret marriage (probably in 1683) the king's wife, Mme de Maintenon[17] would have a place in Protestant demonology. In fact it seems that her main concern was with the education of Huguenot children. If anything, she thought that Louis was too superficial in his approach. 'Louis thinks too little about God', she wrote. Harlay and La Chaise were more important.

THE EDICT OF FONTAINEBLEAU

Harlay de Champvallon had been archbishop of Paris since 1671. Erudite, worldly, a sound administrator and a tenacious negotiator, he seems to have been the kind of ecclesiastical politician who impresses government more than he wins hearts.[18] Bossuet, opposed in personality and policy, was his most severe critic. Harlay's master principle was to serve the king and to defend his Gallican rights. He, not Bossuet, had been mainly responsible for the manipulation of the Assembly of 1681–82 which had led to the Four Articles.[19] He was indeed an assiduous courtier. He had become, in a contemporary view, 'the sole minister of the king in ecclesiastical affairs and the repository of royal authority'. The king valued his advice on appointments and management of the church assembly though he surely realised that Harlay would not go the wire to secure the best possible financial deal for his fellow clergy.

By July 1685 it is possible to see concerted action towards an agreed end, with Harlay going between Assembly and *conseil de conscience* – 'councillors of Babylon' according to the Pope – and the old chancellor, Le Tellier, expediting the legal business. Early in July the Assembly asked that the post of advocate (the last to be left to them) be barred to Huguenots. On 11 July it was put into effect by edict. The role of La Chaise is harder to identify because it is wrapped in the secrecy of the confessional. As Bayle[20] pointed out, however, the confessor alone 'could inform the king of what he would answer for in his conduct'. It is certain that Louis needed assurance that it was no sin to revoke his grandfather's edict. Bayle added: 'Monsieur de Paris acted in concert with the confessor.'

Such strenuous endeavours for the faith could not be ignored at Rome. Pope Innocent XI, elected in 1676, was a strong personality, with ambitious plans. He was interested in negotiations with German Lutherans and with plans for a crusade of European powers against the Turk. He blamed Louis XIV for blocking the grand ecumenical initiative of Rojas y Spinola.[21]

Because he was embroiled with the king over the rights of the Gallican church, Innocent could not approve a conversion campaign financed by the *régale*. 'Of what use', he asked in 1682, 'is the demolition of so many temples if all the bishops are schismatic?' He was sceptical about Louis's claim to be striking a blow for the church by the seizure of Strasbourg and was disgusted by his failure to join in the operation to save Vienna. The impasse between king and Pope affected the events that led to Fontainebleau. Seeing support in Germany fading Louis felt that he had to assert his claim to be a good Catholic. Archbishop de Cosnac told a sceptical Europe that Holland and Germany served as a theatre, not for his victories alone but for those of Jesus Christ.[22] In 1683 Louis's agent informed the Pope that Spinola's proposal was 'incompatible with the purity of our faith and our principles'.

Now Louis paraded his orthodoxy. He repudiated the negotiations of Governor Noailles with the Huguenots of Languedoc. He sensed – or let himself be persuaded – that it was time to come forward as head of the Catholic party in Europe. The great-grandson of Philip II saw France assuming the place vacated by Spain. Could he not do what Philip II had failed to do: destroy heresy in Europe? William of Orange, a hostile but perceptive critic thought, in 1682, that he was already thinking in these terms: 'There is no doubt that it is the intention of the king of France to make himself master of Europe.' Is it significant that the names of Constantine and Charlemagne were now being invoked by Frenchmen so constantly? If such hopes had a place in Louis's estimate of the Huguenot situation they were not wholly unrealistic. Protestants looking for reunion were surely admitting defeat. The accession of a Catholic king, James II, to the English throne, was surely a sign from heaven? That was the view from the windows of Versailles. Every day reports from the *intendants* conveyed, with impressive statistics, the message that the king and the *conseil de conscience* wanted to hear: Huguenotism was disintegrating. Had not the *dragonnades* done their work?

In March 1681 Louvois had authorised Marillac, *intendant* in Poitou, to billet a regiment of dragoons on Huguenot families. There were precedents for such billeting. It was a normal feature of life in frontier provinces. After the death of Bishop Caulet of Pamiers (1680) *intendant* Foucault had lodged cavalry on anti-*régale* families in the diocese. Marillac had already tried out selective taxation when *taille* rolls in Poitou were made out in three columns: 'Old Catholics', discharged in part; 'New Catholics' wholly exempt; Huguenots who made up the deficit. Soldier–missionaries promised better returns. By the end of the year Marillac reported 38,000 conversions. The figures may be doubted; also the sincerity of those who did convert. The unpleasantness – and expense – of soldiers' lodging were enough to persuade many to attend a mass. Perhaps some were dragged there. Tales of horror may have been exaggerated. Benoît,[23] first of a school of Protestant historians to specialise in the listing of atrocities, admitted that terror was more widespread than the violence that caused it. But there were grounds for Catholic concern about the blasphemy of sham conversions and ministerial anxiety about the impact on European opinion at a sensitive time. Jurieu roused feeling in England and Holland with his work, *Derniers efforts de l'innocence affligée*, which was to be the model for a torrent of such propaganda. The Elector of Brandenburg anticipated his later 'open door' policy by declaring that 'he looked with anguish at the persecution of people whom he regarded as brothers and the world as innocent'. Louis answered evasively 'that only chapels built since the Edict have been destroyed'. Louvois was never a prime mover in the process.[24] He was concerned about the effect on the discipline of soldiers, and the reaction of Huguenot officers. Seignelay halted the proselytising activities of De Muin, *intendant* at La Rochelle, which were causing some of the best seamen to emigrate. Louis paused. He recalled Marillac. But he noted that *dragonnades* were persuasive. Meanwhile there was no letting up in the legal campaign.

Barriers to emigration; curtailing of the rights of pastors; the progressive exclusion from legal and other professions: these were the main themes of anti-Huguenot measures between 1679 and 1685. Along the way Huguenot midwives were forbidden to practise; magistrates were required to visit sick Huguenots to attempt conversion. Conversion from Catholicism to Protestantism was forbidden; any minister who accepted a convert from Catholicism was to be banished; a place was to be reserved for a police informer in each temple. Protestant services were banned in places where there were less than ten Huguenots. In 1660 there were 800 Huguenot temples; in 1685 barely a quarter of that number. Ingenuity was required to harass what was assumed to be a remnant. Marriages abroad were forbidden; places of worship where the pastor had used expressions offensive to Catholics were to be demolished. Half an emigrant's goods confiscated were to be given to the informer. That witnesses to increasing concern over emigration. Meanwhile the *dragonnades* were resumed and *intendants* competed for favour, with reports of mass conversions in Béarn, Montauban and Poitou. Following rather than leading the crowd, and with misgivings, Louvois reported, in September, to his brother, the archbishop of Reims: 'the last reports from the Saintonge and Angoumois convey that all is Catholic'. But he had an afterthought: 'His Majesty recommends that you be accommodating to the bankers and manufacturers.' The last discussions in council centred on economic considerations. Seignelay and Colbert de Croissy, legatees and guardians of Colbertism, warned of the dangers of emigration to commerce. More urgent, however, was the cost of compensating all the New Catholics, an intolerable burden, it was held, on the Old Catholics and the state.

It may be held that Louis failed, in 1685, several tests of mature states-manship. He was right to see a trend but he was naive to believe in all the reports; he might have listened more carefully to ministers like Louvois and Seignelay who knew about the realities of life in the provinces and of the concerns of *intendants*. Accepting plaudits uncritically, believing what was easi-est to believe, he lacked the foresight, maybe moral courage, to rein in the zealots – as Richelieu had done – and let time do his work for him. Would not another fifty years have seen the demise of Protestantism in France or, with an unforced trickle of emigration, its reduction to an insignificant sect? That broadly is the case against Louis, whether presented as a crime and a blunder, or more cautiously, as an abuse of power.

The case is, of course, reinforced by our knowledge of the real state of affairs – and of what was to ensue from Louis's misjudgement of the situ-ation. In modern terms it is hard to refute. In late seventeenth-century terms it is less cogent. Louis deserves to be judged in the context of the political and religious culture of these last decades before the Enlightenment (for which the Revocation would be seminal). Into the reckoning should come, not only his ingrained and tutored sense of what was right, but the advice he was receiving, the near-universal applause at the time, and the lasting appre-ciation of the majority of his Catholic subjects, many of whom had little else to be thankful for. Louis would have been a man of exceptional independ-ence of mind, and moral courage, an enlightened autocrat before his time, to have resisted the pressure to enforce the conformity which was generally held (no less in contemporary Britain) to be desirable – and attainable.

Historical processes create their own momentum, with one decision lead-ing inexorably to another, with principal characters less in control than might at first appear. In 1679 Louis might not have envisaged revocation within a given time. It was never a grand design, only a grand idea, not the object of his planning, rather a pious hope. In his unreflective, wholly unmystical fash-ion, Anne's son was a *dévôt* who needed no persuading of the evils of heresy; Mazarin's pupil also had enough of the *politique* in him not to act unless he saw political advantage as well as spiritual merit. Behind the stern rhetoric of public pronouncements we can see a cautious man, still capable of listening, up to a point sensitive to foreign reactions. His views would be as dogmatic as when he had taken his coronation oath to extirpate heresy; his approach would be empirical, weighing advantage and cost. He required evidence and by 1685 it was compelling: that to continue to tolerate the remaining Huguenots would be to protect a subversive element in the community. If they were now subversive, as they had not been before, it was, of course, because of the way they had been treated, cut off from opportunities to serve in official positions, deprived of the opportunity to worship in their temples and therefore reduced to private gatherings to escape surveillance. That would be dangerous to the state, offensive to the church, and prejudicial to the interests of the Catholics who had to live alongside the remaining Huguenots. In other words the acts of the previous five years had created a situation in which it would be not only illogical, but also risky, to delay administering the *coup de grâce*. Even Seignelay, the legatee of Colbertism and concerned with naval issues, who had opposed discriminatory measures, could accept this argument. It brought Louis to the point of decision: 'I cannot doubt but that it is the Divine Will that I should be his instrument in bringing back to his ways all those who are subject to me.' For those, the overwhelming majority in court and country, for whom Revocation was not only expedient but also right, all signs were that the hour was at hand. For them there was a kind of glorious inevitability about the Edict of Fontainebleau:

> The best and greatest part of our subjects of R.P.R. have embraced the Catholic faith; and as by reason of this the execution of the Edict of Nantes is useless, we have judged that we cannot do better, to efface entirely the memory of the troubles, the confusion, and the evils that the progress of this false religion have caused in our realm . . . than to revoke entirely the above edict.

The pious spirit and sacrificial courage of numerous émigrés, with the women often in the lead, the tenacity of many that remained, soon gave the lie to the legal fiction. The Edict assumed that Huguenotism no longer existed. For the time being, however, ministers had to allow that Huguenots did still exist; they soon found that they had no intention of giving up. Ministers were to convert within two weeks or leave the kingdom. Huguenot children were to be baptised, brought up and educated in the Roman faith. Émigrés could take advantage of a four-month amnesty to recover their confiscated property. Stern penalties reinforced the previous ban on lay emigration: 'the galleys for men and confiscation of all worldly goods for women.'

Vauban protested: 'Kings are masters of the lives and goods of their subjects but never of their opinions.'[25] It was exceptional. *Premier président*

Lamoignon spoke for *Parlement*: 'the king has done in a single year what others have been unable to do in a century'; not, in the opinion of the Jesuit Robert, 'by fire and sword but by his gentleness and wisdom'.[26] Bossuet, whose previous experience might have induced caution, saluted 'this miracle of our times' and invited all 'to dote upon the piety of Louis; let our acclamations soar to heaven'. Mme de Sévigné may represent typical court opinion in her bland complacency (or can irony be detected?):

> many people have been converted without knowing why. He [Père Bourdalue] will explain it to them and make them good Catholics. Up till now the dragoons have been good missionaries. The teachers that are being sent out will complete the work.

Harlay directed the missionary effort; the crown provided funds. Translations of the New Testament, catechisms and breviaries were distributed, half a million volumes in all. Squads of missionary priests were recruited to aid stumbling *curés*. Louis XIV's letter to Harlay (November 1685) evokes the earnest mood beneath the rhetoric: 'We must . . . give every consideration to *nouveaux convertis* of good faith, arouse the ardour of the indifferent through education, and use the law against those who relapse.' The effort exposed differences. Le Camus, now cardinal, produced an uncontentious formula for the remaining Huguenots, was challenged by Robert for his unorthodoxy but upheld at Rome. Fénelon instructed his priests in the Saintonge 'not to rouse the Huguenot by argument but to expound the Gospel with authority at once gentle and persuasive'. A third of ministers in his area were converted. But generally the pace was slow. Many, believing that the edict meant the end of the dragonnades, renounced their sword-point conversions. The government was made to look ridiculous. In December Louvois ordered that 'those who want the stupid glory of being the last to resist be driven to the last extremity'. To set the example, Huguenots on his own estate were to be 'properly maltreated'. In December 1685 he ordered the destruction of émigrés' houses in La Rochelle.

A party grew round bishops shocked by reports of violence and sacrilege. Matignon, bishop of Condom, protected the local Huguenots from the troops. At Orléans, De Coislin lodged the soldiers at his own expense. In February 1686 Jurieu published two letters of Montgaillard, bishop of Saint-Pons, condemning the orders to drive all without exception to the altar, even those 'who spit and trample upon the Eucharist'. Jansenists, whose methods were grounded in the attack of Pascal and Arnauld against mechanical treatment of the sacraments, condemned the *dragonnades*. Harlay replied with hints about Jansenist sympathies with the converted – and unconverted

– and banned Le Tourneau's translation of the breviary. Jurieu recalled the promises of 1685. Was this 'Catholic unity'?

Even more serious for Louis, and his standing abroad, was the equivocal position of the Pope. When Queen Christina,[27] former ruler of Sweden and most remarkable of converts, declared that the *dragonnades* were worse than St Bartholomew's Eve, Innocent reproached her – but with tears of embarrassment. Was he relieved, at any rate, that Louis had chosen this way rather than the Gallican, even with an accommodation with the Huguenots? He was still not prepared to make any concession on the issue of the *régale* and he refused to make any of Louis's candidates cardinals. As he became aware of the receding hopes of a peaceful reunion of the churches, he returned to his original view that Louis 'looked more to the advantages of his realm than to the kingdom of God'. Louis held that as defender of the faith he deserved as much as those who had saved Vienna but the Catholics of Germany were more impressed by the Emperor's continuing campaigns against the Turks. Leopold also sought to create a union of German princes: a pre-condition was that the Pope would disavow the persecution in France. Still fearful of Gallican schism, Innocent could not do this. After 1688 the French were at war with William of Orange and the Emperor. By then the German states had lost interest in reunion or in the Pope's companion project, crusade against the Turks. In Holland the Jesuits were threatened with expulsion and appealed to Père La Chaise to use his influence to re-establish the Edict of Nantes! Even in the short term the diplomatic fallout was clearly damaging to France. How dangerous it would continue to be may be judged in the light of what followed from the accession of William III to the English throne.

Louis XIV was not directly responsible for James II losing his throne. His policies and methods were enough to arouse opposition. But the Revocation ensured that his Catholic sympathies would appear in the most sinister light. To the royalist John Evelyn, who knew France and detested revolution, 'The French persecution of the protestants raging with the utmost barbarity seemed to exceed even what the heathen used.' More persuasive even than the literature of atrocity and denunciation flowing from the presses of Amsterdam were the refugees bringing to Britain little but their faith, skills – and stories. The link between them and James's Catholic faith and absolutist tendency would have been noticed even without the tactless observation of the bishop of Valence: 'God seemed to raise the French king to this power, and magnanimous action, so that he might be in a capacity to assist in doing the same there [England].' In Holland the Revocation had already helped William to heal the serious rift between the Stadtholder and the regents of

Amsterdam, on whose mercantile interests and political moderation Louis had relied to constrain William and keep the Dutch neutral. The burgomaster of Amsterdam testified that it was the Huguenots who persuaded them to come to terms with the Prince of Orange. Throughout his wars William was able to rally support, not only as the defender of frontiers but as guardian of Protestantism. Even the War of the Spanish Succession had for many Britons and Dutchmen a religious dimension.

In 1685 the Elector Frederick William of Brandenburg made a treaty with the Dutch and invited to his realm any French fleeing from persecution. To the complaints of the French ambassador he retorted that he 'could not be prevented from being as zealous for his religion as the French king was for his kingdom'. Well attuned as always to the mood of the time, Bossuet was admitting, by 1689: 'Your so-called Reformation was never stronger. All the Protestant peoples are now united in a single bloc. . . . Abroad the reformers have never been more united in a single bloc.' The revocation had not blurred but emphasised the moral division of Europe. 'Today', wrote Leibnitz, 'it is virtually the North that is ranged against the South, the Teuton races challenging the Latin.'

EMIGRÉS AND REBELS

'My realm is being purged of bad and troublesome subjects.' Louis affected to be unmoved by the emigration which his officials found so hard to prevent. If he really believed that it was not unduly harming the economy – or that periodic distress had other causes, in war or in the vagaries of climate – he has been supported recently by economic historians who have made that case. No one would now seriously suggest that there was a crippling of manufactures or the scale of financial loss that Levassor (in 1689) ascribed to refugees taking 'immense sums which have drawn dry the fountain of commerce'. Some rich Huguenot financiers and merchants opted for conversion and remained. They established commercial links with Protestants settled elsewhere in Europe.

That the loss was substantial can, however, be gauged by the clear gains for the host countries. It is also important to place the economic effects in a wider context. If it can be shown that the Huguenots made a significant contribution to the success of allied armies, and to the financial mechanism that supported them (given that French finances suffered badly from the prolongation of the war) it follows that the cost to France of the loss of 200,000 subjects was greater than can be measured by the effect on particular manufactures and trades.[28] That was local and short-term, but severe, more so than might appear from the reports of *intendants* who, if they had been keen to implement the policy, might wish to minimise its ill-effects.

Some of the emigrants were entrepreneurs and artisans recruited by Colbert to develop manufacturing. Towns like Reims, Tours, Nîmes and Rouen lost half their workers; Lyon all but 3,000 out of 12,000 silk-workers. Clothworkers, hatters, papermakers, clockmakers, jewellers, shipwrights – the list could be longer. According to a French agent there most of the 65,000 who went to Holland were clothworkers. Over the years other workers would come forward. The French economy was one of chronic under-employment. It was also starved of cash after years of price recession. The loss of men who had substantial capital and expertise in making capital work for them was therefore significant. Here the English example is telling.

About 40,000 Huguenots got to England, a number exceeded only by those who settled in Holland. By 1700 twenty churches had been established. Some Huguenots had relations there already, or other contacts. The existence of a well-established French-Walloon community from earlier flights gave some a good start. The records of the Bank of England and the East India Company, for example, borne out by studies of prominent individuals in Huguenot congregations, show investment by Huguenots on a large scale. In this period when the availability of money for investment in loans played a crucial part in the war effort, Huguenot investment in the funds, of the order of at least 10 per cent of the total is noteworthy. Important too, though harder to quantify, is the contribution made by their financial expertise, European contacts and individual enterprises such as the fitting out of privateers. Some brought to their adopted country a hatred, not of France but of the régime which had driven them out. Some nursed memories of insults and cruelties, of hardships and perils in flight, with imprisonment or death the price of failure. Some left women and children behind; most left relations and friends in France to yearn for the freedom that they believed could only come with the defeat of Louis. The experiences and convictions of such Huguenots added sharpness to political debate and Protestant culture. It is especially significant in the role of the army and navy that secured first a degree of parity, in William's wars, and then the preponderance of the age of Marlborough.

Marshal Vauban reckoned the loss to the French army as at least 500 officers and 10,000 soldiers; to French shipping, 8,000 seamen. Many came to England and Ireland, as offering the best chance of service and, in a rapidly expanding force, promotion. No one envisaged the small English army of 1689 as being ready, in experience or training, to play a leading role in the forces of the League of Augsburg. In Ireland, notably at Limerick and the Boyne, Huguenots helped defeat the Jacobites and their French allies and secure William III's throne. 'There are your persecutors, forward, lads, forward', shouted a Huguenot officer, pointing at the French beside the Boyne. Huguenot cavalry fought with frantic courage to cover the allied army's retreat at Landen. On one occasion, at Almanza, when Cavalier's Huguenots recognised a regiment that had last been seen terrorising the Cévennes there was a blood bath as they threw aside muskets to fight at bayonet point. Beside fighting spirit and example, the Huguenots brought to the raw English army a French professionalism and battle experience, with the vital specialist skills, which Vauban would particularly miss, in gunnery and engineering. They bought time while the English adjusted to the challenge of sustained war. In 1690 Schomberg declared that the king got better service from his three French regiments than from twice the number of any others. Neither William III nor Marlborough (who employed a Huguenot, Adam de Cardonnel as secretary and aide) undervalued their services. Add the contribution of Huguenot seamen, in the navy or as privateers, and the parallel experience of the Dutch as the other major beneficiary, and it seems reasonable to assert that the Louis XIV could not have been defeated without the Huguenot presence in the camp of his enemies.

The French were not, in the main, keen colonists. What was lost to Colbert's vision of an overseas empire by the exclusion from New France of Huguenots, is therefore highlighted by the enterprise shown by Huguenots, under duress. The diaspora saw families travel far for freedom and fortune. Emigrants found their way to Massachusetts, the Carolinas and New York to bring new life to colonial Protestantism. Benjamin Franklin used to recall a childhood memory of a preacher denouncing Louis XIV, the 'anti-Christ'. Under the shadow of French power and threats the Swiss could only take a few thousand. In 1686 Marshal Catinat ravaged the Vaudois; an object lesson but one that would have distressed François de Sales. The clockmakers who went to Geneva stayed to create a famous tradition. Some seamen ventured to Scandinavia. A number of La Rochelais enlisted under the Genevese soldier Lefort in Peter the Great's Russia. There were settlements all over Protestant Germany. The most important, favoured by the Great Elector, were in Brandenburg–Prussia. In Magdeburg, depopulated in the Thirty Years War, a thousand evolved a separate community, with its own surgeons, lawyers and pastors. At Berlin, alongside the garrison, grew a busy French township of some 4,000 souls, the real beginning of the capital city of the future. Some of their descendants would be among those marching into Paris in 1871 and 1940.

Richelieu had well understood the importance of public understanding of policy and the need to ensure the most favourable interpretation of controversial acts. Bitter experience taught Mazarin the same lesson. Louis came to realise it – but too late. It is hard, however, to imagine that the most skilful propaganda could have made much difference in 1685. Reduction in the number of presses, privileged treatment of those that remained, control of paper supplies and examination, in the Chancellor's office, of manuscripts, added up to an impressive system of domestic control. Meanwhile, the royalist theme, so majestically personified by the king, so strongly advertised in the routines of the court and through its obedient writers and artists, however impressive to Frenchmen and sympathetic foreigners, was actually counter-productive when viewed by the ever-growing number of foreign enemies. It is hard to imagine, therefore, that the most skilful propaganda could have made much difference in 1685 – nor that any system of censorship could do more than limit the damage to Louis's reputation at home. The combination of a tense international situation, fluent writers with shocking stories to tell, printers hungry for copy, and an avid readership, produced the greatest paper war since the Reformation. As early as 1685 Le Camus complained about the entry into France of the *Pastorales* of Jurieu, 'undoing in a day the work of months'. The authorities were unable to prevent it. Bayle's style reflected the confidence that came from his encyclopaedic learning and gift for communication: 'If people only knew the force and present meaning of the expression, no one would envy France the distinction of being "wholly Catholic" under Louis the Great. The Roman church is nothing but a fury and a whore.'

One consequence of Louis XIV's policy was to bring together, sharing common exile, Bayle, the pastor Claude[29] (Bossuet's old antagonist), Gilbert Burnet and John Locke (the last two finding the air of Holland beneficial in years of royalist reaction in England). The influence, on English opinion, of events in France is typified by Burnet, the Scottish broad churchman soon to be an English bishop. Already his *History of the Reformation* had sought to justify English schism. Now he enlarged on the dangers of Romanism. His work brought a retaliatory barrage from Bossuet. In his *Histoire des Variations* he condemned the 'variations', 'subtleties' and 'artifices' with which Protestants sought to heal differences and hide errors in the face of immutable truth. His charge could be answered. The rivalry of Jesuit and Jansenist showed that Rome had its 'variations'. Le Vassor's more profound argument, one that anticipates the liberal churchman's argument for toleration, was that 'disunity was necessary to penetrate to the depths of truth'. The Catholic ideal had been presented with the eloquence and logic that made Bossuet such a formidable protagonist. It was discredited by the imposition of revealed truth on a defenceless minority. The ordeal of the Hugenot roused disturbing questions about the nature of a God, in whose name men persecuted others who claimed also to know their God.

Revocation was an act of faith, but it was also an act of state. Criticism of the idea and the act led inevitably to criticism of the authority behind it. Exiles like Claude left France with an acute sense of grievance: their faith had been reviled, their professional integrity belittled. They rebelled not only against a church, but also against the establishment of which it was an integral part. 'Catholicism', wrote Fénelon, 'gave France its soul.' If that were so, exiled Huguenots would want a different France, would fight for it and hope to return to it. So their revolt went beyond the mandate of the French church to the very nature of authority, spiritual and secular, personified in a king who, by atrocities committed in his name, had released the ties of loyalty. It went beyond the person of Louis to the ideal of the unified state implied in his understanding of Divine Right Monarchy.

As the War of the League of Augsburg went on its costly way, conversion funds dried up, troops were sent to the front and policy toward the Huguenots became increasingly incoherent.[30] Those staunch or discreet enough to stand firm were sustained by the *Pastorales* and their belief that the League would save them. They clung to straws: first the coming of a Dutch fleet, then the expected death of Louis XIV. In fact, after his potentially dangerous operation for a fistula, in 1686, he remained in robust health.[31] Measures might be more half-hearted but he did not waver in his main idea. 'The king will never renew the Edict of Nantes, even if the enemy are at the Loire', wrote Maintenon in a later emergency. He was sustained by his amour propre, the conviction that he had acted properly, and by the parochial piety of the *dévôts* around him. His grandson Burgundy, Fénelon's protégé expressed a typical view: 'the recall now of the Huguenots would offer to the whole of Europe a pitiful inconstancy of principle'. Less obvious to us – but a weighty consideration – was the thankfulness, constantly expressed, of Catholics up and down the land. These included those in formerly Spanish territories where officials found that the Edict had helped the process of assimilation. However, coercion was abandoned.

In 1698, prompted by Cardinal Noailles and Pontchartrain, a minister since 1690 and about to become Chancellor, the council called for an inquiry;

in the following January secret instructions were given to *intendants* and clergy to desist from violence. In Languedoc, where Huguenot communities were most tenacious and communities most bitterly divided, Villars reported that the *curés* of Languedoc could not lose 'their habit of browbeating their parishes'. One such *curé* stopped a caravan of refugees and imprisoned them; his house was surrounded by a mob and he was killed. Retaliation provoked the traditional spirit of resistance: hunger and anger brought ready recruits. Old scores were paid off. Preachers emerged to arouse peasant passions. Guerilla bands formed wearing the white shirts, *camisards*, that gave the rising its name. A leader was found in 20-year-old Jean Cavalier. There had already been a small rising in the Cévennes in 1682,[32] after Huguenot resistance to the closure of temples was met by a brutal *dragonnade*. There had since been a spread of 'prophesying'. Now insurrection flamed in an atmosphere of nervous tension and Biblical fervour. The Huguenots called their assemblies the 'Desert', an allusion to the Hebrews who had waited for forty years in Sinai to enter 'the promised land'. They were further roused by the pamphlets of émigrés and the colourful imagery of their preachers. As happened in Commonwealth England, when traditional social structures and discipline dissolved, the Cévenols responded ecstatically to the visionary and apocalyptic, to *illuminés* who foamed at the mouth, fell into trances, delivered messages of wild hope – and incited them to righteous war.

In harsh and mountainous terrain the revolt posed a severe military problem. When the troops failed to come to grips with the skulking bands, they burnt their villages. Louis formally ordered it in 1703. The revolt diverted 20,000 men and several of Louis's best generals. Villars was there in 1704, the year of Blenheim. It took three years and some royal concessions, to secure the region. Though the allies were not, as Louis feared, able to open up another southern front, the Huguenots of the Cévennes contributed materially to the allied cause and the defeat of France. That is only part of the significance of the rising.

Royal policies had succeeded in destroying institutional, clerical Protestantism in France. They had destroyed, in the remnant, whether stayers or leavers, compromisers or resisters, the respect for authority and the king which had been so marked before; also any lingering wish for a rapprochement with Rome. The hypocritical gestures which sufficed, apparently, for 'the converted' were a shock to those Huguenots who had been attracted to the devotional movement in the church but had remained wary of the miraculous elements in its teaching. What did Catholic veneration for the Real Presence amount to if the sacraments could be treated as a civil test?

So Huguenotism recovered that element of protest against the mechanical and formal aspects of ritual which the work of De Sales, Bérulle and the Jansenists had done so much to dispel. The Huguenots had escaped from the clammy grip of a theology of compromise; they were back in the heroic age, and issues were clearer. As Vauban put it, 'the blood of martyrs has always been an infallible means of enhancing a persecuted faith'. An individualist sect, drawing its vitality from the Bible, would not be blotted out by the destruction of buildings or removal of pastors.

It was in a mood of resignation, in March 1715, that the crown made an empty gesture of acceptance: 'The Huguenots' long stay in France is sufficient proof that they have embraced the Catholic faith, without which they would have been neither suffered nor tolerated.' It was a limp formula and few could have been deceived, certainly not the Huguenots who benefited from the first fruits of toleration. On 21 August 1715, Antoine Court presided over a Provincial synod. It was a few days before the death of the king; almost thirty years after the Edict of Fontainebleau. That had been hailed by Catholics as Louis XIV's supreme act of statesmanship. It had certainly had the most profound and wide-ranging effects, but not those looked for by its apologists. The Huguenot body had survived: slimmer, indeed, and scarred, but, in its own terms, undeniably fit.

Notes

1. For the Edict and its significance see N.M. Sutherland, 'The Huguenots and the Edict of Nantes, 1598–1629', in I. Scouloudi (ed.), *The Huguenots in Britain and their French Background* (London, 1987), pp. 158–68.

2. The theme is developed in J. Parker, *La Rochelle and the French Monarchy* (London, 1980).

3. Élitist, zealously puritanical, charitable, this secretive body was suspected by Mazarin as a front for political activity and by some bishops as a cell in the church. It was losing its influence by 1660 when *Parlement* proscribed all assemblies which met without the king's authorisation, but its members were influential in the stifling of Molière's *Tartuffe* (1664) and its satire on religious hypocrisy.

4. Like all demographic exercises in this period there is room for doubt about any precise figure. This is offered as a middle estimate between Labrousse, 1.2 million in 1598 and Mours, 856,000 in 1670. E. Labrousse, *Un Foi, une Loi, un Roi* (Paris/Geneva, 1967), p. 28. S. Mours, *Le Protestantisme en France au XVIIe siècle* (Paris, 1967), p. 86. It is possible that there was a modest increase in the early years of the century; likely that there was already a declining trend by Louis XIV's personal reign, which then certainly accelerated.

5. Lamoignon de Bâville, 'king of Languedoc', *intendant* from 1685 to 1719, came from the high robe nobility, with strong connections at court and in *Parlement*. He was an outstanding administrator but had no illusions about the difficulty of implementing

the edict. Beik, op. cit., pp. 116–17. He knew, for example, that few priests would be effective missionaries since they would not understand the local Occitan *patois*.

6. For such rhetoric – in this case that of the *co-adjuteur* of Arles (Huguenot country) – for the role of church assemblies and the ecclesiastical background, in particular moves towards reunion, see J. Orcibal, *Louis XIV et les protestants* (Paris, 1951).

7. Jacobus Arminius taught that Christ died for all believers. If sinners repented and believed they could become elect of God. His liberal views were condemned at the Synod of Dordt (1619) but they gained ground at the expense of Calvinist orthodoxy and the doctrine of predestination.

8. *Epistle to the Romans*, 13: 12.

9. Professor at Sedan, he left for Rotterdam in 1681. Thence he strove to maintain discipline and orthodoxy among fellow Huguenots while maintaining the attack on Louis XIV. With Benôit he created a massive machine for propaganda.

10. For Bossuet, see also p. 39 and pp. 87–8.

11. Pierre Bérulle (1575–1629), writer, preacher and teacher, may be called the father-figure of the *dévôts*. François de Sales and Vincent de Paul were among his disciples. The object of the Oratory was to establish a new model for the priesthood. The rift between him and his protégé Richelieu over the latter's foreign policy foreshadowed the painful dilemma implicit in the statesmen's attempts – Mazarin's and, at times, Louis XIV's – to be both *bon français* and a good Catholic.

12. For Arnauld and Jansenism, and their quarrel with the Jesuits see p. 219 and pp. 316 et seq.

13. The *real* presence of Christ in the Eucharistic elements, Bread and Wine, after consecration.

14. For Grotius in the context of international law, see pp. 153–4 and 177, n. 4.

15. For Leibnitz in other contexts, see p. 176 and p. 179, n. 25.

16. See pp. 316 et seq.

17. For the character and influence of Mme de Maintenon, see also pp. 325–6.

18. He also impresses historians. For Briggs he is 'the most impressive, purcly clerical politician of the century' (*Communities of Belief*, Oxford, 1989, pp. 211–12). To his secretary he was 'the Pope on this side of the mountains'. Louis had helped promote the authority of the archbishop of Paris when, in 1674, he attached the *duché-pairie* of Saint-Cloud to the see.

19. See also p. 87. Bossuet actually drew up the Articles, representing a more moderate view than that of Charles-Maurice Le Tellier, archbishop of Reims (with his war minister brother's interest behind him), who wanted a General Council. The gist of the Articles, embodying the theory of the 'Two Kingdoms' is contained in the first: 'St Peter and his successors in the Church at large have only God's authority to act in spiritual matters.'

20. Pierre Bayle (1647–1706) was briefly a Catholic before coming to a liberal Protestant stance and becoming professor at Sedan, then at Rotterdam (1681). His journal, *Nouvelles de la République des Lettres* (started in 1684) was an influential vehicle for the ideal of tolerance, both against Louis XIV and rigorous fellow-Calvinists led by Jurieu. See also pp. 326 and 329, n. 11.

21. For the sustained efforts of the Franciscan friar, see R.J.W. Evans, *The Making of the Habsburg Monarchy* (Oxford, 1979), pp. 305–6. As the Pope knew, there was opposition to Spinola at Rome and Louis's attitude was realistic.

22. The zealous and impulsive archbishop of Valence is here quoted by Orcibal, op. cit., p. 105.

23. Élie Benôit (1640–1728), a former pastor at Alençon, ministered to a congregation in Delft. Refuees' experiences, with many other letters and documents (some originals now lost, so his collection is a valuable source of evidence) were brought together in his immense *L'Histoire de l'Edit de Nantes* (5 vols, 1695). With Jurieu (p. 236, n. 9) he helped create a formidable propaganda machine.

24. I am following here the argument advanced in R. Mettam's article, 'Louis XIV and the persecution of Huguenots: the role of the ministers and royal officials', in Scouloudi, op. cit., pp. 198–216.

25. He would be particularly aware of the effect on the army since a significant number serving in the artillery and engineering units were Huguenot.

26. For these quotations and for the reception of the edict – and reaction – see Orcibal, op. cit., pp. 110–25.

27. The queen of Sweden (1632–54) abdicated from the throne she inherited as a child from Gustav Adolf, became Rome's most illustrious convert and spent the rest of her eccentric life (died, 1689) in Rome.

28. As is convincingly argued by R. Gwynn, *The Huguenot Heritage* (London, 1985), pp. 144–59. On the other side of the argument, the way in which merchant networks continued to flourish irrespective of religious affiliation is explored in L.M. Cullen, 'The Huguenots from the perspective of the merchant networks of Western Europe (1680–1790): the example of the brandy trade', in E.J. Caldicott, H. Gough and J.-P. Pittion (eds), *The Huguenots and Ireland: Anatomy of an Emigration* (Dun Laoghaire, 1987), pp. 129–49.

29. Jean Claude, author of the most celebrated of Huguenot pamphlets, *Plaintes des Protestants, cruellement opprimez* had been engaged, almost to the end, in theological debate with Catholics. He was typical of many ministers who held on till forced to leave; in his case to Holland and a pension from William of Orange.

30. For the incoherence of governmental and ecclesiastical actions, see Orcibal, op. cit., pp. 147–56.

31. See p. 280.

32. This was old Waldensian country, one of the few areas where Huguenots, evoking a response where thirteenth-century ideas about a people's church were embedded in folk memory, counted many peasants among their adherents.

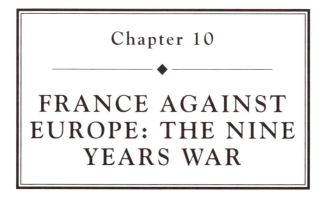

Chapter 10

♦

FRANCE AGAINST EUROPE: THE NINE YEARS WAR

So M. de Louvois is dead – this great minister, so eminent, whose *moi* . . . was so extensive and who was at the centre of so many things.

MME DE SÉVIGNÉ, 1691

The king knows about the misery of his people; nothing is hidden from him.

M. DE MAINTENON, October 1692

LOUVOIS'S WAR

Louis had gained nothing by the moderation and sense of propriety on which he had plumed himself in 1683. German opinion was not impressed by his claim that he had refused to take advantage of the Turkish invasion by attacking Habsburg lands in the east. From his assault on the Huguenots, we have seen, he lost much more. In the diplomatic climate of the post-Revocation years it was inevitable that he should be commonly portrayed as an aggressor. The judicious Leibnitz, in his *Mars Christianissimus* of 1685, called for a union between Holland and the smaller German states. The Great Elector's minister, Fuchs, declared that only understanding between Brandenburg and the United Provinces, and their alliance with England, would be able to deliver Europe from 'the universal yoke of France'. In March 1686 Brandenburg made a defensive alliance with the Emperor. In Holland William exploited to the full the energy and bitterness of the Huguenots, welcomed their soldiers and sailors to his forces, and supported Jurieu's network of spies. Fagel[1] developed a propaganda machine which enlarged upon the menace of France.

Judgements made in these circumstances were plainly affected by previous events and coloured by Protestant propaganda. Inevitably they present the motives of the Emperor, fighting the heathen in the plains of Hungary, and William, working at home to strengthen the party of Calvinist rigour and Orange loyalties, in the most favourable light. But Leopold was not being altruistic when he launched campaigns to secure Hungary for the Habsburgs. As ever, *hausmacht* was stronger than any vague concept of German interest. There was more of dynasticism than of Christian brotherhood in his grudging treatment of his Polish allies. He had not given up hope of recovering Alsace; he thought it possible that he would secure the entire Spanish Succession. For Leopold Ratisbon was but a truce, necessary to give him time to concentrate on exploiting his victories in the east. For William, though his policies might be devious and risky, there was no wavering in his pursuit of what he believed was owed to his dynasty and, it may be added – required by Protestant Europe. He would venture all to win the English throne and strengthen his hand for the next round of war against his mortal enemy. Louis and his ministers were aware of these settled convictions and tended now to think in defensive terms. Unfortunately, at times, their actions belied their intentions. The main intention was to turn Ratisbon from twenty-year truce to definitive peace. Committed enemies would not recognise a fundamental change of policy. Neutral or wavering powers might be impressed, however, by moderate language and cautious moves. Without German allies, or sufficient pretext, William and Leopold would be reluctant to proceed to war. The growing size of armies and navies, the unprecedented resources available to a large alliance, the great issues at stake and the venomous spirit introduced by the Huguenots, made it likely that a war, once engaged, would be intensive and prolonged. The war came – and lasted for nine years. It was not what France needed or Louis wanted. William incurred heavy defeats, overall the allies of the League of Augsburg fared indifferently – and yet they cannot be said to have lost the peace. The resources of states, specially those of England, proved to be as important a factor as the verdict of the battlefield. Given the background and the outcome, it is reasonable to ask of the events that led to war: was Louis's judgement seriously at fault? Was he outmanoeuvred? Was he simply unlucky?

Louis first practised conciliation. In the Palatinate he put forward the strong claim of Madame,[2] his sister-in-law: she was the sister of the late Elector Palatine, whose conversion to Rome had dealt a blow to the Protestant cause and whose death without heir left uncertain the status of a territory of high strategic value. When, in 1685, the Count of Neuberg, the

Emperor's godfather, took possession, Louis renounced Madame's claim and proposed arbitration by the Pope. It was rejected by the German princes, Neuberg stayed in place – and Louis was left to wonder whether conciliation had been the right policy.

Where anything to do with Spain was concerned, with its imminent succession problem in mind, Louis was less amenable. Leopold arranged marriage for his daughter Marie-Antoinette to the Elector of Bavaria, hoping to detach him from his long-term alliance with France. He then tried to secure for him the governorship of the Spanish Netherlands. Louis retaliated by massing troops on the Pyrenees frontier and told Madrid that, 'if His Majesty should give over any part of his states to one who had absolutely no claim, he might find it hard to preserve those lands which touch him most nearly'. The threat sufficed and Spain yielded. But such advantage was dearly bought. Catholic and Protestant states drew together. At Augsburg, in August 1686, Spain, Bavaria, the new Elector Palatine and Sweden bound themselves into a league, on behalf of the various circles in which they had lands, to stop the intrusion of Louis into Germany, and to bind him to the treaties, not only of Nijmegen and Ratisbon – but, significantly, of Münster as well. Saxony and Brandenburg held back, but the latter had already entered into a secret compact with the Emperor and guaranteed his rights in the Empire, specifically in the Palatinate. Louis saw revived the perennial threat of encirclement. The League was nominally defensive – 'to rescue any state attacked or [patently referring to the *Réunions*] troubled by unjust researches or illegal demands'. But he believed that it would become, whenever it suited him, Leopold's war coalition. Acting on this presumption he made pre-emptive strikes – and in the process incited the war which he would have preferred to avoid. The question of responsibility for the War of the League of Augsburg (or Nine Years War) is therefore impossible to answer. As so often, to track the steps towards one of Europe's major wars is to experience a sense of the near-inevitable. As the process develops its own momentum there is needed at least one leading statesman with a powerful motive – and design – for avoiding war. In this period, when the values of princes were formed by an aristocratic court culture whose prevailing idea was of war as an honourable pursuit, not to be judged solely in terms of material profit or loss to state or people, such a ruler would be exceptional indeed. Only after years of defeat and social distress would an influential group at the French court begin to think the unthinkable: that it could be right to sacrifice territories for peace, and, in the writing of Fénelon, to envisage an alternative ideal for monarchy: the avoidance of war and promotion of the arts of peace.

In this situation, as Europe trembled on the brink of war, Louis's long-running quarrel with the Papacy entered a new phase.[3] The old dispute over franchises, never resolved, came to the fore with the appointment of a new ambassador, Lavardin, armed, it was rumoured at Rome, with orders to maintain the traditional rights of the French quarter. Innocent had announced that he would not receive him until these privileges were renounced. Louis responded that the example of other sovereigns was irrelevant to him. God had established him as an example to others; they might be, at least nominally appointed by the Pope; his mandate came direct from God. Louis had reason to be exasperated by a Pope who seemed to obstruct, or to deplore his every move. It was maladroit, however, to allow considerations of prestige to blind him to the ill effects of a squabble over status on his delicate position in Europe. He paid the price when he needed the Pope's support over the question of Cologne.

Here more than prestige was at stake. The little Rhineland electorate, through which Louis's armies had marched towards Holland in 1672, was a prime strategic counter. As a virtual appanage of the Bavarian Wittelsbachs, it had long been amenable to the military requirements of France. When the archbishop died in 1686, Cologne became a test case of the attitude of Pope, Emperor and King, a microcosm of the larger struggle. Louis put forward his long-faithful client Fürstenberg whom he had already installed at Strasbourg. He was opposed by a brother of the Elector of Bavaria, Joseph-Clement, aged 17. The chapter's much-canvassed votes narrowly favoured Fürstenberg but he did not secure a two-thirds majority. The Pope then declared that he would confirm the Bavarian. It confirmed Louis's opinion that a Pope who could act in such a partisan – and uncanonical – fashion was in league with the Emperor and would stop at nothing. Indeed, in a letter to Leopold, Innocent wrote that war against France might be 'the only prompt and effective means of bringing her to compensate all Europe for a part of the wrongs and injustices she has committed'.

So the Pope threw the moral weight of the Papacy into the scales against the king. The king's response was typically robust. He would defend the peace by a concerted display of military force. In a letter to the Pope and cardinals he wrote that 'there is much to show that the conduct of the Pope is going to cause a general war in Christendom'. He went on to threaten Innocent with the occupation of Avignon and Cologne. He followed it with a public declaration in September 1688 to justify his resort to arms. This unusual manifesto recited the injuries that, since Ratisbon, had thwarted his peaceful intentions. His case rested on the unwillingness of Leopold to convert the truce into a permanent peace; the unprovoked formation of the League of Augsburg, the denial of his sister-in-law's rights in the Palatinate, and an elected bishop's rights in Cologne. The strongest argument lay with his troops who moved with striking rapidity to implement Louvois's long-laid plans. Avignon was seized, the Palatinate invaded and Philippsburg taken, with a sector of the Rhine's left bank. These were measures too drastic to be the basis for any negotiation. They were not about peace but strategic advantage.

The accession of the Catholic James II to the English throne in February 1685, after it had long seemed likely that he would be excluded, had been an important part of Louis's picture of Europe and the assessment of religious and political trends which had led Louis to decide upon the Revocation. James II was sensitive about Louis's overt patronage and heavy interest in the Catholic cause in England. He had his own programme for relieving Catholics from disabilities. It was controversial enough without the fears aroused by the influx of persecuted Huguenots. In June 1688 the birth of a son to James and Mary of Modena concentrated the minds of his opponents. The unsuccessful trial of seven bishops for opposition to his Declaration of Indulgence indicated the level of hostility to James and the chance of a successful coup. William of Orange, linked to England through his Stuart mother and by marriage to James's daughter Mary, accepted the invitation of a group of magnates to come to England. It is possible that he did not expect to be placed on the throne but to undertake some form of regency which would give him influence over English policy. The stakes were high. The financial resources of England, her large navy, and potentially effective army together could alter the balance of European power. Alliance between two leading maritime and commercial states was indeed an alluring prospect, but the risk involved was formidable. Invasion by sea, in late autumn, with a large English fleet at sea and an army, also presumed to be loyal, waiting to receive it, was hazardous.

Louis could have made it impossible. He was kept well informed by ambassador Tallard,[4] whose unenviable task was to track and interpret to Versailles the factious intrigues and contests within a political system which the king little understood and instinctively despised. From The Hague D'Avaux[5] sent urgent warnings about William's preparations. Louis suggested to James that the English and French fleets should join in the channel to bar William's way. James demurred. He had to lose his throne before he would be prepared to solicit the aid that could have saved it. There was another possibility. Louis could mount an attack on Holland, or other territory in which William had an interest, and so force him to abandon his project. The issue was debated at Versailles where it was the fashion (reflecting James II's own complacency) to mock the idea of William's invading England. The decision was to be momentous.

William's successful expedition and subsequent elevation to be, with Mary, joint sovereign, were to be significant not only for his adopted country but for Europe. The notion of a 'turning-point' should usually be treated with caution. A decisive change is not readily discernible to contemporaries. Even when it has been understood and noted there have usually been too many subsequent events – here the battle of Blenheim comes to mind – for the original events to be seen, uniquely, to be 'the turning point'. However, in relation to the events of 1688–89, the phrase is appropriate. Marlborough's epoch-making victory at Blenheim only strengthens the argument. What Englishman, in 1688 could have conceived of the country's becoming a great military power, of one of his countrymen leading the army of a coalition of which England's financial and material resources were the main support? Few Frenchmen surely, present at the debate at Versailles, could have had an idea of what would hang on the king's decision. Marshal Villars's account[6] reveals much about political and military attitudes, and the dominant influence of Louvois:

> The court hesitated as to its policy, whether it should aid king James, about to be attacked, or should prevent the peace with the Turks which was being made and which would bring down upon us the whole forces of Emperor and the Empire. M de Louvois . . . decided upon the second course. In effect nothing was more important for us than to secure so powerful a diversion in our favour as that of the Turks. Besides, what prospect was there that so great a revolution could take place in England without great trouble and discord? This suited us better than settled government under king James; the more so that we had already seen England, at peace and under the authority of king Charles II, a devoted ally, compel that sovereign to declare war against us.

At the end of September the French army marched, therefore, not against Maastricht but Philippsburg. Madame, Princesse Palatine, wrote of her misgivings as her husband left for Germany and nominal command of part of the operation. Within less than two months the French had seized most of the strong points on the Rhine from Cologne to Alsace and secured their eastern frontier. But on 5 November William landed unmolested at Torbay. By the end of the year he was master of the kingdom.

Louvois envisaged a mainly defensive war in which France, being encircled and having to fight on several fronts, must limit, where possible, the vulnerable points of entry. It was the lesson, so dearly learned, of France's engagement in the Thirty Years War and its sequel: open frontiers and devastated lands. Louis would need no reminding of the state of Champagne and Burgundy in the year of his coronation. French armies could not cover the whole of its eastern frontiers. Vauban's system of fortifications was not designed to be a Maginot line. A letter from Chamlay,[7] Louis's trusted military advisor, indicates that aggression might sometimes be the best form of defence. The means Louvois proposed 'would make the king absolute master of the Rhine'. The means was the devastation of the Palatinate.

To neutralise that unfortunate land would shorten the front and teach a lesson to the Emperor and his client Elector Philip-William (of the Palatinate). It can be argued – and would be again by supporters of Marlborough – that scorched earth was an accepted convention of warfare. It had been a grim feature of the Thirty Years War. But the pillaging of those years had been as much a matter of indiscipline as of policy. This operation was cold-blooded and thorough. In the summer of 1689 French soldiers sacked the Electoral capital, Heidelberg, Mannheim, newly embellished by the late Elector, Spier, Worms, some fifty castles and many villages. Barns were burned, stores ransacked; refugees spread woeful tales. Saint-Simon, passing through Spier in 1694, noticed the few remaining inhabitants burrowing under ruins or living in cellars. The French general, Tessé, had been unhappy at Louvois's order. Meaning well he sent some ancestral canvases to Madame, but she was inconsolable: her letters speak of her distress at the ravaging of her homeland and her lonely position at a generally unsympathetic court.[8] The action of the king she so much admired made a mockery of his championship of her Palatinate claim.

Louvois would have gone further but Louis stopped the destruction of Triers. The strategic point was gained. The scorched earth of the Palatinate would not sustain an army, Alsace could be left lightly covered; French armies could be concentrated in Flanders and North Italy. Politically it was a serious blunder, evoking in Germany a rare display of public feeling. It took this violation to bring Germans to a sense of nationhood. Pamphlets and broadsheets, some crudely illustrated, described the atrocities of these 'huns' who had reduced warfare to armed robbery. Louis was a monster who claimed to act for God but really ruled on the principles of Machiavelli and the model of the Turk. Some writers claimed that France was an upstart and revived the myth that the real descendants of Charlemagne were the Franks east of the Rhine. The moral was that the German peoples had brought calamity on themselves by their good faith, naivety and indifference to what was happening outside their frontiers. Mazarin's constructive German policy, embodied in the League of the Rhine, was history. One day, a great German historian, Leopold von Ranke, would be asked whom the Germans were fighting in the Franco-Prussian war of 1870–71. 'Louis XIV' was his answer.

TOWARDS TOTAL WAR

The war which Louis had hoped to contain now spread. In May 1689 the Emperor and the United Provinces entered into alliance. Promising support for his Spanish Succession claim William persuaded Leopold to switch his main military effort from the east to the Rhine. The two sovereigns engaged themselves to restore Western Europe to the position of 1659, to restore Lorraine to its duke and Pinerolo to the duke of Savoy. After the death of his French queen Marie-Louise and subsequent marriage to the Emperor's sister-in-law Maria-Anna of Neuberg, Charles II of Spain was tied, for the time, to the Emperor's party. When Louis sent troops to aid James II in Ireland, England promptly declared war. Savoy joined the coalition in 1690. The German states, Brandenburg, Saxony, Hanover, Hesse–Cassel were already pledged by earlier agreement. Sweden later lent assistance to the coalition which, for all its divergences of aim, faced Louis with will and resources equal to his own.

Looking back from 1783 and the Peace of Versailles which ended the fifth major war between Britain and France since 1689, one can look at that fateful year as the start of a second 'Hundred Years War'. The War of the Spanish Succession closely following the Nine Years War; the Seven Years War that of the Austrian Succession – it was as if the intervening years were just a respite, with the chance to re-group, find new allies, rather than a time of settled peace and re-appraisal. For the English or French statesman then there was likely to be, beyond all tactical considerations, an assumption of certain permanent interests, pointing inexorably to further conflict with the state across the channel: the natural enemy in a crucial struggle for power, influence, trade and – ever more important – for colonies. The intensification of this rivalry can be seen as following directly from the relative decline, first of Spain, then of Holland. It has also, at first, an ideological aspect. Crude English slogans like 'Down with Popery and Wooden Shoes' were mob renderings of the more sophisticated, but no less keenly felt revulsion of large parts of a Protestant ruling class from absolutist, Catholic France. 'I hear he [Louis, suffering from a fistula] stinckes alive . . . and so will his memory to all eternity', wrote the young Edmund Verney in 1685.[9] Later, as the value of colonies was perceived and commercial interests became more influential, economic factors become more prominent.

In each war, of course, there were allies with different agendas. Within both countries there were differences over war aims and priorities: in 1701–13, for example, in France about the use of the navy; in England over the costly commitment to continental war. The overall aims of statesmen were, in any case, affected more by traditional values, personal rivalries – and, England's case, by party positions, than may be allowed for in the historian's overview. The most significant group of dissidents in France, the circle of the duke of Burgundy, would espouse a programme as reactionary as it was idealistic. Even in England, countering traditional opposition to standing armies, Marlborough's victories started a minor cult of military glory. Blenheim would be England's Versailles. Less rigid towards the end than his enemies, Louis showed an unexpected ability to trim and adjust in the face of adversity. Reaching, in distress, for a voice to reach his people, he remained the dynast, his view patrimonial: the state was his domain. In the way they came about, were fought, and concluded, the wars of 1689 to 1714 seem to have more in common with the past than with the future. But there are features that anticipate later developments, in the nature of war and its impact on government and society.

The Nine Years War – or War of the League of Augsburg as it is otherwise called – was to prove intense and wide-ranging, with aspects pointing towards the 'total' war of modern times. With ever-larger forces available on both sides, a significant naval dimension, and improved ways of raising money, there was a closer relationship between financial and administrative structures, and the fighting efforts of the major powers. The creation of the Bank of England in 1694, and the credit consequently made available, played a vital part in the defeat of France in a war of resources. The wealth that was making London the financial centre of Europe made England the banker of the coalition. The interacting process of war and state-building can be studied at the fringe, in the wars of the north, in the enlargement of government and new military potential of Brandenburg and Russia, and – providing an object lesson in the penalty for failing to develop – the relative powerlessness of Poland.

For this expansion in the scope and scale of war Louis was most responsible. He set the pace and influenced the tone. The size of the army he maintained, around 300,000[10] during the Nine Years War, and the way in which he used it as an instrument of policy, forced other rulers to answer in kind, copying the French example in recruitment, training and weaponry. 'In effect,

Sire, one might believe oneself to be in the army of Your Majesty', reported D'Avaux at a review of the Dutch army in 1686. After 1689 the size of the forces of what came to be called the Grand Alliance compelled Louis to sustain a level of recruitment beyond what had been thought possible. It is to the credit of his generals, notably Luxembourg and Catinat, and to the mechanisms of control and supply created by the Le Telliers, that the French were generally victorious. When, however, the diplomats met at Ryswick to consider peace, the material state of their respective countries, with the ability to mount further campaigns, was more significant as a bargaining counter than battles won or towns or territories taken. France did not lose an important battle but she cannot be said to have won the war.

On 10 July 1690, William III won a scrambled victory over James II at the Boyne. It was an event of immense significance in Irish history; no less for France. Louis had hoped to keep William out of Flanders by supporting the Jacobites there with troop transports, an escorting fleet and 7,000 soldiers. At first William's expatriate Huguenot general Schomberg fared badly and William had to take command in person. He was there when Luxembourg defeated Waldeck at Fleurus, inflicting 10,000 casualties. Ten days later, however, his victory settled the Irish issue and he was ready to campaign in Flanders. James returned to the hospitality of Louis at Saint-Germain. William was personally unpopular and there was resentment towards his Continental policy and high taxes. Yet French hopes that he would be overturned by another coup soon began to fade. Louis's patronage only harmed the Jacobite cause. His refusal to recognise William as king was consistent with his view of hereditary right. It was also William's strongest political card.

In Flanders, the old prize-fighting ring of Europe, in laborious sieges, occasional ordered confrontations of close-ranked infantry (now with the bayonet to supplement musket and *fusil*), punctuated by ferocious charges of cavalry, the French won several notable, but never conclusive victories. The coalition was hard put to it to match Louvois's well-practised apparatus of war. After the death of Duke Charles of Lorraine in 1690 it produced no general to rival marshal Luxembourg, the *tapissier de Notre Dame*.[11] This fiery little man had stepped into Condé's shoes during the Dutch war and showed much of the great captain's flair for battle. He was quick to size up a battlefield situation and he was ruthless, undeterred by appalling casualties since the enemy suffered worse. The casualties of Waldeck's army who fell at Fleurus were about a fifth of the total engaged.

Attending Vauban's great sieges of Mons and Namur (1691 and 1692 respectively), after the preliminary reviews and marches, Louis was in his element. Inspecting trenches, hearty and oblivious to the dangers from enemy mortars and snipers, fussing about the details of the operation, he may have been an embarrassment to his generals. But he found the experience deeply satisfying. It is easy to ridicule his performance of the part of soldier king. Was it all for show, for palace consumption? Vanity would have been natural enough in these years of victory. The plaudits of his tame historians and poets did not come amiss. Perhaps it is fair, also, to suggest that he found it a relief to be away for a time from the serious debates and hard decisions of council. Also that his constant interest (aided by his excellent memory for names and careers), giving young bloods the impression that he was with them in spirit, sustained them under fire. The steadiness of French troops, the reckless courage of noble officers – without which Steenkerke might have been lost – owed something to his example of devotion to duty. When the authority of the state is embodied in a royal person, his bearing, the way in which he expresses his values and his idea of leadership, have an undeniable effect. The point may be reinforced by comparison with the poor morale of French troops, with more than one shameful rout, during the Seven Years War under the flaccid rule of Louis XV.

After the fall of Namur William retaliated with a sudden attack at Steenkerke (August 1692) which took the French by surprise. On rough ground their cavalry were unable at first to come into action and the infantry were driven back. William seems to have lost control in the smoke and confusion. The battle could have gone either way. It was a counter-attack by the infantry of the king's household that saved the day for Luxembourg. As their officers scrambled into action they were too rushed to dress properly and fought with their cravats loosely knotted about their necks. Soon everyone at Versailles was wearing cravats *à la Steenkerke*. There is much to be learned from the history of fashion.

After the death of Louvois in 1691 the Le Tellier dynasty was represented by his son Barbésieux. Louis did not trust his new war minister's judgement and preferred to take the advice of Chamlay, or that of the last general to catch his ear – or to follow his own instinct. After 1693 he made no further visits to the front but managed all from Versailles. Beside their superiority on the battlefield, the French enjoyed two advantages: interior lines and an undivided command. Yet the main impression of their war effort is one of incoherence. With a growing need for peace, Louis looked for short-term diplomatic advantage, relying on pressure on several fronts to exploit allied disunity. This strategy of dispersal is evident in the campaign of 1693.

William was finding it difficult to raise troops and Luxembourg, with over 100,000 might hope for a crushing victory. Louis directed half the troops to the Rhine front, to follow up the capture of Heidelberg and overawe the German princes. Even so Luxembourg had superior numbers when he attacked William at Neerwinden, in the plain between Liège and Louvain on 29 July. It was another victory gained by furious charges in the face of lethal fusillades and the gradual breakdown of a resolute linear defence. The allies lost 14,000 men and seventy cannon; the French 8,000. Notre-Dame was draped once more with captive standards. There were few at court who did not mourn a family member: the cult of courage took a terrible toll. To mark his appreciation Louis instituted the Order of Saint-Louis, first of modern decorations of valour.[12] Luxembourg went on to take Courtrai and William to defend his policies before Parliament.

Neerwinden marked the apogee of French military dominance. At first stalemate ensued, with no perceptible shift in the military balance. In 1694 Luxembourg fought a skilful defensive campaign: there were no significant actions. Saint-Simon served under him and relieved his boredom by keeping a journal: we may be grateful that it became a habit.[13] In January 1695 Luxembourg died and was replaced by Villeroi, a brave and honourable man but a fumbling general. In this year William was able, at last, to make a substantial gain. The recapture of Namur shocked the French, strengthened William's domestic position and stiffened his resolve to hold out for good terms. Two more years elapsed before the end of the war. The diplomatic process was bound to be complicated when so many powers were involved, and distinct, if not opposed interests were to be satisfied. Looming over the diplomats was the great issue, the Spanish Succession: the potential rewards there were of a different order from what might be gained or lost in the bargaining at Ryswick. It meant that the Ryswick business had a provisional air about it. The players might appear to be intent on their cards – but now and again they looked nervously over their shoulders.

THE NECESSITY OF PEACE

As early as 1693 Daguerre, a French merchant, was used to sound out Dutch opinion in exploratory talks. Because Louis would not recognise William as sovereign, nor therefore his representatives, English interests had to be dealt with indirectly, through his Dutch officials. Louis held to the belief that he could impose succession terms on England; a sine qua non for William was French recognition of his English crown. Progress, unsurprisingly, was very slow. Meanwhile diplomatic efforts to create a 'Third Party' had broken down.[14]

That costly failure reveals how much had been lost in credibility and bargaining power since 1661, and how isolated France had become. Realising that it would be cripplingly expensive, Louis had wanted a short war. He saw the Emperor as the main obstacle to peace. So Colbert de Croissy attempted to bring pressure on the Emperor through a new version of the alliances with Sweden and key German powers which had been so effective in the past. Through baron d'Asfeld, a Swedish soldier of French ancestry, he wooed Charles XI of Sweden, Ernest Augustus, the ambitious duke of Hanover, and the new Elector of Saxony, George William IV (succeeded in 1691). Sweden was offended by the 'reunion' of Zweibrücken and Charles XI was determined to stay neutral and to strengthen his domestic position by the *reduktion*: his recovery of crown lands which was a prime example, in this period, of successful absolutist policy. Hanover soon proved faithless, rightly perceiving Imperial patronage to offer a better chance of securing the coveted Electorate (granted in 1692) than Louis XIV's money. Denmark was brought in to chastise Hanover, but to no avail, since the two powers ended a brief war (1693) with a treaty. Up to that point William had taken the 'Third Party' project seriously; 'I do not see what we can do to stop it', he wrote to Heinsius (November 1693). Croissy made no headway with Saxony but had high hopes of the bishop of Münster, France's ally in the Dutch War. He too played a double game, receiving subsidies but continuing to send troops to the Emperor. A better response might have been expected from the Rhineland princes but Louis XIV forbade any approach there since, he reasoned, they were already either occupied, ravaged or threatened, and that would be enough to persuade them to press for peace. Altogether it was a far cry from the Cardinals' policy and Mazarin's League of the Rhine. It shows how seriously the Dutch War and the *réunions* had affected German opinion. D'Asfeld gave up and took the logical step of joining the French army – and an argument which the French could still win. Versailles was left to ponder the cost – Hanover 1,850,000 *livres* in two years, Denmark, and Münster, both over 2 million in a longer period. Would more money have achieved a better result? It was not a question that Louis appreciated in the grim conditions of 1694–95.

Yearning for peace Louis made the first significant breakthrough in June 1696 with the defection of Victor Amadeus, duke of Savoy.[15] The fact that he had adhered to the League of Augsburg had represented a serious failure on the part of French diplomacy. Like his predecessors, Victor Amadeus would always try to capitalise on his duchy's strategic position. It is likely, however, that he would have inclined to the more powerful neighbour if he had not been treated so insensitively. First Louis had played him off against his mother, then forced him to accept three thousand French troops in the duchy. After the Edict of Fontainebleau he attacked the Vaudois in their Alpine valleys, ordered the duke to support him on his side of the mountains and, when he objected, offered to send troops to assist him. When it came to war the consequence would have been more serious but for the resourceful generalship of Catinat. An unlikely victor in a four-year struggle to contain the ambitious duke, Catinat had started life as a lawyer, without advantage of birth and had made his way through merit. He was a careful general, thorough in planning and in care for his men, unambitious, indeed something of a philosopher. He defeated Victor Amadeus at Staffarde in 1690, then captured Nice and Montmélian. In 1692 he resisted the duke's invasion of the Dauphiné, aided by the local peasantry who were roused by the plundering of the Savoyards and found their Joan of Arc in Mlle de la Tour. In October 1693 Catinat secured victory and a marshal's baton at Marsagli, outside Turin. After rebuffing approaches by Chamlay (the choice of Louis's trusted aide indicates its importance) and Tessé, the duke was left to choose the most profitable moment to desert the League. By the secret treaty of Turin he gained concessions which show the way Louis XIV's mind was turning: towards part, if not all of the Spanish Succession and the importance, in that context, of winning Italian friends. The duke was given command of the French-Savoyard army in Italy and turned swiftly to conquer the Milanese. His eldest daughter Marie-Adelaide[16] was promised to the duke of Burgundy. It was the marriage alliance which had not been made when Mazarin had set aside the idea of Louis XIV's marrying another Savoyard princess in favour of the Infanta of Spain. Nice was restored, with other conquered parts; also Pinerolo and (to the Emperor) Casale. It might seem that the Italian policy of the Cardinals, adopted by Louis, of securing a French presence beyond the Alps, was being jettisoned. But the tactical gain was what mattered: the alliance was broken at its hinge.

The Emperor had two main concerns: securing William's backing for his claim on the Spanish empire, and prosecuting his war against the Turks. Spain was unable to supply money for Spanish Flanders and the Dutch started to take over fortresses for the 'Barrier' which they now regarded as essential for their future security. They carried the heaviest burden of the land fighting. Their navy was in decline and their commerce suffered from the activity of French privateers. Amsterdam was losing financial business to London. It was not only opponents of the house of Orange who now yearned for peace. In England gentry who resented paying the land tax and merchants suffering heavy losses at sea were uniting to demand a settlement. For English and Dutch alike the disturbing new factor was the strength and prowess of the French navy.[17]

On the same day that William was saving his throne at the Boyne Admiral Tourville won a battle which confirmed that the navy of Colbert and Seignelay could command the sea. Off Beachy Head, with some seventy ships, he encountered a slightly smaller Anglo-Dutch fleet under Herbert, sank eight ships and then, thwarted by a change of tide, sailed off to destroy merchant shipping in the Channel. Louis was encouraged by Seignelay and Bonrepas, author of the scheme, to think of invasion, and an army was mustered at Cherbourg under Marshal Bellesfondes for Tourville to escort across the Channel. The affair was poorly organised. Seignelay died in 1690; his successor Jérôme de Pontchartrain was scrupulously efficient but a novice in naval matters; the king's thoughts turned to Flanders and he lost interest. The slight hope of success lay in Tourville's being able to get out to sea before the enemy – or win a decisive victory. After being kept in harbour at La Hogue for a month by contrary winds he sailed out with fifty ships, only to meet Russell with twice as many. The battle of 29 May 1692 was notable for the courage and seamanship of the outnumbered fleet. After twelve hours and great carnage, Tourville's fleet was battered and had nearly run out of ammunition; but no ships had been sunk. At night they broke off to run for home harbours. A pilot's mistake caused Tourville, with twelve ships, to make back for La Hogue where Russell found him and destroyed the ships. So an unlucky disaster turned a moral victory into a material defeat. It put an end to plans for invasion. It was also the end of a grand design, the beginning of a new phase in naval warfare.

La Hogue was one of those battles whose full significance would only become apparent in the light of subsequent developments. It may have changed the course of history.[18] The king does not seem to have been dismayed. When he received Tourville, he surprised courtiers who expected disgrace, or some stern words at least:

> I am entirely happy with your conduct and with that of all the navy. We have been defeated but you have earned glory, both for yourself and for the nation. It has cost us some ships but that will be put right during the coming year, and assuredly we will defeat the enemy.

La Hogue did, however, strengthen the argument of those who maintained that the navy was irrelevant to the real needs of a continental state and consumed resources that could be better used by the army. It is the same argument, navy being changed for army, island for continental state, that Englishmen used – and would have pressed forcibly – if, say, Marlborough had lost the battle of Blenheim. Tourville was the kind of commander who could have lived up to the vision of Richelieu, Colbert and Seignelay – a great navy, defending and promoting the interests of a trading, colonising nation. Now, however, Vauban, the Burgundian, would actually lend his authority to the idea that the navy be put out of commission. Louis XIV resisted this, but the navy ceased to have priority and it was allowed to run down. Deficiencies in naval materials, timber, iron, hemp, pitch, have been suggested as reasons for France's relative naval decline at a time when England and Holland were securing larger supplies from Baltic countries. It was, however, shortage of money rather than shortage of materials which decided naval policy. For the rest of the war and throughout the next, the smaller number of ships kept in commission were used to attack enemy merchant vessels. Increasingly they were supplemented by privateers sailing under royal letters of marque. At relatively small cost to the crown, private enterprise was thus brought into the war effort. In the hands of Forbin, Duguay-Trouin and the legendary Jean Bart, commerce-raiding would prove to be a highly effective weapon. Meanwhile, what might have been achieved if larger fleets had been kept in commission was shown by Tourville's devastating operation against the Smyrna convoy at the battle of Lagos in April 1693. Meanwhile the privateer Jean Bart, based on Dunkirk, was terrorising the northern coastal waters with frigate groups and tactics that anticipated the submarine warfare of the Second World War. In June 1694 he earned his countrymen's gratitude by a bold attack on a Dutch squadron in the Texel. Not only did he secure three Dutch ships but he enabled the large Swedish-Danish convoy, carrying desperately needed Polish wheat, to proceed unscathed to French ports.

A NEW MODERATION

The loss of shipping and trade and its effect on the investing classes in England and Holland is one indication of the importance of economic factors in the conduct of war and moves towards peace. Another, affecting French finance and the capacity of the government to find means and will to maintain the war effort, is the effect of a run of bad harvests and consequent distress in large parts of the countryside. Two sides, for good reasons, anxious for peace – but the difference is instructive. Neither England nor Holland would be unaffected by crop failures (in England, for example, affecting sentiment towards the land tax) but the main influence on government would be that of the merchants and financiers, their willingness or otherwise to lend and invest. In the period 1688–1713, the English government obtained £46 million in loans at rates between 6 and 8 per cent. In France, we have seen, heavily dependent on the taxation of peasants and yield of agriculture, with limits on money that could be raised by other means, the annual harvest became a crucial element in fiscal calculations. Excessive taxation already hurts the peasant producer; after a bad harvest, it becomes unsustainable: the peasant has no purchasing power; the pinching of local markets affects the wider economy; the state loses income. Yet the unprecedented level of war expenditure meant that the state needed a rising income.[19] More offices could be sold, more money borrowed (but at higher rates of interest); the clock was being put back to the early days of the reign, the reforms of Colbert undone.

Intendants' reports convey a bleak picture. It seems that, following several years of unusually cold weather, the start, it was to turn out, of the 'mini ice age', and consequently poor harvests, that of 1694, following an exceptionally severe winter and cold spring, was disastrous. Famine ensued. Government had already reacted to shortages by importing grain.

The king was concerned: 'He knows about the misery of his people; nothing is hidden from him; we are searching for all the means of relieving it', wrote Maintenon in October 1692. Accurate information was sought to assist relief measures. In 1693 Pontchartrain started an inventory of cereal production and census of mouths to be fed. *Intendants* of provinces less affected were asked to provide grain to those suffering more. The differences could be local: Lower Languedoc, using the new Canal des Deux Mers, was required to aid Upper Languedoc. In no large European state could more have been done.

The famine provoked Voltaire's famous lines: 'Men perished of misery to the sound of the *Te Deum*'. It was the background to Fénelon's famous letter of 1694,[20] addressing Maintenon but meant for a king who was 'like a man with a bandage over his eyes', and for ministers whom he accused of misleading the king and sacrificing too much to his authority. That, moreover, at a time when 'Your people are dying of famine. . . . All France is no more than a huge hospital, desolated and without provision . . . there is sedition in all parts.' It offered the first draft of what was to become an alternative policy:

'You have destroyed part of the real resources within the country in order to defend empty conquests outside it.' It was high-pitched and emotional. It was validated by the tax returns that fell alarmingly. But the king was anxious for peace and braced for the necessary conditions. Ministers also deserved better than Fénelon's strictures, for they were already working on plans for the first graduated tax on all classes. It was the *capitation* of January 1695.

For all parties therefore there was urgent need for peace. With the Emperor's troops withdrawn from Italy, and the threat of a French offensive in Flanders, a Bank crisis in London and reports from America, unsettling to merchants, of Frontenac's victories over English settlers, William could not afford to delay. As he told Heinsius he was not prepared to fight on to support the ambitions of Leopold. As for Louis, he was torn between dismay at the prospect of making large concessions and realistic acceptance of the need. For two campaigning seasons operations had been limited by shortage of money to hire waggons. The fiscal prospect for 1697 was bleak. The eventual deficit would be 138 million *livres*. He was resolved to resist Leopold's more extreme claims. Chamlay reported that he had never known the king so angry as when he heard that Vienna proposed that he should give up all gains since Westphalia. 'What!' he exclaimed, 'Am I to give up the work of thirty years, I who have struggled so hard *lest my enemies shall come into my house*? [italics added]' His correspondence, notably that of 1694–97 with D'Avaux, shows how persistently and cogently he had worked to persuade German princes to turn their back on the Emperor. He was disappointed.

There had been a sea change in German views of the Empire since 1648. Even Ferdinand III had enjoyed the advantage, in Evans's words, that his régime 'now represented the only possible embodiment of order in Central Europe'. He died in 1657. Forty years on the cause had been strengthened, most strikingly by the reconquest of Hungary; less obviously by the pervading Austro-Catholic ideology, more appealing to Germans than ultramontane Roman Catholicism and conveyed potently through the native version of baroque architecture and art. The growing Empire offered increasing scope for patronage to soldiers and civilians. There was a strong war party at court. Even the Imperial unitary ideal still had power to attract. Confident in his position Leopold demanded that the treaty should be used to confirm the rights of the archduke Charles to the Spanish Succession. William refused and turned to Sweden for mediation. The Emperor told his envoys to be obstructive. The clear way forward for Louis, therefore, was to collaborate with William. Since William needed it for his domestic audience, he could now turn to bargaining advantage the question of William's sovereignty. Till it was granted, the negotiations begun at William's castle at Ryswick were merely a front. The real negotiations took place between Louis's trusted Marshal Boufflers and the Dutch general Bentinck (in English title duke of Portland). When agreement was reached, in September 1697, the Emperor had little choice subsequently but to accede.

Louis offered up most of the conquests made since Nijmegen, Trier, Freiburg, most of Lorraine and, from Westphalia, Philippsburg and Breisach. They secured the insertion of a clause which guaranteed the religious status of the surrendered lands. The Catholic party in Germany thus became the beneficiary and defender of Louis's 'conquests for the faith', and the German front was split again on the religious question. It was a return to Mazarinist diplomacy which would be rewarded by the adhesion of Bavaria in the next war. To Spain were returned Luxembourg, Ath, Charleroi, Courtrai and – of course – Catalonia. The disputes which had precipitated war, over Cologne and the Palatinate, were settled in favour of the Imperialist candidate. The commercial tariff was mitigated in favour of the Dutch, who were also allowed to garrison a line of fortresses, the 'Barrier' in the Spanish Netherlands. William III was recognised King of England 'by the grace of God'. Of the Huguenots there was no mention.

For the Emperor it was much – but less than he wanted; for William the essential points for which he had fought, which earned a parliamentary tribute: 'he had been given to England to hold the balance of Europe'. Louis had made concessions which appeared to him to be tolerable and timely in view of the impending Spanish Succession crisis, but to soldiers and courtiers disgraceful. They had expected much more after such vaunted victories. For the first time in his reign Louis felt a cool draught of resentment. Vauban, writing to Racine, declared it to be 'more infamous than Cateau-Cambrésis'. Mme de Maintenon considered it 'a shame to restore what had cost so much toil and blood'. 'Blood' is the key word. Casualties had been disproportionately high among noble families. Relatives and survivors felt let down. It was, of course the ministers who were openly blamed.[21] In fact Pomponne had negotiated skilfully from a relatively weak hand. Louis had held on to the most important gain of the *réunions*, Strasbourg. Some lands returned were German, others Spanish, soon to be negotiable anyway. The peace enabled Louis to start the next crucial rounds of diplomacy from a standpoint of moderation. It was no bad example of the old diplomacy at its most effective and – the word is surely allowable when comparison is made with what passed for diplomacy in 1871 or 1919 – civilised.[22]

Notes

1. Gaspar Fagel was Grand Pensionary of Holland before Heinsius, a close ally of *Stadtholder* William and fiercely anti-French.

2. Liselotte von der Pfalz, duchesse d'Orléans (1652–1722). Her life at court is portrayed in her numerous letters which can be studied in E. Forster (ed.), *A Woman's Life at the Court of the Sun King* (Baltimore, 1984). (See also p. 195) The selection records Madame's progression from naive enthusiasm to the frustrations of a wife married to a frivolous homosexual, and a woman high in the court hierarchy but powerless to influence events.

3. See pp. 161–2.

4. Camille d'Hostin, comte de Tallard was a supple diplomat; he would prove to be an unfortunate general.

5. Jean-Antoine de Mesmes, comte d'Avaux, son of Mazarin's chief negotiator at Westphalia, was at The Hague for many years and was well informed.

6. Quoted by Wolf, op. cit., p. 649 (notes). Villars's account is specially interesting since he had been the French agent attached to the Imperial army in Hungary. For the events leading up to this fateful event and for analysis of Louis's actions and motives, see Symcox, 'Louis XIV and the outbreak of the Nine Years War' in Hatton, *Louis XIV and Europe*, op. cit., pp. 179–212.

7. See p. 170. Louis relied heavily on Chamlay who was certainly versatile. During the Cologne crisis he was sent to Rome, disguised as a Flemish gentleman, to influence the Pope's decision.

8. Forster, op. cit., pp. 59–64.

9. M. Verney (ed.), *Memoirs of the Verney Family* (1899), vol. IV, p. 412.

10. Lynn, op. cit., pp. 50–1, estimates 340,000 at the height of the war; on paper 420,000. See also p. 140.

11. François-Henri de Montmorency-Bouteville, duc de Luxembourg (1628–95) was the posthumous son of the man executed in 1627 for defying the royal edict on duelling, and a cousin of the duc de Montmorency executed five years later for leading a revolt. His military career, from flirtation with the Fronde to distinguished royal service, offers a political history in the story of one family.

12. St Louis's Feast day had already been adopted by the king as his own and had become a kind of national holiday. *Bellicae virtutis praemium* was the inscription on the badge of the order: on one side was St Louis; on the other a drawn sword with a wreath of laurel.

13. See pp. 195–6.

14. See Janine Fayard, 'Attempts to build a third party in North Germany, 1690–1694', in Hatton, op. cit., pp. 213–40.

15. For the complicated story of Franco-Savoyard relations see Ralph D. Handen, 'The end of an era. Louis XIV and Victor Amadeus II', R. Hatton (ed.), op. cit., pp. 240–60.

16. Married in 1697, she quickly became a favourite with Louis.

17. The peak of expenditure on the navy was in 1692, 29 million *livres*; three years later it was under half that figure. By 1695 there were 137 vessels; in 1715, 80. For a concise account of the navy in this and the following war, see Lynn, op. cit., pp. 83–104.

Geoffrey Symcox, *The Crisis of French Sea Power, 1689–1687: from guerre d'escadre to guerre de corse* (The Hague, 1974) is authoritative. He concludes that all came down to numbers: 'Ascendancy could only be attained as the result of a long, cumulative process in which one side [the Dutch and English together] built up a crushing numerical superiority; in the end victory became a matter of aggregate numbers.'

18. No French historian can recall La Hogue without regret. Bluche – 'less an allied victory than a triumph of adverse winds and tides' – is more cautious than Michelet, but it was 'a bitter disappointment'. (Bluche, op. cit., pp. 427–36, a good account of the overall French achievement at sea.

19. The letter was not sent to the king – or Fénelon would have gone to the Bastille. It was meant in the first instance for Maintenon who certainly had it in her possession by 1695. Close in some passages to *Télémaque*, on which Fénelon was working by 1695, it gives a foretaste of the book's appeal for a monarchy grounded in traditional principles and concerned primarily with the spiritual and material well-being of the people. The full text is reproduced in Charles Urbain, *Ecrits and Lettres politiques de Fénelon* (Paris, 1920), pp. 143–57. For Fénelon see also pp. 308–10.

20. Evans, op. cit., p. 76.

21. A helpful interpretation of French diplomacy in this period is in V.L. Tapié, 'Quelques aspects généraux de la politique étrangère de Louis XIV, *XVIIe Siècle*, no. 46–7, 1966, pp. 1–28.

22. The words of his letter to archbishop Harlay (January 1698) may be read as more than pious platitudes: 'The moment decreed in heaven for the reconciliation of the nations has arrived. Europe is at peace. The ratification of the treaty which my ambassadors concluded recently has put the seal on this tranquillity which everyone has desired.' Quoted by Bluche, op. cit., p. 439.

Chapter 11

THE GREAT PRIZE

Some very wise men believe that there will not have to be a war
and that we would have a long and difficult one, ruinous for France,
if one [Louis] had insisted on the execution of the Treaty.

MME DE MAINTENON

TREATY OR WILL

From its beginnings in the marriages of Louis XIV to Maria Theresa and of Leopold to Margaret Theresa, the problem of the Spanish Succession loomed over Europe. Through the years of Charles II's precarious growing up and frail adult life, as Charles lived on childless in first and second marriages; through occasional scares, towards its *dénouement*, with anxious precautions in the shape of partition treaties; to the crisis that followed the death of the young prince of Bavaria – it was the great question, the great prize. Even when not directly relevant to a negotiation, the fate of this or that city or province, it was always the brooding presence, the issue which would one day have to be resolved; which had the potential for altering, at a stroke, the balance of power.[1]

The empire of twenty-two crowns comprised as well as Spain itself and the Low Countries, the greater part of Italy (the Milanese, Tuscany, Naples and Sicily), Sardinia and the Balearic islands; Mexico and Central America, the biggest of the Antilles and all South America except Brazil; in Asia the Philippines; in Africa the Canaries and the garrisons of the north, Oran and Ceuta. Its transfer whole to the Austrian Habsburgs was of the stuff of French nightmares: the recreation of the empire of Charles V, the annulment of all that had been won by French arms and diplomacy. On the other hand its transfer from near-moribund Spain[2] to Colbertist France was dreaded by England and Holland alike.

The situation after Ryswick was that no arrangement existed for the disposal of the inheritance among the heir-claimants except the Partition treaty of 1668, now rendered obsolete by subsequent events, Louis's further acquisitions and the Emperor's new-found military strength. In a vague agreement between the Emperor and Holland in 1689 the latter had agreed to support the Austrian claim. That was naturally unacceptable to Louis whose family claim was at least as strong as the Emperor's. Charles II being childless, right to the throne went down to his sisters. The elder, Maria Theresa, had married Louis (himself, a grandson of Philip III). She had renounced her claim but on conditions which were not fulfilled (*casus belli* in 1667). Therefore it was valid still and lay with the Dauphin. The younger sister had married Leopold (also a grandson of Philip III), who, by this marriage, had only a daughter, Marie-Antoinette; she had married the Elector of Bavaria and had a son, Ferdinand-Joseph. Here again, however, Leopold had imposed a renunciation since Marie-Antoinette married outside the family. He intended the Spanish inheritance for a son. By his third wife he had two, Joseph and Charles; the elder was, of course, to be Emperor; the younger, King of Spain. All looked plain and proper from the windows of the Hofburg.

To this conflict of claims, on technical points there was no clear solution. By seniority of daughters, as both son and grandson of an elder daughter, the Dauphin had the better right. If renunciations were to count, the Emperor's family had the better title since neither the Emperor's mother nor his wife had renounced their claim. Then, of course, there was Habsburg family sentiment to urge that the inheritance be kept in the family. For William III, wholly unsentimental but compelled to take an interest, it was a question of the balance of power. The French candidate, as immediate heir, might some day unite the crowns of France and Spain; it seemed more likely than the possibility of the younger son uniting Spain to the Empire. (Actually the Dauphin would die before his father, while Charles became Emperor after his brother's death in 1711.) Either way the balance would tilt unacceptably. Only a neutral candidate, or partition, would prevent it.

William, Leopold and Louis might take a detached view of Spain as opportunity or menace; of Charles II as a helpless pawn in the diplomatic game. The matter looked quite different at the Escurial. In 1689 the king's first wife, Louise d'Orléans, had died and he had immediately remarried. Anna-Maria of Bavaria-Neuburg was daughter of the new Elector Palatine (whom Louis had sought to debar), sister of the Empress and aunt, therefore, of the

Imperial candidate, Charles. The marriage had brought Spain closer to the Emperor and into the war of the League of Augsburg. Charles II, sad, shy invalid, shrank from his young German wife. Nor was her position to be envied. Frustrated and childless she gave her energies, tactlessly, to promoting the German cause.

The Spanish court was one of the two fronts of the Succession struggle; the king's will the prize to be fought for. The other was that of international diplomacy; damage limitation the aim, partition the chosen way. Critics of Louis would hold that he meant the partition treaties to be a blind and that he relied all along on obtaining the whole inheritance by will. This cannot be sustained. He agreed to partition because he feared that he might lose the whole and hoped to avoid war. In 1697 he had sent Harcourt[3] to Madrid to build up a French party at court, but expected little to come from it. In the following year he opted for the partition option to avert war and secure some territory for France. An alternative was to press the claim of the Dauphin, which would lead to war. Or he could put forward a grandson: that might open up a brilliant era for the House of Bourbon but would add nothing to France. He listened carefully to his young foreign minister, Torcy; also to Harcourt, and Tallard, his man in London. Both ambassadors were soldiers, both pessimistic about prospects in a further war.

William had sent Portland to Versailles in March 1698 to complain about the hospitality still shown to James II at Saint-Germain. Hoping to touch old anti-Spanish chords of memory, Torcy stressed the danger that lay in Leopold's ambition to recreate the Austro-Spanish empire. To reassure the Dutch he guaranteed the Netherlands Barrier. Tallard followed up the initiative in London; Villars tried to in Vienna but could make no headway. Leopold believed that what was his by right would be assured by the maritime powers. Like Louis, in 1689, he thought about the future in ways determined by his experience of the recent past. As devout as he was proud Leopold could only see one way forward and he was emboldened by the recent successes of his generals; he neither feared war nor doubted its outcome. William and Heinsius, were, by virtue of their positions more guarded in approach and open to a range of possibilities – including that of a popular Spanish movement in favour of a Bourbon. They were ready to treat. At The Hague in October the terms were made. Prince Ferdinand-Joseph of Bavaria, eight years old, was to have Spain itself and the main parts of the Empire. The Dauphin should receive the Two Sicilies and the *Presidi* (defended forts in Tuscany), Finale and Guipuscoa; the archduke Charles the Milanese. Louis believed with justice that he had subscribed to a plan which the maritime powers would be bound to implement, serving by his statecraft the interests of Europe – of Austria as much as of France. It was all in vain. The little Bavarian would never know the high destiny planned for him. In February he died. Supported by prayers and potions Charles II lived on.

Again Louis took the initiative. Into his concern to save something from the wreck of the first treaty, the unaccustomed speed of the diplomatic process and the generous nature of the new terms, can be read a real anxiety. If the king died without an agreed settlement, Europe would drift into war. In June 1699 England and France agreed on new lines of partition. The main part should now go to the archduke Charles. France should receive in compensation Lorraine (whose duke was to be transferred to Milan) or Nice and Savoy (if Milan were to go to Savoy). Louis hoped to secure a quick signature from Leopold to show Spain that 'it would be of no avail to oppose measures that have already been decided and that their forces are not big enough to stop them being put into effect'. The episode reveals the pragmatic concerns of Louis's diplomacy (and, less surprisingly, William's) that tend to be concealed by its outward show and ritual claims. Louis had stood by the principle of hereditary monarchy in the person of James II; William for the right of a people to choose its own king. Both now collaborated to impose upon the Spanish a king who was neither evidently legitimate nor desired, and slice off part of the inheritance into the bargain.

The Emperor would have none of it. He rejected the treaty that seemed to offer so much. He still believed that he would have the whole inheritance and would not consider sacrificing Milan and Naples to make sure of it. He would commit himself to nothing, wait on events and trust to Habsburg luck. He would call it Divine favour. Is it fair to add that as ruler of a more loosely structured state, with its diversity of races and culture, he was bound to be less affected than Louis by considerations of the well-being of his peoples and the burdens of war upon them? His negative attitude was encouraged by the war party at court led by Eugene von Stahremberg. He declared that it was improper to rule the succession to a still living king. Louis, William and the States General signed the second Partition Treaty in March 1700. By August, Louis heard that Austrian troops were marching to Italy. He could not be sure that he could count on William, who had said that 'having made a treaty to avoid war I do not intend to make war to execute a treaty'. So matters stood when Charles the Sufferer died on 1 November 1700, All Saints Day: it was the one he would have chosen. On 9 November Louis heard that he had left by will the entire inheritance to his younger grandson Philip of Anjou. It was a genuine surprise, indeed *un embarras du choix*.

At Madrid, Harcourt, taking advantage of an upsurge of Castilian feeling and resentment at the overbearing behaviour of the German party at court, had won the diplomatic battle. His ally, Cardinal Portecarrero, had urged upon the king the necessity of finding a king strong enough to hold the empire together. As with France after the Fronde, unity was the prime consideration and, with it, sufficient strength to repel any foreign power seeking to exploit weakness – as had France after the Catalan revolt in 1640. A Bourbon prince offered the best prospect for Spain's future. After a painful life Charles did not fear death. Even in his extremity, however, the issue was plain. Till it was resolved he could not die in peace: he must choose between family tradition and Spain's paramount need. As neighbour to Spain and to the Netherlands Louis had shown that he could attack or defend with equal facility. Under a French prince the Spanish empire would remain intact and a bulwark against the heretic nations who had planned its dismemberment. Since Philip of Anjou was separated from the French inheritance by the Dauphin and by his own elder brother, the duke of Burgundy, he was preferred as prospective ruler of an independent Spain. To ease doubt Charles referred the matter to the Pope. Innocent XII had made his peace with Louis and feared to see the Emperor too strong in Italy. It was, therefore, with the Papal blessing that Charles made his fateful will. Along with material factors, that would weigh with Louis as he wrestled with the implications of the hardest decision of his reign.

Louis was sensitive about any issue in which his personal honour was engaged, meticulous about treaties, strong for the legitimate principle, and respectful towards a sovereign's right to dispose of his own. He could be forgiven if he concluded that in this case the arguments about right and law were so finely balanced that the matter had to be decided pragmatically. To accept the will or stand by his treaty? Which course would bring the greater advantage? Or, as was anxiously pondered, would carry least risk? For two days and during several protracted meetings in Maintenon's room at Versailles, the choice was debated. Far from the popular image of the arrogant king, puffed with family pride, one should envisage a hesitant old man, trying not to be overwhelmed by an excess of fortune, a fulfilment beyond expectation and one which threw into painful relief the policies which had created enemies in Europe when he now most needed friends. He listened to his councillors and was swayed by their views. For the will were the Dauphin and the duke of Burgundy, Pontchartrain urging the commercial advantage of participating in Spanish trade, and eventually Torcy; for the treaty the duc de Beauvillier. The latter argued that adherence to the treaty was the only way of avoiding another, possibly disastrous, war against a European coalition. It would secure a certain and measurable advantage and an addition to its territory. A Bourbon House in Spain would be independent. It would only remain friendly so long as France desisted from any attempt to extend its frontier in the Low Countries. Torcy's eventual view may have been conclusive: France would have to fight anyway, since the Emperor would both reject the will and oppose partition. The Spanish courier had orders, if the succession was refused, to go and offer it to the archduke: France would then have to fight both Austria and Spain, probably without William. Middle-aged and unfulfilled, the Dauphin suffered from being the perpetual heir: responsibility and real authority indefinitely postponed, his sense of purpose blurred through idle days: now at least there was the vicarious experience of power and the honour that accrued. He spoke out for his son's interest. To reject the will would be to betray the interest of the family, an act of dishonour.

Ministers could not agree, but the arguments veered towards acceptance. Whatever the misgivings, the decision was made with style. The Spanish ambassador had already been informed privately when, after his *levée* on 16 November, against all precedent Louis ordered the two folds of the doors of his chamber to be thrown open and the crowd of courtiers to be called inside. Saint-Simon recorded the words: 'Gentlemen', he said, pointing to the young Anjou, 'birth has called him to this crown, and the dead king also by his will. The whole nation wished for his accession and urged me to approve it; it is the will of heaven and I accede with pleasure.' Then to his grandson: 'Be a good Spaniard, this is now your first duty. But remember that you were born a Frenchman so that you may further unity between the two nations. This is the way to make them happy and to keep the peace of Europe.' It was the Spanish ambassador who was heard to say: 'What rapture! Now there are no more Pyrenees!' It was exactly what William and Leopold feared.

Would Louis's simple formula be enough to keep the peace? For the moment it was in the balance. It is argued, as by Beauvillier, that war was inevitable; but also that it was provoked by Louis's behaviour – at least by the way it was reported and interpreted. We should consider, rather, the nature and scope of the ensuing war. Leopold would fight to save at least the Milanese. William was outraged by Louis's decision but he was not a free agent. Many in Holland had good reason to fear the effect of further years of war. In England too there were powerful voices for peace. If Parliament would not vote taxes, if financiers would not lend money, William, hobbled in debate by his own indifferent military record, would not have the means, even if he had the will, to mount effective campaigns. Louis's whole policy should have been directed towards isolating the Emperor. He did not succeed in doing so. Within eighteen months the Grand Alliance had been reconstructed and the stage was set for what would prove to be a disastrous war. Louis's actions during this period have therefore been harshly judged. Yet each move is intelligible when considered in its context.

In letters to the courts of Europe Louis explained his reasons and sought to justify his decision. In his despatch to William he recalled how hard he had tried to bring the Emperor to sign their treaty. He declared that he had been compelled by Leopold's obstinacy to accept the will though it was less advantageous to him than the treaty. English and Dutch shipping would have nothing to fear from Italy, now that the French were not to have Naples. Spain and France would remain entirely separate. That vital assurance, and the integrity of the Barrier, which was guaranteed to the Dutch at the same time, were the tests by which England and Holland would judge Louis's sincerity, and by which they would act.

'All the wisest people think we will have no war', wrote Maintenon in April 1701. England had recognised Philip V as king of Spain. A large part of the English army had been paid off after Ryswick. There were loud demands for lower taxes. William knew that he would gain nothing by trying to force the pace. He had been willing to treat with Louis. But now his sense of personal vocation was renewed, the resentful spirit re-animated. He believed that war was inevitable; it was only a question of timing. As he wrote to Pensionary Heinsius: 'I will drag this people in by prudent and gradual measures without their realising it.' He relied on propaganda. Louis supplied him with material. Philip went to Madrid in January and found the people well disposed. On 1 February *Parlement* registered letters patent reserving his right, and those of his descendants to the French throne. The wording was cautious. If Philip should become king of France he should not cease to be king of Spain. It seems to have been Louis's intention, not that the crowns of France and Spain should be united but that Philip should be able to claim the French throne if the contingency should arise. Similar letters had been granted to an earlier duke of Anjou (afterwards Henry III of France). But these seemed to challenge the stipulation of the will and his own pledge that the crowns should remain separate; if only a formality could have been delayed till a more appropriate moment. It is typical of the fussy parochialism observable at times in Louis, in tune with the expectations of a highly legalistic society, that in doing what seemed proper according to tradition he should underestimate the effect on foreign opinion.

Another trait in Louis's government we have seen. When French troops occupied and scorched the Palatinate in 1688–89, the operation was conceived in military rather than in diplomatic terms. When, without warning, in February 1701, French troops seized the Spanish fortresses of the Barrier in the name of the king of Spain, the argument was again a plausible one. Dutch troops should not stay in Spanish garrisons if they did not recognise the Spanish king. The States General promptly did so and the troops were withdrawn. But an impression lingered. The Dutch were vulnerable and became apprehensive. In England Louis's coup was freely spoken of as the invasion of Flanders.

The complaints of English merchants were supported by news that the French fleet had sailed to guard Cadiz and that the French Guinea Company had gained, by treaty with Madrid, the privilege of the *asiento*, of importing slaves into South America, coveted (later gained at Utrecht) by the English. They did not know that Louis's instructions to Harcourt for the new king were that English and Dutch ships were to be excluded from the Indies and South America. But it did appear that Louis intended to manage the Spanish empire. In so much as he used French muscle to support a vulnerable Spanish position he was acting in the spirit of Charles II's will. The alternative, as he saw it, was to stand aloof while the Spanish empire offered pickings to the financiers and merchants of the maritime Protestant powers.

Louis's letters to his grandson, besides conveying in moral precept and practical advice his own conception of how a monarch should conduct himself, offer clues as to his idea of the future relationship between Spain and France. The young king should take all possible steps to strengthen the state finances and improve conditions for trade. Nothing, the king urged, could be so good for both countries as this 'great union'. In the context of all his other advice it seems that Louis envisaged friendly relations and cooperation, but nothing beyond that. He would have understood that the proud Castilian concerns for their empire's unity which had produced the Bourbon succession would act equally strongly against any sign of excessive French influence in Spanish affairs.

Meanwhile, the Emperor prepared for war. It was therefore a reasonable precaution of Louis, in May 1701, to send troops under Catinat to defend the Milanese. Louis was drawn in by Spain's weakness. His enemies could say that he thought more of extending the power of France. That was the spirit in which, at The Hague, in September 1701, England, Holland and the Empire decided on the terms which became the war aims of the Grand Alliance.

The Emperor had already begun his campaign in Italy where Catinat was retreating before Prince Eugene. William had been given by Parliament the power to conclude alliances necessary for England's safety: a cautious mandate. One aim of the contracting parties at The Hague was to secure for the maritime powers 'particular and sufficient surety for their realms and for the navigation and commerce of their subjects'. They undertook to prevent for ever the union of the French and Spanish crowns and agreed to share any captures in the Spanish colonies between England and Holland. Moreover they bound themselves to procure for the Emperor satisfaction of his claim to Spain. They would restore the Barrier and the Emperor's Italian possessions. Louis was given two months to consider the terms. Here, however, was little inducement to negotiate. Representing the commercial aims of the English and Dutch and the dynastic imperatives of Austria, it amounted to a manifesto of war. The aims would prove discrepant, the partnership uneasy; for the present it served to bring the maximum force to bear on the reduction of France's power.

The Grand Alliance was sealed on 9 September 1701. Nine days later, James II died at Saint-Germain. Moved by the plea of James's widowed queen and Maintenon, though against the advice of his ministers, Louis XIV recognised his son as James III, king of England, Scotland and Ireland.[4] A rider was promptly added to the Alliance terms by which the powers bound themselves to secure satisfaction for this insult to England and her king. It had a significant effect on English opinion and helped William secure the support without which he would not have been an effective ally. So it is usually regarded as a serious blunder. At best it has been seen as a case of misplaced chivalry. Since, however, it reveals the essence of Louis's ideas about right and duty, it requires further analysis.

There was a political calculation. Mazarin's instruction remained influential with Louis – and he had been caught off guard by the Restoration of 1660. In a second restoration the returning king should feel gratitude to France. Louis may be forgiven for thinking that anything could happen in England whence his ambassador reported stormy debate and constant intrigue. But his action is consistent with his whole handling of the Jacobite question. When he suggested James for the elective crown of Poland, vacated by the death of John Sobieski in 1696, he may have been trying to rid himself of an incubus. But he allowed the question of a pension for Mary of Modena to bulk large in the Ryswick negotiations. When, after the treaty, he allowed James to stay at Saint-Germain he caused suspicion by contravening what appears to have been an understanding between Portland and Boufflers. He found it hard to view the matter pragmatically, or solely in political terms. It was for him a question of the honour due from one sovereign to another. We need not be surprised that he acted as if he actually believed in the principles of Divine Right; nor that he had, in consequence, a horror of rebellion. His *amour-propre* too had been hurt by his enforced abandonment of James at Ryswick and by the reaction to it. Writing then in his diary 'We have abandoned the true king of England', De Sourches probably reflected the feeling of most courtiers. Louis may have lost face at court as much by this surrender of principle as by the loss of towns. The court revolved round questions of status. It was in 1701 that Louis issued new instructions on the status of *ducs et pairs*. Maintenon, surely in such matters her master's voice, always referred to William as 'Prince of Orange' and to Anne later as 'Princess of Denmark'. Louis was influenced by the values of the society which he ruled so meticulously. No less were William and Anne by the crude pragmatism of parliamentary politics. In England the sovereign had to work within the constraints of the system reinforced by the revolution which had brought him to power. How volatile and how displeasing that system seemed to French eyes, how much treachery they saw it engendered, how much bribery was involved! All that could be advanced to justify Louis's stand for principle. The political philosophy and practices of the two countries had long been drawing apart. There was now a huge gulf, affecting mutual under-standing and diplomatic relations.

Parliament passed a measure attainting James Edward of high treason for having assumed the title of king. William then dissolved it and secured a Whig majority which promptly voted for 50,000 soldiers and 40,000 sailors. In the following March he died. His spirit lived on in the formidable coalition he bequeathed to his successor, Stuart Anne. Versailles hoped that a change of ruler would bring a change of spirit, but over-estimated the personal authority left to the crown. By 1702 war had become the policy of the dominant groups in Parliament. It was as much due to the actions of Louis as to those of William. Louis had not, however, behaved with the reckless arrogance so often attributed to him but with that mixture of sagacity and naivety, of moderation and rashness, principle and opportunism, which makes his statecraft so hard to judge. Voltaire's judgement may be pondered: 'There has never been a more legitimate war.'

Notes

1. This vital period in diplomatic history is explored by M.A. Thomson in a number of articles, notably 'Louis XIV and the origin of the War of Spanish Succession', T.R.H.

series 5. no. 4, London 1954, reprinted in R. Hatton and J.S. Bromley (eds), *Louis XIV and William III* (Liverpool, 1961), pp. 140–61. See also his 'Louis XIV and the Grand Alliance', *Bulletin of the Institute of Historical Research*, 89 (1961).

2. For this period of Spanish history, see Henry Kamen, *Spain in the Later XVII Century, 1665–1700* (London, 1980). Also R.A. Stradling, *Europe and the decline of Spain* (London, 1981): both offer a refreshing corrective to the more extreme views of the country's decline.

3. Henri, marquis (later duc) d'Harcourt, was to be one of the most influential men at court during the next fifteen years.

4. The wider subject of Louis XIV's relations with the Jacobites is dealt with in Claude Normann, 'Louis XIV and the Jacobites', in Hatton, *Louis XIV and Europe*, op. cit., pp. 82–111.

Chapter 12

◆

THE GREAT WAR

War is a continuation of policy by other means.

CLAUSEWITZ

War shows itself as the bankruptcy of policy.

RUSSELL WEIGLEY, 1991

A WAR ON FOUR FRONTS

Louis faced Europe almost alone. The climate of opinion was generally hostile. An English official manifesto accused him of aspiring to 'universal monarchy'. The Diet of Ratisbon (September 1702) was told that 'the king had done all that he could to enfeeble and entirely ruin the German people'. The Elector of Hanover, bound by his new Electorate (1692) and claim on the English throne, the Elector of Saxony, Imperial candidate for the throne of Poland in 1697 and now fighting for it against Charles XII of Sweden, and the Elector Palatine nursing a justifiable grievance against the despoiler of his lands, were Leopold's principal allies in Germany. Others supplied contingents of troops. Only the Wittelsbachs stood by France. For the Elector of Cologne to allow passage of French troops to the Low Countries was a lesser evil than occupation by German troops. His brother, Max-Emmanuel of Bavaria was Leopold's son-in-law but his wife had no claim on Spain, his son had died and he now looked for French support in his ambition to become Emperor. He undertook to ban the passage of Imperial troops and raised 10,000 troops in exchange for a large subsidy. With Savoy, Louis was less successful. As ever, Victor Amadeus was determined to get the maximum from his strategic position. Louis promised money and a second French marriage: that of Philip V to his younger daughter. The Emperor offered Montferrat and more money. After 1703 Savoy stayed in the allied camp, an important factor in the Italian campaigns. At first Portugal too favoured France, but in 1703 signed the Methuen treaty with England. In the north, Charles XII, a potential ally, would be courted by both the French and by Marlborough after his victory at Fraustadt over Augustus of Saxony and Poland in 1706. Fatefully, after already six years of successful fighting, he elected to invade Russia. After his defeat at Pultawa in April 1709 and subsequent sojourn in Turkey he was no longer of significance to the western powers. Denmark, after 1700, was also nominally neutral, but sold serviceable contingents of troops to Marlborough's army.

This bare recital of diplomatic engagements suggests that France started the war at a serious disadvantage. There were weaknesses too in the allied position. The Emperor fought mainly to impose his son on Spain; after the development of the Hungarian revolt under Ferenc Rákóczi (1703–7), his interests and activity in the west were limited to Spain and Italy. The Dutch became increasingly defensive-minded as the war went on and their concern, understandably, did not stretch beyond the Barrier and the ruin of France's trade. Their preferred strategy, which imposed thwarting limitations on Marlborough's campaign plans, was to advance piecemeal, securing fortress towns for a larger Barrier. With heady military triumphs to savour, English ministers were prepared to lavish gold upon their allies and back the Habsburg claim to Spain – so long as it seemed attainable and necessary to maintain the balance of power. But the country's long-term interests, as can be seen in the terms of the peace of Utrecht, lay in the extension of trade and furtherance of naval power. Meanwhile, because of the high proportion that fell on the landed class, taxes were a political issue from the start. A faction opposed to continental involvement on principle and advocating a 'blue water' strategy, concentrating resources on the navy and colonies, would have come to the fore long before the Tory victory of 1710 but for Marlborough's unprecedented victories. One significant French victory – and the Grand Alliance would have been fractured. In 1703 Louis had reigned for sixty years; his army had never been defeated in a full-scale battle. But now it faced war on four fronts.

Prodigious exertions were called for. Only five years had elapsed since Ryswick, insufficient time for the recovery of army or treasury. Louis knew this well for his ministers constantly reiterated the themes of poverty and disorder. From the start the allies were heartened by knowing that Versailles would be responsive to proposals for peace – and by knowing that they could raise the price with each victory. In 1702 France still had over a quarter of a million men under arms, of whom three-quarters were infantry, but many were raw levies, inexperienced, poorly fitted out, hastily mobilised and rushed to the frontiers.[1] The cavalry were ill mounted and armed; the shortage of horses was alarming. To encourage emulation or draw on an apparently rich pool of talent, Louis marked the start of war by promotion on the grandest scale: in December 1702 he created twenty-four lieutenant-generals. From nine the number of marshals rose to twenty. Several of the new creations, like Marsin, Tallard and Villeroi, would have unfortunate records. They were seen as 'palace generals' on whom Louis thought that he 'conferred capacity along with his patent.' Louis would see Villeroi, for example, as a safe man, who would heed the instructions from Versailles. There was, however, a serious problem of overall control of so widespread a war. It was an even greater problem for the allies. The experience of Marlborough in the years between his famous victories is instructive. In 1703 he was held back from attacking at a favourable moment by the caution of the Dutch field deputies. In 1706 an ambitious plan for a thousand-mile march to Italy to aid the beleaguered duke of Savoy had to be abandoned (fortunately it transpired) because the Imperial general, Louis of Baden, could not guarantee cover through the Rhineland.

Marlborough's victories may leave a misleading impression. His correspondence shows repeatedly how pessimistic he was about campaigning prospects, as much because of difficulties with his allies as of misgivings about his abilities to defeat the opposing generals. He out-performed Tallard at Blenheim, Villeroi at Ramillies, even Vendôme (though the latter was illserved by his co-commander Burgundy) at Oudenarde. But Vendôme was a fine fighting general; so conspicuously was Villars; Berwick proved his capacity in successful campaigns in Spain. This great European war does not exhibit a consistent trend; it cannot be reduced to a simple pattern. Taking extraordinary personal risks under fire, anticipating enemy moves, reacting swiftly to new situations and maintaining, in some degree, control over the confused scene, Marlborough imposed the stamp of genius on the battlefield.[2] Little, if at all, his inferior in ability and fighting spirit, Prince Eugene – who might so easily have been serving Louis[3] – contributed notably to the allied success. Louis already had reason to believe that he was unfairly judged in his efforts to avoid war. It was his misfortune, when he was thwarted in efforts to make peace, that his armies should be confronted, with disproportionate political effect, by two of the greatest soldiers of the age.

History was made spectacularly in the decisive actions of a single day, the murderous encounter of the battlefield. Less evidently it was being made in the preparations for war, the paying of troops (and subsidies for foreign troops), provision of men, horses, equipment and food. Marlborough's quartermaster-general Cadogan is rightly credited with the efficient supply of Marlborough's men, notably, for example in his march to the Danube before the battle of Blenheim. On the other hand, the main reason why Marlborough was unable to exploit further his victories in the field was that the work of Vauban, maintained with no expense spared over forty years, had created a fortress chain in depth that made it dangerously impracticable to proceed far without siege. Vauban's forts saved France from invasion and, as in the case of Strasbourg for the Rhineland, provided secure bases for manoeuvres deep in enemy territory. Louvois's arrangements for commissariat, maintained by Chamillart and Voisin,[4] facilitated recovery after the disasters of Ramillies and Oudenarde. The resilience of French armies after defeat was a matter of organisation as much as of morale. Perhaps Chamillart, who combined the portfolios of finance and war from the outset till 1709, faced with the restoration of shattered armies, deserves better of posterity than the usual charge of mediocrity. Desmarets, his right-hand man and successor as *contrôleur-général*, had talents worthy of his great uncle. In the department of *matériel de guerre*, France, which maintained the struggle till 1714, secured the throne of Spain and ended on a victorious note, was not obviously the loser.

The one French general who exhibited a war-winning capacity, with offensive spirit tempered by sound judgement, was Villars. Catinat had been unable to prevent Louis of Baden from taking Landau in September 1702, but in the following month Villars crossed the Rhine after a successful feint and defeated Louis in a spirited action at Friedlingen. His excited troops proclaimed him marshal on the spot. Had he been able to persuade Max-Emmanuel of Bavaria to march with him on Vienna, then almost empty of troops, he might have struck a more decisive blow. But they were at odds from the start and the chance was lost. Villars, covering Bavaria, won a second victory, at Höchstädt, in September 1703 over the main German army under Styrum but was then recalled, at his own request and in pique with the Elector, to deal with the Camisard revolt.[5] It illustrates the significance of the revolt in a war from which the Huguenots were to derive little benefit for themselves. After the second battle of Höchstädt (Blenheim), Villars would boast that he could tame Marlborough. We can only speculate on the possible outcome if he had commanded on the fateful day, 13 August 1704, when

Marlborough and Eugene inflicted a crushing defeat on the French generals Marsin and Tallard: such a defeat that the battle has to be seen, not only as a catastrophe for French arms, but a turning-point in the history of Europe. With Tallard prisoner in Marlborough's coach, and thousands already dead on the battlefield, eleven thousand French infantry cooped up in the village of Blenheim were compelled to surrender and so humiliation compounded defeat. The French would fight stoutly in future battles but without the confidence that they would conquer. As they fell back towards Alsace they left 30,000 French or Bavarians dead or captive behind them. In the following years the main French forces would be fighting to save their homeland.

There is little doubt that Louis XIV's wisest course, after 1704, would have been to instruct his generals to avoid open battle and rely on political developments. The glory of Blenheim would not silence Marlborough's critics at home indefinitely; nor did it lessen the resolve of the Dutch deputies to confine him to local operations. The Hungarian revolt continued to be a serious distraction to the Imperial war effort. The revolt in the Cévennes being eventually crushed, Villars was able to guard the Rhine. 1705 was a frustrating year for Marlborough. In North Italy Eugene forced Vendôme back to the line of the Adige but Vendôme created there a strong defensive position. With something like a return to his old self-confidence the king was encouraged to return to the offensive. Villeroi was ordered to seek battle in Flanders. La Feuillade[6] was supplied with lavish equipment to besiege Victor Amadeus's capital Turin. It was playing into Marlborough's hands. He knew that he could only succeed by bringing the enemy to battle. Defensive tactics might have forced him to fight – as later at Malplaquet – under unfavourable conditions. The strategy of Versailles was also flawed at the human level. As the king aged he came to value his friends more, becoming more liable to mistake loyalty for talent. He liked Chamillart and appreciated his immense efforts to fund and supply the still formidable engines of war. He might have done better to listen to Vauban. The veteran siege-master offered to assist La Feuillade at Turin. That conceited courtier, Chamillart's son in-law refused him.

Villeroi,[7] an honourable man but a consistently unsuccessful commander, was Louis's friend. Three years before he had earned ridicule when he was captured by the Austrians during their attack on Cremona. Now keen to impress, he interpreted Louis's mandate all too impetuously. If he had waited for Marsin to come up with reinforcements he would have had superior numbers. At Ramillies, on 23 May 1706, he faced an army of equal strength, about 50,000. To make matters worse he allowed a large part of his force to be immobilised behind a marsh which he reinforced in response to Marlborough's feint attack. The main action developed in the centre where Marlborough achieved critical mass after drawing troops off from his right. At the climax of the day the finest French troops, the *maison du roi*, were worsted in a fierce encounter. The French army would never again take the field in such fine array. They left 12,000 on the field, dead or wounded; another 6,000 were captured in the ensuing rout. An unusual feature of the battle of Ramillies was that it was fought so early in the year. It gave Marlborough time to exploit his victory. For weeks there was hardly a French army in the field while the great towns of Flanders, Louvain, Ghent, Oudenarde, Antwerp and Brussels surrendered to Marlborough. A town like Menin, fortified by Vauban, should have obstructed the allies for months. Its fall in a previous war might have been held to justify a campaign; that it surrendered, in August, days before in Marlborough's view, it was necessary, indicates low morale. At Menin Marlborough stood on French soil. The king received Villeroi with a courtesy and sympathy, as of a friend sharing in a cruel blow of fate, that is impressive: 'at our age we must not expect good fortune'. But Villeroi was dismissed and Vendôme[8] was brought in from the Italian front. He came to find the Allied ascendancy complete: 'every one is ready to doff his hat at the mention of Marlborough'. Ramillies affected the country near to home – at least to the seat of government – where it obviously hurt most and aroused uncomfortable memories. With Louis now giving priority to the north-eastern frontier, it also had a distorting effect on a previously coherent overall strategy. Villars's promising operation in the Rhineland was suspended. Ramillies had a particularly unfortunate effect in Italy.

La Feuillade diverted troops from his siege of Turin to chase Victor Amadeus in the mountains. Already twice unlucky, Marsin came to replace Vendôme convinced that he was going to die; the duc d'Orléans was in nominal command but could do little to avert disaster. Eugene pierced the lines of the Adige without difficulty, attacked the French at Turin on 7 September before they could concentrate their troops and gained a victory much easier than Ramillies but nearly as important. The French who had been cramped in their tactics by orders from Versailles to stay on the defensive, lost 9,000 troops, their commander Marsin, all their siege equipment and, as it turned out, Italy. La Feuillade retreated precipitately to the Alps. In 1707 the Austrians were on French soil, besieging Toulon.

'THERE ARE MURMURS AT HIS VERY DOOR'

Up to this point events in Spain had brought Louis further anxiety. The challenge here was two-fold: to bring some order into a lethargic and casual government, and to defend Philip V's throne against the archduke Charles. Only seventeen when he came to the throne, Philip was unsure of himself at first and content apparently to be led by those around him, Marie-Louise-Gabrielle, his Savoyard wife, the princesse des Ursins who ran his household and became his mistress, Cardinal Portecarrero who had mobilised the pro-French faction in the battle for the will, and successive French ambassadors and administrators. As government had faltered in the last Habsburg years, the pride of grandees and the separatism of the provinces had grown. Catalonia had been held like an eel's tail; relatively prosperous Barcelona was virtually independent. Portecarrero was reduced to the usual expedients of Spanish ministers: nepotism and inaction. Traditional taxes yielded little; new wealth in ports like Bilbao was hard to tap. Even the court could hardly pay its bills. It was reasonable that Spanish policy should be directed from Versailles since French troops were fighting for Spanish possessions; inevitable that French officials be sent to oversee the government of a country that could not govern itself. Louis was forced, as Torcy wrote, 'to enter into the details of Spanish government and its dependent states'. Orry reorganised the finances, Louville advised the king. They and their successors, Cardinal d'Estrées, Grammont and Amelot de Cournay encountered obstruction at all points. The Spanish who seemed to have expected miracles from Versailles liked neither the methods nor manners of the miracle workers. The *grand seigneur* D'Estrées offended by his hauteur; *bourgeois* Orry by his presumption. Within the French party frustration and overlapping of authority caused quarrels.

When archduke Charles landed in Catalonia in 1705, he found support at all levels. In the veteran Galway[9] and the eccentrically gifted Peterborough, he had enterprising commanders. Throughout, the English navy, assisted after 1703 by the alliance with Portugal, played a crucial role. In October 1702 an English fleet destroyed the annual bullion fleet from America while it lay in Vigo Bay, and with it most of a year's revenue. The French navy was highly effective in commerce-raiding,[10] yet France paid a high price for the council's strategic decision to concentrate resources on the army. The naval power which Colbert and Seignelay had managed to equal paid a lucky dividend to England when Admiral Rooke, by chance, found himself in possession of Gibraltar, a fortress then supposed, and afterwards proved, to be impregnable. In March 1704 a fleet of transports and men of war brought the archduke to Lisbon. His march on Madrid was checked by Berwick but while the English controlled the Mediterranean he could rely on supplies for his more successful landing in Catalonia. Berwick was recalled at the request of the queen who was irked by his cold manner. In 1706 Philip V's attempt to recover Barcelona failed and for a few weeks he had to abandon Madrid. But he was now showing spirit, eliciting some Spanish response. It was enough for some Castilians to know that the enemy was based in Catalonia. Patriotic spirit and the Bourbon cause was further helped by reports of destruction and sacrilege at the hands of the archduke's mainly Protestant soldiers. The 'war of the two kings' would soon take a different turn.

In this great war there was no consistent trend. In each year between the great actions which tend, particularly for English readers, to dominate the picture of the war, the French held their own, gained small advantages, brought misgivings to the allied leaders and enabled Louis to see some point in maintaining the war of endurance. This is illustrated by the events of 1707. In the Low Countries Vendôme ceded nothing to Marlborough. On the Rhine Villars manoeuvred and fought in the Turenne tradition, carried the 'Lines of Stolhofen' and captured Heidelberg, Stuttgart and Mannheim. Between this year and 1713 there would be no major battle in the Rhineland. Here was conducted 'war as process'[11] (as opposed to 'war as event'). Battle and siege are plainly indecisive; the tempo of operations is slow; war is expected to feed war. That comes across plainly in Louis XIV's instructions about foraging. The underlying principle is that attrition will eventually produce the desired result; meanwhile, overtly or covertly there will be negotiation as diplomats seek to make the most of what the generals can give them. Only in Spain was there a prospect of dramatic change – for there was an extra factor, that of national feeling inspiring a popular response.

There was a surge of sentiment for Philip. He played his part. When informed of the allied demand that he abdicate he responded with well-publicised words: 'I shall only quit Spain when I am dead. I would prefer to perish fighting for it foot by foot, at the head of my troops.' Castilian hatred of Portugal, Catalonia and the English and German troops that made up the bulk of the allied armies was strengthened by stories of pillage and desecration. There was a natural loyalty to the successor chosen by their own king and it animated the popular, priest-led movement which swept Charles out of Madrid and harassed his armies in defeat. In April Berwick, who had been restored to command, won the battle of Almanza against Galway and saved Spain for the Bourbon king. The *Te Deum* ordered by the king (and another for the birth of an heir, the prince of the Asturias) was more than a routine piece of propaganda. Louis was far from despairing of the outcome of this war of fluctuating fortune.

The French provided another example of effective popular resistance when a large Savoyard-Imperialist army invaded Provence and reached Toulon. The Austrians had never been keen on the enterprise which had been urged on them by Marlborough who was swayed by the value of Toulon as a naval base. In the face of an opposition of peasants and militia, skilfully organised by Tessé, Eugene was driven back with much loss. Shipping and naval installations were damaged by Admiral Rooke's bombardment of Toulon but the allies lost their chance of dominating the Mediterranean from this harbour. Not till September 1708, by the capture of Minorca, did they achieve their aim of securing a base for winter operations.

Almost from the outset Louis had shown willingness to treat for peace. As before, in dealings with Holland, an unofficial envoy was entrusted with the delicate task of taking soundings without giving the impression that France had special need of peace. Mesnager, a Rouen merchant, could make no headway. In England the general election of May 1708 confirmed the Whig faction in power, with the objective expressed in the slogan, 'No peace without Spain', that is without Philip V's being replaced by Charles. That still suited the financial and mercantile interests on whose support they relied but only for as long as Marlborough could deliver the victory that would make it feasible. Whig ministers wanted to put more resources into Spain, Louis to concentrate his troops in Flanders to secure counters for negotiation. He also hoped much from the presence, with Vendôme's army, of his grandson the duke of Burgundy. His earlier memories of campaigning in the Fronde, when Mazarin had rightly believed that his presence would hearten the troops, had been reinforced by his happy experience of sieges – though, in reality, the generals would have preferred him not to be there. Grounded in the traditional practice of French monarchs, exemplified in recent times by his grandfather fighting for his throne, and by his father at the siege of La Rochelle, it had become an article of faith that the presence of a royal prince raised to the highest pitch the ardour of noble officers and the men they led. Unfortunately the complicated character of Burgundy, his capricious and moody temper only partly subdued by Fénelon's tutelage and a growing sense of political responsibility, did not command general respect among the soldiers. His heart was not in the war. He lacked the knowledge or flair for successful generalship. By contrast Vendôme knew Flanders and his adversary. Battle-hardened but tending to be lazy about detail, resourceful, a soldier's soldier, he shared the command in a way which was fatally ill-defined. He had little rapport with the proud but inexperienced prince.

The campaign was crucial to Louis's prospect of an honourable peace. It began well with the defection to the French of Ghent and Bruges, a signal that southern cities found Dutch over-lordship no more palatable than French. When Marlborough forced an action at Oudenarde on 11 July, he took a risk in crossing the Scheldt when the French were near enough to attack the first troops across. It was mistakes by Vendôme that allowed the bold thrust to develop into a piecemeal engagement. It was then Burgundy's failure to come into the battle, despite repeated requests from the furious Vendôme, that assured Marlborough's victory; and it was Burgundy's decision to retreat to Ghent that gave defeat the appearance of a rout. More were captured than killed and wounded: the total of French casualties, around 12,000, was more than three times that of the allies. While the troops divided into Vendômists and Burgundians in charge and counter-charge, alleging incompetence and worse, their bitter commanders took the war to Versailles. Vendôme was recalled in disgrace, though not till after the fall of Lille. Slandered and ridiculed by Vendôme's friends, the proud and sensitive Burgundy suffered more, being in a weaker position to advocate peace from his compromised record in battle. Sourness and disillusion spread through the palace: the reiterated themes of paint and plaster were of war, victory and royal glory, but the talk was of defeat, disgrace – and peace.[12]

At the front, when the allies besieged Lille, Vauban's masterpiece and France's strongest fortress, nothing was at first done to aid the city which Boufflers, Governor of Flanders, defended with 16,000 men. Two great convoys of siege equipment were allowed to trundle through unmolested. A third was attacked unsuccessfully at Wynendael where the French suffered a sharp defeat. Louis felt that his prestige was engaged at Lille. Was it not the great prize of his first war? Chamillart was sent in person to order Vendôme to seek a general engagement. His failure to profit by Marlborough's exposed position when a large proportion of the allied troops were engaged in the siege speaks volumes for the moral effects of his defeat at Oudenarde. Marlborough could have marched direct upon Paris, though it would have been risky with waning supplies, the risk of autumn rains and mud – and a strong garrison in his rear. Had he done so the French would surely have been roused to resist. He took the cautious course, accepting very high casualties and huge expense.[13] The French left Lille to be slowly strangled. Boufflers did not capitulate till 9 December. With Lille fell also Bruges and Ghent. But Boufflers's epic effort underlined the value of Vauban's fortress strategy. Above all it restored pride and made possible the huge effort of the following year.[14]

The terrible year 1709 displayed several aspects of war: economic and social pressures intensifying; diplomatic exchanges in which high professional skills could not disguise a sense, on the French side, of desperation; a military effort on both sides on an unprecedented scale. It followed the most severe winter in living memory as prolonged frosts paralysed the country and brought misery to the people already suffering from the poor harvest of 1708. Rivers froze, even the swift-flowing Rhône. Olives and vines were caught in the south, everywhere early wheat sowings were trapped under the ice. Wine froze in bottles, the water mills were still and wolves came down from the hills. It was said at court that 'the common people were dying like flies'.[15] *Intendants*' reports bore out the extent of the tragedy and its implications for the war effort, since taxes could not be collected from starving peasants. There had been a running deficit since the start of the war. Between 1708 and 1715 receipts were barely a quarter of expenses.[16] Corn had to be imported from the Baltic, at high cost. Britain declared it contraband and sent a squadron to the Danish Sound to prevent it. The price of bread rocketed. In Picardy it quadrupled in a year. In cities across the land shopkeepers and bakers were pillaged. Religious houses that were suspected of hoarding were sacked by wandering bands of peasants, beggars and deserted soldiers. One evocative *intendant*'s report described savage bands 'squatting in the fields who scattered like wild animals when he approached'. A report from Quercy suggests panic: there were 30,000 men under arms, Cahors was besieged. He, the *intendant*, was imprisoned in his coach 'and escaped only by a miracle'. He knew the authors of the disturbance but 'they are so many that it would be dangerous to make an example of them'. It is reminiscent of 1636 – and the same area that had seen the *Croquant* risings. Parish registers of 1709 show often the laconic entry: *fame periit*. In the register of Vincelles in the Yonne, the *curé* wrote of men, women and children scratching at the earth with their nails, searching for roots. 'Others less industrious scrabble the grass along with their animals, others completely broken lie along the roads waiting to die.'

Followed by shivering courtiers, Louis, strode about the gardens of Versailles, majestically indifferent to the elements. He was at his best when others seemed to be losing heart. He seems to have been making a deliberate and defiant effort to convey the idea of 'business as usual'. Did he sense, beyond the emergencies of the moment, a new tendency to criticise, not just particular decisions but the whole trend of policy and the thinking that had informed it? The military crisis was, potentially, a political crisis. The king wanted peace but it was not available. So, as Marlborough pondered plans for invasion, he had to concentrate on plans for resistance and revival: at stake were northern France and the capital itself. Meanwhile hungry Parisians learned to chant a bitter *Paternoster:* 'Our father which art in Versailles, thy name is hallowed no more, thy kingdom is great no more, thy will is no longer done on earth or on the waters. Give us this day thy bread which on all sides we lack.' The king reduced his table at Marly and sent gold and silver plate to the mint. Yet, wrote Maintenon,

> He is reproached for his expenditure. . . . They would like to take away his horses, his dogs, his servants. . . . There are murmurs at his very door, they would like to stone me because they imagine that I never tell him anything unpleasant for fear of grieving him.

In fact the most impressive thing about the king at this time of defeat and distress was his realism in the face of compelling evidence. At the height of the famine his new *contrôleur-général*, Desmarets, reported in sombre terms: 'the armies cannot be properly paid . . . we are on the point of a total break-down and may fear the most terrible uprisings . . . to all these evils no remedy can be found but prompt peace'. That was what Louis had long wanted. Yet he had hoped for a victory which could enable him to emerge without significant loss of lands or honour. He had inclined to the soldier's view that Marlborough could still be beaten. But now the pessimists held sway. 'It is wretched', wrote Vendôme to Chamillart, 'that you are so hopeless about the prospects of campaigning. I am sure that the Dutch will hold their feet on our throats when they see we are in no state to enter a campaign.' Chamillart had been backed in council by Beauvillier and Chevreuse. The Maintenon group was solid and strong. So Louis could not escape the defeatist mood in his own chamber.

Mme de Maintenon saw the hand of God in the victories of France's enemies. 'How can you say', she asked the princesse des Ursins, 'that God has not declared Himself against us, when He sends us a winter such as has not been seen for five or six hundred years?' Maintenon's mood was one of pious, introspective pessimism.

> Our king was too glorious, He wishes to humble him in order to save him. France was overgrown and perhaps unjustly; He wishes to confine it within narrower bounds and perhaps more solid. Our nation was insolent and unruly; God wishes to punish it and to enlighten it.

It is the language of Fénelon and his pupil Burgundy: the authentic voice of the *dévot*. Inward-looking, concerned with *la France profonde*, it was not without its own kind of pride. An analogy comes to mind in the mood (though more cynical and self-serving) of Vichy after the defeat of 1940. Shocked by defeat men comforted themselves with the reflection that there was more to France than the ability to win battles. Since his disgrace over the Quietist affair[17] the archbishop had been confined to his diocese, but Cambrai lay in the path of the moving armies. He was visited by the great and his eloquent pen could not be stopped. He was a prophet for the little group at Versailles who planned for a better future. He argued now for a bold stroke for peace. 'It would be better to sacrifice Franche-Comté and the Three Bishoprics than to risk the whole of France.' He would not even hope for a victory 'such as can only flatter us with vain hopes and prolong our misery'. In similar vein Burgundy was philosophical about the loss of Lille: 'has not the state subsisted for whole centuries without this town, indeed without Arras and Cambrai?' It was to dismiss as relatively worthless the main gains of the reign.

'CONDITIONS SO CONTRARY TO JUSTICE'

Louis saw matters quite differently but he too sought peace. He hoped that the allies would be divided. In Torcy's words: it was the general view that the only way of securing peace was to approach Holland. Feelers had already been put out, through unofficial envoys like the Dutchman Helvetius, Chamillart's private doctor. Chamillart had himself written to a Dutch politician that the realm was on the edge of a precipice and it was not in the interest of the Dutch to let it fall. In March 1709 Rouillé, an experienced diplomat, was sent to test the waters. He returned with stiff terms and the message that they were not for negotiation. When the council debated them Beauvillier is said to have painted so tragic a picture of the state of the country that Burgundy burst into tears. 'It would be difficult', wrote Torcy, 'to picture so melancholy a scene.'

Torcy was sent to The Hague. It is a mark of earnest intention, but also probably a tactical error, because the allies regarded him as the king's chief minister: the French must indeed be in desperate straits. When Torcy arrived, in May, Marlborough and Eugene, now operating together again, had started their campaign. The allied mood was arrogant. Heinsius was gratified by France's plight; Eugene boasted that he would soon be in Paris. Yet the hard winter and shortage of supplies compelled them to restrict their operations to siege warfare. While the allies presented their demands in forty articles, 'The preliminaries of The Hague', the logistics of war showed that they would have been wise to be more moderate. Rejecting their proposals Louis began to look less the arrogant dynast, more the statesman with a sound grasp of a changing situation, the sovereign with an instinctive feel for how his subjects might respond.

He was prepared to go a long way: to abandon, on Philip's behalf, all the Spanish dominions; to allow the Dutch a new Barrier, including the French fortress of Lille and Tournai; even, at one point, to cede Strasbourg; to destroy the port and fortifications of Dunkirk; and to give up Hudson's Bay and Newfoundland. Reaching so far, the allies added what they should have known Louis could not accept: that the Spanish crown should go to Charles with all the lands that Charles II had possessed – or ought to have possessed by the will of Philip IV; and that Louis should employ his army in enforcing the settlement on Philip V if he did not comply within two months. The first clause meant Louis renouncing his gains from Spain at and after the peace of Aix-la-Chapelle; the second was meant by the allies to ensure that Louis was acting in good faith. It also gave away the fatal flaw in their position. To re-conquer Spain in the face of popular support for Philip V would be costly and hazardous. An order from Louis to his grandson would avert the necessity. Louis's response to such an offensive demand could have been predicted: 'Since I have to make war I would rather fight against my enemies than against my own children.'

Though it was far from clear in the summer of 1709, as Villars built up his forces and campaigned with watchful caution, the diplomatic episode was to prove a turning point in the war and in Louis's fortunes. It is therefore worth a closer look. It is easy to see that the allies overreached themselves. Does it therefore follow that Louis could claim a superior moral position? Both Heinsius and Marlborough were later to express misgivings over the fatal restitution clause (though not at the time). The allies should have taken more note of the recent upsurge in Spanish sentiment towards Philip V and of the king's determination to die sword in hand rather than surrender his throne. But they may be forgiven for suspecting Louis's motives. His efforts to negotiate during the war looked to them insincere or inept. From the start his agents, including both neutrals and Dutchmen, were putting out peace feelers. The Dutch, always the most vulnerable and sensitive to the possibility, assumed that he was trying to divide the allies: arguments before 1704 and events after 1710 show that they were justified. The Dutch intelligence service was better than the French realised and the activities of French agents were closely monitored. Louis blundered in the choice of Rouillé, a man known to be unacceptable to the Dutch. He would have done better to leave negotiations in the hands of Torcy. Instead Chamillart, minister of war, was supervising simultaneous separate negotiations. Torcy was exasperated and Dutch misgivings increased by such conduct. It helped to obscure the king's fundamental, immutable position. Louis wanted peace but not so much that he would sacrifice to it the master principles behind his understanding of government.

The principle of Divine Right on which he refused to turn out his grandson was that on which he had refused to recognise Anne as queen of England. At the same time, with a confidence grounded in his sense of moral superiority, he went back to the oldest tradition of the monarchy: the protection of his people. In an open letter to be read aloud by the *curé* in every church, he explained the case for war and appealed to his subjects for their support. The royal letter was an extraordinary moment in the history of the monarchy. As his *Mémoires* show Louis was keenly aware of the need to set the record straight – and to ensure that it would be his record. He now showed an instinct for leadership and a tactical adroitness that would elude his successors. The paternal wording of the letter evokes the spirit of the Hundred Years War.

> Although my affection is no less than I feel for my own children and although I share all the sufferings inflicted by war upon my faithful subjects, and have plainly shown all Europe that I wish sincerely that they should enjoy peace, I am convinced that they themselves would scorn to receive it on conditions so contrary to justice and to the honour of the French name.

A ballad of the time of Joan of Arc's time had incited resistance: 'Let each of you village folk who love the king of France take courage to fight the English. Let each of you take a hoe, the better to uproot them; if they will not go, spoil their faces with your fists.' During the fifties there were reports of peasant bands in Burgundy standing up for themselves and ambushing Spanish troops. The peasants of Provence had recently helped thwart Eugene's invasion and save Toulon. Popular risings had shown the same willingness to take up arms. Now again the enemy was not the tax collector but the Englishman, German or Dutchman, the issue was simple, at least to the peasants of Artois and Picardy who were within range of the enemy's cavalry patrols. But Paris could not be saved by royal words or by a few gallant local initiatives. All depended on Villars, guarding the north-east frontier with the last effective army of France.

With militia units serving with professional soldiers it could be called a national army.[18] To pay for it the king and at least some nobles melted down plate; ladies pawned jewellery; peasants released hoarded *sous*. Bullion was taken from the Spanish treasure fleet sheltering at Saint-Malo. Villars had found the army in poor shape, discipline neglected, ragged soldiers selling their weapons for food. He set about restoring morale. His style was flamboyant, his self-confidence infectious. The stakes were high. 'The salvation of the state rests in your hands', wrote Maintenon in June. Louis backed him now without reservation and provincial governors were ordered to give priority to the army's needs. Recruits were not hard to find. Young peasants from ravaged villages followed the bread waggons and stayed to enlist. Villars's heroic spirit and drive gave the troops a new will to fight. Perhaps for the first time in the war – and it was rare in any war in *ancien régime* Europe – ordinary soldiers felt a genuine identity with their general and their cause. Fighting to defend their native soil they would show a tenacity and élan that anticipates the spirit of armies of the Revolution. The supply problem remained grim, however. When cavalry horses were dying at the picket lines there could be no thought of an offensive. Instead Villars created the lines of La Bassée, covering forty miles with trenches and redoubts. Marlborough spent two months building up his forces to achieve the superiority in artillery and cavalry required for the decisive victory which would open the way to Paris and compel Louis to make peace. In June his scouts revealed the strength of Villars's lines and he turned instead to besiege Tournai, reputed the strongest fortress in Europe. Villars would not be drawn from his lines to attempt a relief. After its fall, however, in early September, he edged forward and dug in to fight a defensive battle.

On 11 September, where the gap of Malplaquet, the gateway to Hainault, lies between the woods of Sars and La Lanière, his 75,000 men, drawn up in concave pattern over a front of three miles, faced Marlborough's 86,000 on what is nearly the line of France's modern frontier. The French held their own with courage against repeated attacks. Marlborough and Eugene turned the French left flank with a well-executed assault through the woods but it fell back in good order, sustained by Villars's reserves from the centre. Marlborough counted on breaking through the weakened centre before sending in his massed cavalry to roll up the flanks. But this was not to be another Blenheim. The Dutch were checked on the French right, then driven back by furious bayonet charges. When Marlborough at last carved a passage through the French centre, the battle had degenerated into separate and desperate struggles. Here indeed was the 'art of war' as Voltaire described it: 'like that of medicine, murderous and conjectural'. French cavalry charges and infantry pushes at point of bayonet frustrated the allies and enabled Boufflers, who took over, when Villars was wounded, to conduct an orderly retreat, with drums beating, flags waving and artillery drawn to safety. Significantly, few prisoners were taken. Marlborough commanded the battlefield at the end of the day but could take little comfort from it. 'I have never seen so many dead in so small a space . . . piled two and three high', wrote a French officer. The allies had lost 20,000 in killed and wounded, the Dutch having fared particularly badly after heroic attacks, with 5,000 killed in the first half-hour. The French had lost barely two-thirds that number and the next day they were in battle formation again. Marlborough and Eugene could not follow up their 'victory' and knew that it had not achieved its prime objectives. The effect on French morale was dramatic. Reporting to Louis, Boufflers did not hesitate to write of a 'glory greater than words can express'. He could assure his king that 'the title of French has never been held in higher esteem nor more feared than it is now among all the allied armies. . . . They say that they saw the old French in action'. Marlborough would be constrained after 1710 by a change in the political situation, with the Tories in power and looking for a way to discredit him and end the war which, they alleged, he pursued for his own gain. It is still significant, however, that he did not attempt to engage Villars in open battle.

The Tories made much in parliament of the 'butcher's bill', though English losses in the battle were relatively light. They played on insular prejudices aroused by the Barrier treaty of 1709 in which the English guaranteed Dutch claims in the Netherlands. The Austrians feared that Holland aspired to control, if not to annex the southern Netherlands and its trade. When, therefore, negotiations were resumed in March 1710 the French had some cards to play. They found the allies as intransigent as ever. 'From the start', wrote Torcy, 'the enemy showed more arrogance than ever, less readiness for peace.' For Louis the French envoys, Huxelles and Polignac, offered more than ever: the suggestion that Philip might receive Naples and Sicily in return for giving up Spain; even, at one dispirited moment, financial aid towards turning Philip off the Spanish throne. The allies insisted, however, that Louis use his own army. By their unyielding stance at Gertruydensburg the Dutch gained nothing; ensuring that Louis would fight on, they let the initiative slip to the English, with the eventual consequence they most feared: the separate peace between England and France that left them to the uncertain patronage of Austria and the certain prospect that they would lose trade to the English and French.[19]

In the campaign of 1710 Marlborough played his game of military chess with his usual skill but did not manage to get Villars away from his defences to fight the only kind of battle that he could contemplate: out in the open, with the possibility of surprise. So disabled by his shattered knee that he had to be strapped on his horse, Villars showed moral courage too in resisting the king's demand for the field action which he knew that Marlborough longed for. Meanwhile laborious, expensive sieges yielded Douai, Béthune, Saint-Venant and Aire, but not Arras which was Marlborough's main objective. Between him and Paris lay Villars's great trench system, the *Ne plus ultra* lines. Meanwhile the prospect that the French would cave in receded with news from Spain. There French victories had secured beyond question the Bourbon throne and rendered futile the main allied demand.

In 1708 Philip V had defied the diplomats: 'I would rather die at the head of my troops in the defence of my states, than weakly abandon them.' His subjects responded with enthusiasm. The towns found money for an army; partisans, often urged on by their priests, harried Imperial troops and raided their baggage trains. In December 1710 Vendôme, who had been recalled from resentful retirement at Philip's request, caught the allied generals Stanhope and Starhemberg apart and defeated them in successive actions at Brihuega and Villa Viciosa. Stanhope had been forced to surrender; Starhemberg lost most of his force of 12,000. With 5,600 prisoners, 22 artillery pieces and 'a prodigious number of flags, standards and drums', Vendôme was entitled to boast: 'never a battle so glorious for the king's arms, no victory so complete as Villaviciosa'. Torcy understood its significance: it 'changed beyond doubt the affairs of Spain and . . . those of Europe as well'. Louis had already signalled his resolve to fight on by imposing the *dixième*,[20] a tax on nobleman and commoner alike. Now he could lift his head from gloomy accounts of debt and distress to order a *Te Deum* to be sung at Versailles; a message to courtiers that their unprecedented sacrifice was worthwhile.

PEACE AT LAST

More important than victory in battle in deciding how France would fare in future negotiations was the policy of England's Tory ministers.[21] The diplomacy of William III and Marlborough had underpinned the Grand Alliance; the defection of Bolingbroke and Harley broke it up. Before Christmas 1710 Torcy was informed that the English would not insist on the entire restoration of the Spanish monarchy to the House of Austria: 'we shall be content provided France and Spain will give us good securities for our commerce'. Bolingbroke's case was strengthened by the death, in April 1711, of the Emperor Joseph I, elder brother of Charles, would-be king of Spain, now to be Emperor. So fighting ostensibly to prevent a Bourbon union of crowns, the alliance was now fighting to create a Habsburg union. So England carried out a phased withdrawal from the war. There was to be a military standstill in Flanders and Spain; meanwhile a separate negotiation with France in which the interest of England was to be pursued without regard to recent compacts with the Emperor or Dutch. French diplomacy was offered something to work on at last.

As often in diplomacy, the crucial preliminaries, creating the conditions, even determining the outcome, were the work of an obscure figure. The abbé Gaultier had been chaplain to Tallard and accompanied him in captivity to England. There he stayed, worked for Torcy and the Jacobite Jersey. In July 1711 he went to Paris with the English demands. Bolingbroke then took over, bargaining fiercely with Torcy. Certain extra propositions, those in England's interest eventually embodied in the peace of Utrecht, notably the recognition of Queen Anne, the Act of Settlement and the neutralisation of Dunkirk were to remain a secret. The matter of Lille and Tournai was deferred to the conference. Bolingbroke gave up his claim for 'cautionary' towns in the Spanish Indies in return for an extension of the *asiento* for thirty years. On 8 October Nicholas Mesnager, for Louis XIV, signed the preliminaries. The open clauses, to be communicated to Heinsius, were a guarantee of the barrier fortresses and an undertaking not to unite the crowns of France and Spain under a single monarch.

Now it was Villars who yearned for action, Louis who was cautious. In the summer campaign of 1711, Villars, still outnumbered, stayed behind his lines. Without the support of Eugene (in Germany to provide a show of strength during the Imperial election) Marlborough operated with a relatively small army and showed that he had lost none of his resourcefulness and daring. The great tapestry commissioned to celebrate the capture of Bouchain may exaggerate the importance of the event but not the brilliance of the manoeuvre. After an elaborate bluff and hectic night march, he pierced the *Ne plus ultra* lines, crossed the Scheldt and besieged Bouchain under the eyes of Villars. He constructed a fortress ring round the city to provide cover before its eventual fall. With the prospect of a successful invasion of France receding it was as if he wished to display his mastery of the military art before leaving the field. At the end of the year he returned to England to face dismissal, followed by charges of corruption, even cowardice. Even the polemical genius of Swift, whose devastating pamphlet, *Some Remarks on the Barrier Treaty*, stated the case for 'little England' and the primacy of domestic over continental concerns, cannot redeem the sordid aspects of an attack on the character of the greatest soldier in Europe. For Bolingbroke it was an essential part of the operation of making a separate peace with France. To France it gave new hope. Louis XIV, who had treated even unsuccessful generals more generously, and Villars with extraordinary favour, must have found the episode distasteful. But his comment was apposite: 'the affair of displacing the duke of Marlborough will do all we desire'.

1712 saw two interdependent campaigns: the diplomatic which started in January at Utrecht, whose commitments and evasions influenced the morale of the troops and the moves of their generals; and the military, on which depended the outcome of negotiations. Here, as Eugene besieged Landrécies, the key to the valley of the Oise and the north-eastern heartlands of France, Villars knew that he could win or lose the war in a day. For peace was inevitable and imminent. A heavy defeat – and only some desperate action could save Paris and prevent humiliating losses at Utrecht; victory – and the Dutch, even the Emperor would tire. No one was more aware than Louis of the need for Villars to proceed with caution, but to strike hard if he saw the chance. The seventy-two-year-old king had his own appalling trial, and grief to master. In April 1711 the dauphin had died. In the following February the duchess of Burgundy died, followed quickly by her husband, the new dauphin, and their elder son. At his pre-campaign briefing Villars was moved by the king's dignity and spirit. He declared his trust: 'I hand into your charge the troops and the safety of my realm. I know your zeal and the valour of my troops.' But he did not shrink from the possibility of defeat. 'If there should be a disaster to the army you command what do you think my part should be?' He answered his question in words which, as recalled by Villars, have the ring of truth: the courtiers would want him to retire to Blois but he knew that armies so large were not beaten so badly that it could not effect a withdrawal to the Somme. Then – and it might have been Louis XIII speaking in the year of Corbie, but it is an old man who has known glory but now recalls his anxious youth and campaigns scarcely less critical: 'I know that river; it is very difficult to cross; it has strong places and I should count on being able to get back to Péronne or Saint-Quentin to rally what troops remain and make with you a last effort, perish together, or save the state.'

Villars was neither crushed by his responsibility nor forced on to the defensive. Since Ormonde's British troops had been ordered out of action (orders which were communicated to the French), he saw that Eugene was stretched to protect his communications. He decided to teach him the lesson he had recently learned from Marlborough. By an elaborate feint he persuaded Eugene to concentrate his troops around Landrécies; then after a night march (23–24 July 1713) he stormed the thinly held entrenchments and carried Denain at the point of the bayonet. The allied casualties, killed, wounded, captured were about 6,000, the French a third of that number and those mainly in the front line of the daring assault. A small action seemingly – but it had momentous effects. The victory severed Eugene's line of communication, ruptured his invasion plan and, in Napoleon's words a hundred years later, 'saved France'. Louis was elated: 'My troops displayed such courage as I cannot adequately praise; in it I recognise the whole valour of the nation.' Torcy's bargaining hand was strengthened, the Dutch were now keen to settle and Villars could concentrate on following up his victory and bringing the Emperor to the table.[22]

Now urged on by the king Villars followed up his advantage. Town after town was recaptured with the supplies collected for the allied invasion: Marchiennes in July, Douai in August, Quesnoy and Bouchain in September. With such reminders of France's revived power the diplomats edged their way towards peace. The idea of a partition of the Spanish empire which had been revived by the English (and considered seriously by Louis) was discarded when Bolingbroke secured that Philip should renounce his claim to the throne of France and that his act be registered by *Parlement* and by the *Cortes* of Madrid. In November Louis gave way over Tournai, a bitter pill: he had presided over its siege in the heady days of 1667. The obstinacy of Heinsius delayed the last stages. The French failed to secure compensation for their unfortunate ally Bavaria in the form of either Belgium or Sicily. A typical delay was caused by a quarrel between the lackeys of Holland and France: few conferences passed without such incidents. England acted as arbiter in disputes arising out of the claims of lesser powers, Savoy, Prussia and Portugal. Bolingbroke had to send an ultimatum threatening the renewal of war before Torcy would concede to Portugal her rights in Brazil against the encroachment of the French from Guiana. We are reminded that he was Colbert's nephew. As in the case of the Asiento, and fishing rights off Newfoundland so keenly desired by British merchants (and granted to them) at the end of this first world war, the commercial and colonial interests of the maritime powers can be seen vying with traditional concerns.

On 11 April 1713, Heinsius resolved, in his own words, 'to drink the chalice of peace'. Did he sense that Utrecht was a requiem for the end of Holland as a great power? Bolingbroke had better reason to celebrate a treaty in which England had been the prime mover and had bargained with reference exclusively to her own strategic and commercial interests. Between France and the Empire the war dragged on for Charles VI, deserted by his allies, refused to accept the fait accompli of Utrecht. Not till Villars had won further victories on the Rhine and taken Landau and Fribourg did he resign himself to peace. For two months Eugene and Villars negotiated; eventually, at Rastadt, on 6 March 1714, a treaty was signed. Significantly it was not couched in the Latin of traditional usage but in French.

EUROPE'S CHANGING FACE

It is clear that France's war had ended on a high note and that the state had fared better than might have been thought possible in 1709. It can be claimed for Louis that he had returned in his last years to the realism of the cardinals and the ideal expressed in the inscription on the triumphal arch of 1659: *Arbitriis pacans omnia regna suis.* Yet he was plainly not in a position to arbitrate as – up to a point – Mazarin had been after the peace of the Pyrenees. If any power can be said to have 'given peace' to Europe it was England – if only in a negative way through abandoning the alliance which made continued war possible. In fifty-five years the position of France in relation to other powers had undergone a radical change. This was partly due to events beyond even the long reach of Louis's diplomacy: for example the failure of John Sobieski to turn his victory at Vienna to the advantage of Poland and the victory of Tsar Peter over Charles XII of Sweden in 1709. Other trends, however, were more directly related to Louis's actions, such as the rapprochement of German princes with the Emperor. They should be considered in any estimate of Louis's overall achievement in the sphere of foreign policy which – he would be the first to acknowledge – was his life-long, and prime concern.

There is no doubting the power that Louis had wielded for most of his reign and that Denain had shown could still be a formidable instrument of policy. Had he used it well? He had imposed on Europe his interpretation of the peace of Westphalia and he held Alsace with Strasbourg. He held the Franche-Comté and the *réunion* gain of Saar-Louis. He had secured his frontier by the retention of the inner ring of northern fortresses, notably Lille. He kept Dunkirk, though compelled to raze its fortifications. Above all, a Bourbon still reigned on the throne of Spain. Is that enough for a favourable verdict? Before it is reached there is needed a wider view of Europe and France's place in it. Also a look at the cost to the country, what was destroyed or what was not achieved. Drawing up any kind of balance sheet of loss and gain has to be an artificial exercise when its items are not comparable. How many lives lost in war, or peasant farmers ruined, trade not secured, ships sunk, business lost, or *livres* of state debt, is Strasbourg worth, or the Franche-Comté, as a permanent acquisition? Even to pose the question is to reveal its artificiality. Yet it was some of those closest to the king who were most keenly aware that Louis's subjects paid a high price for Louis's policies. The duke of Burgundy, preparing to be a king of a very different kind from his grandfather, Fénelon advising him, Beauvillier voicing misgivings in council and Maintenon musing in the privacy of her chamber, would not have expected the historian to shrink from trying to find a balance, if not in material terms, at least in the overall picture of the reign.

Utrecht–Rastadt represented an alteration in the terms of power that was greater than the text of these treaties might suggest. In 1659 the staring fact had been the decline of Spain as an international power, its corollary the rise of France as a cohesive state with the military capacity to dominate Europe. Now France was checked in her expansive course and definite limits had been set to her further advance. She would still, however, be expected to play a leading role in international affairs. She had been checked, not by a single state but by a coalition. France remained the greatest country on the Continent. The serious disorders and discontents that lay beneath the surface are not what the diplomats of Europe saw; rather they saw a state that was still pre-eminent in population, natural resources and efficient government; a country which had withstood the onslaughts of the most formidable alliance, and survived intact.

Thanks, in part, to the overreaching of his enemies, in part to the spirited propaganda counter-offensive mounted by Torcy, Louis could point to a significant alteration in the perception of France in Europe. In England the Dutch could now again be portrayed as aggressors, seeking to control the world through their commerce. In Germany it was possible once more to see France as a benevolent influence. Meanwhile her cultural ascendancy was reinforced as one princeling after another built his imitation Versailles. In the weary aftermath of war it was more absurd than ever to see Louis as the sovereign bent on universal monarchy, but easier to see him, as he had always claimed to be, primarily concerned with the security of his frontiers. There was now a fair wind for policies of *entente*. The ground was prepared for the sane policies of Orléans, Dubois and Fleury. That this was the work of Louis XIV's last years is too often overlooked.

Of the Grand Alliance Austria, already enlarged by the conquest of Hungary and free at last of the threat from Transylvanian rebels, might seem to have secured most: most of former Spanish Flanders; Milan, Naples. From Antwerp to Oltenia in far Wallachia; from Silesia to Neapolitan Calabria; her possessions were not only more extended than those of any other state; there was, as events had shown, both the political influence and military capacity to defend and profit from them. Austria still belonged however to the old, scattered type of political organisation whose disadvantages had been exposed in the century's wars.[23] It can be argued that her very acquisitions, complicating the question, whether to concentrate on development in the east or in the west, prevented her at first from becoming a great power in the eighteenth century. Frederick the Great's invasion of Silesia (1740) would concentrate Austrian minds on the question. Its logical consequence was the 'enlightened' programme of constitutional and administrative reform which enabled Austria to compete militarily in the climate of realpolitik associated with the ruthless Prussian and so far removed from the scrupulous world of Louis XIV and emperor Leopold.

The continental future would lie with the compact, militarist state of which Sweden had been a precursor and Prussia was to be the prime exemplar. Contemporaries might not, however, have seen the recognition by France at Utrecht of the new royal status of Frederick I (the Elector of Brandenburg became king of Prussia in 1701) as having the significance that it was to acquire with the energetic government of his son Frederick William I (1713–40). They would have been struck more by the decline of her neighbours. Sweden, which had been the object of such expensive diplomatic cosseting since Richelieu's alliance of 1631 but had rebuffed Louis XIV's efforts to draw it in to redress the military balance in the west, was never to recover from Charles XII's decision to go east instead, and from his defeat at Pultawa (1709) at the hands of Peter the Great. He had previously defeated the coalition ranged against him. One of its members, Saxony, had little energy or prestige left after her defeats by Charles. It was reduced by 1714 to the level of a Polish province, its duke Augustus given more trouble than benefit by his election to the Polish crown in 1697 (against the French candidate, Louis's cousin Conti[24]). John Sobieski's failure to turn his military renown to advantage by creating a hereditary monarchy was to prove terminally damaging to Polish aspirations. It is easy of course to be wise after the event – in this case first partition (1772) and eventual dismemberment. Meanwhile the elective crown was still reckoned to be worth playing for in the marriage stakes. Louis XIV would still have been surprised that Maria Lescinska was thought to be a suitable bride for his successor. Beside the great stake of the Spanish Succession for which his marriage had put France in play that of Poland might seem to be an empty honour, alliance with the country of little value.

It was a sobering commentary on five decades of diplomacy that France went to war in 1701 with only two allies. Of those Bavaria was a spent force after Blenheim. Max-Emmanuel was, like his brother Wittelsbach elector of Cologne, on French insistence, reinstated in his 'estates, offices and dignities'. He was, however, in relation to Brandenburg–Prussia, even Hanover (which gained from the English connection after 1714), much diminished in wealth, standing and independence. The other French ally, Savoy, soon defected and contributed much to allied victory in Italy. From its political see-saw it won parts of the Milanese, and Sicily. The latter emerged from a typical exercise in the diplomacy of balance and compensation, an echo of the partition treaties and foretaste of much transferring and exchanging to come. Milan and Naples meant recognition of the need to compensate the Habsburgs for loss of Spain; Sicily represented the need to keep some balance in the peninsula.

The British ambassador in Spain was bullish: 'there is no nation that can raise itself more easily and never more so than now' (1715). Spain had already gained from Bourbon administration and the patriotic spirit roused by successful resistance to the Anglo-Austrian party. It would gain too from the amputation of limbs, especially that of Flanders. Parts of the country and several industries were flourishing again. In the next decade, under the stimulus of Philip V's enterprising wife, Spain played an adventurous diplomatic hand with a policy directed towards the recovery of the Italian states. 'Spain breathed again under Philip V'; but by the time Voltaire wrote this the revival had proved to be illusory. Spain would derive little benefit from her 'Family Compact' with France when drawn into successive wars in which she had no real interest.

England and Holland had been the main props of the Grand Alliance, and of them undoubtedly the latter had given most. When Louis XIV had launched his invasion in 1672 the United provinces had been been a great maritime and commercial power and – which Louis had found hard to accept – had played the arbiter between warring states. The aggression of that year had fostered a spirit of militancy and empowered the House of Orange in the person of William III to make resistance to France the central, all-consuming aim of government. The war party had displayed to the end a remarkable tenacity, tinged with the vindictive spirit that had sought to make Louis bend and scrape for peace. The piled dead of Malplaquet represented part of the cost of such commitment – and reason for Dutch determination to get something for their blood and treasure. In 1713 they gained nothing beyond the right to garrison the forts of the Barrier. In the French invasion of 1745 these would prove of little use. For them they had sacrificed their commercial supremacy and much of their financial strength. In 1700 the debts of the province of Holland alone came to 30 million florins; in 1713, to 173 million. The direction of European policy passed meanwhile largely to the English. As a future Pensionary, Slingelandt, was to comment: 'the English, while amassing to themselves the advantages of peace, left to the Dutch only the sad resource of complaining of the injustice and infidelity of the court of London'.

As would become apparent during the eighteenth century, those advantages were substantial. Promoting peace, it could be said that Bolingbroke served Europe well – and France in particular. His exclusive concern was, of course, the well-being of Britain.[25] That he was able to negotiate from strength was due largely to the genius of the general he vilified and the strength of the financial interest that he had denounced as pursuing war for the sake of gain. A war fought through the agency of a national Bank, more upon loans than taxation, helping to ensure rates of interest consistently lower than those that obtained in France, had enriched merchants and financiers (some Huguenots among them) who were now able to turn their gains to account. London outstripped Amsterdam. Britain gained from France a foothold in Canada and, from Spain, Gibraltar, the key to the Mediterranean. It had shown that it could be a continental power to be reckoned with. Though such an outcome was far from inevitable, for France had equal opportunities for overseas commerce and colonies, it would turn out that Britain would play an increasingly significant role in Europe on the basis of an expanding empire.

Notes

1. At its peak (1707) 255,000 effectives out of a paper total of 373,000 suggests Lynn, op. cit., p. 271, running counter to the traditional view that the army was at its largest during this war. At different times Spanish troops were available and, at the outset, Bavarian. For the role of the militia see pp. 141–2.
2. Marlborough is rightly seen, as by David Chandler, *The Art of War in the Age of Marlborough* (London, 1976), as proponent of the big battle as the only means of breaking an enemy's military power, therefore his will to resist. But even he found himself constrained by the conditions and conventions: alongside his five major field battles should be counted the thirty fortresses he besieged and took.
3. Eugène-François de Savoie-Carignan was the son of Mazarin's niece Olympe Mancini and the comte de Soissons. His career was fuelled by deep resentment towards the king. Like his brother, he had grown up at the French court but when he petitioned Louis for a position in the royal army it was refused.
4. Michel Chamillart, *parlementaire*, protégé of Mme de Maintenon and much valued by the king (see p. 281) was *contrôleur-général*, 1699–1708; from 1701 and the death of

Barbésieux he was also war minister. The abler Daniel-François Voysin succeeded him as War Minister; he was Chancellor from 1714 till his death in 1717.

5. For the rising of the Cévennes and its impact on the war see p. 233.

6. François d'Aubusson, duc de la Feuillade, had earned promotion, critics might say, through his eager sponsorship of the Place des Victoires and its equestrian statue of the king.

7. François de Neufville, duc de Villeroi, was the son of Louis's governor and the king's friend from boyhood.

8. Louis-Joseph, duc de Vendôme, was Louis's first cousin once removed. Since his military record is patchy and his uncouth personal habits were memorably portrayed by Saint-Simon – 'he lay about with dogs all over his bed' – a tribute deserves space: 'he was devoted to his prince with such dedication that his private affairs suffered greatly for it. Adored by his soldiers he served only for his glory and that of the king and his country' (Quincy, quoted by Bluche, op. cit., pp. 310–11).

9. The earldom of Galway, conferred by William after his signal service in Ireland, conceals the identity of the Huguenot nobleman, marquis de Ruvigny who would have preferred to fight for France – but would not abandon his faith for that privilege (see p. 226).

10. In 1707 the English admitted the loss of 1,146 merchant ships in five years. When in 1709 Duguay-Trouin of Saint-Malo was ennobled for his services, he had already captured 16 warships and above 300 merchantmen. For his remarkable odyssey, from slave trader to lieutenant-general and chevaliero of the Golden Fleece, for Duguay-Trouin's brilliant (Drake-like) marauding expedition to Rio (1711–12), and for the consistently successful escorting of convoys across the Atlantic, also for the picaresque career of the Basque filibuster, eventually captain-general of the king of Spain, Jean-Baptiste Ducasse, see Bluche, op. cit., pp. 559–63. His well-supported conclusion is that 'If the war took a turn in the Bourbons' favour in 1712 this was because Ducasse had won the battle of the convoys.'

11. The term is used by Lynn, op. cit., p. 2 and 367–76 to denote the characteristics outlined above and developed in my narrative.

12. See also p. 145 and 272.

13. 12,000 killed or wounded in the own siege; several thousand more before the citadel fell (Lynn, op. cit., p. 322).

14. Louis-François, duc de Boufflers, was the epitome of heroic service, a man whose single-minded career suggests much about the values and moods of Versailles. He was constantly in action and repeatedly wounded. To the end, guided by two twin principles, loyalty and obedience, he asked only to serve.

15. Madame Palatine reported (2 February 1709): 'In Paris alone 24,000 have died since 5 January.'

16. For the financial situation generally see pp. 299–301.

17. For Quietism and its relevance to Fénelon's career see pp. 324–6.

18. For the purpose and use of the militia see pp. 141–2.

19. Some Dutch realised it: All gained 'at the price of so much blood, sweat and money' was 'now thrown away by the loss of one accursed night'. Quoted by P. Geyl, *The Netherlands in the Seventeenth* Century, vol. ii (Utrecht, 1973), p. 370.

20. For the *dixième* in the fiscal and social context see pp. 303–4.

21. The Tory ascendancy followed an election in October 1710. War-weariness was a prime factor.

22. Torcy (see also p. 157) was stronger, after the dismissal of Chamillart and the death of the Dauphin, His complete ascendancy came with the death of Burgundy in February 1712 and the decline in Beauvillier's influence. The king was both appreciative and supportive. Matthew Prior referred to him as 'the first minister after Mme de Maintenon' and abbé Gaultier addressed a letter from London 'to the *premier ministre*'. See J.C. Rule, 'Colbert de Torcy', in *Louis XIV and Europe*, op. cit., pp. 277–83. It was not the least of his achievements that he brought up to date the crown's traditional use of official historiography to record and defend the actions of the king. See Klaits, op. cit., pp. 35 ff.

23. In Evans's (op. cit., p. 446) appropriately heavy sentence, 'a complex and subtly balanced organism, not a "state" but a mildly centripetal agglutination of bewilderingly heterogeneous elements'.

24. François-Louis, prince de Conti, nephew of the great Condé, acting in the family tradition: in 1669 Condé was an unsuccessful candidate.

25. After the Act of Union (1707), 'a union of policy' as Defoe called it, not of affection, it is appropriate to write of 'Britain', though English – and London's – interests continued to be prominent in diplomacy.

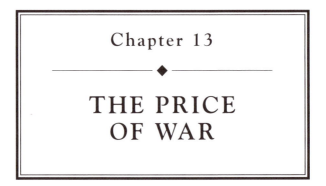

Chapter 13

◆

THE PRICE
OF WAR

The king is only a man of the people, and worthy of his crown only so far as he
gives himself to their good.

FÉNELON

THE MONEY FAMINE

After the experience of the Nine Years War and, in particular, the acute
distresses of 1693–95, and the financial deficits which had led to the
capitation of 1695, Louis had sincerely wished to avoid a further war. If he
had known that it would be such a protracted ordeal and that it would bring
the state close to bankruptcy he would, no doubt, have tried harder to avoid
the provocations which played into his enemies' hands. The main factor in the
yearly worsening of the royal finances after 1701 was the cost of maintaining
war on several fronts against a powerful coalition united, for most of the war,
in the determination to persist *à outrance*. Its effect can be measured in terms
of the proportion of royal expenditure, averaging over 70 per cent, allocated
to war, and in steadily rising annual deficits. Between 1708 and 1714 the average annual expenditure, which had been 99 million *livres* during the Dutch
war, was 218 million. By then the disposable income, what was available to
spend after all charges, had fallen to 35 million. The aggregate debt had risen
by 1715 to at least 2,000 million *livres*.[1] It shows how urgent was the necessity of making peace, but also how remarkable was the war effort of the
years after 1708 and – it should be added – the achievement of Desmarets.[2]
Colbert's nephew and disciple, he was forced to operate in a fiscal situation
created by a national emergency that was surely beyond the great minister's
worst nightmares.

The history of France and the reputation of the king would have been different if Louis had lived out his last fifteen years in peace, with the frontiers established by Ryswick, and budgets returning to the Colbertist balance. That was not, however, what would have been expected by Louis's admirers; nor, indeed, by his enemies. No more would the decisive defeats of his armies have been predicted; nor indeed a prolonging of the war to the point where he was prepared to surrender the recent acquisitions for which so much blood and treasure had been spent. Historians who have seen Louis as specially reprehensible have also depicted in darkest tones the ruinous condition of France and even seen in this earlier crisis some warning signs of the greater storm that would destroy the monarchy.[3] From that position it is a short step to ascribing to Louis XIV some responsibility for the revolution of 1789.

It is a false position and it would be a misleading step. The situation of France from 1708 to 1713 – from Oudenarde to Denain – can be better understood by reference to an earlier crisis, that of the Mazarin years. Politically, of course, there was a world of difference. There was no danger of a Fronde. The stability of the Orléans Regency, in significant contrast to that of Anne, illustrates the transformation that had taken place in sentiment and in notables' perception of their interest as partners, in a sense, in the operations of government – and its spoils. The absolutist consensus was challenged only by a few dissident voices – and then not as to the nature of sovereign power but the ends to which it should be put. Moreover the experience of the years 1715–40, with fast-growing trade, financial reform and reduction of debt, suggests that a leading role in Europe was compatible with a sound financial position. Even after 1763, and two debilitating wars, matters were by no means irremediable. With growing commercial activity and an efficient administration eighteenth-century France, once more a naval power, had the potential to be prosperous and strong. It was involvement in the American war of 1778–83 that would strain the finances to the point at which reform was inevitable – and dangerous to the régime. Looking to traditions rather than to the interests of the state, having less reason than Louis XIV to make war, and exhibiting a greater recklessness, Louis's successors and their ministers would fail to profit from his painful experience or his last advice to his great-grandson.[4]

The drive to create a powerful army and navy, requiring a larger revenue and more effective ministerial control, had a crucial role in the development of the absolutist state. Nor, as we have seen, was the process confined to France. Between 1667 and 1714 the wars in which France was a major player became more extensive, saw the deployment of larger armies and involved ever greater expenditure. More than ever war played the main part in determining the financial health of the country, having particularly damaging effects when, as in France, unlike England, there had not evolved an efficient way of tapping surplus wealth. The lack of an institution comparable to the Bank of England[5] must rank high in an assessment of the impact of war on France. It should also be placed in context. Colbert's policies, influenced largely by his awareness of the shortage of specie, had helped to obviate some of the worst effects of the monetary famine – but it had persisted. His successors, Le Pelletier, Pontchartrain, Chamillart and Desmarets, had to search for expedients to deal with a situation which was largely beyond their control. They struggled to meet the bills of war from resources attenuated by deflation. The downward trend of prices reflected the diminishing flow of precious metals entering Europe. The percentage annual increase in the amounts of gold and silver had halved during the century: in 1700 it was only 0.5. Against that background, and as it affected a financial system which was being reduced, in Beik's words, to 'a competition for the effective possession and use of rare liquid capital',[6] the Revocation is seen to have been specially unfortunate. There was a substantial loss of capital to the banks of Amsterdam and London and reduction in the bargaining power of ministers when it came to contracting over tax farms or negotiating loans.[7]

The effects of Revocation could have been foreseen. Nature's contribution could not. Yet its role was crucial in the pre-scientific agrarian economy. The impact, just over halfway through each war, 1693–95 and 1708–9, of exceptionally severe winters, cold springs, wet summers and spoiled crops, had an effect which can be measured not merely in terms of weak demand and falling revenue, but in a sharp reduction in population: around 2 million in the first case, 1.5 in the second. The distress and loss helped tilt the balance against mercantilism.[8] The *laboureur* was widely seen, even idealised, as the type of worthy peasant, thrifty and industrious, potentially beneficent as employer and investor, but also, in relation to his resources, the prime taxpayer in bad times. His plight stirred the consciences of those, whether coming from the secular anti-Machiavellian, or Christian agrarian tradition, who saw, in Colbert's policies, not significantly modified by his successors, a perverse misapplication of the power of the state. Fénelon was not alone in questioning whether France could maintain a military power sufficient to defeat a coalition on the basis of so vulnerable an economy.

The money problem was much aired. The Protestant pamphlet, *Soupirs de la France esclave*, spoke of a shortage of money so remarkable that transactions were being stopped because 'those who have bread cannot buy wine nor those who have wine, bread'. At the receiving end of virtually static returns from the *taille* and the tax farms, ministers would see the problem in less picturesque terms. They followed Colbert in relying upon statistics. The great inquest ordered by Beauvillier for the duke of Burgundy in 1697 was only one of several. A census was carried out in 1693, another in 1709. Outside government Vauban – no man knew the country better – and Boisguilbert,[9] a southerner but an official in Rouen, offered thoughtful analyses of the country's plight. Both departed from strict mercantilist doctrine in proposing some test other than precious metals for the health of the community: Vauban's concern in *Dîme royale* was population, Boisguilbert's in *Détail de la France* was agriculture, ruined, as he saw it in Normandy, by the *taille personelle*. 'It was the ruin of goods, bodies and souls.' But both attributed to money the vital economic role. In Boisguilbert's phrase it was 'the valet of commerce'. One remedy favoured by ministers was turning back gold and silver into currency. Always aware of the need to set an example Louis ordered, as early as 1689 that silverware be sent to the mint: eventually his palaces were stripped of their ornaments of silver and gold. Even the silver throne at Versailles, so recently installed, was sent to the mint. Bishops were asked to donate unused church plate. Even if the wealthy had responded more generously, there would only have been a marginal effect on the world of cash and credit within which ministers had to operate.

DESPERATE MEASURES

Every year after 1701 saw a gap between the crown's income and its expenses. As short-term expedients brought further charges on revenue, it widened remorselessly till policy was reduced to a race, hard for ministers to conceal, between peace and bankruptcy. From the outset the crown had a limited range of options. It could increase existing taxes or create new ones. The nature of the *taille* and of an inelastic agrarian régime meant that even in good harvest years, it could not be made to yield much more. The systematic raising of *subsistance* reduced somewhat the cost of the armies but made it harder to raise much from new taxes. The low level of domestic demand and the further effect of war on trade curtailed what could be raised in indirect taxation through the tax farms. The *gabelle* held steady but revolts had shown that it could not be extended. New taxes would only have a substantial yield if they tapped hitherto immune or in some way privileged individuals. That was the thinking behind the *capitation* and the more radical *dixième*,[10] both imposed at a time of national emergency, without which it might have proved impossible to secure cooperation. It also provided an argument for new tenders for sale of offices as a covert form of tax, justified by its being taken from those who were usually exempt, when the crown accepted payments in lieu by existing office holders to preserve their own rights.

The main attraction of office creation was that it tapped a seemingly inexhaustible fund of social aspiration. As Pontchartrain memorably observed: 'each time Your Majesty creates an office God creates some fool to buy it'. It has been estimated that offices of value 1,570,000,000 *livres* were created between 1600 and 1715. Nearly half that total accrued during the last twenty-five years. It added hugely to the state's expenses in salaries and tax exemption. 16.4 million in 1683, the cost of *gages* had risen to 37.6 million in 1715. No less crippling was the continuous borrowing operation through issues of *rentes* and the seductive but ultimately damaging device of the *tontine*,[11] and consequent rise in payment of interest. Colbert had reduced the total of charges on the revenue to 22 million *livres*; it was 48 million in 1706, 90 million in 1713. The church paid a larger *don gratuit* but it was too influential at court to allow a payment commensurate with its wealth.

Finance ministers in difficulties usually defer payment of interest and salaries. No less short-term was the manipulation of currency. Colbert had eschewed the method. Le Pelletier revived it. In 1692–94 coinage was called in and re-minted, using a smaller amount of precious metal. In 1689 and on four subsequent occasions the *contrôleur-général* announced that the coins in circulation were worth a different amount. The main advantage to the crown, being the largest debtor in the land, was that it wiped out lenders' profit on short-term loans. But it encouraged hoarding and discouraged investment.

It is customary to point to the lack of a central note-issuing bank and of soundly backed paper money as fundamental weaknesses of the old financial régime. The apparent reluctance to adopt what was plainly successful in England is usually traced to France's 'bubble' experience of 1721 and the resulting failure of John Law's system in that year. But there was already prejudice because of the government's irresponsible use of credit instruments in the previous thirty years. Because transporting cash was dangerous and costly, tax collectors followed mercantile practice in using letters of exchange drawn on private individuals to transmit funds from the provinces to the capital. In wartime government needed cash more urgently, refused to accept instruments of exchange but ventured into the system itself by issuing paper to pay its debts. Payment orders, *mandements*, from the *Épargne*, bearing the royal signature, were commonly used: they authorised payment to a creditor from tax receipts. In 1701 the crown took the process a step further by issuing *billets de monnaie*: at first they were certificates, valid as cash, in return for old coins; after 1704 they were issued more regularly and no longer backed by metal.

More promising for the future was the revival, in 1702, of Colbert's loan bank, *caisse d'emprunts* (abolished by Le Pelletier).[12] It might have flourished in a more favourable climate. But defeats and the postponement of peace saw confidence wilt, interest rates rise and certificates losing half their value. The next stage was the forced loan – under other names, as government forced holders to convert their bills into claims on other revenues, into annuities and even new certificates, defined as cash in the Paris region. When Chamillart, over-worked and desponding, resigned (1709), Desmarets inherited a situation not wholly dissimilar from Fouquet's in the 1650s. He showed skill in exploiting his wide connection at home and abroad to raise loans and farmers for the indirect taxes and he set up a new *caisse* based on the resources of twelve *receveurs-généraux*: it issued interest-bearing certificates supported by the income from various taxes and money-raising devices. Before the end of the war its paper was worth 600 million *livres* on top of the old *rentes*. Living dangerously Desmarets could assure the king that his soldiers would be paid. But the failure of peace talks in 1710 convinced him that a new initiative was needed if the war effort was not to collapse.

The *capitation* of 1695, a direct tax of universal application, was important, as a departure from time-honoured practices of tax exemption, an assault on the principle that underlay them and a mark of the authority of the king. It was maintained until 1699, and renewed in 1701, but with so many exemptions and special deals, that its yield was negligible. The *dixième*[13] of 1710 was tougher: it was a levy on wealth in land, town property, office, loan interest and manufactures. Its preparation was shrouded in secrecy, the work of a group of Desmarets' relatives and clients – an illustration of the value, if not necessity, of this feature of government. *Intendants* were responsible but their *subdélégués* played a vital part, as men with local knowledge. With difficulties of verification, concealing and haggling, and arguments about privacy, the tax offered a challenge to those determined to evade it. The church secured a large concession. By December 1711 three-quarters of the nobility of Auvergne had simply refused to declare. The merchants of Lyon were particularly obstructive. Lawyers prospered accordingly. As usual the south-west proved most awkward. Yet there was only one case of rioting, in distant Béarn.

The *dixième* cannot be called a failure. It can be cited as evidence for a real advance in government, the way in which it was perceived and could operate.

It raised 18 million *livres* in 1711, 96 million in four years. The army received recruits, weapons and food. The *dixième* did not turn privileged Frenchmen into conscientious taxpayers but it did introduce the germ of an idea of civic responsibility into a system which had long exhibited so much that was inefficient and unfair. It offered hope for the future. Colbert might have found some consolation in his nephew's achievement. Meanwhile Colbertism was being rejected. Coming from different sources, reflecting varied concerns, philosophical, theological and social, opposition went beyond demanding a more equitable tax system and calling for free trade; it questioned the aims of government.

A CRISIS OF MORALE: COLBERTISM CHALLENGED

In relation to financial issues alone it is inappropriate to use the much overused word 'crisis': the situation was never so dire or politically destabilising as in the 1640s. Louis remained visibly in charge and that helped keep his ministers steady. In respect, however, of the morale of the régime in the years that separated the defeat of Oudenarde from the peace of Rastadt it can be justified: at a time of disillusion and soul searching 'crisis' accurately reflects the sense of being on a course to disaster, together with a readiness to think about change and sacrifice. Through respected figures at court the spirit of enquiry touched council and king. Between spokesmen for different interests, offering distinctive solutions, there were patches of common ground and some evident cooperation. The revolt of the merchants evoked sympathy among nobles and churchmen: defeats and deficits provided supporting evidence for the general case for change. Yet there never developed a concerted movement of opposition. Throughout, the ideological conflict, like the position adopted by individuals, was affected by separate issues. Mme de Maintenon turned from Fénelon to Noailles because of the furore over Quietism.[14] Seignelay's spirited defence of the naval interest and advocacy of the war of commerce envisaged by his father must be viewed in the context of the rivalry of the ministerial clans. More nobles surely were moved by hostility to the *capitation* than by the reasoning and rhetoric of the Christian agrarians. A serious grievance of the bishops was the scale of the *don gratuit* which made the church resort to the alienation of lands. Each interest, tradition and agenda therefore requires separate treatment.

Seventeenth-century merchants believed in a limited free market – limited to their own area of interest and potential profit. Some merchants attacked protectionism because their own trade had suffered. Others, beneficaries from tariffs and from privateering, and now eager investors in Colbert's trading companies, sought to use their wealth to bring pressure on government. The remarkable careers of men like Thomas le Gendre[15] and Samuel Bernard[16] show how enterprising individuals with international connections, taking advantage of the crown's increasing need of loans and advances on taxes, could move from trade and banking to positions of power and influence. Le Gendre inherited interests ranging from Canada to Morocco and the Guinea coast. The *intendant* at Rouen reported: 'The Sieur Legendre has correspondents in every possible place and his wealth runs from four to five millions.' He converted to Catholicism in 1685 but continued to work closely with the older branch of the family, still Huguenot, in Amsterdam and maintained other contacts with Huguenots abroad. He was ennobled but, stated the revealing royal letter, that rendered him 'equal to the nobles with whom he may associate, without . . . impeding him from carrying on his trade'. When in 1693–94 there was a severe grain shortage it was to him that Pontchartrain turned to relieve it. Those ships sailing into Le Havre from Protestant Holland and Scandinavia 'for the account of Thomas Le Gendre', his presence at the conference table where, in 1697, the Franco-Dutch tariff reduction was negotiated, show us aspects of reality behind the face of royal power. Another was the appearance of Samuel Bernard at Versailles, as Louis XIV's honoured guest. Bernard's story is even more remarkable. He too became Catholic but exploited his contacts with staunch Huguenots. Religion rarely interfered with trade. His contacts helped secure naval supplies and his investment in privateers brought huge profits. In 1696 Pontchartrain secretly gave him authority to provision all France's maritime forces. After 1701, with interests now all over the world, in grain dealings, and war supplies of all kinds of munitions, entrusted by successive ministers with confidential missions, leaned on for essential loans, he was one of the most powerful men in the land. A fortune estimated at sixty million *livres* enabled him to act as chief banker to the embattled state. In 1709 he could claim, like the Paris brothers who were similarly patriotic in the year of Denain, to have saved the state. He also became bankrupt to the extent of 30 million and had to be propped up by the state – a situation that would have seemed incredible twenty years before – and survived to make a second fortune.

The prominence of such financial giants, and the aspirations of merchants right down to single ship owners, small investors and contractors, leads to a phenomenon of the last two decades of the reign: a shift in real power: the crown's overall control of policy was never threatened, but ministers had to listen to, sometimes bend to those who had capital, could increase it – and could lend it. Le Pelletier had wanted to re-establish a traditional *conseil de commerce*. His rival Seignelay, wanting to preserve his father's régime of overall economic control , opposed it: 'this council could only multiply the diversity of advice and cause difficulty'. In 1700 Chamillart established it in a form intended to provide ministers with expert advice from leading merchant-bankers elected by twelve leading towns to represent their interests. Armed with grievances and keen to exploit opportunities, delegates took advantage of uncertainty in ministerial ranks compounded by the division of responsibility for commerce between the marine minister, Jérôme de Pontchartrain, and the inexperienced Chamillart. The very setting up of the council in peacetime was taken as an invitation to launch an onslaught on Colbertism. Everything, deputies claimed, had been conceded to monopolies; the privileged companies had killed the spirit of enterprise. The policy of the favourable balance has been taken too far and it had led to war. The deputy from Languedoc called for the abandonment of Colbert's doctrine that France must surpass the world in and by her trade, and that foreigners could be made to have recourse to her.

To the protectionist such men were provincial, unable to appreciate the larger picture and the longer term; they started from a different position; they could not appreciate the needs of the state. They did, however, know about trade. They tested Colbert's policies by their damaging effects. His tariffs had invited retaliation while the privileges of his monopolist companies had driven foreign ships from French ports and prejudiced the prospects of French ships in foreign ports. These arguments fitted so closely the concerns of the agrarian reformers that 'Liberty of Trade' became their battle cry in the heated debate of the time. There was a fairly general revolt against Colbertism. Traders chafing at the restrictions imposed by the state and nobles feeling the effects of peasant poverty that affected their rents, anticipated the arguments of the *physiocrates* of the eighteenth century. Fiercely loyal to Colbert's memory, but a pragmatist, sobered by financial experience, *contrôleur-général* Desmarets wrote to Mesnager, who was charged with a trade mission to England, that he did not believe that there was a risk to French commerce in giving 'all countries reciprocal equality': for 'the more facilities we give to foreigners to send their goods to us the more we will be able to sell of our own. Uniformity and freedom in commerce always creates wealth in the countries in which they are established.' The free traders might indeed seem to have won the argument. It was in this spirit that the government signed with the Dutch the commercial treaty of Utrecht, and a similar treaty with Prussia. Only the opposition of Whig merchants in London prevented Bolingbroke from carrying through the business on which Mesnager was engaged: the treaty with France that the Whigs themselves would achieve after the Hanoverian succession and the death of Louis XIV.

Arguments about economics had their counterparts in – and were affected by – the fierce contemporary debates about science, political theory, theology and morality. Today they would be seen as compartmentalised disciplines. In the age of Locke, Leibnitz and Baylehen they could still be studied as connected aspects of a single body of truth based on principles of universal relevance. So St Augustine, Machiavelli, Descartes and Nicole are found to be fellow lodgers in the house of mercantilism. Augustine's teaching about Divine Grace was scrutinised and repeatedly re-interpreted in the conflict over Jansenism; so was *Il Principe*, in arguments over international morality and the proper role of the state. Descartes was crucially important in promoting a mechanistic view of the universe whose main casualty was the idea of a God-ordered cosmos, every part created for a determinate cause. For the Jansenist intellectual Pierre Nicole man, without divine grace, is necessarily corrupt. Yet he held that in a kingdom organised according to Cartesian physics, its people, like those envisaged by Machiavelli, being motivated by the instinct to survive, could still glorify God. Though true justice and charity in the individual could only come by grace, through nature's laws a corrupt society could still conform outwardly to the rules of justice. The sanctions in such a society, inevitably competitive and potentially self-destructive, were those ordained by an overriding secular authority. So here was another route to absolutism, the utilitarian, concerned with 'enlightened self-interest'.

There were other reasons for those, like Fénelon, who spurned the utilitarian idea of society to oppose Jansenism. There were, we have seen, other arguments against mercantilism besides its being derived, supposedly, from Machiavelli's idea of a world of hostile, self-contained political units. Colbertism, in project and propaganda, was intimately bound up with the idealisation of the state and with its expansion. But there were grounds for concern about the condition of the peasant masses beyond the idea (a misreading of Colbertism, though apparently its effect) that to subordinate economic activity to the requirements of foreign trade was to sacrifice domestic well-being to increase the power of the state. Opposition groups interacted and became bolder when that power seemed first to have been abused, misdirected, and then found wanting. It is easier to identify the reasons why disparate groups might become critics of the régime than to judge their effectiveness. But when there was a prominent churchman of high character, with the imagination to see an alternative way forward, then various arguments for reform could become a significant movement.

AN ALTERNATIVE VOICE: FÉNELON

François de Salignac de la Mothe-Fénelon (1651–1715), of a noble but impoverished family in Périgord, had risen swiftly to eminence in church and palace, through his ability and pastoral zeal as converter of Huguenots, and the patronage of Bossuet and of Mme de Maintenon. She welcomed him into her circle of *dévôts* and appreciated the humane idealism expressed in his treatise on the education of girls (1687). Scholarship lightly worn; a rare imagination; single-mindedness in pursuit of his ecclesiastical and political aims, a fervent spirituality that won many hearts; the independence of mind that made him a rebel at the heart of the establishment – there is enough to make him a compelling figure. The classical humanist who prefigured romanticism; the prophet of agrarianism whose pastoral vision seems to have derived as much from Virgil's *Georgics* as from knowledge of peasant farming; the academician who proposed that taste rather than dogma should be the guiding principle in the art of writing; the *dévôt* and mystic who can also be seen as a precursor of Enlightenment: several men in one, Fénelon defies neat definition. He provoked the conventional: Bossuet over Quietism, Maintenon after her first enthusiasm veering towards orthodoxy and her husband's view, and, inevitably, Louis XIV himself. The king might have tolerated the 'chimerical spirit' of the young abbé whom he had made tutor to the duke of Burgundy (1689) and archbishop of Cambrai (1695), had he not also offended by criticising the régime which had promoted him to a position where such criticism could hurt.

The king may not have read the text of Fénelon's emotional letter of 1694, in which the archbishop described a stricken realm, 'one vast hospital' and denounced ministers who served a king 'like a man with a bandage over his eyes'. Its main themes were developed in *Télémaque*[17] which the king certainly did read.

Fénelon described *Télémaque* as a 'fabulous narration in the form of a heroic poem like those of Homer and Virgil'. Into it he had put 'the main instructions which are suitable for a young prince whose birth destines him to rule'. The audacity of the work, written for the young prince but published (1699) illicitly by an enterprising printer, is contained in Fénelon's next words: 'In these adventures I have put all the truths necessary to government and all the faults that one can find in sovereign power.' Louis XIV read only the faults described in Fénelon's account of the misrule of king Idomeneus and, by implication, throughout the book. Mentor, the tutor, condemns the king for failing to listen to disinterested advisers, preferring war to peace and luxury to simplicity. He should change while there was yet time. 'Hasten to repair these faults, suspend all your great works . . . let your people breathe in peace.' Beyond rebuke and repair it is, however, the forward-looking and constructive side to this unique experiment in political education which could have been so important, but left only sadness and the frustration of wondering what might have been.

After exile to Cambrai (1697) Fénelon remained, through his letters, the inspiration of those who criticised the régime, and Burgundy the focus for all who looked for change. When Fénelon heard that the duke was 'too content with his obscure life' he reminded him that 'the realm of God does not consist in a scrupulous observance of minute formalities. A great prince ought not to serve God in the same way as a solitary or simple individual.' He should follow the example of St Louis. His policies should be based upon avoidance of war, therefore of excessive taxation, which would offer to France the blessings which Fénelon attributed to the mythical republic of Salente. All there engaged in agriculture and lived in peace and plenty. The legislator's purpose was to secure a natural increase in population, not by conquest but through good farming and an increase in the food supply. In his *Examen de conscience sur les devoirs de la royauté*,[18] drawn up for the duke, he impressed on Burgundy the horrors of war. His first-hand knowledge of conditions in the Cambrésis, with its refugees and ransacked farms, complemented Burgundy's own unhappy experience of military command. Fénelon's liberal values and an unfettered imagination brought fresh thinking to familiar topics. He contrasted, for instance, the lot of the beggar who steals a *pistole* because he is hungry, and that of conventional heroes who rob neighbouring states of their liberty: magistrates crush the hungry individual while poets laud the feats of the army which has injured thousands. The humanitarian appeal is grounded on a wider view of human rights. In the *Dialogue des Morts*[19] we read:

> each individual owes incomparably more to the human race, which is the great father-land, than to the particular country into which he is born. As family to nation, so is nation to universal commonwealth. Therefore it is infinitely more harmful for nation to wage war on nation than for family to wrong family.

With ideas ranging so boldly it is not surprising that the archbishop had to stay in his diocese. His thinking was more subversive, however, when he questioned what lay behind the misdirection of royal policy. Here he revealed himself the nobleman. The ills of the realm resulted from the error of the king in excluding its rightful counsellors from government. He pronounced that the ideal state was an aristocracy, in which birth, the distinction which all could respect, should be the first qualification for office. As if blind to the evidence of the events of the past century he maintained that aristocratic government would be more stable and balanced than absolutism because – a revealing notion which would be taken up by the *philosophes*, though not for the same purpose – it was not artificial. There was in Fénelon's thinking, whether about politics, religion or education, a sentimental leaning towards the natural, what seemed to conform to man's instincts, that would endear him to Rousseau. He saw hypocrisy at Versailles and a mercenary trend: especially offensive was the sullying of noble title and values by *mésalliances*, secret investment in financial syndicates, and sales of nobility. In the taming of nature in which Louis took such pride, and the acquiescence of nobles in the cult of royalty, he saw mere artificiality. Fénelon rationalised the prejudices which can be seen in every page of Saint-Simon and were, undoubtedly one common factor in all the murmurs and intrigues at court against '*bourgeois*' ministers. Louis was mainly concerned about Fénelon as an influence on Burgundy. But Burgundy was not his immediate heir till 1711, after the untimely death of the Dauphin, and then only for a year. Meanwhile, critics of the régime, those excluded from the networks around the current ministers, those with grudges and those who wanted to be near to the seat of power in a future reign, clustered in loose, secretive groups. Under the sharp eye of the king there could be no open disintegration at Versailles. His stoical bearing stiffened patriotic resolve and isolated the defeatist. But there were recognised pressure groups at court who speculated and planned for the future. With reform in the air, intrigue was a tonic to nobles long deprived of any genuine part in political life but still nostalgic for imagined days when the nobility helped the king to govern. Ever sharp and forthright in her comments on the surface of affairs Madame described 'the vastly pretty comedy' to her fellow German, the duchess of Hanover:

> the entire court is in a ferment of intrigue. Some try to win the favour of the all-powerful lady [Maintenon], others again that of M le Dauphin, others again that of the duc de Bourgogne. He and his father have no love for one another; the son despises the father and would like to rule.

GREAT EXPECTATIONS – AND TRAGIC LOSSES

Nearest to the centre of affairs was 'the cabal of the nobles', long-serving courtiers, associated with earlier successes, respected as soldiers, like Marshal Boufflers or diplomats, like Harcourt. Loyal to the king they blamed ministers for military disasters. The 'cabal of Meudon', under the wing of the Dauphin, was more detached and conspiratorial, indeed faintly *frondeur*. Again it was concerned more with personalities than with principles. Here simmered the familiar illegitimacy grievance. Prominent figures were the princesse de Conti and duchesse de Condé, daughters respectively of La Vallière and Montespan, determined to secure the legitimisation of the royal bastards. It became a more urgent issue after 1712 and the disturbing possibility of the duc d'Orléans coming to the throne.

Quite different from the others was the clique that formed round Burgundy. Aged 29 when his father's death, in 1711, made him heir he had already made more mark than his dutiful father. The latter's long waiting in the wings, without a leading role either in war or council, had dulled his spirit and any inclination he might have had for independent thought or action. His strong-willed son, given to moodiness and fits of rage, had been given, with his younger brothers Anjou and Berry, a secluded and intensive education. His governor, the *dévôt* duc de Beauvillier, Louis's trusted adviser and the first nobleman to enter the *conseil d'en haut*, is a man hard to comprehend outside the intense spiritual and moral climate of French Catholicism: of his nine daughters seven took the veil at the same convent. He worked with Fénelon to impress on his charge that a king lived for his people, not the people for the king.

'Our princes have not been taught to live', wrote Madame. Certainly Burgundy cut an uneasy figure, often abstracted and introspective, more interested in physics and metaphysics than in the conventional pastimes of court and camp. He was an unwavering supporter of anti-Huguenot measures when many were becoming doubtful about them and distressed about their consequences. After Oudenarde he avowed a lonely, serious pacifism which the typical courtier foolishly construed as cowardice or what might be expected of a humourless prig. Did his wife Marie-Adelaide of Savoy see a lighter side? She brought charm and gaiety to the court and some comfort to the old king.

Promise and hope turned to tragedy in February 1712 when first the duchess, then Burgundy and their elder son died, victims apparently of measles – and, surely, the treatment of the court doctors.[20] 'History is disarmed before his memory', wrote Michelet. One can only guess what kind of ruler he would have been. Some contemporaries thought that his training, as boy and adult, had made him too scrupulous. He could have been a Joseph II,[21] too rigid and unrealistic a reformer. He could have found a happy medium between the political reforms that were so badly needed and the sentimental conservatism that coloured the aristocratic reformers of the period. He could have found that the militarist tradition was too strong to resist. He could also have found that the force of aristocratic reaction was incompatible with the programme of reform in which he was interested. Absolutism, without its arbitrary elements, aristocratic government with a responsible notion of service to the state: only a remarkable sovereign could have brought off so desirable a balance.

The death of Burgundy brought prominence to the personality and claims of Philippe duc d'Orléans, son of Monsieur, Louis's brother, who had died in 1701.[22] Both men advertised themselves by outrageous behaviour. For both the same excuse may be made: they were allowed too little scope for ability and energy. The son was genuinely talented. In 1707, repeating the pattern of his father's military career, he showed initiative and courage campaigning in Spain, only to be recalled. As if to prove his critics right he plunged into dissipation. 'Never was man so gifted, yet no man's life was ever so flat, vain, empty', said Saint-Simon, who turned to him as reformer in the aristocratic interest after 1712. He would turn restlessly to music, to painting, to fashionable chemistry, to one of a succession of mistresses. His mother recited the list of his accomplishments in a letter to her sister and yet concluded: all that does not keep him from being bored by everything. It offended the king that he obviously preferred louche parties in Paris to the more formal occasions at court. He rebelled against the slow and stifling routines and the jealous dominance of the king. He loved, perhaps needed, to shock. He was once seen at Midnight mass on Christmas eve, deeply immersed in what appeared to be his missal – and afterwards announced that he had been reading Rabelais. Louis had despised the father; he detested the son. Orléans invited distrust and rumour: that in Spain he had been planning to subvert his brother Philip V; that at Versailles he was poisoning his way to the throne.

He could not be accused of the death, in May 1714, of Berry, Louis's third grandson; he had internal bleeding after a fall from his horse. But this death meant that only a child of three stood between Orléans and the throne. If power over the child who was to be Louis XV were not to come into the hands of the bastards, Maine and Toulouse, Orléans must take a lead.

As minds turned to the prospect of regency a faction formed: disgruntled courtiers, conservatives who argued for hereditary right in the face of illegitimacy, and *parlementaires* who hoped to use the chance of a regency to claim political privileges that they had lost – or had never possessed. Meanwhile, however, in July 1714, *Parlement* registered without demur a royal edict declaring Maine and Toulouse fit to inherit the throne in default of a legitimate prince.[23]

It was an extraordinarily bold step, born of the king's anguish after tragic family deaths and his justifiable concern about the future. As an extreme statement of the absolutist idea that royalty was a race apart it shocked conventional courtiers into realising that there was a potent idea behind the iconography of Versailles. To ministers it was a precautionary measure justified by circumstance and valid as an expression of the royal will. To Saint-Simon it was an immoral act. He wrote of the clique of the bastards 'making a mockery of the crown and trampling on this nation'. The king, as 'head of a unique line', should have been doubly anxious to preserve its sanctity 'since he was king solely by right of inheritance' but was caused to 'dishonour and overthrow its most ancient laws in order to make possible the crowning of the offspring of a double adultery'.

Notes

1. Usually now accepted though estimates vary according to the method used. Based on figures for the years 1701–6 that sum represents thirty years' revenue from the direct and farmed taxes. Revenue figures are assessed by R. Bonney in 'J.R. Malet: historian of the finances of the French monarchy', with useful tables and graphs, *French History*, V, pp. 180–233. See also the graphs in R. Briggs, op. cit., appendix.

2. Nicolas Desmarets, *contrôleur-général* 1708–15 earned rare, if somewhat double-edged, praise from Saint-Simon: 'he had gone to the heart of all its [financial and government] aspects. Since everything passed through his hands no one knew better all the tricks of the financiers and all the profits they had made.'

3. For example, P. Sagnac and A. de Saint-Leger, *Louis XIV 1660–1715* (Paris, 1949), pp. 647–9. It is still in the Michelet–Lavisse tradition. A revealing introductory sentence refers to his 'deliberate design . . . for the submission of all Europe to his design'. For a balanced view of France's economic condition, see J. Meuvret, 'The condition of France, 1688–1715', in The New Cambridge Modern History, VI, 1970.

4. (Allegedly) 'I have loved war too much. Do not follow me in that or in over-spending.'

5. Founded in 1694, it was a private company offering a limited range of financial services, one of which was to provide paper credit for the government. Its fortunes (and interest rates) were tied to those of the war (a deputy governor was killed in the Namur trenches on a visit to the king). Its rates were always higher than those

for other loans. But – significantly – they came close to the market rate in the Spanish Succession war. That marked the crucial difference between England and France.

6. W. Beik, op. cit., p. 247.

7. But for mitigating factors, see Jean Bouvier in 'The Protestant bankers in France from the Revocation of the Edict of Nantes to the Revolution', *Louis XIV and Absolutism*, op. cit., pp. 263–80 and a review article of Luthy, *La Banque protestante en France*, 2 vols (Paris, 1959, 1961). See also p. 237, n. 28.

8. On which whole development, along with other aspects of the opposition to Louis XIV's régime, the main authority is L. Rothkrug, *Opposition to Louis XIV: The Political and Social Origins of the French Enlightenment* (Princeton, 1965). For Christian Agrarianism see in particular pp. 234–98.

9. Pierre de Pesant de Boisguilbert (1646–1714). The basic contention of the *Détail* was that the velocity of monetary circulation varied directly with the volume of agricultural (not industrial) consumption. Wealth consisted of wheat, wine, salt and linen: in all of those France was rich.

10. The *capitation* had been levied on a rough sliding scale and yielded about 20 million. The privileged managed increasingly to avoid payment.

11. So called after the Italian Tonti who invented it and introduced in 1653. Loans were raised through groups classified by age. Lenders, in effect, gambled on their outliving fellow syndicate members. For survivors the rewards could be considerable. For the state the loss was assured.

12. Louvois's ally in council, Claude le Pelletier was *contrôleur-général* 1683–89. His abolition of Colbert's *caisse d'emprunts* owed more to party prejudice than to financial calculation.

13. Richard Bonney's article, 'Le secret de leurs familles: the fiscal and social limits of Louis XIV's *dixième*', *French History*, vol. 7, no. 4, 1993 pp. 383–417 is illuminating on the whole area of government finance and the financiers at this time.

14. For Quietism see pp. 324–6. Louis-Antoine, Cardinal de Noailles, was archbishop of Paris 1695–1729: for his role in the Jansenist quarrels see pp. 323–5. His elder brother, Anne-Jules, duc de Noailles, head of a family much favoured by Louis, was a general, successful in several minor engagements.

15. For the career of Le Gendre, see Rothkrug, op. cit., pp. 230–1 and 395–400.

16. See Jacques Saint-Germain, *Samuel Bernard, le Banquier des Rois* (Paris, 1960).

17. For the much-debated question of the letter see p. 258, n. 19. After the Bible, *Télémaque* was the most read book in eighteenth-century France. Cherished by Rousseau it was profoundly influential in his thinking about nature and education. His Emile was allowed only *Robinson Crusoe* to read when young, *Télémaque* when adult. See Judith N. Shklar, *Men and Citizens: a Study of Rousseau's Social Thought*, (Cambridge, 1990), pp. 4–6. It is accessible now in a good translation: Patrick Riley (ed.), *Telemachus* (Cambridge, 1994).

18. For the text of this important work see Urbain, op. cit., pp. 29–96. There will also be found his memoirs (concerted with Chevreuse) on political action, *Plans de Gouvernement* and *Mesures à prendre après la mort du duc de Bourgogne*: he did not give up hope after his pupil's death.

19. A recent study of the *Dialogues* is in G.A. Kelly, *Mortal Politics in Eighteenth Century France* (Waterloo, Canada, 1986.) A standard text is B. Jullien (ed.), Paris, 1900.

20. Their remedy, repeated letting of blood through leeches, was the worst imaginable for the fever accompanying a severe case of measles. Only the spirited action of his nurse who removed him from the doctors' care saved the younger son, the future Louis XV.

21. Austrian Emperor, co-ruler with Maria Theresa, 1765–80, sole ruler 1780–90. The most dogmatic and thorough-going of enlightened autocrats.

22. For this complicated man and his performance as Regent, see J.H. Shennan, *Philippe duc d'Orléans* (London, 1979).

23. In May 1715 they were given the title of Princes of the Blood in preparation for entry to the regency council. Saint-Simon expressed an orthodox royalist view which has resonance even today. For Bluche, op. cit., pp. 592–4, the king had renounced his own principles with respect to the supremacy of the fundamental laws about succession (see p. 163) expressed at the time of the War of Devolution: 'the Louis XIV of 1714 repudiated the honest and juridically knowledgeable Louis of 1667'.

Chapter 14

◆

FAITH, REASON AND AUTHORITY

You are as pure as angels and as proud as Lucifer.

ARCHBISHOP PÉRÉFIXE to the nuns of Port Royal

I assure you that I have been overwhelmed by this divine solitude.

MME DE SÉVIGNÉ on the solitaries of Port Royal des Champs

JANSENISM

The gulf between Saint-Simon's view of monarchy and that implied by the legitimisation edict is one indication of the weakening of the royalist consensus. Another, also with implications for the future, was the furore over Jansenism.[1] In September 1713, after Louis had had referred the matter to Rome, the Pope issued the bull *Unigenitus* condemning essential Jansenist propositions. *Parlement* refused to register the bull and the reign ended with a constitutional impasse. The old king suffered self-inflicted wounds. Gallican principles which had contributed so significantly to the authority of the crown, and had been so useful to the king in his dealings with the Pope, were now deployed against him. How had this paradoxical situation arisen? Why was Jansenism so important to Louis?

The story of Jansenism, starting with a new interpretation of the theology of St Augustine and appealing at first to a few *dévôts*, seeking certainty and inspiration in a troubled world, might seem to belong to the sidelines, of interest mainly to historians of the church. However, the ways in which it came to matter first to Richelieu, then Mazarin, then, towards the end, obsessively, Louis XIV, point us to central political issues. Like Puritanism in

England, Jansenism cannot be viewed in religious terms alone. Seeking to assess its political impact the reader may mark the clues along the route from the posthumous publication (1640) of Cornelius Jansen's *Augustinus*. He was bishop of Ypres in Spanish Flanders, and author of tracts hostile to Richelieu and to the policy which had led to war against Spain. His associate Saint-Cyran was a mystic, an experienced confessor with a fashionable following and a *dévôt* of the most extreme kind. When Richelieu had imprisoned him (in 1638) he thought that he was nipping a schismatic, possibly treasonous movement in the bud. Becoming already a resource from which various individuals could draw what sustenance they needed, indeed as much a state of mind as a movement, Jansenism could not be so easily extinguished.

Scrupulous in a legalistic way, exclusive and, above all, spiritual perfectionists, early Jansenists might see themselves as reformers in a corrupt society, or pioneers yearning for the vitality of the primitive church; as rationalists seeking truth by following the rules of Descartes, or guardians of true doctrine against those who sought to compromise. They had in common the bracing conviction that they lived in a state of grace. As Augustine defined it, that was a predetermined gift, a special intervention of God to save a favoured individual from the common state of fallen man, so corrupted by the consequences of original sin that he could not hope for salvation. The evidence, following Augustine and Jansen, that they could find in the Bible was marshalled by rational method to provide a message of appalling clarity. It left no room for human reason or will, for the mystic's idea of Divine grace seen 'as in a glass darkly', or for an instinctive trust in the generous nature of Divine Love. Any such obscuring of the message spelt to those spiritual absolutists mere weakness, worldliness and evidence of an irredeemably fallen condition. It was noticeable that Jansenists appeared to derive from predestination a compulsion to behave in ways that would convince others – and, more importantly, themselves – that they were saved. A feature of the sect was the inclination among its lay men and women to live apart from the world and to censure its ways. Their condemnation of dancing and gambling challenged the culture of the court.

Jansenists belonged at first to close-knit *parlementaire* families, to articulate men versed in subtle argument, and to devout nuns, mostly from the same stock. They were well served by art. Philippe de Champaigne's incomparable series of paintings of Jansenist nuns provides a glimpse of their severe world. The plays of Jean Racine, orphan and early Jansenist pupil, breathe the spirit of Port Royal, high-minded, grand in theme and gesture, restrained in use of language, disciplined in argument, strictly rational.[2] In a relatively small intellectual world, where Cartesian method was the prevailing fashion, such families could be disproportionately influential. When they were associated with a history of opposition to the Jesuits, they could expect hostile attention from government. From there, though their record does not fully support the charge, it was a short step to labelling them *frondeur*. Several leading *frondeurs*, like Luynes and La Rochefoucauld and, most blatantly De Retz, had had links with Port Royal. Jansenist tenets certainly led some to a subversive political view: if political institutions were but the attempt of Fallen Man to find security they did not necessarily reflect the divine order; nor were their edicts necessarily binding on Christians. In a city where style counted and was closely observed even Jansenist style encouraged suspicion. They had 'secret habits', used code names; to the anxious eyes of government they were only half-visible.

The home of Jansenism was Port Royal, two institutions but one in spirit. Both the Paris convent in the Faubourg Saint-Jacques, where Jacqueline (mère Angélique) and Agnes Arnauld had reformed the discipline according to the precepts of Saint-Cyran, and the male community of the *solitaires*, Port Royal des Champs, a house of retreat for devout laymen, were dominated by a few families. Six Arnauld girls had entered the convent by 1640. When in 1643 their brother Antoine Arnauld wrote *De la fréquente communion* he was not only presenting the Jansenist case to his own sophisticated *bourgeois* world – and that in the year of Louis XIV's accession, with all its uncertainties. He was also following family tradition in attacking the Jesuits, for his father, in Henry IV's reign, had led the opposition in *Parlement* to the return of the Jesuits to France. Antoine argued that the Jesuits debased the sacraments by allowing easy penance and encouraged the idea that salvation could be won on easy terms. That, in the Jansenist view, was the natural consequence of too liberal a view of Divine Grace. The Jesuits attacked the book as an indictment of their methods, a threat to their existence – and, in so far as it started from Jansen's premise about the nature of grace – a fundamental questioning of the role of the church. If most persons are denied salvation of what value is the worship they offer to God? Are they members, in any meaningful sense, of the church? Much therefore was at stake in the battle precipitated by Arnauld's book. A sub-plot in the great play of the Fronde, linked loosely through the Jansenist sympathies of some leading *frondeurs*, it centred on five propositions, alleged by the censors of the Sorbonne to be contained in Jansen's *Augustinus* and to be heretical, and condemned as such by Papal bull in 1653. The typically legalistic Jansenist defence was based on questioning the *fact* that the propositions were contained in the original work; so they hoped to avoid questioning the *right* of the church to condemn them.

The quarrel was raised to a higher level by the intervention of genius, in the shape of the mathematician Blaise Pascal.[3] His *Lettres provinciales*, the first of which appeared in January 1656, the month in which his friend Arnauld was formally censured by the Sorbonne, purported to be letters from a country gentleman, staying in Paris, to a friend. Pascal's weapons were intimate knowledge of the doctrinal issues, an understanding of the power of ridicule and, above all, the style, elegant, lucid, ironic, which makes the *Lettres* so memorable. Though scrupulous about facts Pascal played teasingly on the Parisian xenophobia from which Mazarin had suffered so much. The *Lettres* were in a literary class of its own – but they were still in the tradition of the *Mazarinades*.[4] Pascal's view of the Jesuits, heroic missionaries and committed teachers, was distorted because he concentrated on their role as confessors, in particular their use of moral case law and what he saw as the lax standard of those who claimed to be saving souls by offering absolution on easy terms. The Jesuits were clearly vulnerable on that score; moreover their efforts to discredit Port Royal were ill-judged and crude. But those 'soldiers of Christ' could not be worsted so easily. Port Royal would pay dearly for Pascal's paper triumph. His stinging onslaught could not be forgiven. It is relevant to the outcome that Louis XIV had a Jesuit confessor throughout his reign. It was not hard for père Annat, père Lachaise or, most insistently, père Le Tellier to present the Jansenists as a blemish on the church and a danger to the state.

The virtue in the Jansenist position was finely expressed in the *Lettres*. Jansenists scorned any form of intellectual dishonesty. The sectarian pugnacity and pride of Port Royal was also in evidence. Pascal wrote in the confidence of his new found certainty of faith and did not pause to think of the damage he was doing to the church. This quarrel can be said to have marked the first check to the broad advance of French Catholicism. Contrasting Christian positions had been exposed in a dramatic and public fashion. The damage would continue so long as Jesuits and Jansenists attacked each other over points which seemed irrelevant to the larger questions about Christianity. No wonder Voltaire so enjoyed the letters. In the short term, however, Pascal helped create the climate of opinion in which the conscience-saving formula of 1669 left the Jansenist nuns who accepted it free to enjoy the 'Peace of the Church': they signed 'purely and simply' instead of 'sincerely'.

'Truce' might be a more apt word than 'peace'. The legacy of Arnauld and Pascal was the certainty that the Jesuits would counter-attack. With what effect on Jansenism and with what consequences for church and state would still depend on the king. Here, as with the Huguenots, we see his direct, entire responsibility for the course of events. Louis was most determined in action when his conception of duty coincided with his personal preferences and suspicions. Now his sense of proportion seems to have deserted him. Perhaps he was affected, his judgement undermined, by the insistent message, from coronation to last unction, that he, the God-given, was responsible for the well-being of the church. If ever this stoical man, so surprisingly reasonable and realistic in years of misfortune, could appear touched by paranoia, it is over Jansenism.

AN UNEASY PEACE

After 1669 Jansenism continued to make converts, with some ardent sympathisers like bishops Pavillon and Caulet. Their resistance to Louis XIV's extension of the *régale*[5] to the whole of France (1673) intensified Louis's determination to have Jansenism declared heretical. At the same time it enjoyed papal favour because of its stand against the *régale*. It was even rumoured in 1680 that Arnauld would be made a cardinal. The Jesuits dubbed Innocent XI 'the Jansenist Pope'. The movement remained small, if measured by the number of open supporters of Port Royal and exponents of Augustinian theology. But through certain town parishes, for example in Rouen and Orléans, it was finding its way into the mainstream of French religious life. It received a significant extension and new characteristics through association with the Oratory. Founded by Bérulle, Richelieu's stern critic, the Oratory had become influential through its seminaries for the training of priests on Cartesian principles. Their leading exponent was Pierre Nicole,[6] author of a book on logic for Jansenist schools, a gentle scholar, reduced by his theology to a profound pessimism about the human condition. Jansenists of his generation were busy practical men, teaching, translating the scriptures, working on reform of the liturgy, seeking the assurance of salvation through good and useful lives. They had renounced Saint-Cyran; now, with Bossuet's encouragement they turned on the new school of mysticism. In his *Réfutation des principales erreurs de Quiétisme* Nicole attacked Mme Guyon's[7] idea of direct inspiration from God: the best that fallen man could do was to work out his salvation reasonably and without sentiment. To the true Jansenist Christianity was not mysterious; it was all too agonisingly plain.

In 1679 Jansenism lost two powerful protectors: by death, the duchesse de Longueville and, by his fall from office, Pomponne, Arnauld's nephew, and foreign minister. In the same year, archbishop Harlay turned the screw on the convent of Port Royal. The nuns were told to take no more novices; their confessors were dismissed. Nicole and his fellow Oratorian, Pascal Quesnel, left for the Low Countries where they sustained the Jansenist case but in terms now less academic, more combative and so more provoking to government. The Revocation and its aftermath diverted its attention but the very success of the Jansenists in converting Huguenots and their zeal in after-care roused jealous suspicions: 'New Catholics' – but good Catholics? Were not the Jansenists little better than Calvinists?

Arnauld died in 1693, Nicole in 1695. Taking their lead from the activist Quesnel, and heartened by the appointment of Noailles[8] to succeed Harlay as archbishop of Paris, Jansenists became bolder. They knew that he would be sympathetic but he had lost the support of his patron Mme de Maintenon and was powerless to prevent the Jesuit onslaught. It focused on Quesnel's *Réflexions morales sur le Nouveau Testament*. This important book owed little directly to Jansen and drew widely on orthodox theologians. It had been published first in 1678. Enlarged and re-published in 1692 it won much praise. However, it contained Jansenist assumptions which, the Jesuits felt, should be challenged: the irresistible power of Divine Grace and the futility of human effort; the identification of sin with self-love; the glory of persecution for righteousness sake; the need for access to scripture for all Christians. All that could be labelled Calvinist.

The Jesuits could point to an implicit defiance of authority in one sentence in the *Réflexions*: 'An unjust excommunication ought not to prevent us from doing our duty.' There was also a democratic tendency in Jansenists like Jacques Boileau. His writing aroused echoes, disturbing to the hierarchy, of Richer and his advocacy, earlier in the century, of the rights of the lower clergy against the bishops. So the Jesuits could count, in the main, on the episcopal hierarchy, and not least on Fénelon, championing Mme Guyon. Mme de Maintenon had turned against Noailles, her former *protégé*; more ominously for the Jansenists, after 1693 and the settlement of the *régale* issue, Pope Clement XI was reconciled with the king.

The last two decades of the reign saw the French church in disarray. As sometimes within political parties zealous doctrinaires may fight self-destructively for principles and power – and seem to lose sight of what the power is for – so we see churchmen engaged so intensely that compromise had become impossible and the issues could only be resolved by some kind of coercion. Affecting all was the church's embarrassment in the aftermath of the Edict of Fontainebleau (1685), with differences of opinion over the treatment of *nouveaux catholiques* and tactics to be employed against the remaining Huguenots. The sheer stature of Bossuet and Fénelon meant that their impassioned argument over Quietism also had political implications.

SELF-INFLICTED WOUNDS

The Jansenists brought matters to a head when they submitted to archbishop Noailles a question of conscience arising from the case of a Parisian *curé*: could a confessor absolve an ecclesiastic who condemned the Five Propositions but refused, 'with respect and silence', to attribute them to Jansen? The hounds found scent. The old hares, 'fact' and 'right', lying low since 1669, were started: neither Bossuet nor Noailles could prevent the Jesuits from giving chase. Pope Clement XI, to whom the question was referred, decided against the Jansenists. On his orders, in 1703, Quesnel was arrested in Brussels. He escaped, but his papers were handed over to the French government. They revealed that many Jansenists still saw themselves as an elect body, under a special dispensation; they were not bound to obey Pope, bishop or king. They also witnessed to the existence of a widespread network of committed and sympathetic Jansenists. Louis, in tense wartime mood, saw them as a danger to the state, demanded from Rome a bull condemning Jansenism, and promised to use his secular powers to destroy heresy. In July 1705 the Bull *Vineam Domini* condemned the Jansenist attitude of 'respectful silence'. The formulary could now be enforced in letter as in spirit.

Turning to Rome for the theological verdict Louis had revived the spirit of Gallicanism. The Articles of 1682[9] had affirmed the right of the French church to be consulted before the publication of a bull in France. Despite the reconciliation of Pope and king the articles were still alive, not least in the mind of Bossuet, their principal architect. The successful assertion of the principle that the Pope could not make a final pronouncement on doctrinal questions without the approval of a general Council might yet save Jansenism. During the *régale* crisis the Jansenists had taken an ultramontane stand against the crown. Now, with the king and Pope working together, they sheltered behind the Gallican view of the relationship of church and state: Arnauld would have approved. However the king persuaded *Parlement* to accept the bull. His authority was sufficient – this time. Noailles sought compromise. He persuaded the clergy to accept *Vineam Domini*, but with the reservation that a Pope might be fallible on a point of fact. This left a loophole for Port Royal since the right of clergy to adjudicate on points of doctrine was preserved. But the nuns and solitaries refused to accept the Bull, reservation or no. Noailles could not save them. In the year of Malplaquet the king ordered the suppression of the two houses. The year after, in 1710, to prevent its becoming a centre for pilgrims, the very building of Port Royal des Champs was destroyed and the Jesuits were given licence to dig up the remains of notable Jansenists from their graves. There were left in Paris only nineteen of the original seventy nuns; this unhappy group was dispersed to other houses. The communal symbol of Jansenism was shattered. In a critical year in France's history, with the enemy near the gates, a domestic war had ended, apparently with a triumph for the Jesuits and for intolerance. Meanwhile the heart of Jansenism remained intact. Doctrines proved tougher than buildings.

In 1711, determined to complete the business, Louis asked Rome for a bull condemning Quesnel's *Réflexions morales*. In 1713 the bull *Unigenitus* anathematised 101 propositions extracted from the book. Noailles now had to stand firm. From a cautious Jansenist he became a resolute Gallican and he was widely supported, among others by chancellor Pontchartrain and foreign minister Torcy. Old alliances re-formed, *refusés* among the lower clergy, *appellants*, a strong minority among the bishops. Among them was the aristocratic bishop Coislin of the frontier diocese of Metz. His Pastoral Letter, subtly balanced but sympathetic to Jansenism, was suppressed by royal *arrêt*. Pontchartrain seized the opportunity to resign the chancellorship. The Sorbonne was buzzing. *Parlement* was more active than it had been for sixty years. The narrowly partisan père Le Tellier, who had succeeded the more diplomatic Lachaise as confessor in 1709, was strongly opposed to Noailles: he urged the king to stand by his new principles. Discontented Parisians seized on the issue: anything to voice anger and disillusion with the régime. As would become apparent in the next reign, it was going underground; the more popular, the more diffused it became, and the harder to define. Meanwhile a mass of pamphlets poured from the press. There was talk of a General Council, even of schism. Jansenism was the talk of the markets and Noailles, another (but worthier) De Retz, found himself the hero of a popular movement.

Louis had managed for fifty years to have the best of both worlds. He had used Gallicanism to strengthen his arm against the Pope; he had become ultramontane to prove himself a good Catholic. Now, in the last months of his reign, he was forced to decide between the claims of Rome and the traditions of the French church he had sworn to uphold. If he were to turn his back on those traditions they might become the instrument of opposition to the crown. Louis had grown up with that opposition. Did spectres of the Fronde haunt the sleep of the old and ailing king?

It is no wonder that he hesitated, groaned and blustered. *Procureur-général* Daguesseau came out boldly with a condemnation of the 'idol of Roman grandeur' and saluted Noailles – mark the words – 'as the man of the nation'. Daguesseau had been told by his wife to face imprisonment rather than give in to Louis, who shouted to him that it was not far from his room to the Bastille: if *Parlement* refused to register he would make them 'crawl on their bellies'. But Louis remained a Gallican at heart. A sovereign in the French absolutist tradition could hardly be otherwise. Only the pursuit of Jansenism could have put him into this false position. Separatist by instinct, ready to defy any authority that doubted its claims, now associating itself with the idea of a national church, it threatened Pope and king alike. Louis's pride and pre-judices wrestled with his persisting sense of himself as the embodiment of the realm. So he wavered before accepting *Unigenitus*, in the last month of his life, on behalf of church and kingdom. He proposed a national council that should obtain the submission of Noailles and the clergy. On 30 August he died. Five years later *Parlement* registered *Unigenitus*.

QUIETISM

Quietism, like Jansenism, exhibits certain perennial features of religious psy-chology; like Jansenism it stems directly from the experience of Counter-Reformation. Both movements were opposed to the orthodoxy imposed by the Council of Trent. Both provoked government to intervene. Both led to high-profile conflicts of leading churchmen. Both therefore played a part in the subtle undermining of authority in church and state. Similarities end there. The aspiration of Quietists was utterly opposed to the precise spirit of Jansenism and its utilitarian social tendency. Fénelon was drawn to the one for the same reason that he fought against the other. His ideal, 'the disinter-ested love of God', was irreconcilable with a self-interested concern with personal salvation. Man's 'glory and his perfection consist in going out of himself, in forgetting himself, in losing himself, in being swallowed up in the simple love of infinite beauty'. Already out of favour for his criticism of royal policy, Fénelon was disgraced because he came out openly in support of Mme Guyon. Her story could only have been possible in the culture of court and salon in this troubled *fin de siècle*.

Prejudice surrounded her from the start because of the precedent of Molinos, the Spanish priest condemned by the Inquisition in 1687. The mystical path commended by St Ignatius, and therefore the model for Jesuits and very precisely directed, aimed to turn the soul, by deliberate psychological effort, to see itself in the light of eternity. Another kind of mystic would rather bypass this arduous exercise, to find 'loving attention to God present in the soul'. This mystic was not controlling the process: he or she was called by supernatural voice to 'the prayer of quiet' in which God required the subject to adhere to Him. Molinos, whom some thought a charlatan and false prophet, taught this approach. By 1687 a Quietist following had grown, with small and secretive groups, looking to him for inspiration. On his arrest he had 12,000 letters from his devotees. The church feared the spread of groups operating by their own rules but linked in a way that made them a force for subversion. There was a presumption of hysteria in this kind of enthusiasm. There was also the possibility that those who claimed a special relationship to God would think themselves dispensed from normal moral rules.

Mme Guyon's serene conviction that she was a saint, capable of miracles, but also no more than the passive instrument of God's will, did nothing to allay these concerns. A wealthy widow with noble connections (distantly related to both Fénelon and Arnauld) she was a formidable woman, iron-willed and manipulative. In *Spiritual Torrents*, a typical work, she seemed to relate herself in a literal and sensuous way, to God. She claimed in all her books that she merely moved her hand to write what God directed. Her impact on otherwise worldly people suggests the power of her personality and also a yearning for religious experience. In 1680 she claimed that she had arrived, by various travels and trials (which included an embarrassing association with a Barnabite priest later consigned to a madhouse), at the 'Peace of God'. She soon enjoyed the patronage of Mme de Maintenon who introduced Mme Guyon to Fénelon and to her girls' school at Saint-Cyr. But the mystic's ascendancy over the pupils led Maintenon to ask Bossuet to enquire into Quietism. To Fénelon's chagrin Bossuet's commission found that Quietism was incompatible with Catholic belief. Fénelon believed that the commission allowed too little for the value of mystical experience and was too intellectual in its analysis. Maintenon saw, however, that the church was closing ranks against Quietism, and drew back. Fénelon's continued espousal of Mme Guyon was the main cause of his dismissal from court and enforced stay in his archdiocese of Cambrai (1698).

Mme de Maintenon, the ex-Huguenot, had been demonised by Huguenots as a malign influence on the king. She was tactfully unobtrusive in the early years of her unacknowledged marriage but that did nothing to lessen the suspicion that she was, in religious matters, a power behind the throne. In fact she had little to do with the Edict of Fontainebleau. But she was increasingly involved over Jansenism. Her likes and dislikes, her personal stake in education, and her periodic interventions and shifts of patronage, made her a significant player. She could not manipulate the king. He was his own man to the end. But it seems that she encouraged his sense of responsibility for the church in France and stiffened his resolve to act.

Fénelon, advocate of a religion of the heart, was also Fénelon the critic of Louis's policies. Bossuet was the high priest of Versailles[10] and keeper of its conscience: the man to whom Louis would naturally turn for moral support or definition of faith. He had started negotiations with Lutherans and corresponded with Leibnitz but without ceding essential Catholic positions. He believed passionately in unity and saw schism as self-perpetuating: 'variations' would lead to further and debilitating 'variations'. He had managed to be a good Gallican and a good Catholic; guardian of morality and a good courtier. He was sympathetic towards Jansenism but wary of its excesses. He had remained remarkably level-headed, as rational in argument as eloquent in the pulpit. Now, approaching old age, he took it on himself to defend the citadel of Catholicism against enemies outside and inside.

Outside the citadel they could be treated as open foes of faith and a proper view of history. There were the sceptical rationalism of Bayle,[11] the relativism engendered by travel and archaeology, the taste for travellers' tales describing ancient civilisations that owed nothing to Judaism or Christianity, the evidence of the geologist's trowel for an older world than Bossuet believed to have been created in 4004 BC. The classical doctrine still ruled the world of letters but the intellectual assumptions on which it rested were being abandoned. The process was not so dramatic as is conveyed by Paul Hazard's celebrated aphorism: 'One day most French were thinking like Bossuet; all of a sudden they think like Voltaire. It is a revolution.'[12] Furiously engaged on several fronts Bossuet could hardly stand back and take a detached view of the changing scene. But he knew, for example, that he had to change his estimate of the date of the foundation of the world to accommodate recent discoveries about Chinese and Egyptian history. He could see that the fixed frame was starting to crack. The method of Descartes had shown a potential which the philosopher's own prudence and faith had veiled; he had educated thinking men to follow the dictates of reason – and some of his followers were less cautious than he. Reason had been on the side of authority in church and state; now it was changing its allegiance. As authority came also to be discredited by its abuses and failures, most evidently in the sphere of religion, champions of reason and research became more critical of the established rules of life and politics. 'All the ills that affect a man proceed from one sole cause, namely that he has not learned to sit quietly and contentedly in a room.' Pascal's dictum well describes the inward-looking, classical state; one that is reluctant to travel, content to accept rule and prefers to search for truth in the human mind than in the outside world. But now men were travelling. Reasoned faith was becoming reasoned humanism. Soon the ascendancy of French thought would pass. Already the empiricism of Locke and Newton was rousing interest. Meanwhile moles within the walls were doing visible damage. 'You did not see', wrote Fénelon to Malebranche, who wrote to refute Spinoza, 'that what you were really doing was to subordinate religion to philosophy.'

Touching more directly on his sphere of responsibility, also following lines of enquiry which he, the good Cartesian, could hardly disavow, those who challenged orthodoxy from within were harder to refute. Specially troubling were the Oratorian Malebranche, author of *Recherche de la Vérité* and the biblical scholar Richard Simon. Speculating in the same area as English deists, like Toland, author of *Christianity not Mysterious*, Malebranche managed so to build God into the natural order as to displace the God of revelation and to reduce miracles to superstition. Sifting myth from history, Simon sought to identify the core of what could be believed, or found relevant, in the Old Testament. Such men, motivated by religious spirit, working at the heart of the Catholic establishment, forced the 'eagle of Meaux' on to the defensive. Defending orthodoxy against all comers Bossuet did not lack courage. Over Quietism, which was not so much threat as diversion, he might seem, like his royal master over Jansenism, to have lost his sense of proportion. But here he was in his element, fighting on familiar ground and confident in his arguments.

Fénelon could have bought peace by disassociating himself from Mme Guyon but he was not the man to detach person from principle. In Mme Guyon he saw a woman who went to the heart of the matter: mysticism was 'the touch of God experienced in the human spirit'. Bossuet could accept neither the style nor conclusion of a woman who could give no reason for her conduct – but could claim: 'I act infallibly so long as I have no other principle than the infallible one.' The misgivings of Bossuet and others led to informal conferences at Issy from which emerged the Articles (1695) which, it was hoped, would establish rules for the church to follow. The prayer of simple regard and the claim that extraordinary states of prayer were the only way to perfection were both disallowed. Fénelon signed the articles, but proceeded to explain his different interpretation. His *Maximes des Saintes* attempted to define the authentic tradition of Christian mysticism. Bossuet felt that the heresies of Mme Guyon were still detectable in Fénelon's work. In 1697 Fénelon appealed to Rome. While Rome pondered, the literary battle continued to the point of Fénelon's composing 'A Reply to Bossuet's remarks on Fénelon's Reply to Bossuet's Relation'. No wonder that Pope Innocent XII complained about 'the inexhaustible fecundity of the French genius'. It was not being seen at its best. While Fénelon elaborated his meanings Bossuet, 'the great simplifier', searched for their sense. He also descended to using documents entrusted to him privately. While a fascinated public learned of Mme Guyon's eccentricities, Bossuet's nephew badgered the pontiff for a favourable verdict. Louis was persuaded to write five letters to 'sustain' the Pope. We have for us, writes Bossuet the elder, 'God, truth, our good intentions, the king, Mme de Maintenon.' There is something sad about the list of powers arrayed in such a cause, as if a mocking echo of nobler days.

'The archbishop of Cambrai erred through loving God too much; the bishop of Meaux sinned through loving his neighbour too little': the Pope's words make it clear where his sympathies lay. Fénelon's eventual censure was gentle, avoiding the word heresy. Bossuet died (in 1704) without his bull. Fénelon too had the last word, announcing to his own Cathedral congregation the terms of the Papal judgement and his own defeat – then preaching a sermon on the importance of submission to Papal authority. It was magnificent, a touch of theatre, worthy of the *grand siécle*. Fénelon never returned to court but devoted himself to war-afflicted Cambrai, giving money to relieve the poor, caring for refugees and wounded. He died in the same year as his king.

Notes

1. Jansenism has inspired a considerable literature: see Bibliography. Some, like R.A. Knox, *Enthusiasm* (Oxford, 1949), pp. 176–230, tend to judge it severely. L. Cognet, *Le Jansénisme* (Paris, 1961) is concise and dispassionate. No historian doubts its significance. For a good résumé, see R. Briggs, op. cit., pp. 183–93. Also, for their influence and, specially, Puritanism, his *Communities of Belief* (Oxford, 1989), pp. 339–63.
2. The 'little schools' of Port Royal instilled Jansenist ideas in their pupils and challenged the Jesuit near-monopoly in the education of the Parisian élite.
3. Blaise Pascal (1623–62) was a loyal but uneasy member of Port Royal. Another mathematician, Descartes, could accept doubt as the initial situation of the philosopher. Pascal knew it, and expressed it in the *Pensées*, as the constant torture and stimulus of his spiritual life. Certainty came only through a mystical experience.
4. One of the most powerful of those pamphlets, *La Vérité tout nu*, had been written by Arnauld's cousin, Robert Arnauld d'Andilly. It was the sort of link which coloured Louis's view of Port Royal.

5. For the *régale* see p. 39, n. 27, pp. 85–7.
6. For Pierre Nicole (1625–95) in the context of opposition to the régime, see also p. 307.
7. For Mme Guyon in the context of Quietism, see p. 324.
8. For Noailles, see also pp. 323–4.
9. For Gallicanism and the background to the Four Articles, see pp. 85–7.
10. For this aspect, see p. 181.
11. Pierre Bayle, 'first of the sceptical philosophers' (Voltaire) was hugely influential as editor of (and prime contributor to) *Nouvelles de la République des Lettres*. His massive *Dictionnaire historique et critique* was banned in France in 1697. For the Huguenot context, see pp. 222 and 236, n. 20.
12. P. Hazard, *La Crise de la conscience Européenne (1680–1715)*, vol. I (Paris, 1935), Preface, p. i.

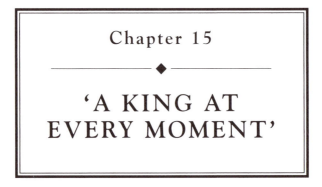

Chapter 15

'A KING AT EVERY MOMENT'

I am leaving you, but the state remains for ever.

LOUIS XIV (quoted by Dangeau)

A BRAVE END

Several routes have led us to the king's last days: diplomatic initiatives reasserting his authority after a peace more favourable than could have been expected before the battle of Denain; the frustrating tussle over Jansenism and *Parlement*'s belated defiance; the weary anti-climax of the Huguenot story; the radical provision for the succession. We have seen Louis buffeted, at times stubborn, at times compliant, readier to listen; much distressed but stoical and dignified. He might bend, but he did not break. In 1712, his blackest year, Madame Palatine wrote that she was surprised by his strength. She later wrote that he would have enjoyed a few more years of life but for the heavy attentions of his physicians.[1] They did their worst – but it may have made little difference. After a lifetime of large eating, a variety of ailments and the regular emetics that suggest mainly how tough he was, his digestion began to fail him. He was already spending more time in relative privacy. Council meetings might be held in Mme de Maintenon's chamber, she watchful but discreetly silent in a corner. He probably realised that policy was being made increasingly in ministers' chambers and that he was presented, if not with fait accompli, often with arguments too well prepared and compelling to require more than formal assent. She knew of his private misgivings and frequent tears. The public image was as stiff and unbending as ever. There was a touch of his former hauteur when the British ambassador came to complain that the French had been slow to fulfil their treaty obligation to destroy the fortifications of Dunkirk: 'Mr Ambassador, I have always been master in my own house, sometimes of others too. Do not cause me to remember it!' One of his last letters dealt with a plan to assist the Jacobites recover the British throne. On 9 August 1715 père Le Tellier conferred with the king about the registration of *Unigenitus*. That afternoon he went stag-hunting for the last time.

On 13 August, though carried to Mass in an armchair, he stood through-out a long audience for the Persian ambassador. There is pathos in Coypel's painting[2] of a tableau of faltering royalty: Louis, upright but haggard, stands beside his little grandson and his governess Mme de Ventadour. He after-wards presided over the *conseil des finances*. It was as if the pain and exhaustion were a challenge to be overcome, a last chance to set an example of duty. The pattern was maintained almost to the end, formal meetings, private consulta-tions, his favourite chamber music solacing days of increasing pain. The gan-grenous patch on his leg spread and Fagon, who had talked of sciatica and administered purges now talked of amputation. Louis declared that he was too old to bear it and prepared to die. On 25 August he awoke to the sound of drums and oboes, saluting the Feast of St Louis. That evening he asked for the viaticum. Witnessed by the princes and household officers he received the last unction. On the succeeding days he devoted his last energies to his faith, his family and closest friends. The faithful Dangeau described how each person was received separately and given a personal message. 'He acted and gave instructions like a man about to die but with a strength, a presence of mind and a grandeur of soul never before witnessed.' Madame spoke of his 'courage beyond description. He gave his orders as if going on a journey.' The little Dauphin received words that were certainly meant for a wider audience:

> My child, you are going to be a great king, but all your happiness will depend on your submitting yourself to God and on the care that you take in bringing relief to your people. This means that you should avoid, as far as possible, making war. It is the ruin of the people. Do not follow the bad example that I have set you. I have often gone to war too lightly and pursued it for vanity's sake. Do not imitate me but be a prince of peace.

The confessional style reflects the influence of Maintenon who had long agonised over the human cost of war, reinforced, no doubt, by the insistent voice of père Le Tellier, now his constant attendant. Louis had lived proudly but always, as he believed, under the eye of God; he would now die humbly, with words of contrition, placing his trust in God's mercy.

When the highest courtiers gathered round his bed to hear words of farewell, along with humbler servants, they heard him express his gratitude for their services, and regret that he had been unable to reward them better. He urged them to serve the Dauphin, 'a child, five years old, who may encounter many difficulties, with the same affection they had given him'. Would his listeners not feel the pathos in the old man's recalling his own five-year-old plight? Then: 'I am leaving you, but the state remains forever. Bind yourselves to it faithfully and you may set an example for all my subjects. Be united and in conformity with one another, for in this lie the unity and strength of the state.' Dangeau may have polished the words but there is no reason to doubt their substance. Louis knew what convention required of the dying statesman;[3] he was always concerned too about the verdict of posterity. He remembered acutely what difficulties a Regency could bring. There is also a strong and characteristic message here. At the heart of his idea of the state as a permanent interest, lies the older idea of personal service to the king. For king and subject, as for any other patron and client, it implied mutual rights and obligations, but there seems to have been something stronger. If Louis now sensed a genuine affection it was surely because he too could be affectionate. If the loyalty was heart-felt it was because he had shown himself to be conspicuously loyal to those who served him. It is among his most admirable traits.

When all allowances are made for *parti pris*, for the respect of courtiers and the love of friends, accounts of his last days ring true. As always an immaculate performance was expected of him and he did not fail to give it. From birth he had been the focus of aspiration for a secure monarchy and for order in the realm. From childhood he had been closely watched. From the age of 22 he had sustained, without respite, the awesome responsibility of personal rule. For more years than most could remember, he had been the human embodiment of absolute sovereignty, supreme judge, executive and patron. In practice too, as Fénelon said, he had been more head of the French church than the Pope. In the performance of the part to which he had been born and to which he had given his all, he had excelled the highest expectation. The rhetoric had become reality. There had been no king like him, no European sovereignty so exalted. Wherever the stage, he had been at the centre: at court, in council, in church; at war, in tent or trench, compelling attention by the mere fact that he was king, in Saint-Simon's words, 'a king in every place, a king at every moment, a king who reduced everyone to respect and breathless anticipation'. It would not be different as he approached death. He endured, but at each stage controlled, a protracted and public parting. Every symptom, every medical report of pulse or defecation, every vain remedy, down to the Provençal gentleman's nauseous concoction 'guaranteed to cure the gangrene',[4] every relapse or recovery: all were marked by those who ached to think of the greatness that was slipping away, or took position for a new régime. He died on 1 September, four days short of his seventy-eighth birthday. Within hours the papal nuncio, Bentivoglio was penning a eulogy of the king 'in whom were united all the royal and Christian virtues'.

> Whilst commanding men he remembered that he was a man himself, and he had a talent for winning the hearts of all those who had the honour of approaching him. In him, also, were great piety and justice, an excellent and rapid ability to distinguish the true from the false, moderation in prosperity and strength in adversity, no less capable in the arts of war than in those of peace. In the midst of the disorders of war he made good government flourish and spread the sciences and arts throughout his kingdom.

With more in the same vein and 'constancy in the true religion' we are left with the picture of a king 'who will live in the centuries to come, when it will be difficult to find his equal'. A very different king was the 'patron of the money-lenders, the slave of an unworthy woman, the sworn enemy of peace', to celebrate whose demise Parisians drank in their *cabarets*, lit bonfires and sang their cruel *chansons*;[5] different too from the misguided tyrant envisaged by a country *curé* who would not repeat all the verses, all the songs, or all the unfavourable comments which had been written or said against his memory:

> Louis XIV, king of France and Navarre, died on September 1 of this year, scarcely regretted by his whole kingdom, on account of the exorbitant sums and heavy taxes he levied on all his subjects. . . . During his life he was so absolute that he passed above all the laws to do his will. The princes and nobility were oppressed, the *parlements* had no more power; it was obligatory to receive and register all edicts, whatever they were, since the king was so powerful and so absolute.

The reader will no doubt allow for fulsome funerary language and Bentivoglio's sympathy towards the king who had done so much recently to gratify the Pope. Also worth recalling is the Parisian tradition of rude and radical comment (*Mazarinades* had not sprung up from nowhere). But it was surely disturbing that it was directed not against a minister but the king. In the *curé*'s strictures there are distinct echoes of Fénelon who had an important following among the clergy. They often knew, at first hand, of poverty and famine. So it would be right, in each case, to be on guard against exaggeration. Most important is to make the distinction, which contemporaries found it hard to make, between the personal and the political achievement, the one so distinctive and influential, the other still impressive in many aspects but marred by errors which had serious consequences. Where one man can see only grandeur and virtue and another only desolation and pain, where there were wholly different criteria, one cannot expect objective judgement. It is useful, then, to return to the facts, specifically at what happened in the immediate aftermath of the reign. Like Richelieu's legacy in the record of Louis XIV's own minority, his may be assessed in that of Louis XV.

POST-MORTEM: ANOTHER REGENCY

Three weeks after the registration of the edict of legitimisation (2 August 1714) the king's will had been deposited in the *chambre de greffe* of *Parlement*. An iron door and iron grille were triple locked, *premier greffier*, *procureur-général* and *premier président* having keys to separate locks. At the same time an edict informed the country that the king had provided for a regency during the minority of his great-grandson. Informed opinion might guess that the newly legitimised Maine and Toulouse would be on the Regency council. They would soon learn besides that Orléans was to be head of the council, which would also include the chancellor, the head of the *conseil des finances*, the secretaries of state, the *contrôleur-général* and marshals Villeroi, Harcourt, Huxelles, Villars and Tallard. Maine was to look after the well-being and education of the young king. All matters were to be decided by majority, Orléans having the deciding voice when opinions were divided. It was the sort of provision that Louis might be expected to make, traditional and cautious, with ministers balanced by his loyal friends and the regent granted only limited freedom to act. Louis must have had his own minority in mind when he drew up his will. It was secure only so long as he lived. No more than his father had, could he expect to control affairs from the grave.

The aristocratic reaction that followed the king's death, which went some way to fulfil the hopes of the circle of Saint-Simon, lies beyond the scope of this study of royal power. More, however than a postscript, the Regent's immediate actions, and *Parlement*'s response, do provide a significant commentary on the reign. Orléans, seeking release from Louis XIV's intended constrictions, and *Parlement*, liking Orléans' assurance that he would rule 'assisted chiefly by their counsel and wise remonstrances', worked together to effect a bloodless *coup*.

At the crucial meeting of *Parlement* on the day after Louis's death, with peers and princes of the blood in attendance, soldiers ringed the Palais de

Justice to prevent a counter-stroke by the duc de Maine. Inside, the regent claimed – and *Parlement* approved – the full powers of regency, by right of birth and in accordance with precedents. He had already secured the support of carefully chosen notables by promising them key posts in the aristocratic administration that would come to be known as the Polysynodie.[6] Villars was to be president of the war council, Noailles of the finance council; his brother, the archbishop, was also secured for the cause, a shrewd move given the volatile temper of Paris and the Jansenist sympathies of many clergy. Orléans was free to appoint to high office and to keep the household troops under his command – in effect to rule. This he did with some skill, until his death in 1723. There would be no serious challenge to royal authority during this period, nor popular disturbances.

The social tone of the Regency provides a further commentary on the reign it followed. Reaction and release were its keynotes. The presence of the old king had ensured decorum, his piety had set the tone. Frustrated libertines could now say, write and do what they wanted, knowing the Regent to be one of themselves. Corresponding to the flight from Versailles, the preference of many courtiers, like the Regent, for the less formal ways of Paris, and its uninhibited *demi-mondaines*, artists enjoyed and depicted a world apart from the classical rule of commissioned art, its serious themes and weighty symbolism. The delicate, playful art of Watteau and Lancret represents the régime at its most attractive: for the rococo artist prettiness was all. The ostentatious dissipation of the duchess of Berry, Orléans' unstable daughter, and her circle, was typical of the less salubrious aspects of the emancipation, with the flaunting of bad manners and potential for scandal that the old king, believing above all in example, had resisted to the end. Another representative figure was Orléans' friend, the poet Fontenelle.[7] When he died, in 1757, aged a hundred, the finicky *littérateur* and assiduous propagator of scientific ideas had lived long enough to see the publication of the first volumes of the *Encyclopédie*. By then the gap between official, clerical attitudes to religion, and prevalent modes of belief and conduct, had widened so far that it is possible to identify two distinct upper-class cultures. Scepticism and materialism had so pervaded the fashionable world that monarchy was being visibly weakened by association with the church which had provided, for Louis XIV, the vital sanction and support.

Dissolute, cynical, too clever to be satisfied with the orthodoxies, theological or political, but too restless in spirit to put much of consequence in their place, Orléans had shown, as titular commander in Italy and Spain, the knowledge of tactics that could have made him a fine general. Under the abbé Dubois's tutelage he had shown the aptitude for philosophy and science that earns him recognition as a plausible representative, in these seminal years, of the spirit of Enlightenment.[8] When he had emerged, after Burgundy's death, as a possible regent, his teasing style developed into a serious programme for an alternative régime. Saint-Simon and his friends rallied to the man they hoped would restore to the princes of the blood and the peers their rightful place in government. Nor, up to a point, did he fail them. He made shrewd, soothing concessions to magistrates and high nobles without surrendering his liberty to act decisively. The Polysynodie gave a few notables a share in policy-making and to some more the illusion that, by sitting alongside experts, they were so sharing. Meanwhile continuity was maintained, through firm direction and informal reference to the relevant ministers. In two vital areas Orléans retained complete control. Torcy lost his ministerial post, but was put on the foreign affairs council in 1716. Orléans needed his expertise and the files accumulated from his control of the diplomatic postbag. Dubois was the main architect of his foreign policy, seeking the peace with security which had been the main concern of Louis's last years. European peace had never seemed more secure than after the entente with Britain which developed into the Quadruple Alliance of 1718.[9] One can imagine that Louis XIV would have found alliance with Austria hard to swallow, but he would surely have approved the policy of building *entente* on the terms of the peace of Utrecht. It can as fairly be called his legacy as can the more damaging results of war.

In the last two years of Louis's reign Desmarets had pursued an orthodox deflationary policy; with the reduction of demand had gone that of commerce. Money was hoarded, debts and bankruptcies mounted; troops went unpaid and roamed about seizing what they could find. Noailles's finance council adopted the expedient, so fruitfully employed by Colbert in 1661, of 'making the blood-suckers disgorge'.[10] There were individual casualties but the old financial system and most of its seasoned operators survived. Yet the war had demonstrated the power of credit and value of state banks. As Orléans was sufficiently perceptive to realise, radical reform was called for. In John Law he found the man to undertake it. Law's system[11] – and its failure – is explicable in terms of Colbertism and the economy that underlay it. Again the apparent postscript is found to be a commentary on the reign. Law could rely less than the financiers of England and Holland on the generation of economic activity through the manipulation of the money supply. He was planning for a society in which the mercantile values were overlaid by the structure and mentality of absolutism, erected, as we have seen, above a society of orders and corporations, of many-tiered venal office, not readily malleable, tenacious of rights. To implement his schemes Law needed greater intervention by the state. That had been powerfully resisted during Louis's reign. During the regency, when the full authority of the crown was wanting, the current flowed even more strongly against innovation.

To the old king's discomfort *Parlement* had begun to flex its muscle over Jansenism and the Gallican issue that arose from the king's policy towards the sect. Louis XIV had never done more than suspend *Parlement*'s right of remonstrance. He had not needed to. Taxation of the privileged classes had been presented as exceptional, a wartime expedient. When the Regent restored some latent powers to *Parlement* he was giving away less than some magistrates hoped. They pushed hard. In 1717 they refused to register a financial edict and secured from government a detailed account of the state's income and expenditure and nominated a commission to inspect it. In 1718 successive remonstrances against financial policy compelled government to resort to a *lit de justice*. To reinforce the lesson three *Parlementaires* were arrested. In 1720, after *Parlement* had refused to register another financial edict the regent ordered the whole body to be exiled to Pontoise. At the same time it was made to accept *Unigenitus*. In that sequence of events can be seen a contrast with events in Louis XIV's own experience of regency which speaks volumes for what he had achieved.

ENVOI

It is generally accepted that Louis XIV was a highly accomplished performer in the skills and style of kingship. All would allow that he was dignified and stoical, diligent, methodical, endowed with an excellent memory, ability to master detail and – that other valuable gift in a sovereign – genuinely able to impress, to please and to evoke loyalty. There, however, agreement ends. To admirer and detractor he is still a very different kind of king. Given the varying lines of approach there is unlikely to be anything approaching a definitive account, let alone a common verdict. The Republican France of today is still, in some respects, the France of Louis XIV.[12] The nostalgia for monarchy is still powerful. It is also the France of the Revolution and of Napoleon. After two centuries of dispute about its place in the state French Catholicism is still, latently, political; anti-clericalism is still potent wherever there is religious fervour. It is therefore to be expected that a French historian, writing about the *ancien régime*, will allow political and religious principle, if not overtly to guide the pen, at least to predispose to a certain colour of ink. To the Anglo-Saxon historian the challenge is different: it is to enter imaginatively into a world of unfamiliar values while preserving the necessary degree of objectivity. He is helped by the immense literature around the subject, including some monographs of the highest quality. He must still select and judge in such a way as to help the current generation of readers to make their own informed judgements. If only to provide a starting point for discussion he may also feel that he should risk an overview of the reign.

Before the seventeenth century France was a country broadly similar to others in terms of sovereignty: political authority was widely diffused, royalism strong in sentiment but weak in practice. In the seventeenth century there developed a distinctive form of absolute monarchy, widely admired and copied. The first half of Louis XIV's personal rule, and the ministries of Colbert and Louvois, saw the most intense phase of that process. Though for various reasons it attracted more criticism during the later years, the process was not reversed. New measures – like the *dixième* – tested royal authority to the limit. Louis appeared then to be less aware of traditional constraints and, to conservatives at court and in *Parlement*, to be crossing the line that divided the legally absolute from the capriciously arbitrary. He not only thought the unthinkable – but acted on it, taxing the wealthy and legitimising the illegitimate. In so doing he bequeathed a lesson to his successors. The potential for reform existed, along with the mechanism for implementing it. Responsibility for the failures in government that were to lead eventually to revolution surely lies, not within the system but with those who set the tone, and made the decisions, principally Louis XV and Louis XVI.

When Louis died there was still a fund of good will towards monarchy. The Regency showed that government could act effectively even when the king was a minor. The subsequent régime of Fleury[13] demonstrated some of the best aspects of Louis XIV's government, along with the commitment to peace which brought financial stability and a widening spread of prosperity. And yet it is still possible to argue that there were defects in the political system and in its supporting apparatus that could only be overcome by a statesman of exceptional ability and strength – such as Hohenzollern and Habsburg were fortunate to have.[14] An extreme way of expressing that view – too reductionist in my opinion – is that all the power that monarchy had managed to amass enabled it to do little more than to fight longer wars, with larger armies and with more ample resources; to postpone bankruptcy for longer than previous régimes; to ensure a greater degree of security against foreign invasion and domestic revolt. The reader will have realised that it is not my view. To remove the word 'little' puts the achievement in a fairer light.

The questions remain: not just how much 'more', but why not so much more that there would be no need for further investigation?

The reductionist view appears to be strengthened by evidence for the relative failure of some of Colbert's commercial and industrial enterprises. It gains force from the financial difficulties of the later years and the distressing effects of famines, together with the highly articulate criticisms of government policy that accompanied them. It can lead to a bleak conclusion: given the inelastic conditions of the economy there was little that the strongest government could have achieved to improve the lot of the people: increased regulation, in these circumstances, could only fail to do more than to protect the state against civil disobedience.

A main trend in modern scholarship is to expose the large gap between the high pretensions and claims of royal government and the reality, what its agents could actually do.[15] In a sense the constitutional conflict was won by the crown. In the general submission and cooperation of the privileged classes after the Fronde can be seen the justification for calling Louis XIV's monarchy absolute. To secure loyalty, however, and to be effective, the crown needed to work with the grain of an aristocratic society, to show that there were tangible rewards for any perceived loss of political influence. In other words, a government that was strong in terms of military strength and internal security had to accept a degree of complicity with the privileged élites at the centre and in the provinces. *Parlement* might not be able to mount a political challenge to the crown but its judicial position was strengthened; *les grands* might not aspire to a place in council but they, and a number of those prepared to be serious members of the enlarged court, could find new ways to wealth and influence through patronage and financial deals. In the provinces *intendants* found that they had to work with the main authorities in church and state if they were to achieve anything. We can say that absolute monarchy was imprisoning itself by the terms on which it secured its authority.

It is within that frame that Louis XIV's kingship should be judged. It is possible, we have seen, to point to certain errors of judgement. Even allowing for the fact that he did not expect the later and most costly wars to last so long – though he should have made allowances for it after the six-year Dutch War – he can be criticised for acts of omission and commission that helped bring those wars about. Acting sometimes on grounds of *raison d'état*, while proclaiming dynastic right, he had only anticipated the conduct of eighteenth-century rulers. Nonetheless it accounts for much of the hostility he aroused. Not, of course, all. It is easier to explain than to commend his policy towards the Huguenots. His pursuit of Jansenism came to look like a serious loss of a sense of proportion And yet, at the end of a long reign, he showed himself capable of listening, of adjusting. There was a heroic quality in his bearing; it stiffened the resolution of ministers, impressed the court, inspired his soldiers and helped to save the state. In 1715 it was significantly larger and more secure, and more efficiently governed, than in 1661. It was, beyond question, the most powerful state in Europe.

The argument returns again to his personal qualities. It could rest there. Those closest to him had most cause to admire him. His responsibilities had been awesome. His power, we have seen, was not unlimited but it was sufficient: in military terms for one country to stand up to a coalition; in civil terms to maintain internal security in the worst of times. History is littered with the sordid or pathetic ends of statesmen whom power has corrupted absolutely. Going towards his Christian death, defying pain, considerate to the needs of state and the feelings of those around him, Louis XIV seems impressively to be the same man essentially as the intense and committed young king who took the Coronation oath and Christian sacrament in the Cathedral of Reims sixty-two years before. In the spirit of that oath and the symbolic actions that surrounded it, he had been a good Catholic and a good Frenchman. Within the bounds of possibility, material and psychological, he had been a good king. Because he rarely showed the imagination or independence of judgement to break free of those bounds some may deny that he was a great king. That was the formal title bestowed on him in 1680 by the city of Paris. It did not become common European currency. That was to be the distinction of Peter and Catherine of Russia, and Frederick II of Prussia. But it was a German, Leibnitz, Protestant and fierce critic of Louis's policies, but well acquainted with the French cultural scene, who wrote that 'Louis XIV was one of the greatest kings who ever lived'.

Notes

1. Louis's chief physician, Guy Fagon, was, according to Saint-Simon, 'one of the great minds of Europe, a great botanist and a good chemist'. He was also a mathematician and Superintendent of the Royal Botanic Gardens. His performance says more about the state of medicine than about his ability.
2. It can be seen today at Versailles.
3. Richelieu – 'I have no enemies but those of the state' – and Mazarin, asking to be treated as an ordinary penitent 'for there is but one gospel for the great and humble alike', were models. Louis was present at Mazarin's deathbed, and much affected by it.
4. The *sieur* Brun's elixir was 'made from the body of an animal' and stank. Louis took it in wine.

5. *'Ci-gît le roi des maltôtiers/Le partisan des usuriers/L'Esclave d'une indigne femme/L'ennemi juré de la paix/Ne priez point Dieu pour son âme/Un tel monstre n'en eût jamais.'*

6. The Polysynodie was a system of six councils for war, navy, finance, home affairs, foreign affairs and religion. Each had ten members, half official, half noble. It was suppressed in 1718 and the old system restored. Saint-Simon, its ardent promoter, confessed that its failure was due to the frivolity, ignorance and lack of application of a nobility good for nothing except to get itself killed in war. This judgement was unfair to some – notably Noailles, head of the finance council.

7. See p. 198, n. 11.

8. The term is useful to convey the intellectual ferment of the decades before and after 1700. Centring on Paris and London, it was stimulated by the dispersal of Huguenots after 1685, the foundation of scientific societies and by travellers' accounts of a wider world. Faith in the power of reason, interest in scientific research and a critical attitude towards religious dogma were among its main features.

9. The Quadruple Alliance represented the victory of the party of diplomatic realism over those who valued particularly the family connection with Spain. It was made necessary by the reckless adventurism of Alberoni. Spain's temporary isolation was an ironic outcome to the diplomacy which had secured a Bourbon succession and a war fought to avert the supposed threat of a union of crowns.

10. Through the time-honoured instrument of a *chambre de justice*, providing an opportunity to government to distance itself from the financial dealings of previous years, to make money from fines (to general applause) and to bargain from strength with rival syndicates (see pp. 115 and 132, n. 7).

11. By the time the enterprising Scotsman became *contrôleur-général*, in 1720, he had gained the ultimate monopoly: maritime and colonial trade (through Mississippi and Senegal companies), together with a bank of issue empowered to raise taxes, to coin and print money. To maintain this empire he made regular issues of shares; their value soared, then collapsed when figures showed what were the real trading prospects of the companies. Meanwhile, he had been undermined by those with an interest in the old system, *trésoriers*, *fermiers* and *traitants*, who had most to gain from his failure. The way in which he failed, so unnerving to the Regent and his successors, helps explain why France never achieved what he worked for, the abolition of financial privilege and enhancement of the power of the state and its ability to mobilise credit.

12. If this is thought to be far-fetched by the reader more used to reference to Napoleon in this context, let him consider the role of *clientèles* in modern French government, the faith in theoretical models, the sense of hierarchy that pervades society, the respect for rule in the cultural sphere, the disrespect towards authority when it comes to taxation and the readiness to obstruct and resort to violence when supposed rights are infringed.

13. André-Hercule de Fleury (1652–1743), cardinal minister in the Richelieu mould, *dévôt*, far-thinking and realistic diplomat, ruthless towards opposition, was able to secure harmony among conflicting interests and get the most out of able ministers without sacrificing essential elements of royal authority. His sway ended with

France's entry into the war of the Austrian succession – which he opposed – in 1741.

14. One thinks particularly of Frederick the Great and Joseph II. Both these sovereigns, however, owed much to their able predecessors, Frederick William I and Maria Theresa.

15. As notably in Mettam, *Power and Faction*, op. cit.

GLOSSARY

———— ◆ ————

aides. A variety of indirect taxes, mostly on drink, levied by the state.

arrêts de conseil. Royal orders which did not require registration to give them force of law.

arrière-ban. See *ban* below.

avocât-général. One of *gens du roi*, royal representatives in *Parlement*.

bailliage. Royal judicial district, having court in first instance, and appeal for minor cases: headed by *bailli*.

ban et arrière-ban. Traditional summons to muster nobles for military service: becoming method of taxing nobles by making them provide substitutes.

banalités. Seigneurial rights obliging tenants to use mill, oven and winepress of *seigneur*.

bourgeoisie. Non-noble members of the upper echelons of society (commonly urban society) sufficiently well off not to work with their hands and possessing privileges, as distinct from the mere *habitant* – but the distinction is blurred at the lower level: it was common for working men to term the employer *bourgeois*.

bureau des finances. Sixteenth-century creations in the *géneralités*. Administered by *trésoriers-généraux* (q.v.).

cahier des doléances. A list of grievances and wishes drawn up by representatives of each estate on the convoking of Estates General.

caisse des emprunts. A loan bank.

censitaires. Statutory providers of *cens*, labour or other dues on the *censives* or tenures.

Chambre des Comptes. Sovereign court, having important rights and duties: e.g. registration of royal marriages, peace treaties.

chambre de justice. Special financial court set up to confiscate financiers' gains and teach political lessons.

chambre des requêtes. Court of appeal in *Parlement*. (See *maître de* below).

champart. A feudal tax in kind, payable by the peasant to the *seigneur*, constituting around a twelfth of produce.

charge. A public office.

clientèle. In political usage, a close-knit group of dependants, bound to *patron* by mutual interest in advancement.

coadjuteur. Ecclesiastical title, denoting assistant to bishop.

commissaire départi. Royal official given a specific brief by letter of commission: so, a term used for *intendants.*

comptant. Cash payment made by the crown.

conseil d'en haut. See *conseil d'état* below.

conseil d'état. The original royal council out of which evolved, with the growth of government, several bodies with specialised functions and, by Louis XIV's reign, the executive *conseil d'en haut.*

contrôleur-général. Financial officer with supervisory powers. With the appointment of Colbert became supreme financial officer, with powers ranging over the whole economy.

corvée. Statutory labour laid down by custom.

Cour des Aides. Sovereign court of appeal in matters of taxation.

créature. In political usage a person in dependent but often well-established relationship to the *patron.* (See *clientèle* above.)

Dauphin. Title of heir-presumptive to throne. At court he is *Monsieur*, his wife, *Madame.*

dérogeance. Loss of status by nobles participating in certain occupations: notably manufactures and many trades.

dévôt. Member of zealous Catholic party, traditionally sympathetic towards Habsburgs, still critical of aggressive foreign policies, tending towards intolerance (as towards Huguenots) and censure of moral laxity.

dixième. Royal direct tax levied from 1710 on wealth in land, office and business.

droit annuel. A form of premium enabling an *officier* to transmit his office in return for one-sixtieth of its estimated value. See also *office, charge.*

duc et pair. Nobleman of highest rank below princes of the blood. As a peer – possessing a fief erected into *duché-pairie* (as opposed to mere *duc*) – enjoys right to attend *Parlement.*

écu. A gold crown whose value depended on its declared value in terms of money of account (the *livre tournois*): typically three *livres.*

écuyer. Title, often – because easily – usurped, at the lowest level of the order of nobility.

élection. Fiscal area presided over by an *élu*, responsible for apportioning the *taille* (q.v.) on the basis of personal income. See also *pays d'* below.

élu. See *élection* above.

émeute. A popular demonstration or rising, typically violent, but short of a full-scale revolt.

Épargne. Central treasury: place of receipt of taxes and other state dues.

enquêtes. One of the three main courts of *Parlement*.

états. Estates. Assemblies representing the three Estates, having administrative and financial powers. See also *pays d'* below.

faubourg. A suburb, as in Faubourg Saint-Antoine.

fermier. Leaseholder responsible, for a consideration, for collecting dues, seigneurial or royal.

fleur de lis. The lilies of France. Triple (in honour of the Trinity) stylised device on a blue shield: the royal arms.

franc-salé. See *gabelles* below.

gabelles. Salt taxes levied on a basis which varied according to regions, exemptions and privileges. *Franc-salé*: a province free of salt tax.

gages. Guarantees and benefits of office.

gentilhomme. Common usage denoting noble status (real or understood), not specific rank.

généralité. One of the major administrative areas (23 in 1643) into which the country was divided, and the seat of an *intendance*.

Grand Conseil. A branch of the *conseil d'état* (created in 1497) dealing with judicial business in which *Parlement* might be considered to be an interested party, therefore not proper to judge.

les grands. Collective, informal name for highest nobles.

hobereau. Poor country gentleman: in court, *salon* parlance signifying uncouth.

intendant. Royal commissary empowered to oversee financial, military and concomitant administrative affairs in the provinces. The *intendant de l'armée* had more specialised functions, but matters of discipline, supply and billeting had implications for the civilians in his field of operation.

journalier. A day labourer.

laboureur. A prosperous peasant farmer.

lettre de cachet. A letter emanating from the sovereign, signed by a *secrétaire d'état*, containing an order relative to an individual (commonly for imprisonment) or a particular case.

lit de justice. A ceremony in which the king, attending personally, could enforce registration of edicts in *Parlement* or other sovereign courts.

livre. Money of account comprising twenty *sous*: each *sol* contained twelve *deniers*.

lods et ventes. Seigneurial dues charged at the time of transfer of tenures, either by inheritance or sale.

maître des requêtes. A royal judge attached to the *conseil du roi*.

manant. Villager; collective term for the peasantry below the level of *laboureur*.

menu peuple. Common people: often used in a derogatory sense.

métayer. Share-cropper (*métairie*: farm held on that arrangement, or *métayage*).

noblesse d'épée. Nobility of the sword: the military, not necessarily *ancien* nobility, privileged supposedly by virtue of feudal service.

noblesse de robe. Nobility deriving from office in the higher ranks of judiciary or administration.

noblesse de clocher. Nobility (lowest level) derived from municipal office in larger cities.

octrois. Urban sales taxes.

office. A permanent government post (as distinct from temporary commission. See *commissaire* above.); generally for sale, sometimes conferring nobility on *officier* (see also *charge* and *gage*).

Parlement. Sovereign, final court of appeal with wide powers of *police* (the word conveys both justice and administration). The *Parlement* of Paris, with three main chambers, had jurisdiction over more than a third of the realm, with responsibility for registering royal edicts. Besides Paris, in 1643, there were nine provincial *parlements*: Toulouse, Bordeaux, Grenoble, Dijon, Rouen, Aix, Rennes, Pau and Metz. Besançon and Douai were added during Louis XIV's reign.

partisan. Financier involved in *parti* or *traité* (see *traitant* below), a contract to collect indirect taxes.

paulette or *droit annuel.* A form of premium enabling an *officier* to transmit his office in return for annual payment of one-sixtieth of its estimated value.

pays. An area having own distinct identity, as *Pays de Caux*.

pays d'élection, pays d'état. See *élection* and *état* above.

politique. Term used, originally during religious wars, to denote one who might put French political concerns before those of religious allegiance.

premier président. Presided over *Grand Chambre* or plenary meeting of *Parlement*. The only post in *Parlement* (not an *office* but a *charge* and revocable) nominated by the king.

président à mortier. One of eight judges of highest eminence in the *Grand Chambre*.

prévôt des marchands. Principal official of the municipality of Paris: like a mayor.

princes du sang. Immediate relative princes of the blood royal.

procureur-général. One of the *gens du roi*, royal representatives in *Parlement*.

régale. Royal right of disposing of revenues of vacant bishoprics.

rente. Interest paid to *rentiers* on government bond issued on the security of municipal revenues.

robin. A lawyer, man of the *robe*: pejorative sense – 'mere commoner' – when used by noble.

roturier. Of the common people.

secrétaire d'état. From original secretarial role holders of this venal office have become heads of ministerial departments, each with responsibility for designated provinces. (Only those who were summoned to sit regularly in the *conseil d'en haut* were designated *ministres.*)

seigneurie. The basic economic unit in most of rural France. The obligations of the tenant to the *seigneur* involved a widely varying range of dues and services. A *seigneur* enjoyed rights of jurisdiction within his lands.

subsistances. A tax paid by townspeople to exempt them from billeting troops.

surintendant des finances. Under the *contrôleur-général* (post Colbert's appointment) the head of financial administration.

taille. The main direct tax, levied either on income, the *taille personelle*, in the *pays d'élection*, or on property, *réelle*, in the *pays d'états* (q.v.).

traitants. Financiers who had made a *traité* (contract) with the crown, usually to raise taxes or sell offices.

trésoriers de France. Financial officials who headed the *bureau des finances* in each *généralité*.

BIBLIOGRAPHY

———— ◆ ————

Compiling this selection of books and articles from a vast field, I have had in mind several kinds of student or general reader. One may wish to know my sources, general or particular; another may look for signposts before embarking on some specialist study; another may simply want to read further. In this situation – given that the serious student will in any case want to consult a more extensive bibliography, starting perhaps with the volumes of the *Bibliographie annuelle de l'histoire de France* – I hope that it will be helpful to readers that I have been highly selective. I have also, in the main, listed only works published during the last half century during which our knowledge and understanding of Louis XIV and his France have been enriched, in many areas re-directed, by scholars on both sides of the Atlantic. Where an English translation exists I have given it preference to the French original.

For the institutions of France M. Marion, *Dictionnaire des Institutions de la France aux 17e et 18e siècles* (Paris, 1923), is still indispensable. R. Mousnier, *The Institutions of France under the Absolute Monarchy, 1598–1789*, 2 vols (trans. from the French of 1974, 1980, London, 1979, 1984) is authoritative though grounded in his idea of society as a hierarchy of orders. (This interpretation, along with alternative models, is discussed in an article by J.M. Hayden in *French History*, vol. 10, no. 3, 1996.) See also, for the phenomenon of office-holding, R. Mousnier, *La plume, la faucille et le marteau* (Paris, 1970).

Biographers of this period are well served by contemporary writers of letters and journals. Seventeenth-century journals are deliberately similar to historical narratives. They tend to describe the public lives of people who seem to have little or no private life and write as observers of their own career or that of someone whom they have served. Rarely, though it may be unwittingly revealed, is there apparent awareness of the inner self. The subject is well treated by J.M.G. Blakiston, *Reminiscing in the Seventeenth Century* (Winchester, 1985). Some narratives are printed in the collective work of Michaud and Poujoulat, *Nouvelle collection des Mémoires pour servir à l'histoire de France, 2nd and 3rd series* (Paris, 1838–39). Here, for example, are Mme de Motteville, La Rochefoucauld, Turenne. In a category of their own are the *Mémoires* of Louis XIV. Published and analysed in several French editions, they are available in English, ed. P. Sonnino (New York, 1970). Interesting light is shone on Louis's early years in Saint-Maurice, Marquis de, *Lettres sur la cour de Louis XIV, 1667–1670*, ed. J. Lemoine (Paris, 1910). In the series *Le Temps retrouvé, Mercure de France*, are those of Marie and Hortense Mancini, ed. G. Doscot (Paris, 1965) and the letters of Princesse Palatine, ed. O. Amiel (Paris, 1981). The latter may also be enjoyed in *A Woman's Life in the Court of the Sun King*, ed. E. Forster (Baltimore, 1984). Mme de Sévigné may be approached through *Lettres*, 3 vols, Pleiade edn (Paris, 1953–63), Fénelon through *Écrits et lettres politiques*, ed. C. Urbain (Paris, 1920). *Sui generis*, at both ends of the reign, are the profoundly egotistic and often mendacious *Mémoires* of Cardinal de Retz, ed. M. Allen and E. Thomas (Paris, 1956) and –

alongside numerous selections – the more valuable historical source, the *Mémoires de Saint-Simon*, ed. A. de Boislisle, 43 vols (Paris, 1879–1930). A fine English edition, with most essential material, is that edited and translated by Lucy Norton, 2 vols (London, 1967–70).

There are a number of books directly concerned with the life of Louis XIV. Two good, short studies, for student use, with concise accounts of the main aspects supported by helpful bibliographies (and in the latter case some documents) are: D.J. Sturdy, *Louis XIV* (London, 1998) and P.R. Campbell, *Louis XIV* (London, 1993). Among more ample biographies pride of place must belong to the richly detailed J.B. Wolf, *Louis XIV* (New York, 1968) and F. Bluche, *Louis XIV* (Paris, 1984; trans. M. Greengrass, London, 1970). The former has relatively little to say about the social and administrative context of royal power; the latter is particularly good on the human aspects of king and his government. It may be noted that his bibliography contains no works in English, necessitating a separate list by Greengrass of the numerous works which have contributed to a more balanced view of the reign. A different French tradition, that of the *Annales*, with great stress on the condition of the people and the factors limiting absolutist policies is represented by P. Goubert, *Louis XIV and Twenty Million Frenchmen* (trans., London, 1970). Between Bluche and the severely critical Goubert is the judicious *Louis XIV* of J.-C. Petitfils (Paris, 1995). Also valuable is P. Sonnino, *Louis XIV and the French Monarchy* (New Brunswick, 1994). Louis's ideas about government are explored in Jean-Louis Thireau, *Les idées politiques de Louis XIV* (Paris, 1970). W.F. Church, *Louis XIV in Historical Thought* (New York, 1976) considers past interpretations. N. Barker, *Brother to the Sun King; Philippe Duke of Orleans* (Baltimore, 1989) illustrates the significance for the future of the vast fortune accumulated by the family. It goes a little way towards rehabilitating him; further towards explaining why he has appeared to be so futile.

The background to the reign may be approached through P.R. Campbell, *The Ancien Régime* (Oxford, 1988) and R. Briggs's succinct and masterly *Early Modern France* (Oxford, 1977). G. Treasure, *Seventeenth Century France* (new edn, London, 1981) is more detailed. For the European context, see A. Corvisier, *La France de Louis XIV: Ordre intérieur et Place en Europe* (Paris, 1979), R. Mandrou, *Louis XIV en son temps* (Paris, 1973), W. Doyle, *Europe of the Old Order, 1660–1789* (Oxford, 1978), G. Treasure, *The Making of Modern Europe* (London, 1984), R. Hatton, *Louis XIV and his World*. See also relevant chapters in *The New Cambridge Modern History*, vol. VI, ed. F.L. Carsten (Cambridge, 1961) and vol. VII, ed. J.S. Bromley (Cambridge, 1970). Valuable for the history of the royal state leading up to Louis XIV are J.R. Major, *From Renaissance Monarchy to Absolute Monarchy* (Baltimore, 1994) and J.B. Collins, *The State in Early Modern France* (Cambridge, 1995). A classic work is still valuable: G.N. Clark, *The Seventeenth Century*, 2nd edn (Oxford, 1947) ranges widely in its essays.

Louis's minority and the Fronde have received more attention in recent years. Following the influential account in G. Lacour-Gayet, *L'Éducation politique de Louis XIV* (Paris, 1923), the childhood and education of the king may be studied in Henri Carré, *L'Enfance et la premier jeunesse de Louis XIV (1643–1661)* (Paris, 1944), also in Wolf, op. cit., and in his chapter in J.C. Rule (ed.), *Louis XIV and the Craft of Kingship* (Ohio, 1969); also, from his mother's standpoint, in the early chapters of R. Kleinman, *Anne of Austria* (Ohio, 1985). The Fronde is covered in Orest Ranum, *The Fronde, a French*

Revolution (New York, 1993), H. Méthivier, *The Fronde* (Paris, 1994): Ranum is especially good on Paris, Méthivier more comprehensive. E.H. Kossman, *La Fronde* (Leiden, 1954) offers valuable insights. Though narrower in focus, as the title suggests, the essential and influential introduction to the crisis is that of Lloyd Moote, *The Revolt of the Judges; the Parlement of Paris and the Fronde* (Princeton, 1971). R.M. Golden, *The Godly rebellion: Parisian Curés and the Religious Fronde 1652–1662* (Chapel Hill, 1982) shows how Jansenism, associated with withdrawal from the world, could also be a source of revolt appealing to clergy. G. Treasure's *Mazarin* (London, 1995) is the most recent book on that statesman – and the first in English for ninety years. P. Goubert was drawn to write his *Mazarin* (Paris, 1990), as he wrote, from his study of the people and the sufferings caused by war. G. Dethan's *Mazarin, un homme de paix à l'age baroque* (Paris, 1981) benefits from his extensive knowledge of Mazarin's Italian roots and connections. Dethan's *La Vie de Gaston d'Orléans* (Paris, 1992) and Simone de Berthier, *La Vie du Cardinal de Retz* (Paris, 1990) offer balanced accounts of those flawed characters so important during Louis's boyhood; the latter does not replace J.H.M. Salmon, *Cardinal de Retz* (London, 1969). There is a need for a new study of Condé. At present he is better known as soldier than as political magnate. Meanwhile, there is the massive work of the duc d'Aumâle, *Histoire des princes de Condé pendant les XVIe et XVIIe siècles*, vol. V (Paris, 1885).

Notable among collections of articles, indicating the current state of research or offering starting points for discussion of particular aspects of the reign, beside J.C. Rule, op. cit., are: P.J. Coveney (ed.), *France in Crisis, 1620–1675* (London, 1977): it has a particularly good introduction; R. Kierstead, *State and Society* (New York, 1975); R. Hatton, *Louis XIV and Absolutism* (London, 1976) and *Louis XIV and Europe* (London, 1976); J.F. Bosher (ed.), *French Government and Society, 1500–1850* (with the editor's important essay, 'Chambres de Justice'); M.P. Holt, *Society and Institutions in Early Modern France* (Georgia, 1971); J.P. Labatut, *Noblesse, Pouvoir et Société en France au XVIIe siècle* (Limoges, 1987); K. Cameron and E. Woodrough (eds), *Ethics and Politics in Seventeenth Century France: Essays in Honour of Derek A. Watts* (Exeter, 1996). R. Bonney, *Limits of Absolutism in Ancien régime France* (Aldershot, 1995) is an invaluable collection of his own articles. P. Sonnino (ed.), *The Reign of Louis XIV: Essays in Celebration of A. Lossky* contains some useful summaries of the state of knowledge, little that is new. There are several valuable collections of documents: R. Mettam (ed.), *Government and Society in Louis XIV's France* (London, 1977, with particularly good introductions); O. and P. Ranum (ed.), *The Century of Louis XIV* (New York, 1972); R. Bonney (ed.), *Society and Government under Richelieu and Mazarin* (London, 1988); A. Lossky (ed.), *The Seventeenth Century* (New York, 1967).

The imagery and presentation of monarchy has received much attention. Two seminal works were: E. Kantorowitcz, *The King's Two Bodies: A Study in Mediaeval Political Theology* (Princeton, 1957) and M. Bloch, *The Royal Touch: Sacred Monarchy and Scrofula in England and France* (trans., 1973). For recent understanding of ritual, reflecting anthropological contributions, see Edward Muir, *Ritual in Early Modern Europe* (Cambridge, 1997). O. Ranum, *Artisans of Glory; Writers and Historical Thought in Seventeenth Century France* (Chapel Hill, 1980) deals with the royal patronage of amenable writers. Coronation procedures are the subject of R. Jackson, *Vive le Roi! A History of the French Coronation from Charles V to Charles X* (Chapel Hill, 1984). Another ritual event is examined by L.M. Bryant, *The French Royal Entry Ceremony* (Geneva, 1985). Sarah Hanley, *The Lit de Justice of the Kings of France: Constitutional Ideology in Legend, Ritual and Discourse* (Princeton, 1983) shows how important was the ceremony but, controversially, denies its mediaeval origins. The title, *The Fabrication of Louis XIV* (London, 1982) conveys the theme of P. Burke's persuasive book. Its lavish illustrations should not, however, mislead. Such propaganda was new only in scale. The subject may be pursued in J.M. Apostolides, *Le Roi-machine: Spectacle et Politique au Temps de Louis XIV* (Paris, 1982), E. Le Roy Ladurie, *Versailles Observed* (Brighton, 1981), Y. Bottineau, *Versailles, miroir des princes* (Paris, 1989), L. Marin, *Portrait of the King* (London, 1988) and M. Martin, *Les Monuments équestres de Louis XIV: une grande entreprise de Propagande Monarchique* (Paris, 1986). N. Elias, *The Court Society* (London, 1983) completes the grand thesis developed in *The Civilising Process*, 2 vols (Oxford, 1987, 1982). It may be held – as by J. Duindam, *Myths of Power: Norbert Elias and the Early Modern European Court* (Amsterdam, 1996) – to ascribe too much significance to court ritual. For a wider view of court life, see A.G. Dickens (ed.), *The Courts of Europe: Politics, Patronage and Royalty, 1400–1800* (New York, 1977). A good straight account is J.-F. Solnon, *La Cour de France* (Paris, 1987). R. Asch (ed.), *Princes, Patrons and the Nobility* (Oxford, 1991) has much relevant to France. See especially Asch's introductory essay.

R.W. Berger, *A Royal Passion. Louis XIV as Patron of Architecture* (Cambridge, 1994), lavishly illustrated (and with a full bibliography for art historians) shows how the king contributed to the images of grandeur through his own interest in architecture, painting and sculpture. See also his *Versailles: the château of Louis XIV* (Pennsylvania & London, 1985). A good guide to the evolution of the palace is G. Walton, *Louis XIV's Versailles* (Chicago, 1986). The politics of architecture is a subject of H. Ballon, *Louis Le Vau, Mazarin's Collège and Colbert's Revenge* (Princeton, 2000). For the king as gardener, see W.H. Adams, *Les Jardins en France. Le Rêve et le Pouvoir* (Paris, 1980) and T. Mariage, *The World of André le Nôtre*, trans. G. Larkin (Philadelphia, 1999). For Paris, see L. Bernard, *The Emerging City: Paris in the Age of Louis XIV* (Durham, NC, 1970). For other aspects of the capital see below.

In no area has revision been more striking than in historians' recent treatment of French society, government – and their interrelation. Feeding it have been the local studies in depth in which French historians have long excelled. Dijon and its hinterland is the subject of G. Roupnel's influential *La Ville et la campagne au 17e siècle: étude sur la population Dijonnais* (Paris, 1922). P. Goubert, *Beauvais et le Beauvaisis de 1600 à 1730* (Paris, 1960) is fundamental; so is E. Le Roy Ladurie, *Les paysans de Languedoc* (1966). See also R. Baehrel, *Une croissance; La basse-Provence rurale* (1961), J. Jacquart, *La crise rurale en Ile-de-France, 1550–1670* (Paris, 1975), P. Deyon, *Amiens, capitale provinciale* (Paris, 1967). Much of the work of these pioneers is synthesised in two collaborative volumes: F. Braudel and E. Labrousse (eds), *Histoire économique et sociale de la France, ii, 1660–1789* (Paris, 1971) and G. Duby and A. Wallon (eds), *Histoire de la France rurale, ii, l'âge classique des paysans, 1340–1789* (Paris, 1975). But the reader should not miss the insights of Marc Bloch's classic, *French Rural History* (trans., 1966). A rich and eclectic source for the understanding of France is F. Braudel, *The Identity of France*, vols I and II (trans. S. Reynolds, London, 1990; original, Paris, 1986). The pre-eminent importance of Paris in the period is well brought out in R. Mousnier, *Paris, capitale au temps de Richelieu et Mazarin* (Paris, 1978) and O. Ranum, *Paris in the Age of Absolutism* (New York, 1968). There is also G. Dethan, *Paris au Temps de Louis XIV* (Paris, 1990). Much in J. Roche, *The People of Paris.*

An Essay in Popular Culture in the Eighteenth Century (1981, trans. New York, 1987) is applicable to Louis XIV's capital; P. Benedict (ed.), *Cities and Social Change in Early Modern France* (London, 1989) deals with different questions arising out of urbanisation.

Wendy Gibson, *Women in Seventeenth Century France* (London, 1989) gives a well-documented account of a – till recently – neglected area. There is much to explain the feminine influences on Louis XIV in C.C. Lougee, *Le paradis des Femmes; Women, Salons and Social Stratification in Seventeenth Century France* (Princeton, 1976). Much of the material in the comprehensive *History of Women, Renaissance and Enlightenment Paradoxes*, ed. N.Z. Davis and A. Farge (Cambridge, MA, 1993) is from France. Vol. III, *A History of Private Life, Passions of the Renaissance*, ed. R. Chartier (Paris, 1989; trans. A. Goldhammer, Cambridge MA, 1993) is also of absorbing interest and copiously illustrated. Much of O. Hufton, *The Poor of Eighteenth Century France* (Oxford, 1974) is also relevant to this period. Little had changed. See also P. Ariés, *Centuries of Childhood: A Social History of Family Life* (Paris, 1960; trans. R. Baldick, New York, 1962).

The causes and character of popular risings become somewhat less controversial the more is known about them. Y.M. Bercé, *The History of Peasant Revolts, The Social Origins of Revolts in Early Modern France* (Paris, 1986; trans. A. Whitmore, London, 1990) is a condensed version of his influential history of the Croquants. For interesting comparative perspectives (with Russia and China), and rebuttal of the Marxist analysis of Porchnev (see also articles in Coveney, op. cit.) see R. Mousnier, *Fureurs paysannes, Les paysans dans les révoltes du XVIIe siècle* (Paris, 1967). Also Y. Garlan and C. Nières, *Les révoltes bretonnes de 1675* (Paris, 1975) and R. Pillorget, *Les mouvements insurrectionnels de Provence entre 1596 et 1715* (Paris, 1975). C. Tilly, *The Contentious French* (Harvard, 1986), is wide-ranging and thought-stimulating. W. Beik, *Urban Protest in Seventeenth Century France* (Cambridge, 1997) treats this distinctive feature of life in French cities.

Among the most important of the books that have shaped present views of Louis's government are R. Bonney, *Political Change in France under Richelieu and Mazarin, 1624–1661* (Oxford, 1978) for essential background, illustrating the changing role and growth in the power of *intendants*; A. Smedley-Weill, *Les intendants sous Louis XIV* (Paris, 1995) for their role in Louis's government. Important also for a realistic view of Louis's government and its limitations – are W. Beik, *Absolutism and Society in Seventeenth Century France; State Power and Provincial Aristocracy in Languedoc* (Cambridge, 1985); A.N. Hamscher, *The Parlement of Paris after the Fronde, 1653–73* (Pittsburgh, 1976); R.C. Mettam, *Power and Faction in Louis XIV's France* (Oxford, 1988); R.R. Harding, *Anatomy of a Power Elite: the Provincial Governors of Early Modern France* (New Haven, 1978); S. Kettering, *Patrons, Brokers and Clients in Seventeenth Century France* (Oxford, 1986). Also her *Judicial Politics and Urban Revolt in Seventeenth Century France: the Parlement of Aix, 1629–1659* (Princeton, 1979); J.B. Collins, *Classes, Estates and Order in Early Modern Brittany* (Cambridge, 1994) and D. Bohannan, *Old and New Nobles in Aix-en-Provence, 1600–1695; Portrait of an Urban Elite* (Baton Rouge, 1992). For the history of one important family in government, see D.J. Sturdy, *The d'Aligres de la Rivière* (London, 1986). Contentious issues arising out of the relationship of central government and provinces are the theme of E.L. Asher, *Resistance to the Maritime Classes* (Berkeley, 1960).

The following deal more specifically with economic questions: *Histoire de la Population française*, 4 vols (Paris, 1988); R. Davis, *The Rise of the Atlantic Economies* (London, 1973).

E. Labrousse et al. (eds), *Histoire economique et sociale de la France, ii. Des derniers temps de l'âge seigneurial aux préludes de l'âge industriel 1660–1789* (Paris, 1970) ; J. Meuvret, *Études d'histoire économique* (Paris, 1971); also his chapter in New Cambridge Modern History, vol. 7, op. cit., 'The condition of France, 1688–1715'. R. Bonney, *The King's Debts, Finance and Politics in France, 1589–1661* (Oxford, 1981) established the author, with D. Dessert, as the leading authority on this difficult subject. Dessert gives copious detail about financiers in *Argent, pouvoir et société au Grand Siècle* (Paris, 1984). See also his *Fouquet* (Paris, 1987). J. Dent, *Crisis in Finance: Crown, Financiers and Society in Seventeenth Century France* (Newton Abbot, 1973) pioneered and anticipated some of his conclusions. J. Meyer, *Colbert* (Paris, 1984) soundly combines biography with policy analysis and replaces the weighty and still authoritative C.W. Cole, *Colbert and a Century of French Mercantilism*, 2 vols (New York, 1939). Two important studies by T.J. Shaeper deal with the period after Colbert: *The Economy of France in the Second Half of the Reign of Louis XIV* (Montreal, 1980) and *A Study of Mercantilism after Colbert* (Columbus, 1983). For the debates over mercantilism, their origins and significance, see L. Rothkrug, *Opposition to Louis XIV: the Political and Social origins of the Enlightenment* (Princeton, 1965). An example of a local study offering wider understanding – in this case of the effect of Colbert's efforts to foster textile manufacture – is J.K.J. Thompson, *Clermont-de-Lodève, 1633–1789: Fluctuations in the Prosperity of a Languedocian Cloth-making Town* (Cambridge, 1982).

Louis XIV's biographers – Bluche, op. cit., Wolf, op. cit. and others – devote much space to his diplomacy, now usually regarded in a more sympathetic light than was the case fifty years ago. Partly responsible for this was R. Hatton, approaching the topic from a broad European perspective. The essays in R. Hatton (ed.), *Louis XIV and Europe* (London, 1976), including her own, 'Louis XIV and his fellow monarchs', are essential reading. D. Croxton, *Peacemaking in Early Modern Europe: Cardinal Mazarin and the Congress of Westphalia* (Susquehanna & London, 1999) adds to our understanding of the tortuous processes of diplomacy and of the interrelation of war and diplomacy. A new edition of Abraham de Wicquefort, *The Ambassador and His Functions*, ed. M. Keens-Soper (Leicester, 1997) reveals much about the way in which political rivalries and interests affected foreign policy. After a long period of neglect French historians have returned to the study of international relations. Foremost has been L. Bély, *Espions et ambassadeurs au temps de Louis XIV* (Paris, 1990) and *Les Relations internationales en Europe (XVIIe et XVIII siècles)* (Paris, 1992). French diplomatic practice is the subject of W. Roosen, *The Age of Louis XIV: the Rise of Modern Diplomacy* (Cambridge, MA, 1990). P. Sonnino, *Louis XIV and the Origins of the Dutch War* is revealing about the pressures on ministers and the complexity of the issues. It follows similar treatment in the valuable *Louis XIV's View of the Papacy (1661–1667)* (California, 1966). See also C.J. Ekburg, *The Failure of Louis XIV's Dutch War* (Chapel Hill, 1979). J. Black (ed.), *The Origins of War in Early Modern Europe* (Edinburgh, 1987) has two essays on Louis XIV's wars. Still authoritative is M.A. Thompson, 'Louis XIV and the origins of the War of the Spanish Succession' (reprinted (from T.R.H.S., series 5, no. 4, 1954) in R. Hatton and J.S. Bromley (eds), *Louis XIV and William III* (Liverpool, 1968). A. Lottin's essay, 'Louis XIV and Flanders' in *Conquest and Coalescence*, ed. M. Greengrass (London, 1991), and the latter's introduction, deal with the important topic of assimilation of new lands. An older work, still of inerest, is G. Zeller, *L'Organisation défensive des frontières du Nord et de l'Est au XVIIe siècle* (Paris, 1928).

Taking the subject on from the much-debated question of the Military revolution – best approached through G. Parker, *The Military Revolution: Military Innovation and the Rise of the West, 1500–1800* (Cambridge, 1988) – there has been much recent work on the French army and its use. A. Corvisier, *Louvois* (Paris, 1983) supplements (but does not replace) L. André, *Michel Le Tellier et Louvois* (Paris, 1942). Corvisier's *Armies and Societies in Europe, 1494–1789*, trans. A. Siddall (Bloomington, IN, 1979), John Childs, *Armies and Warfare in Europe, 1648–1789* (Manchester, 1982) and F. Tallett, *War and Society in Early Modern Europe, 1660–1815*, among others, witness to the interest in the nature and effect of *ancien régime* war. The student is well served by J.A. Lynn. Following his important *Giant of the Grand Siècle: the French Army 1610–1815* (New York, 1997) there is the narrower but well-documented volume, *The Wars of Louis XIV* (London, 1999). See also David Chandler, *The Art of Warfare in the Age of Marlborough* (New York, 1976) and, for the vital topic of fortification, C. Duffy, *Fire and Stone: the Science of Fortress Warfare, 1660–1860* (Newton Abbot, 1975) and *The Fortress in the Age of Vauban and Frederick the Great, Siege Warfare*, vol. II (London, 1985). The revived emphasis on the achievements of Louis XIV's navy is shown in D. Dessert's authoritative treatment: *La Royale: vaisseaux et marins du Roi-Soleil* (Paris, 1996). For the transition from fleet to privateering warfare see G. Symcox, *The Crisis of French Sea-Power 1688–97: from guerre d'escadre to guerre de corse* (The Hague, 1974).

Religious subjects that mattered so much to Louis XIV and his subjects have naturally received much attention. They cannot be taken out of context, for which see (among many) J. Delumeau, *Le Catholicisme entre Luther et Voltaire* (Paris, 1971) and L. Châttelier, *The Europe of the Devout: the Catholic Reformation and the Formation of a New Society* (Cambridge, 1989), R. Taveneaux, *Le Catholicisme dans la France Classique, 1610–1715*, 2 vols (Paris, 1980) and E. Préclin et E. Jarry, *Les luttes politiques et doctrinales aux XVIIe et XVIIIe siècles*, vol. 19 in *Histoire de l'Eglise* (Paris, 1955); also H. Phillips, *Church and Culture in Seventeenth Century France* (Cambridge, 1997). Though dealing with the period before Louis's personal reign, J. Bergin, *The Making of the French Episcopate, 1589–1661* (London, 1996) reveals much about the hierarchy of the church of his day – and the processes which created it. The essays in R. Briggs, *Communities of Belief: Cultural and Social Tensions in Early Modern France*, (Oxford, 1989) have much to say about religious and social attitudes, Jansenism and – his phrase – 'agencies of control'. Relationship between Louis and Rome is the subject of P. Blet in *Les assemblées du Clergé et Louis XIV de 1670–1693* (Rome, 1672) and *Le clergé de France, Louis XIV et le Saint Siège de 1695 à 1715* (Rome, 1989).

L. Cognet, *Le Jansénisme* (Paris, 1961), concise and informative, is a good starting point for that elusive subject. See also A. Sedgwick, *Jansenism in Seventeenth Century France* (Charlottesville, 1977) and F. Hildersheimer, *Le Jansénisme en France aux XVIIe et XVIIIe siècles*. A. Sedgwick, *The Travails of Conscience: the Arnauld Family and the Ancien Régime* takes one admirably into the Jansenist mentality. L. Cognet sheds perhaps too clear a light on mysticism in *Crépuscule des Mystiques* (Paris, 1991). There is also J.-R. Armogathe, *Le Quiétisme* (Paris, 1973). Though there is much about him in the general histories, Bossuet may best be approached through his work, as through a recent edition, ed. P. Riley, of *Politics Drawn from the Very Words of Holy Scripture* (Cambridge, 1998), with its helpful introduction. The same is true of Fénelon (needing, like Bossuet, a new biography?) In this case Riley's introduction to his edition of *Telemachus* (Cambridge, 1994) is of service. From the numerous letters of Fénelon (10 volumes in the recent edition by J. Orcibal (Geneva, 1993)) there is a good selection, translated by J. McEwen, with 'reflections' by Thomas Merton (London, 1964). P. Janet, *Fénelon* (Paris, 1914) stands the test of time. See also J.-L. Goré, *L'Itineraire de Fénelon: humanisme et spiritualité* (Paris, 1957).

The background, theological and political, to the Huguenot question is provided by D. Ligou, *Le protestantisme en France de 1598 à 1715* (Paris, 1968) and the essays, ed. M. Prestwich, in *International Calvinism (1541–1715)* (Oxford, 1985). There is also G.A. Rothrock, *The Huguenots; a History of a Minority* (Chicago, 1979). J. Orcibal, *Louis XIV et les Protestants* (Paris, 1951), J. Garrison, *L'Édit de Nantes et sa révocation. Histoire d'une intolérance* (Paris, 1985) and E. Labrousse (also marking the tercentenary), *La révocation de l'Édit de Nantes* (Paris, 1985) are sure and balanced guides to the ever-controversial event and policies behind it. For the still disputed economic consequences of the revocation see W.C. Scoville, *The Persecution of the Huguenots and French Economic Development* (Berkeley, 1960). For the diaspora M. Magdelaine and R. von Thadden, *Le Refuge Huguenot* (Paris, 1985) and I. Scouloudi (ed.), *Huguenots in Britain and their French background, 1550–1800* (London, 1987), for the Cévennes, C. Almeras, *La révolte des Camisards* (Paris, 1960) and P. Joutard, *La révolte des Camisards* (Paris, 1977) and for the pressures on Huguenots in one area, O. Martin, *La Conversion protestante à Lyon (1659–1687)* (Geneva, 1986).

There are a number of good introductions to cultural aspects of the period. D. Maland, *Culture and Society in Seventeenth Century France* (Cambridge, 1970) surveys the whole scene. A. Adam, *Grandeur and Illusion: French literature and Society, 1600–1715* (London, 1972) is magisterial – and highly readable. A. Blunt, *Art and Architecture in France, 1500–1700* (London, 1953) wears its years well, as does V.L. Tapié, *The Age of Grandeur: Baroque and Classicism in Europe*: he is particularly good on baroque symbolism and staging. An older book, A. Tilly, *The Decline of the Age of Louis XIV* (Cambridge, 1929) is a full study of the literature of the later years. Highly influential, dealing with the same period, has been P. Hazard, *La Crise de la conscience Europeéne, 1680–1715* (Paris, 1935; trans. by May as *The European Mind* (London 1953) but the original title suggests the thrust of his argument: the roots of the Enlightenment lie in the various challenges to traditional beliefs. H.-J. Martin, *Livre, Pouvoirs et Société à Paris au XVIIe siècle (1598–1701)*, 2 vols (Paris, 1969), deals, among other aspects of publishing, with government controls. E.J. Kearns, *Ideas in Seventeenth Century France* (Manchester, 1979) is a study of the intellectual climate through the leading thinkers. L.W.B. Brockliss, *French Higher Education in the Seventeenth and Eighteenth Centuries: a Cultural History* (Oxford, 1987) shows how the maintenance of a position in the élite continued to require conformity to religious and political orthodoxy. R. Hahn, *The Anatomy of a Scientific Institution: the Paris Academy of Sciences* (Berkeley, 1971) reveals the integration of scientific endeavour into government through its control of funding and choice of research projects. J. Klaits, *Printed Propaganda under Louis XIV* (Princeton, 1976) is mainly concerned with the ministry of Torcy and his efforts to recover ground in the war of ideas. (See also Ranum, *Artisans of Glory*, op. cit.). Also R. Chartier, *The Cultural Uses of Print in Early Modern France* (Princeton, 1988); R. Muchambled, *Popular Culture and Elite Culture in France, 1400–1750* (Baton Rouge, 1985).

The following articles are specially relevant or interesting:

B. Barbiche, 'La hiérarchie des dignités et des charges', *XVIIe Siècle*, 157, 1987, pp. 359–70.

N. Barker, 'Philippe d'Orléans, frère unique du Roi: founder of the family fortune', *French Historical Studies*, XIII, no. 2, 1983, pp. 145–71.

D.C. Baxter, '*Premiers commis* in the war department in the later part of the reign of Louis XIV', *Western Society for French History: Proceedings*, 8, 1980, pp. 69–80.

F. Bayard, 'Les financiers et la Fronde', *XVIIe Siècle*, 145, 1984, pp. 255–62.

W. Beik, 'Urban factions and the social order during the minority of Louis XIV', *French Historical Studies*, 15, 1987, pp. 36–67.

P. Benedict, 'La population reformée française de 1600 à 1685', *Annales* ESC, 42, 1987, pp. 433–65.

J. Black, 'Louis XIV's foreign policy reassessed', *Seventeenth Century French Studies, X*, 1988, pp. 199–212.

P. Blet, 'Louis XIV et le Saint Siège', *Dix-septième siècle*, 123, 1979, pp. 137–54.

R. Bonney, 'Cardinal Mazarin and the Great Nobility during the Fronde', *English Historical Review*, 96, 1981, pp. 818–33.

R. Bonney, 'The French civil war, 1649–53', *European Studies Review*, 8, 1978, pp. 71–100.

R. Bonney, 'J.R. Malet: historian of the finances of the French monarchy', *French History*, 5, pp. 180–233.

L. Ceyssens, 'Autour de la Bulle Unigenitus: son acceptation par l'Assemblée du Clergé', *Revue d'histoire ecclésiastique*, 80, 1985, pp. 369–84, 732–59.

J.B. Collins, 'Sur l'histoire fiscale du XVIIe siècle', *Annales* ESC 34, 1979, pp. 325–47.

J.M. Constant, 'La troisième Fronde; les gentilshommes et les libertés nobiliaires', *XVIIe siècle*, 145, 1984, pp. 341–54.

A. Corvisier, 'Guerre et mentalités au XVIIe siècle', *XVIIe Siècle*, 148, 1985, pp. 219–32.

J. Delumeau, 'Le commerce extérieur français au XVIIe siècle', *XVIIe Siècle*, 70, 1966, pp. 81–104.

J. Dent, 'An aspect of the crisis of the seventeenth century: the collapse of the financial administration of the French monarchy (1653–61), *Economic History Review* (2nd series) 20, 1967, pp. 241–56.

R. Descimon and C. Jouhaud, 'La Fronde en mouvement', *XVIIe siècle*, 145, 1984, pp. 305–22.

D. Dessert, 'Finances et société au XVIIe siècle: à propos de la chambre de justice de 1661', *Annales* ESC, 29, 1974, pp. 847–84.

D. Dessert and L. Hjournet, 'Le lobby Colbert: un royaume ou une affaire de famille?' *Annales*, ESC, 1974, pp. 847–82.

F. Dubost, 'Absolutisme et centralisation en Languedoc au XVIIe siècle', *Revue d'Histoire Moderne et Contemporaine*, XXXVII, 1990, pp. 384–406.

H.A. Ellis, 'Genealogy, history and aristocratic reaction in early eighteenth-century France: the case of Henri de Boulainvilliers', *Journal of Modern History*, 58, 1986, pp. 414–51.

N. Ferrier-Caverivière, 'Louis XIV et ses symboles dans l'histoire métallique du règne de Louis-le-Grand, *Dix-Septième siècle*, 134, 1982, pp. 19–30.

A. Frostin, 'Le Chancelier de France, Louis de Pontchartrain, "ses" premiers présidents et la discipline des cours souveraines', *Cahiers d'histoire*, 1982, pp. 9–34.

R. Golden, 'The mentality of opposition; the Jansenism of the Parisian *curés* during the Religious Fronde', *Catholic Historical Review*, 64, 1978, pp. 565–80.

P. Goubert, 'The French Peasantry in the seventeenth century: a regional example', *Past and Present*, 10, 1956, pp. 55–77.

A.N. Hamscher, 'The Parlement of Paris and the social interpretation of early French Jansenism', *Catholic History Review*, LXIII, 1977, pp. 392–4.

S. Hanley, 'Engendering the family; family formation and state-building in early modern France', *French Historical Studies*, 16, 1988, pp. 4–27.

D. Hickey, 'Innovation and obstacles to growth in the agriculture of Early Modern France: the example of Dauphiné', *French Historical Studies*, 15, 1987.

J. Jacquart, 'French agriculture in the seventeenth century', in P. Earle (ed.), *Essays in European Economic History, 1500–1800* (Oxford, 1974), pp. 165–85.

J. Jacquart, 'La Fronde des princes dans la région parisienne et ses conséquences matérielles', *Revue d'histoire moderne et contemporaine*, 7, 1960, pp. 257–90.

E. Kaiser, 'The abbé de Saint-Pierre, public opinion and the reconstitution of the French monarchy', *Journal of Modern History*, 55, 1983, pp. 618–43.

S. Kettering, 'Patronage and kinship in early modern France', *French Historical Studies*, 16, no. 2, 1989, pp. 406–35.

S. Kettering, 'The decline of Great Noble clientage during the reign of Louis XIV', *Canadian Journal of History*, 24, 1989, pp. 157–77.

R. Kleinman, 'Changing interpretations of the Edict of Nantes; the administrative aspect, 1643–61', *French Historical Studies*, 10, 1978, pp. 548–71.

P. Lefebvre, 'Aspects de la fidelité en France au XVIIe siècle: le cas des agents du prince de Condé, *Revue historique*, 201, 1973, pp. 59–106.

P.K. Leffler, 'French historians and the challenge to Louis XIV's absolutism', *French Historical Studies*, 14, 1985, pp. 1–22.

A. Lossky, 'The absolutism of Louis XIV: reality or myth?', *Canadian Journal of History*, 19, 1984, pp. 1–15.

A. Lossky, 'The general European crisis of the 1680s', *European Studies Review*, 10, 1986, pp. 177–98.

D.S. Lux, 'Colbert's plan for the Grande Académie: Royal policy towards science, 1663–67', *Seventeenth Century French Studies*, XII, 1990, pp. 177–88.

R. Maber, 'Colbert and the scholars: Ménage, Huet and the royal pensions of 1663', *Seventeenth Century French Studies*, XII, 1985, pp. 106–14.

R.C. Mettam, 'Louis XIV and the persecution of the Huguenots: the role of ministers and royal officials', in I. Scouloudi (ed.), op. cit., pp. 198–216.

R.C. Mettam, 'Power, station and precedence: rivalries among the provincial élites of Louis XIV's France', *Transactions of the Royal Historical Society*, 38, 1988, pp. 43–62.

J. Meyer, 'Louis XIV et les puissances maritimes', *XVIIe siècle*, 123, 1979, pp. 155–72.

A.L. Moote, 'The French crown versus its judicial and financial officers', *Journal of Modern History*, XXXIV, 1962, pp. 146–60.

D. Parker, 'Sovereignty, absolutism and the function of the law in seventeenth century France', *Past and Present*, 122, 1989, pp. 36–74.

D. Parker, 'Class, clientage and personal rule in absolutist France', *Seventeenth Century French Studies*, IX, 1987, pp. 192–213.

D. Parker, 'The Huguenots in Seventeenth-century France', in A.C. Hepburn (ed.), *Minorities in History* (London, 1978).

J. Plainemaison, 'Qu'est ce que le Jansénisme?', *Revue Historique*, 553, 1985, pp. 117–30.

O. Ranum, 'Courtesy, Absolutism and the rise of the French state, 1630–1660', *Journal of Modern History*, 52, 1980, pp. 426–51.

D. Roche, 'Aperçus sur la fortune et les revenus des princes de Condé à l'aube du XVIIIe siècle', *Revue d'histoire moderne et contemporaine*, XIV, 1967, pp. 217–43.

W. Roosen, 'How good were Louis XIV's diplomats?', *Studies in History and Politics*, 4, 1985, pp. 125–36.

H.H. Rowen, 'Arnauld de Pomponne: Louis XIV's moderate minister', *American Historical Review*, 61, 1956, pp. 531–49.

G. Rowlands, 'Louis XIV, aristocratic power and the elite units of the French army', *French History*, 13, no. 3, 1999, pp. 281–303.

J. Rule, 'The *commis* of the department of foreign affairs, 1680–1715', *Western Society for French History, Proceedings*, 8, 1980, pp. 81–9.

J.C. Rule, 'Gathering intelligence in the reign of Louis XIV', *International History Review*, XIV, 1992, pp. 732–52.

J.H.M. Salmon, 'Venal office and popular sedition in seventeenth-century France', *Past and Present*, 37, 1967, pp. 217–43.

J.H.M. Salmon, 'The Audijos revolt: provincial liberties and institutional rivalries under Louis XIV', *European History Quarterly*, 14, 1984, pp. 119–49.

J.M. Smith, ' "Our sovereign's gaze": Kings, nobles and state formation in seventeenth century France', *French Historical Studies*, 18, 1993, pp. 396–415.

P. Sonnino, 'The dating and authorship of Louis XIV's Mémoires', *French Historical Studies*, 3, 1964, pp. 303–37.

R. Taveneaux, 'Jansénisme et vie sociale en France au XVIIe siècle', *Revue d'histoire de l'église de France*, 14, 1968, pp. 27–48.

There are some valuable special issues of *Dix-septième siècle*: 'Serviteurs du roi: quelques aspects de la fonction publique au XVIIe siècle', 42–3, 1959; 'Aspects de l'économie française au XVIIe siècle', 70–1, 1966; 'La mobilité sociale de XVIIe siècle', 122, 1979; 'Louis XIV et l'Europe', 123, 1979; 'Fénelon', 19–21, 1951–52. A special number of *Annales*, ESC, 41e année, 1986, is largely given to the rituals of French monarchy.

INDEX

Absolutism, 15, 28, 35, 36, 110; theory of, 74–8, 84–5; and Divine Right, 87–9; Bossuet and, 87–9; challenged, 89; practice of, 116, 121, 215, 324, 333, 338–9; and armies, 135, 141, 300; and Huguenotism, 214, 218; consensus about, 299

Académie française, 77, 285; and language, 45, 66 n.5

Académie des Sciences, and Colbert, 130

agriculture, condition of, 44ff., 47, 48–51, 66 n.8, 300

Aides, cour de, 70; indirect taxes, 28, 80, 103

Aix-en-Chapelle, treaty of, 159, 165, 187

Aix-en-Provence, 15, 33

Alais, Grace of, 214

Almanza, battle of, 277

Alexander VII, Fabio Chigi, Pope, and Louis XIV, 161–3

Alsace, 81, 125, 244; at Westphalia, 159; and *réunions*, 160, 203–5; held by France, 291

Ambassadors, 'Affair of', 73, 161

Amsterdam, printing at, 228; Huguenot influence on, 228–9; and London, 252, 295

America, colonised by French, 127–8; Canada and Talon, 127; and Colbert, 127–8; Louisiana, 127–8; Huguenots not in, 231; warfare in, 255; Spanish, 259

Amyraut, Moise, Huguenot, 217–18

'Ancients and Moderns', dispute, 186–7, 198

Anjou, duc d', see Philip V of Spain

Angers, 62

Anna Maria of Bavaria-Neuberg, 2nd wife of Charles II of Spain, 260–1

Annat, père, confessor, 166

Anne of Austria, queen, queen-mother and Regent, 35, 37 n.2, 150, 299; Character and beliefs, 1, 3, 7, 22, 192; Louis XII's wife, 1, and Louis XIV, 1, 3, 5, 6, 15, 32, 150, 192; and Fronde, 10, 12, 13, 16; as Regent, 3, 10, 13, 16, 18; and Mazarin, 6, 7, 13, 22

Anne, queen of England, 'Princess of Denmark', 268; Louis recognises, 290

Apafi, Prince of Transylvania, 179 n.24

Arminius, 217, 236 n.7; and followers of, 217

Armies, in general, 134–7, 239; French, reform of, 70, 134ff.; 'Military revolution' 135–7; size of, 136, 148 n.3, 247, 257 n.10, 272; intensification of warfare and, 146, 164; and society, 131–322, 136–7, 272; feudal spirit in, 137; levelling effect of, 138; casualties, 143–5; commissariat 146–7; loss of Huguenots from, 230–1; weaknesses in, 272 (see also Le Tellier, Louvois)

Arnauld, Antoine, 219, 221; *Fréquente Communion*, 219, 318; on Jesuits, 318ff.; and family, 318ff.; and Gallicanism, 322; and *Parlement*, 318; died, 321

arrière-ban, 9, 27, 28, 40 n.36, 54, 140, 141; and militia, 141

Artillery, French, 143

Artois, 285

Asiento, privilege of, 266, 290

Augsburg, League of, 207; formed, 240; War of ('Nine years War') 133, 231, 239; Confession of, 220

Auvergne, Jours d', 101–2
Augustine, Saint, and Jansenism, 317
Augustus II, duke of Saxony, king of
    Poland, 293
Austria (see also Habsburgs, Empire),
    297 n.23; in Dutch War, 172; pressure
    of Turks on, 175; conquest of
    Hungary, 292; gains from Utrecht-
    Rastadt, 292–3; extensive possessions,
    292–3
Avignon, Papal seizure of, 162, 204, 241;
    seized, 242

Balzac, J.L. Guez de, 84, 106 n.21,
    218
Bank of England, 246; Huguenot
    investment in, 230, 300; compared to
    France, 300, 313–14 n.5
Barbésieux, Louis-François, marquis de,
    war minister, 248
Barrier, Dutch, 173–4, 251, 256, 266,
    271, 272, 286
Bart, Jean, privateer, 253
Bavaria, and France, 205, 240; and
    Emperor, 240; and Spanish Succession,
    261; at Utrecht-Rastadt, 290; future of,
    294
Bâville, intendant, and Languedoc, 103;
    and Huguenots, 103, 216–17,
    235–6 n.5
Bayle, Pierre, 222, 236 n.20, 329 n.11;
    exile, 232; rationalism of, 326
Beachy head, French victory at, 252
Beauvais, 47
Beauvillier, Paul duc de, and Louis XIV,
    94, 107 n.33; and Saint-Simon, 191; for
    Partition Treaty, 263–4; in council,
    311; dévôt, 311; for peace, 281, 293
Bellièvre, Pomponne de, 25, Premier
    Président, 34
Benôit, Élie, 224; on atrocities, 237 n.23
Bentivoglio, Papal nuncio, on Louis XIV,
    333
Bernard, Samuel, financier, 305, and
    Louis XIV, 305

Bernini, architect, 197 n.7; and Louvre,
    181; and Louis XIV, 183, 189
Berry, Charles, duc de, died, 312
Berry, Marie-Louis-Elizabeth d'Orléans,
    duchesse de, 335
Berwick, James Stuart, duke of, marshal,
    commands in Spain, 277
Bérulle, Pierre, Oratorian, 219, 235,
    236 n.11, 320
Besançon, 81; besieged, 171; in réunions,
    205
Bignon, Jerome, political philosopher,
    94–5
Boileau – Despréaux, Nicolas, 45, 186;
    influence of, 66 n.4
Boisguilbert, Pierre de Pesant de, and
    Détail de la France, 301
Bolingbroke, Henry St John, viscount,
    and English diplomacy, 287, 288, 290,
    295, 307
Bossuet, Jacques-Bénigne, bishop, tutors
    Dauphin, 4, 220; and Divine Right, 18,
    35, 76, 77–8, 87–8, 219; career, 39
    n.24, 77, 87; style, 45, 87, 169; Political
    Theory, 87–8; and Louis XIV, 88, 180,
    181, 209, 220; works of, 87, 219, 220,
    223, 232; sermons of, 172; on Turenne,
    172; and Huguenots, 219, 220–1, 232;
    and Gallicanism, 219, 322; and Burnet,
    232; and Quietism, 322, 324ff., 327–8;
    defends orthodoxy, 327–8; dies, 328
Boufflers, Louis-Francois duc de,
    marshal, 267, Louis' emissary, 250;
    at Malplaquet, 286; defends Lille,
    279
Bouillon, duc de, 81
Boulogne, 70
Boulonnais, revolt in, 52, 66–7 n.9, 70,
    100–1
Bourgeois, 59ff.; haute, wealth of, 59;
    aspirations, 59–60, 64, 66; and office, 60,
    61; organisations, 63; and trade, 64;
    values of, 60–1; Huguenot, 213
Brandenburg, 36; rise of, 136; nature of,
    170, 171, 173; and return of

Pomerania, 174; Grench alliance with, 205

Brest, docks at, 130

Brienne, Henri-Auguste de Loméwnie de, Secretary of state, 35, 41 n.47

Brinvilliers, Mme de, 183

Brittany, 23, 47; secured, 45, 66 n.3, 79; revolt in, 118, 173; Mme de Sévigné in, 57, 148 n.6; nobility in, 56; *Intendant* in 66 n.3; Estates of, 79, 84

Broussel, Pierre, *parlementaire*, 9, 24, 38 n.14

Burgundy, Louis, duke of, as Dauphin, (1711), 292; and pacifism, 311; at Oudenarde, 272, 279, 309; character of, 279, 282; and Fénelon, 281–2, 309–10, 314 n.18; and reform, 292; death of, 289, 311–12; significance of, 312, 336

Burgundy, Marie-Adelaide, duchess of, character, 311; marriage of, 251, 257 n.16; death of, 289, 311

Caisse de conversions, 221

Callières, Francois de, diplomat, 158

Cambrai, gained, 174

Camisards, Hugueot rebels, 234

Canal of the Two Seas, 124–5, 254

Capitation, 255, 298, 301

Casale, seized, 207

Cassel, battle of, 173

Catalonia, and France and Spain, 176, revolt of, 159; returned to Spain, 256

Catholicism (see also Gallicanism); and the state, 19; and Huguenots, 22, 213–14, 216, 225–6; and absolutism, 77; revival of, 217, 218ff.; and sacrilege, 227, 234, Austrian, 255

Catinat, marshal, *roturier*, 138, 142, 231

Cavalier, Jean, Camisard leader, 234

Cavalry, 139, 142, 285

Cevennes, 47; revolt in, 233–4, 237 n.32, 273; in 1715, 133–4, *Pastorales* in, 233; effect of rising, 273–4; crushed, 274

Chambre de Saint Louis, 9

Chambre des Comptes, 25; under Colbert, 117

Chamillart, Michel, minister, 295–6 n.4; and war, 273, 279; defeatism of, 281, 282, 303; negotiates, 283–4; establishes *conseil de commerce*

Chambre des Comptes, 25; under Colbert, 117

Chamillart, Michel, minister, 295–6 n.4; and war, 273, 279; defeatism of, 281, 282, 303; negotiates, 283–4; establishes *conseil de commerce*

Chamlay, Jules-Louis, marquis de, advisor to Louis XIV, 147, 170, 244, 257 n.7, 248, 251, 255; quoted, 173

Champagne, character of, 15, 17, 20; regiment of 140

Champaigne, Philippe de, painter, 317

Champlain, Samuel, explorer, 125, 126

Charenton, temple of, 216

Charlemagne, and imperial tradition, 78, 223, 244

Charles, archduke (later Emperor Charles VI), claims Spanish throne, 260ff.; and second Partition treaty, 262, in Spain, 276ff., 287–8, 290–1

Charles II, king of England, 31; restored, 36; dishonest, 159; and Dover treaty, 167; allied to France, 167ff.; Louis's pensioner, 175

Charles II, king of Spain, born, 160–1; physical frailty, 161, 167, 259, 261; marriages, 260–1; dies, 262; will, 262

Charles duke of Lorraine, 167, 172; stateless, 175

Charles XI, king of Sweden, absolutist policies of, 250

Charles XII, king of Sweden, invades Russia, 271; defeated at Pultava, 293

Charleroi, siege of, 139; given up, 174, 256

Chavigny, Léon Bouthillier, comte de, 1

Chevreuse, Marie de Rohan, 7, 15, 38 n.10

Chevreuse, Charles-Honoré, duc de, 94, 107 n.33, 281

Church Assembly, 70, and Gallicanism, 222; and Huguenots, 217, 222

Christina, Queen of Sweden, and Revocation, 228, 237 n.27

Claude, Jean, pastor, 232, exiled, 233, 237 n.29

Clientèles, 28, relationship, 51–2; Colbert's; in government, 83, 93, 102 n.19

Clement XI, Pope, reconciled to Louis XIV, 321; decides against Jansenists, 322; and Louis, 323

Clivet, Bernard Postel, sieur du, 52

Colbert, Jean-Baptiste, 27, 30, 32, 48, 196, 339; and Mazarin, 35, 71–2, 113, 115, 117; and Louis's *mémoires*, 42 n.49; and Louis, 94–5, 110, 114, 126, 161, 186; family of, 57, 97, 107 n.33, 110, 226, 299; and Bordeaux, 61–2; and Boulonnais, 66 n.9; and Fouquet, 71–3, 111, 115; as patron of art, 110; *contrôleur-général*, 71, 93, 97–8; and *offices*, 84, 115–17, and Le Telliers, 114; character, style method of, 111, 114, 123, 154; and statistics, 111, 301; vision and ideas of, 110, 113, 114, 119, 120, 121, 123, 124, 128, 188, 307, 336; achievement of, 97, 107 n.34, 109, 128–31, 131 n.1, 215; and war, 165–7, 178 n.16; and finance, 97, 102, 109, 111, 115–17, 118, 132 n.10, 167, 172, 299, 303; and communications, 124–5; and navy, 97, 119, 129–31, 154, 253, 276; and manufactures, 111, 113, 115, 118, 120, 121–3, 124, 132 n.13; and commerce, 97, 111, 113–15, 123, 124, 128–9, 174, 208; and colonies, 125–9, 231; and household, 97; and agriculture, 119–20; and law, 110, 124, 154, 184; and science, 110, 130, 185; cultural programme of, 180ff.; and Paris, 183; and Versailles, 185, 188; death of 89, 128, 176

Cologne, 128, 154; ally of France, 172; succession to, 207, 241–2

Colonies, French in India and America, 125, 126, 127; Colbert and, 125–9; Louis XIV and, 126

Concini, Concino, assassination of, 2, 37 n.1

Condé, Louis de Bourbon, prince de, and generalship, 4, 142, 146, 247; as governor, 8, 144; and Louis XIV, 10, 18, 91; in Fronde, 10, 12ff., 22, 56, 216; failure of, 21; and reinstatement, 100; invades Franche-comté, 146, 165; leads in Dutch war, 168, 169, 171, 172; at Senef, 172; retirement of, 169, 172; at Chantilly, 172; and Polish crown, 297 n.24

Condé, Charlotte-Marguerite, princesse de, 7

Conseils: d'en haut, 94; Spanish succession debate in, 263–4; *des finances*, 94; *des dépêches*, 95; *de commerce*, 95, 120; *de conscience*, 22, 95, 221, 223, 235 n.3, 306

Conti, Armand de Bourbon, Prince de, 13, 39 n.20, 15; and Polish crown, 24

Contrôleur-général, Colbert as, 73, 111ff., 115–18, 118ff.; Le Pelletier as, 302; Chamillart as, 273, 281ff., 306; Desmarets as, 273, 281, 298

Corsican Guards affair, 161–2

Corvées, 46, 51; and roads, 48, 103

Couperin, Francois, composer, 6

Court (see also Versailles), international influences, 155–6; and status, 268

Coysevox, Antoine, sculptor, and Louis XIV, 189

Créqui, Charles duc de, ambassador, 155; and Corsican Guards affair, 161–2

Croissy, Charles, marquis Colbert de, career, 176, 204; foreign minister, 98, 157, 203ff.; and the king, 176; and *réunions*, 203; and Revocation, 225; and 'Third Party' negotiations, 250

Daguesseau, *procureur général*, condemns Rome, 324

D'Argenson, *lieutenant-général*, policing Paris, 183–4

Daugnon, comte de, 16

Dauphin, see Louis de Bourbon, Burgundy

Dauphiné, province of, 23, 79; Huguenots in, 216

Denain, French victory at, 289–90, 305, 330; significance of, 291

Dérogeance, 53

Descartes, René, 77, Cartesian logic, 77, 85, 106 n.2, 307, 317, 327; and Malebranche, 87, Bossuet and, 87

Deshayes, Catherine, 'la Voisin', sorcerer, 183–4

Desmarets, Nicolas, *contrôleur-général*, 273, 281, 298, 313 n.2, 334, 336; in financial crisis, 281; and trade, 306

Devolution, law of, 154; war of, 163–4

dévôts, 21, 22, 316; Richelieu as, 152; and Huguenots, 214; Louis XIV as, 225

Dijon, 44, 61, 103; Colbert and, 123; world of, 132 n.15

Diplomacy (see also treaties, Westphalia etc); professionalism, 151; development of, 157; growth in resident, 151; congresses, 152–3, 203; precedence and honour in, 155–6, 249, 290; and international law, 153–4, 203; moral climate of, 156; pragmatism in, 156–7; ambassador's role in, 157–8; French expertise in, 173; and peace, 176; at Nijmegen, 173–4; Ryswick, 249–52, 255–6; Louis XIV civilised; before Utrecht, Preliminaries, 282–3; Utrecht-Rastadt, terms, significance, 292ff

Divine Right, 17, 18–19, 35; and healing, 39 n.25, 85, 87–9; and Louis XIV, 18–19, 85, 87–9, 192–3, 200,; Bossuet and, 87–9; outmoded, 192

Dixième, tax, imposed, 287, 301, 303–4, 314 n.13

Don gratuit, 304

Douai, captured, 164; recaptured, 287; law court at, 205 Dubois, abbé, 292

Dragonnades, 223–4, 227, 228; Ducasse, and battle of convoys, 296 n.10

Duelling, 57, 67 n.14; Soissons and, 70; and honour, 156

Duguay-Trouin, René, privateer, 296 n.10

Dunes, battle of, 31, 32

Dunkirk, fortified, 130; and Vauban, 144; and piracy, 131; forts destroyed, 283, 291

Duquesne, Abraham, seaman, 131, 133 n.18, 208; victories of, 174

'Dutch War' (see also United Provinces), causes, 165ff; aims, 166–8; course of, 169–73; end of, 173–4

East India Company, 123

Élus, 26; and *taille*, 100, 102, 117

Empire, Holy Roman (see also Austria), authority of, challenged, 218; German princes and, 205, 210, 211, 228; France seen as enemy, 238; as benevolent, 150, 292

England, civil war in 11, 81, 122; as ally of France, 31, 167, 172; as enemy, 121, 245ff; finance in 116, 136, 246, 254; colonial enterprise, 125, 126; trade and navigation acts, 126, 129; navy of, 128, 154; rivalry with Dutch, 130; the flag question, 154; corrupt politicians of, 158; and Popish plot, 175; religion in, 220; permanent interests of, 245; and Continental war, 246ff.; cult of glory, 246; backs Habsburgs for Spanish crown, 271; separate peace talks, 286, 288; gains at Utrecht, 294–5

Escurial, palace, 260

Estrées, Francois duc de, 207, 208

Estrées, César, Cardinal d', advises Philip V, 276

Eugène de Savoie-Carignan, Prince, 295 n.3; in Spanish Succession War,

267, 274, 275, 282, 285–6, 289–90; talent of, 272
Evelyn, John, 14; on Revocation, 228

Fabert, Abraham, marshal, 138
Fagel, Gaspar, 239, 257 n.1
Fagon, Guy, physician, 330, 331, 340 n.1
Famines, 43–4, 140, 254–5
Félibien, André, 165, 167
Fénelon, François de la Mothe de Salignac, 333; family, 308; and Huguenots, 221, 227; on catholicism, 233; and peace, 241, 281–2, 309; 'alternative' policies, 254–5, 300; and Quietism, 87, 282, 308, 322ff.; letter to Louis XIV, 254–5, 258 n.19, 308; and Burgundy, 292, 308, 309, 310, 314 n.18; opposes Jansenism, 307; exile, 282, 308–9; and girls' education, 308; and Télémaque, 308–9, 314, n.17; and Bossuet, 326–8; on Spinoza, 327; condemned by Pope, 328; dies, 328
Ferdinand II, Emperor, 152
Ferdinand-Joseph of Bavaria, and Partition treaties, 260; dies, 262
Ferrier, père Jean, 166
Ferry, Paul, pastor, and Bossuet, 219
Feudalism, and dues, 51–3; spirit of, 83; and réunions, 203
Filles de charité, 44
Finance (see also Fouquet, Colbert, etc), and Fouquet, 71–3; and Colbert, 115–17; and war, 298; and Desmarets, 298; end of reign, 298ff., 313 n.1
Financiers (see also Colbert), and land, 54, 58, 97, 115, 116; Huguenot dimension, 229–30; end of reign crisis, 305
Flanders, (see also Devolution), war in, 142, 143, 144, 164, 203; towns gained in, 165, 205; 'invaded' by French, 266; towns surrender after Ramillies, 275
Five Great Farms, 125
Fleur de lys, 34, 88, 121, 129, 145, 155
Fleurus, battle of, 143

Fleury, Cardinal, statesman, 292
Fontenelle, Bernard de, poet, 'modern', 186, 198 n.11, 335
Fontainebleau, forest of, 125; Edict of, 212, 226, 321, 322
Fouquet, Nicolas, 52; ministry of 71–2, 115, 117; and Colbert, 71–3; patronage of, 72; dismissal of, 36, 72–4, 93, 96, 97, 104 n.7, 117; significance of, 73–4, 93
Franche-Comté, 53, 203; invaded, 165, 171; restored, 165; and Alsace, 203; held, 291
Frederick William, 'Great Elector', 136, 170ff. (and see Brandenburg)
Frederick William I, king of Prussia, 293
Fronde, 7ff., 56, 81, 83, 137, 191; start of, 10, danger of, 24, 37 n.4; failure of, 23, 134; aftermath of 20–3, 24, 28, 100, 101; assessment of, 25, 27; effects of, 29–30, 135
Fouquet, Nicolas, 52; ministry of 71–2, 115, 117; and Colbert, 71–3; patronage of, 72; dismissal of, 36, 72–4, 93, 96, 97, 104 n.7, 117; significance of, 73–4, 93
Franche-Comté, 53, 203; invaded, 165, 171; restored, 165; and Alsace, 203; held, 291
Frederick William, 'Great Elector', 136, 170ff. (and see Brandenburg)
Frederick William I, king of Prussia, 293
Fronde, 7ff., 56, 81, 83, 137, 191; start of, 10, danger of, 24, 37 n.4; failure of, 23, 134; aftermath of 20–3, 24, 28, 100, 101; assessment of, 25, 27; effects of, 29–30, 135; women in, 38 n.10; in provinces, 13 (see also Ormée); Huguenots and 214–17; Jansenism and, 318, 324
Frontenac, governor of Quebec, 127, 255
Fürstenberg, Egon von, 206, bishop of Strasbourg, 206
Fürstenberg, Wilhelm von, 167, 169

Gabelle, 28, 100, 301; variations in, 80; exemption from, 81, 118

Gallicanism, 316ff., of bishops, 22; and Jansenism, 25, 316; and *régale*, 39 n.27, 221, 223, 322; and Rome, 85–7, 161–3, 221, 223, 322; 'liberties', 85; and *Parlement*, 86, 162; Four Articles of, 86, 87, 236 n.19, 322; and Jesuits, 86; and Huguenot question, 219, 20, 223

Galway, marquis de Ruvigny, earl of, 296 n.9, 276

Gaston, duc d'Orléans, 2, 3, 15, 18

Gaultier, abbé, 288

Gazette, 4, 197 n.5, on Louis XIV, 36, 182; quoted, 221

Genoa, bombarded, 155, 208

Ghent, 173, 174

Gibraltar, 276; significance of, 276–7

Gloire, la, notion of, 90, 172, 176, 246, 286; Louis XIV and, 90, 92, 143, 170–1; Colbert and, 110, 114, 120, 131; nobles and, 143, 176; Vauban and, 145

Gobelins, les, workshops, 121, 122, 188, 190

Godefroy, Denis, antiquarian, 204

Gondi, Paul de, archbishop of Paris, Cardinal de Retz, in Fronde, 10, 12, 15, 16, 20–1, 31, 70; and Pope, 162

Governors, provincial, powers, patronage of, 13, 59, 70, 103, 156

Grand Alliance, formed, 265; aims of 266; sealed, 267; vulnerable, 271 (see also Spanish Succession)

Grands Jours de l'Auvergne, 101

Grands, les, 8, 55–6 (see also Versailles)

Grotius, Hugo, 2; and international law, 153–4; and *mare liberum*, 177 n.4; on Christian reunion, 220

Guyon, Mme, 320–1; and her teaching, 325; supported by Fénelon, 327

Habsburgs (see also Austria, Spain), family interest, 155, 163, 263, 288; German princes and 205, 210, 211; Austrian, 163, 338; Spanish, 163 (see

also Spain); threat to France, 163, 238; and Spanish Succession, 259ff., 294

Halles, les, 11

Hanover, and English connection, 274, 294; France and, 250

Harcourt, Francois de Lorraine, comte de, 16

Harcourt, Henri, duc d', ambassador in madrid, 261, 263, 269 n.3; and Louis XV, 334

Harlay, Francois de, archbishop of Paris, 236 n.18; and the king, 221; influence of 221; and Jansenists, 321; and Huguenots, 221, 227; in *conseil de conscience*, 222; and Gallicanism, 222

Heidelberg, sacked, 244

Heinsius, Grand Pensionary, 255, 261, 265, 282, 283

Hémery, Particelli d', *surintendant*, 10, 25

Henrietta of Orléans ('Minette'), and Dover treaty, 167

Henrietta Maria, queen of England, 11

Henry IV, king of France, 2, 4, 9; assassination of, 2, 12, 18, 38 n.19, 81, 82; reign of 5, 69, 78, 81, 86, 118–19; and Edict of Nantes, 212ff

Hobbes, Thomas, political philosopher, 76

Hochstädt (see Blenheim)

Hocquincourt, Charles de Monchy d', 31

Hohenzollern, house of, 335

Holland, see United Provinces

Holy League, 81; and Huguenots, 213

Honnêté, ideal of, 186

Hôpital-général, 30, 41 n.43, 44, 185, 198–9 n.8

Horses, in war, 142–3, 145, 146, 149 n.10

Hôtel de Ville, administration of, 24; massacre of, 11

Hungary, and Turks, 142; and Emperor, 206, 209; reconquest of, 255; revolt under Rákócsí, 271, 274

Huguenots, Huguenotism, aggression and resistance of, 22–3, 213, 216; special status of, 213; and Edict of

Nantes, 212ff.; changing character of, 215, 217–18, 223; Louis XIV and, 70, 201, 211, 215, 217, 221ff.; legislation against, 103, 201, 211; respond to Colbert, 123; numbers of, 214, 235 n.4; persecution of, 130, 215, 223ff.; propaganda of, 184; excluded from colonies, 231; reunion of churches and, 218, 219, 220; after Revocation, 226ff.; emigration of, 228–30, 231, 237 n.28; military effect, 230–1; Louis's reputation and authority and, 232–3, 238; in Cevennes, 233–4, 237 n.32, 273; in 1715, 233–4; vengeful spirit, 239; compared to Jansenists, 320, 322

Hungary, 175ff., 179 n.24, 206, 208–9, 239

Île de France, 30, 52

Innocent XI, Pope, and Emperor, 209; character of, 22; and siege of Vienna, 209–10; and Louis XIV, 201, 210, 211, 221, 222, 223, 228, 241; and Huguenots, 201, 223, 228; and *régale*, 221, 223, 228; and Jansenism, 320 (see also Papacy)

Innocent XII, Pope, blesses Charles II's will; 263; and Quietism, 328 (see also Papacy)

Intendants, 34, 101, recruitment of, 100; and taxes, 9, 100, 102, 103, 117, 303; recall of, 10, 100; restoration of, 25; control of villages, towns, 50, 59, 67 n.16; rôle and powers of, 89, 99ff., 107 n.36, 131; *de l'armée*, 141, 146ff.; Huguenots and, 223ff., 230; in 'great winter', 280; and famine relief, 254; and *subdélégués*, 103, 303

Invalides, Hôtel de, 142, 185;

Issy, articles of, 327–8

James II, king of England, accession of, 223, 242–3; expulsion of, 228; at Saint Germain, 247; dies, 267

Jansen, Cornelius, 20–1

Jansenism, 10, 20–2, 25, 216, 219, 221, 335; and Louis XIV, 70, 147, 162, 316; missionary efforts of, 221; and Jesuits, 221, 232; and *dragonnades*, 227–8, 235; and *Unigenitus*, 316, 337; *and 'Peace of the Church*, 319, 320; *and Gallicanism*, 322–41

Jesuits, (Society of Jesus), 325; and Jansenism, 21, 221, 232, 319ff.; as confessors, 22, 221; as teachers, 87, 186, 198–9 n.12; as missionaries, 127; and Louis XIV, 221–2; and Fénelon, 321

Kara Mustapha, Grand Vizier, 208–10

La Bassée, lines of, 285

Laboureurs, 4, 9, 54; plight of, 300

La Bruyère, Jean de, on poverty, 44; on Louis XIV, 192; on Huguenotism, 201

La Chaise, père Pierre de, Cofessor to Louis XiV, 221, 222, 319 La Hogue, battle of, 252; significance of, 252–3, 258 n.18

La Feuillade, Francois Aubusson, general, besieges Turin, 274; routed, 275; flatterer, 296 n.6; Laffemas, Barthélemy, 112, 132 n.5, 119

La Fontaine, Jean de, 73, 104 n.6, 198 n.11

Lamoignon, Guillaume de, *premier président*, 73, 104 n.5, 227

Landen, battle of, 231

Languedoc, province of, 8, 23; Estates in, 45, 124; cloth trade in, 123, 306; Huguenots in, 216, 223, 233; rising of Camisards in, 233; famine in, 255

La Reynie, Gabriel Nicolas de, *lieutenant-général*, policing Paris, 183–4, 197 n.8

La Rochefoucauld, Francois duc de, 14, 15, 39 n.21, 24

La Rochelle, siege of, 62, 82, 214, 227; prosperous, 123, 129

La Salle, cavalier de, and Louisiana, 127–8

La Vallière, Louise de, mistress of Louis XIV, 90, 106–7 n.28, 164, 166, 182

Law, diversity of, 90; Roman, codifying, 55, 80, 82, 83, 124; Customary, 80; Colbert and, 124; International, 152, 153–4, 202; of Nature, 153; Fundamental, 92; and *réunions*, 202; and Huguenots, 213

Law, John, financier, 336–7

Le Bret, cardin, political philosopher, 35, 41 n.48; and Absolutism, 76, 84

Le Brun, Charles, painter, and Colbert, 121; at Versailles, 186, 188; and Louis XIV, 180, 189, 190; and Gobelins, 188

Le Camus, bishop of Grenoble, and conversions, 221, 227, 232

Le Gendre, Thoma, trade and wealth of, 305, 314 n.15

Le Havre, 130

Leibnitz, Gottfried Wilhelm, 307; and crusade, 176, 179 n.25; and church reunion, 220; and Revocation, 229; and German political union, 238, 340

Le Nain, Louis, 49

Le Nôtre, André, gardener, 187; and Louis XIV, 189–90

Le Pelletier, Michel de Souzy, manipulates currency, 302, 303, 314 n.12

Leopold, Emperor, and Turks, 36, 175, 201, 202, 205, 208–10, 228, 239; and Louis XIV, 161, 175, 209, 210, 211, 241, 250; builds Schönbrunn, 181, 207; and German princes, 205, 210, 211, 228, 239; and Hungarians, 206, 271; war against France, 164, 170, 174–5, 228; and Spanish Succession, 163, 164–5, 167, 239, 245, 255–6, 260, 261; *hausmacht*, 239, 255, 271; Pope supports, 209–10, 241; marriages of, 260, and Hofburg, 260; pride, stubbornness of, 261, 262; militancy of, 261, 262, 265, 266

Le Tellier, père Michel, confessor, 319, 323, 331

Le Tellier, Michel, in Minority, 11, 146, 38 n.17; War Minister, 30, 73, 93, 94, 96, 97, 98, 134–5; reforms of 137ff., [see also Louvois] 141; *clientèle*, 96, 97; influence of , 111; His commissaires, 138; Chancellor, 176, 222

Lettre de cachet, 10, 28; crown's use of, 85

Le Vassor, on 'Variations', 232–3

Le Vau, Louis, architect, and Versailles, 91, 165, 187, 188

Lille, 61, 103, 288; captured, 164; fortified, 178 n.15; besieged, 279; retained, 291

Limousin, 45, 47, 100

Lionne, Hugues de, diplomat, 31; Foreign Minister, 73, 94–5, 157, 159, 165, 168–9; and Spanish Succession, 160, 164; and Rome, 161–3; before Dutch war, 165, 166, 167, 168, 178 n.14; death of, 95, 168–9

Literacy, 46, 66 n.4

Lit de Justice, 3, 8, 10, 18, 24, 26

Locke, John, *Journal*, 307, 66 n.2, 108 n.40; quoted, 102, 103, 122, 190; in Holland, 232; philosophy of, 327

Lorraine, invasion of, 167, 168

Longueville, Anne, duchesse de, and Jansenism, 21, 320; 39 n.21

Longueville, Henri d'Orléans, duc de, 13, 39 n.20

Lorraine, duke Charles of, at Vienna, 210; restoration of, 245; in Spanish Partition treaty, 262; died, 247

Louis IX, 'Saint Louis', 78, 82; invoked, 309

Louis XIII, king of France, 289; as minor, 18, 75; and Anne, 1; and Louis XIV, 2, 3; character, 2, 3; and Richelieu, 6

Louis XIV, king of France, birth of, 1, 2; accession of, 3, 4; and queen Anne, 1, 2, 3, 5, 13, 32, 34–5; early days and education of, 1ff., 5–6, 15, 82; appearance and manners of [see also Court], 14, 90–91, 155, 275; accomplishments of, 5–6, 17, 90–1

[see also 'at war', government etc.];
minority of, 10–14; and Mazarin, 5, 6,
13, 15, 16, 17, 20, 31–4, 89, 151, 152,
160–1, 164; and family, 1, 2, 3, 4, 5, 6,
11, 13, 32, 34–5, 70, 87, 150, 160–1,
164, 260, 310, 311–12, 313; achieves
Majority, 14, 17; Coronation of, 17–20,
88, 226, 340; temperament and
personality of, 2, 3, 4, 6, 10, 17, 32–3,
69, 90ff., 158, 162–3, 174, 192, 221–2,
225–6, 247–8, 281, 301, 335; health of,
32, 233, 245, 330; principles of, 20, 25,
36–7, 87–8, 92ff., 101, 138, 139, 147,
152, 182, 190, 214, 233, 241, 247, 263,
268, 284, 284, 287, 301, 304, 332–3
[see also 'assessments']; faith and
values of, 8, 18, 20, 23, 36–7, 92ff.,
87–8, 181, 209, 222, 225–6, 233, 236
n.11, 241, 247, 268, 284 [see also 'and
Huguenots' etc]; descriptions of,
young, 14, 90–1; old, 283, 289; image
of [see also Versailles] 117, 127, 145,
170–1, 186, 188, 189, 190, 231, 241,
265, 270, 284; portraits of, 186, 189,
190, 208; and culture, 38 n.8, 68 n.17,
91, 182–3, 185, 186, 189, 190, 194;
and court, 35, 90ff., 139, 148 n.6,
166, 182ff., 190ff.; and buildings
and gardens, 180, 182, 183, 186–8,
188–90; and government, 14, 23, 25,
28, 33, 35–6, 69ff., 75–7, 83, 83, 89,
90ff., 99, 100–1, 117, 137, 145, 147–8,
176, 200–1, 272ff., 277, 288, 340; and
diplomacy, 73, 95, 110, 132 n.3, 150ff.,
155, 156, 157, 158–9, 161, 166, 173–5,
176, 178 n.12, 179 n.24, 202, 203, 206,
208, 209–10, 223, 238, 241–2, 250ff.,
255–6, 267–8, 278, 281–3, 286, 287ff.;
and Parias, 11, 13, 17, 24, 34–5, 150;
and ministers [see also government]:
Fouquet, 72–4; Colbert, 72–3, 110,
120–1, 126–8, 134, 182; Louvois,
134–5, 138, 169, 176; marriage of,
32–3, 34, 88, 150, 156, 260; and
Maintenon, 89, 176, 222, 254, 106 n.26;

and mistresses, 90, 106–7 n.27 and 28,
164, 166, 176, 182, 184; at war, 17, 20,
30–1, 90, 144, 147, 148, 164, 170–1,
178 n.13, 206, 247, 248; and papacy,
86–7, 161–3, 178 n.11, 201, 210, 211,
221, 222, 223, 241–2; and Huguenots,
23, 70, 88, 95–6, 201, 211, 215, 217,
221ff., 232–3, 238; and Jansenists,
20–2, 25, 70, 147, 162, 3165, 320,
323, 324; propaganda, for, 68 n.17,
92–3, 144–5, 231, 241, 265, 270, 284;
against, 232, 238, 244–5; *mémoires* of,
36, 41–2 n.49, 70, 93, 101, 147, 161,
165, 166, 169, 171, 174, 215, 284; and
Spanish Succession, 147, 151, 159,
160–1, 240, 251, 256, 260ff., 264, 283,
287ff.; and old age, 280–1, 289, 324,
330ff., 335; in crisis, 281, 282–3, 284,
287, 301, 304; realism, moderation of,
95, 255–6, 258 n.22, 281–3, 291, 298;
death of, 332–3; assessments of, 232,
235, 291ff., 299, 309–11, 332–4,
337–40

Louis XV, and succession, 311, 312, 331;
character of, 299

Louis de Bourbon, Dauphin, 4, 70;
education of, 87; Spanish Succession
claim of, 260; beneficiary of partitions,
261, 262; claims for son, 264; and *cabale*
of Meudon, 311; death of 310

Louisiana, 127–8

Louise of Orléans, wife of Charles II of
Spain, 260

Louvois, Michel le Tellier, marquis de, 93,
96; character of, 134, 168, 169; war
minister, 96, 121, 134–5, 141, 168, 171,
176; disciplinarian, 138, 139, 148 n.5;
and recruitment, 140; and uniforms,
141; and weapons, 142–3; 'great
victualler', 145–6; rivalry with Colbert,
141; ascendancy, 114, 168, 169, 176;
and Huguenots, 141, 224, 225, 227,
237 n.24; and *bâtiments*, 176, 187; and
réunions, 203, 204, 206; and Palatinate,
242, 243–4; death of, 248

Louvre, palace of, 11; compared to Versailles, 181; Bernini's design for, 183; Le Vau and Perrault's design for, 184

Loyseau, Charles, jurist, 55, 67 n.11, 75, 76, 84

Lully, Jean-Baptiste, composer, 6, 38 n.8; at court, 91, 185; Louis XIV befriends, 194

Luxembourg, county of, 159, 160; and *réunions*, 203, 205; siege of, 206

Luxembourg, marshal, 171; victories, 173, 247, 248, 249; reputation of, 247; died, 249

Lyon, 61, 65, 122, 125; and Colbert, 123; effect of Revocation on, 230; merchants of, 303

Maastricht, siege of, 144

Machiavelli, Nicolo, political theory of, 307

Maine, Louis-Auguste de Bourbon, duc de, legitimised, 312, 313, 334; and Regency, 335

Mainz, Elector of, 164; and France, 178 n.25

Malebranche, Nicolas, 87, 106 n.25, 327

Malplaquet, battle of, 143, 285–6; casualties at, 143, 294; invasion threat, 151; significance of, 286, 294

Mancini, Marie, loves Louis XIV, 32–3; *mémoires*, 33

Mansard, Jules Herdouin, architect, and Versailles, 166, 188, 189, 192, 201; and Clagny, 188

Marguerite, Princess of Savoy, and Louis XIV, 32

Marlborough, John Churchill, duke of, 246; learns generalship, 146; at Blenheim, 243, 272, 273, 274; after Blenheim, 246; at Ramillies, 272; at Oudenarde, 145, 272, 279; at Malplaquet, 151, 285–6; after, 288–9; has logistical problems, 295 n.2; and scorched earth, 244; has Huguenot

secretary, 231; political problems, 272, 274, 286, 289; his genius, 272, 288, 295 n.2; and peace question, 283

Marly, palace of, 187, 197, 281

Marseille, 33–4, 61, 64, 65, 140, 190; repression of, 62, 70; obstructs Colbert, 123

Maria Lescinska, marries Louis XV, 293

Maria Teresa, queen, as Infanta, 32–3; marries Louis XIV, 34, 150, 156; as wife, 164; rights of, 160–1, 163; and Spanish Succession, 260

Marie de Médicis, Regent, 2, 56

Marillac, René de, *intendant*, and Huguenots, 103, 224

Marsin, Ferdinand, comte de, Marshal, 272, 275

Martin, Francois, in India, 129

Martinet, Jean, 139

Mary of Modena, widowed, 267; and Louis XIV, 267

Max-Emmanuel of Bavaria, 294, ally to France, 270, 273

Mazarin, Jules, Cardinal, early life, 38 n.9; *clientèle* of, 15, 144, 37 n.4; and Anne, 6, 7, 13, 32; in Fronde, 10ff., 20, 23, 24, 36; *premier ministre*, 3, 5, 7, 8, 10ff., 17, 23, 26, 31, 32–3, 34, 62, 82, 89, 94, 217; and Louis XIV, 5, 6, 15, 16, 17, 20, 32, 34, 89, 152; diplomacy of, 5, 6, 22, 26, 31, 32–4, 35, 151, 152, 158, 159, 160, 169, 251, 256; and Jansenism, 21–2; *Mazarinades*, 12, 38 n.18, 13, 291; and Fouquet, 71, 72; and Colbert, 771–2, 113, 115, 120; and Westphalia, 159–60; and League of Rhine, 150, 164, 245, 250; and Pyrenees, 160; and Rome, 153, 161; 'good European', 210; and Huguenots, 22, 23, 210, 214–17

Medals, commemorative, 167, 178 n.17, 190

Mediterranean, trade in, 113–15; pirates in, 129, 208; naval war in, 129–31; France in, 208, 210

Menin, 275

Mercantilism, 112, 132 n.6, 110; and Colbert, 113–14 [see also Colbert], 120; and power, 115; reaction against, 300, 304–5

Mercoeur, Louis de Bourbon, duc de, 15, 39 n.20

Messina, 173, 179 n.23

Métayer, métayage, 51, 58

Metz, 160, *parlement* of, 168; in *réunions*, 204, 205

Michaud, code, 99

Mignard, Pierre, painter, and Louis XIV, 190

Milan, 165; Spanish in, 207, 259; partition treaties and, 261, 262

Militia, in action, 141, 284

Minorca, captured by English, 278

Molière (Jean-Baptiste Pocquelin), 67 n.16, plays of, 91, 185, 194; Louis supports, 194

Molinos, Fr., Spanish friar, 324–5

Mont-Louis, fortress of, 145

Montchrétien, Antoine de, 112, 130 n.5

Montbéliard, annexed, 205

Montecucoli, Imperialist general, 171, 176; and St Gothard, 171

Montespan, Mme de, mistress of Louis XIV, 90, 107 n.28, 164, 166; repudiated, 176; sorcery allegations about, 184

Motteville, Francois de Bertaut, Mme de, on Maria Teresa, 34, 41 n.46; on Louis XIV, 91

Moyenvic, 160

Munster, treaty of (see Westphalia), 152, 240; bishop of, Louis's ally, 250

Naples (and Sicily), 105, 165, 259, and Spanish partition, 259ff., 261, 262, 286; and Emperor, 264

Nantes, 65, 226, 129; Edict of, 2, 23, 212ff., 235 n.1; terms and nature of, 213–14; Revocation of, 81, 89, 96, 201, 207, 212, 224–5; results of, political,

228–9; economic, 229–30, 300; reaction to, 227; and ideas, 232–3

Navy, French, galleys in, 101; forestry for 119; Colbert and, 129, 131; victorious, 174; Seignelay and, 130–1, 252; strength of, 252, 258 n.17; and Tourville, 252–3; Pontchartrain and, 252; changing role, 253; privateering, 253, 276, 296 n.10

Nicole, Pierre, 307; Jansenist, 320; self-exile, 321; died, 321

Nijmegen, treaty of, 155, 173–4, 176, 188, 202, 203, 205, 215, 240, 256; Louis's view of, 174

Nîmes, effect of Revocation on, 230

Noailles, Louis-Antoine de, Cardinal, archbishop of Paris, 321, 322, 323, 324; and Huguenot question, 233

Noailles, Anne-Jules, duc de, governor of Languedoc, 222; and finance counmcil, 336

Noblesse: d'Epée, recherches into, 28, 54, 102; grievances of, 27, 28, 40 n.36, 56; lawlessness of, 29; in villages, 53–4; distinctions within, 54ff.; privileges of, 55ff., 79; at court, 55–7, 191, 193, 195; values and manners of, 57–8; *campagnard*, 58–9, 103; casualties of, 57; étrangères, 81; in Fronde, 83; *de robe*, 10, 56, 58

Normandy, Fronde in, 13, 29, 45, 47; nobles in, 55, 59, 67 n.13; Huguenots in, 216

Offices, and *officiers*, 7, 9, 25; effect on government, 84; characteristics, 103; Colbert and, 116; number and value of, 302

Olier, Jean-Jacques, 220

Oppède, Henri de Forbin d', 33

Orange, 81

Ordinances, Civil and Criminal, 124

Orléans, 102; communication to, 124, 125; Huguenots in, 227; Jansenism in, 320

Orléans, Philippe duc d', Monsieur, 2; and Louis XIV, 3, 91, 191; soldier, 173, 275

Orléans, Philippe, duc d', son of above, regent, 292; regency of, 299, 334ff., character of, 312; and Louis, 312; as soldier, 312; and *Parlement*, 334–5, 337

Ormée, 8, 23, 40 n.31

Oudenarde, battle of, 145, 146, 272, 279; secured by France, 165

Ottoman Empire (Turks), and Empire, 36, 139, 201, 208–10; at war, 139, 208–10; and France, 152, 208–9, 210; revival of, 208

Palatine, Liselotte, duchess of Orléans, 'Madame', letters, 195, 244, 257 n.2, 330; her claims to the Palatinate, 239–40

Palatinate, and France, 207; ravaged, 244–5; dispute settled, 250

Papacy (also Rome), and Gallicanism, 85–7, 161–3, 201; 221, 223, 322; and Louis XIV, 85–7, 161–3, 178 n.11, 201, 210, 211, 221, 222, 223, 241–2, 322; and decline of influence of, 153; Corsican Guards affair, 161–3; and Huguenots, 201; and Edict of Nantes, 228

Paris, 125, 159; and Fronde, 8, 10ff., 20, 24; and 'Ecclesiastical Fronde', 20ff.; and king, 13, 14, 17, 24, 150; officials from, 46; government of, 63; policing of, 183–4; size of, 183; threatened by Marlborough, 145; buildings of, 183–4; scandals in, 184, 185, 335; suffering in, 296 n.15

Parlements, provincial, 8, 23, 79, 130; and nobility, 56; offices in 58, 61; of Rouen, 61; of Metz, 204; in Bordeaux, and *Ormée*, 8, 23, 40 n.31; and Huguenots, 214, 215

Parlement, of Paris, 56, 158, 212; and Gallicanism, 86, 162, 322; and Regency (Anne) 3, (Orléans) 313, 334–5; and Fouquet, 71–2; and Louis XIV, 4, 26, 34, 40 n.32, 158; constitutional position, 23ff., 26, 75, 84, 339; and Fronde, 7ff., 12, 70; and taxation, 11; and Jansenism, 20–1, 318, 324, 337; conservatism of, 49; registers Philip V's right to throne, 265

parlementaires, 7, 8, 56, 82, 98, 317

Pascal, Blaise, 15, 328 n.3; and Jansenism, 21; cultural influence, 85, 106 n.2; *Lettres provinciales* of, 319; and Jesuits, 221

Paulette, 10, 26

Paulin, père Charles, 17, 39 n.23

Pays d'états, 28, 306; and tax, 79; and Colbert, 117

Peasantry, life and customs of, 45–7, 66 n.7; farming, 49, 50, 119–20; in Brittany, 52; and dues, 52–3, 118; revolts of, 38 n.11, 118; and famine, 254–5

Pellisson, Paul, historiographer, and Louis XIV's *Mémoires*, 42 n.49; and Huguenots, 221

Péréfixe, archbishop Hardouin de, 5, 6

Perrault, Charles, architect, [with brother Claude], a 'modern', 184, 186

Phélypeaux, see Pontchartrain

Philip IV, king of Spain, 1, 32; and Pyrenees peace, 160; his palace, 181; died, 181

Philip V of Spain (Philip, duc d'Anjou), 263–4, 278, 283, Louis XIV's decision for, 260 ff.; England recognises, 265; right to French throne, 265; Louis XIV's letters to, 266; character and government of, 276, 287; renounces French throne, 290; future of, 294

Philippsburg, 160, 203; given up, 256

Physiocrates, 306

Picardy, 15, 29

Pithou, Jean, 82, 105 n.16

Poitou, 15, 50, 55, *dragonnades in*, 223, 224

Poland, 76, weakness of, 246; partitions of, 135; claims on crown of, 209, 270, 297 n.24

Politiques, 82, 86; Henry IV, 213

Pomponne, Simon Arnauld, marquis de, foreign minister, 93, 107 n.31, 98, 157, 169, 204; and Nijmegen, 173–4; moderation of, 169, 176; in Sweden, 167; dismissed, 176; and Ryswick, 256; and Jansenism, 320

Pontchartrain, Jérôme Phélypeaux, comte de, and navy, 98, 131, 133 n.19, 252, 306

Pontchartrain, Louis Phélypeaux, comte de, *dévôt*, 54; minister, 98; dynasty of Phélypeaux, 98, 107 n.35; chancellor, 98, 263, 373; and censorship, 232; and famine relief, 254; and offices

Population, 30, 43, 66 n.1

Port-Royal, 20, 100, 221, 318; in Paris, 318; dispersed, 323; de Champs, 318, 323; Arnauld, family of and, 318; Pascal and, 319–20; supporters of, 320; and bull *Vineam Domini*, 322–3; suppression of, 323

Portecarrero, Luis Manuel, Cardinal, and Spanish Succession, 263; and government, 276

Portland, Hans Wilhelm Bentinck, earl of; and Ryswick, 256, 267

Portugal, revolt of, 125, 162; loss of empire, 125; rights in Brazil, 290

Poverty, 44–5, 253–4, 300

Prices, 30, 280, 300; and famine, 280; and depression, 11, 300–1

Provence, 47, 79, 284; galleys of, 130

Pussort, Henri de, and law reform, 98

Pultawa, battle of, 271

Pyrenees, peace of, 34, 150, 152, 160–1; as frontier, 126, 203

Quebec, French colony in, 127, 128

Quesnel, Pascal, Jansenist, 321, 322

Quietism, 324ff., and Maintenon, 321, 325, 328; and Fénelon, 87, 282, 308, 322ff.; and Bossuet, 322, 324ff.; and Mme Guyon, 320–1; spread of, 325

Racine, Jean, 32, 45, 256; language of, 145, 187; historiographer, 188

Rákóczi, Ferenc, Hungarian rebel, 271

Rambouillet, marquis de, 194, 199 n.24

Rastadt, peace of, French used at, 153; terms of, 290–4

Ravaulx, Roland de, and *réunions*, 204

Reims, 48; coronation at, 17ff.; effect of Revocation on, 230

Religious Wars, 2, 12, 15, 39 n.22, 59, 81, 86

Rentiers, 9, 25, 59

Réunions, 80, 128, 154, 202ff., 211 n.1, 215, 240, 256; causes and justification of, 154, 202–3; process, 204; gains by, 205, 211; effect on Germany, 250

Rhine, as frontier, 203, 206, 207; and Louis XIV, 126, 128, 159; League of (Rheinbund), 150, 164, 165, 177 n.2

Rhone, river, tolls in, 125; freezes, 280

Richelieu, Armand-Jean du Plessis, cardinal duc de, 1, 55, 122, 151; as *premier ministre*, 2, 3, 4, 6, 8, 69, 177–8 n.10, 207; diplomacy of, 31, 70, 82, 112, 152, 158, 171; fortune of, 38 n.12; and nobility, 56; *émeutes*, during, 62, 81; and Huguenots, 62, 82, 214; and propaganda, 76, 77; and navy, 129; and Colbert, 96–7, 109, 112; and *intendants*, 98–9; and Jansenism, 317; death of, 340

Riquet, Pierre-Paul, engineer, 124

Rochefort, port of, 122

Rochefoucauld, Francois de Marcillac, duc de la, *frondeur*, 191, 199 n.22

Rocroy, battle of, 4, 137; Rousse, curé Jean, 20

Rouen, 61, 65, 81, 114, 116, 125; loss of Huguenots in, 230

Roussillon, 159; secured (with Cerdagne), 160–1

Rouillé, Pierre, Louis XIV's agent, 283

Rueil, Peace of, 12

Russia, 157; military power, 246

Ryswick, peace of, 158, 247; concessions at, 159; negotiations before, 249–52, 255–6; terms of, 256, 299

Saint-Cyran, Jean Duvergier d'Hauranne, mystic, 317, 320

Saint Denis, royal necropolis in, 18; Germain, Declaration of, 10, 12; abbey of, 19; palace of, 1, 11, 15, 91, 166; James II at, 261; treaty of, 174, 205

Saint Louis (see Louis IX), 17, 331; Order of, 249, 257 n.12

Saint-Maurice, Thomas Francois, marquis de, 164

Saint-Sacrement, Compagnie du, 22, 39 n.28; and Huguenots, 214, 235 n.3

Saint-Simon, Louis de Vouvray, duc de, 138; and Louis XIV, 5, 37 n.5, 196, 332; Journal of, 37 n.5, 195–6, 249; and government, 90, 181; and court, quoted, 156, 185, 191; opinions of, 310, 313, 316; on Orléans, 312, 334, 336; on 'legitimisation', 313

Sales, Francois de, 220, 235

Salons, culture of, and Versailles, 194; *honnête homme*, ideal in, 194

Savoy, 32, 80, 245; and League of Augsburg, 245; and france, 207, 250–1, 270; interests and diplomacy of, 250–1, 271; and Partition treaty, 262; at Utrecht-Rastadt, 290–4

Schomberg, general, 231; at Boyne, 247

Sedan, annexation of, 204

Séguier, Pierre, chancellor, 3, 26, 37 n.3, 94; and Fouquet, 73

Seignelay, Jean-Baptiste Colbert, marquis de, minister, and navy, 130, 131, 276, 304; and Revocation, 225; and Louvois, 176; and Le Pelletier, 306; death of, 131

Seigneurs (see also *noblesse*), and popular revolts, 46; and dues, 51, 52–3; new men, 54, 57, 58; oppression of, 54

Senef, battle of, 171; Mme de Sévigné on, 179 n.22

Serres, Olivier de, 119

Servien, Abel, diplomat, 159

Sévigné, Marie de Rabutin-Chantal, marquise de, letter writer, 148–9 n.6; quoted, 111, 139, 172; on Louis XIV, 195; and *gloire*, 179 n.22; on Huguenots, 227

Siege warfare (see also Vauban), and Vauban, 142, 143, 144–5; 170–2, 206, 247

Simon, Richard, Biblical scholar, 327

Sobieski, John, king of Poland, 179 n.24, 291; and Marie Casimir, 209; and Louis XIV, 209; relieves Vienna, 210; death of, 267

Soissons, Eugène-Maurice, comte de, 70, 81

Somme, river, 163

Sorbonne, and Jansenism, 20–1, 34, 319, 323; and Gallicanism, 86, 162

Spain, 80, 81, 83, war against, 3, 16, 29, 31–2, 140, 163–4, 171–3; treaty of Pyrenees, 33–4; and 'Affair of Ambassadors', 161; decline and weakness of, 112, 163, 174–5, 208, 245, 251, 269, n.2, 276, 292; colonies of, 125, 126, 259, 260; and Portugal, 125; manners of, 155–6; succession to, 128, 151, 159, 160, 240, 259ff., 292; in Dutch war, 171–3; power in Italy, 207; extent of empire, 259; need of strong ruler, 266; sentiment towards Philip V, 277ff.; revival of, 294; influence on Versailles, 193

Spanish Succession, issues and politics of, 128, 151, 159, 160, 249, 251, 259ff., 268–9 n.1; and partition treaties, 259; war of, 229, 245, 270ff.

Spinola, Rojas y, ecumenist, 222, 223, 237 n.21

Spinoza, Baruch, 105 n.10; and sovereignty, 74

States-General, 8, 13, 40 n.37, 83

Steenkerk, battle of, 248; Strasbourg, 204; annexed, 81, 152, 201, 205–6, 211, 223; held, 256, 283

Subdélégués, 50, 103

Sublet de Noyers, minister, 138

Sully, Maximilien de Béthune, duc de, *grand dessein of*, 153

Sweden, 82, 250; in Triple Alliance, 165; in Dutch War, 172; Pomerania restored to, 174, 205; and France, 174, 205, 250; interests of, 205; defeated (1709), 291; effect of defeat on, 293

Taille, 10, 301; in *pays d'élections*, 79; in *pays d'états*, 79; burden of, 28, 40 n.39, 46; *intendants* and, 100; exemption from, 27, 54, 61, 79, 102, 121, 130

Tallard, Camille d'Hostin, marshal, 147, 257 n.4; generalship, 272, 274; ambassador in London, 242, 261; captive, 288; and Louis XV, 334

Taxation (see also *taille*, etc.), 9, 30, 40 n.39, 46, 47, 79; weight of, 51, 82; exemption from, 140; returns fall, 255

Télémaque, 308–9, 314 n.17

Tessé, René de Froulé, comte de, marshal, 251; ravages Palatinate, 244

'Third party' in Germany, 250–1

Thokoli, Imri, and French support, 179 n.24; allied to Turks, 208–9

Tolls, internal, 63, 80–1

Tontine, 302, 314 n.11

Torcy, Jean-Baptiste Colbert de Croissy, marquis de, foreign minister, 157, 276; reforms under, 157; and Spanish Succession, 261, 263, 264; and peace talks, 282–3, 284, 286, 288, 290; Colbert's nephew, 290; propaganda under, 292; ascendancy of, 297 n.2; under Regency, 336

Toul, 160

Toulon, sailors from, 122; canal to, 124; docks at, 130; attacked by Imperialists, 278, 284

Toulouse, 58; archbishop of, 124

Toulouse, Louis-Alexandre de Bourbon, comte de, 313, 334

Tournai, captured, 164, 165; ceded, 206, 290

Tourville, Anne-Hilarion de Cotentin, admiral, 155; victories, 131, 252; at La Hogue, 252–3

Tours, effect of Revocation on, 230

Traitants, financial role of, 71

Trent, Council of, 219

Triple Alliance, 165, 167

Trésoriers, 9, 10, 26–7, 71, 84, 100

Triers, 244; Elector of, 205

Troyes, presses of, 63

Turenne, Henri de la Tour d'Auvergne, prince, marshal, 216; as *frondeur*, 14, 22, 220; as Huguenot, 22; converts, 168, 172, 220; Louis XIV's general, 31, 71, 94, 139, 146; and Louvois 139; influences Louis XIV, 150, 166, 168; wants war, 165–6, 168; *vicomté* of, 81, 105 n.15; and Sedan, 204; rivalry with Condé, 171; death of, 169; reputation of, 172

Turin, secret treaty of, 251

Unigenitus, bull, 316, 323; Louis and, 324; registered by *Parlement*, 324, 332

United Provinces (also Holland), 61; alliance with France, 164; France at war with, 95, 110, 114, 140, 139, 168–74, 246ff.; commercial strength of, 112, 113, 120, 122, 124, 125, 126; and Colbert, 113, 114; bank in, 116, 136; navy of, 129, 131; war against England, 125, 126, 129, 164; Triple Alliance and, 165; trade treaty with France, 307; offends Louis, 165ff.; de Witts fall, 170; William of Orange and, 170ff., 261; and Barrier, 173–4, 251, 256, 266, 271, 272, 286, 288; cost of wars, 175; Huguenots to, 230, 232, 238–9; and Spanish Succession 260ff., 283; and Utrecht-Rastadt treaties, 283ff., 286,

290–1, 294–5; decline of, 245, 251–2, 295, 296 n.19

Utrecht, peace of (see also Rastadt), 290–1; English interests in, 271; gains, losses: France, 291–2; Austria, 292–3; Germany, 293–4; Poland, 293; Spain, 294; Maritime Powers, 294–5

Vauban, Sebastien, marshal, 141; and population, 43, 301; military engineer, 130, 143, 144–5, 204, 206, 274, 275; fortification, science and art of, 145, 171, 279; value of, 145, 149 n.13, 273; and defensible frontier, 163, 203, 244; sieges, 171, 173, 247; on state of army, 173, 230, 231; about Revocation, 226, 230, 235; and navy, 253; and Ryswick, 256; *Dîme royale*, 301

Vaux le Vicomte, 71, 104 n.4

Vendôme, César, duc de, 4, 37 n.4

Vendôme, Louis Joseph, duc de, marshal, 275, 296 n.8, 277, 278, 281; at Oudenarde, 279; victorious in Spain, 287

Venice, 207; trade, 120; glass, 122

Ventadour, Charlotte de la Mothe-Houdancourt, duchesse de, 331

Verdun, 160

Versailles, the regime, 15, 71; early days of, 91, 128, 171, 181ff.; as permanent base, 89, 148, 176; values of, 57, 58, 59, 60, 90, 128, 139, 176, 181, 199, 200, 287; symbolism of, 77, 92, 180, 185, 186, 187, 188ff.; style of, 187, 193–4, 196; arts in, 185ff., 187, 189; routines of, 188ff., 191ff., 193ff.; nobles at, 191; as system, 192–3; Spanish influence on, 156; receptions at, 156, 331; influence of, 181, 193, 201; pleasures of, 182, 193, 201; Grand Trianon at, 187; cost of, 187; faults in, 192–3, 195, 196; crucial debates at, 243, 263–4; imitation of, 292; flight from, 331

Victor Amadeus, 11; duke of Savoy, 207–8; Louis and, 207–8, 250–1, 274; for Emperor, 245, 271; exploits position, 271

Vienna, 155, 207; French envoy at, 158; besieged, 202, 208, 209, 210, 223

Villa Viciosa, (and Brihuega), French victory, 287

Villars, Claude duc de, marshal, 142, 172, 234, 273, 274, 275; and glory, 178–9 n.22; and Versailles debate, 243, 257 n.6; in Cevennes, 234, 273; and Emperor, 261; capacity of, 273; and 'war as process', 277, 296 n.11, 283; at Malplaquet, 286–7; at Denain, 289–90; and 'Ne plus ultra lines', 287; and Louis XIV, 284, 286, 288, 289; in Regency council, 334

Villeroi, Nicolas duc de, 5, 37 n.5, 94

Villeroi, Francois de Neufville, duc de, marshal; king's friend, 296 n.7; generalship, 147, 249, 272, 274–5; and regency of Louis XV, 334

Vincennes, château of, 35

Vincent de Paul, 'Monsieur Vincent', saint, 22, 40 n.29, 100; and Filles, 41, n.41, 44; and Huguenots, 214, 220

Voysin, Daniel, war minister, 273

Westphalia (Munster and Osnabruck), treaty of, 6, 152, 153, 174, 203; terms of, 159–60; sequel to, 203; Louis' interpretation of, 291

William of Orange, *stadholder* of Holland, king of England, 151, 158; ambitions of, 151, 170, 175, 239, 265; *stadholder*, 170, 173; amd Regents, 228–9, 239; generalship of, 170–3, 247, 264; and Louis XIV, 175, 223, 294; Huguenot support for, 231; and England, 202, 228, 242–3; war against France, 228, 247ff.; victory at Boyne, 247; defeated, Steenkerk, Neerwinden, 248, 249